The Muirhead Library of Philosophy

EDITED BY H. D. LEWIS

# A HISTORY OF
# ENGLISH UTILITARIANISM

# MUIRHEAD LIBRARY OF PHILOSOPHY

An admirable statement of the aims of the Library of Philosophy was provided by the first editor, the late Professor J. H. Muirhead, in his description of the original programme printed in Erdmann's *History of Philosophy* under the date 1890. This was slightly modified in subsequent volumes to take the form of the following statement:

'The Library of Philosophy was designed as a contribution to the History of Modern Philosophy under the heads: first of different Schools of Thought—Sensationalist, Realist, Idealist, Intuitivist; secondly of different Subjects—Psychology, Ethics, Æsthetics, Political Philosophy, Theology. While much had been done in England in tracing the course of evolution in nature, history, economics, morals and religion, little had been done in tracing the development of thought on these subjects. Yet "the evolution of opinion is part of the whole evolution".

'By the co-operation of different writers in carrying out this plan it was hoped that a thoroughness and completeness of treatment, otherwise unattainable, might be secured. It was believed also that from writers mainly British and American fuller consideration of English Philosophy than it had hitherto received might be looked for. In the earlier series of books containing, among others, Bosanquet's *History of Æsthetic*, Pfleiderer's *Rational Theology since Kant*, Albee's *History of English Utilitarianism*, Bonar's *Philosophy and Political Economy*, Brett's *History of Psychology*, Ritchie's *Natural Rights*, these objects were to a large extent effected.

'In the meantime original work of a high order was being produced both in England and America by such writers as Bradley, Stout, Bertrand Russell, Baldwin, Urban, Montague and others, and a new interest in foreign works, German, French and Italian, which had either become classical or were attracting public attention, had developed. The scope of the Library thus became extended into something more international, and it is entering on the fifth decade of its existence in the hope that it may contribute to that mutual understanding between countries which is so pressing a need of the present time.'

The need which Professor Muirhead stressed is no less pressing today, and few will deny that philosophy has much to do with enabling us to meet it, although no one, least of all Muirhead himself, would regard that as the sole, or even the main, object of philosophy. In view of Professor Muirhead's long and fruitful association with the Library of Philosophy to which he now also lends the distinction of his name, it seemed not inappropriate to allow him to recall us to these aims in his own words. The emphasis on the history of thought also seemed to me very timely; and the number of important works promised for the Library in the near future augur well for the continued fulfilment, in this and in other ways, of the expectations of the original editor.

H. D. LEWIS

# MUIRHEAD LIBRARY OF PHILOSOPHY
## General Editor : Professor H. D. Lewis
### *Professor of Philosophy, University College, Bangor*

THE ANALYSIS OF MIND  By Bertrand Russell  *6th Impression*

ANALYTIC PSYCHOLOGY  By Prof G. F. Stout  *Two Vols 5th Impression*

COLERIDGE AS PHILOSOPHER  By Prof J. H. Muirhead  *2nd Impression*

CONTEMPORARY BRITISH PHILOSOPHY  Edited by Prof J. H. Muirhead

CONTEMPORARY INDIAN PHILOSOPHY  Edited by Radhakrishnan and Prof J. H. Muirhead

DEVELOPMENT OF THEOLOGY SINCE KANT  By O. Pfleiderer

DIALOGUES ON METAPHYSICS  By Nicholas Malebranche  *Translated by Morris Ginsberg*

ETHICS  By Nicolai Hartmann  *Translated by Stanton Coit Three Vols*

THE GOOD WILL: A STUDY IN THE COHERENCE THEORY OF GOODNESS  By Prof H. J. Paton

HEGEL'S SCIENCE OF LOGIC  *Translated by W. H. Johnston and L. G. Struthers  Two Vols  2nd Impression*

HISTORY OF ÆSTHETIC  By Dr. B. Bosanquet  *2nd Edition 6th Impression*

HISTORY OF ENGLISH UTILITARIANISM  By Prof E. Albee

HISTORY OF PSYCHOLOGY  By Prof G. S. Brett  Edited by R. S. Peters  *Abridged one volume edition*

HUMAN KNOWLEDGE  By Bertrand Russell  *3rd Impression*

A HUNDRED YEARS OF BRITISH PHILOSOPHY  By Dr. Rudolf Metz  *Translated by Prof J. W. Harvey, Prof T. E. Jessop, Henry Sturt  2nd Impression*

IDEAS: A GENERAL INTRODUCTION TO PURE PHENOMENOLOGY  *2nd Impression*  By Edmund Husserl  *Translated by W. R. Boyce Gibson*

INDIAN PHILOSOPHY  By Radhakrishnan  *Two Vols  Rev 2nd Edition*

# A HISTORY
# OF
# ENGLISH
# UTILITARIANISM

BY

ERNEST ALBEE

LONDON . GEORGE ALLEN AND UNWIN LTD
NEW YORK . THE MACMILLAN COMPANY

FIRST PUBLISHED IN 1901
SECOND IMPRESSION IN 1957

PRINTED IN GREAT BRITAIN
BY BRADFORD AND DICKENS
LONDON, W.C.1

TO THE MEMORY OF
S.A. AND R.P.A.

# PREFACE

NOBODY would deny that the History of Ethics is a very essential part of the History of Philosophy, and, so far as ethical theories have formed an organic part of the general systems of ancient and modern philosophers, they may be said to have received due recognition at the hands of the historian. But, as the general tendency of English thought has been (or for a long time was) practical rather than speculative, it has happened, not unfortunately, that the progress of ethical theory in England has, on the whole, been less involved with the rise and decadence of definite systems of Metaphysics than has been the case on the continent. Problems belonging distinctly to Ethics have for the most part been discussed on their own merits— except, perhaps, where theological issues have been raised. And if English philosophers have not always put forth the profoundest theories regarding the nature and meaning of morality, they have at least done inestimable service in the way of clear thinking and consistent reasoning.

Now the result of this comparatively non-metaphysical character of English Ethics is that it has by no means taken its true place in the general History of Philosophy. Properly speaking, we have no history of English Ethics. Dr. Whewell, indeed, published in 1852 his *Lectures on the History of Moral Philosophy in England;* but this book was hardly calculated to serve more than a temporary purpose. It everywhere shows marks of haste, as might perhaps be expected from its mode of composition, and the writer is so concerned to refute theories incompatible with his own, that his expositions, even aside from their necessary brevity, are generally unsatisfactory and sometimes quite misleading. A very different book is Professor Sidgwick's *Outlines of the History of Ethics for English Readers*, first published in 1886. This is all that a mere 'outline' could very well be; but, when it is considered that Chapter iv. of this little volume, on " Modern, Chiefly English, Ethics," is only about one hundred pages long, it will readily be seen that it does not by any means. pretend to be an adequate history of the subject. Other 'outlines' might be mentioned, such as the interesting one contained in Professor Wundt's *Ethik;* but none of these really supply, or pretend to supply, a need which we doubtless all feel.

Since, then, we have no adequate history of English Ethics, the attempt has been made in this volume to cover a part of the ground by tracing the rise and development of Utilitarianism in England. No one of the writers considered — not even Hume or Mill — is individually of such importance for English Ethics as Bishop Butler; but, taken as a whole, Utilitarianism may fairly be regarded as England's most characteristic, if not most important, contribution to the development of ethical theory. This being the case, its history certainly deserves careful and somewhat extended treatment. The author hopes that, whatever may be the shortcomings of the following chapters, he will not be accused of treating the subject either carelessly or in a partisan spirit. The greater part of the matter of the first five chapters has already appeared as a series of articles in the *Philosophical Review* (published from May, 1895, to July, 1897), and for the privilege of using here the matter of those chapters, in a somewhat extended and otherwise modified form, the author is indebted to the editors and publishers of the *Review*. The remaining chapters of the book appear for the first time, except the first section of the final chapter, as indicated in the text. A paper based upon the manuscript of that part of the chapter was read before the American Psychological Association, at the Baltimore Meeting, December, 1900, and was afterwards printed in the *Philosophical Review*.

CORNELL UNIVERSITY,
    *May*, 1901.

# CONTENTS

# INTRODUCTION.

THE barbarous terminology employed in certain modern systems of philosophy has often been censured, and with considerable justice; but the habit of using in a technical sense words that already have a popular meaning, or words that inevitably suggest others having a popular meaning, has its own decided drawbacks. The technical use of the term Utilitarianism, with which we shall constantly have to do in the following chapters, partly illustrates this. Though first used by one of the later exponents of Universalistic Hedonism, as standing for that principle, it has never become entirely divested of certain associations connected rather with the ordinary meaning of the word 'utility,' and with the supposed practical applications of the Utilitarian theory, than with the essential logic of the theory itself. When one speaks of English Utilitarianism, therefore, it is not wholly evident, without explanation, whether one mainly refers to a very important practical movement of English thought, extending through the closing years of the eighteenth century and about the first half of the nineteenth century, or to a very familiar, to us probably the most familiar, type of abstract ethical theory.

There is a reason for this confusion, which should not be overlooked, even apart from the possible ambiguity of the term Utilitarianism. Bentham and James Mill, two of the three "English Utilitarians" to whom Mr. Leslie Stephen devotes much the greater part of his very interesting and valuable work bearing that title, were much more interested in the supposed practical applications of the theory of Utility than in the theory itself considered merely as belonging to Ethics as one of the philosophical disciplines. In a less degree the same tendency may be traced in the writings of J. S. Mill, to whom the third volume of Mr. Stephen's work is mainly devoted, though of the importance of his actual contributions to philosophy proper there can be no serious question.

Now it is this social and political side of the Utilitarian movement that Mr. Stephen has had principally in view in his admirable account of the " English Utilitarians ". A mere examination of the analytical table of contents of his three volumes would show how small a proportion is devoted to theoretical Ethics. Yet the doctrine of Universalistic Hedonism, as Professor Sidgwick aptly termed it, had been largely developed as an ethical theory proper before Bentham wrote, and before he and the two Mills undertook to deduce from it their characteristic views on society and government. And though Utilitarianism as an ethical theory seems to have lost ground, on the whole, during the past two or three decades, it has certainly outlived the practical Utilitarian movement referred to above, and still demands the thoughtful consideration of all students of Ethics.

In truth, this is the one easily recognisable type of ethical theory which has had both a perfectly continuous and a fairly logical development from the beginnings of English Ethics to the present time. Such being the case, it has seemed worth while to trace its development in considerable detail in the present volume. It must always be remembered that we are here primarily concerned with the development of an abstract type of ethical theory, and not with the practical corollaries, social and political, which by some have been supposed to result from the theory. It is important to keep this in mind, for some of the greatest names connected with the practical Utilitarian movement are of comparatively minor consequence for the history of the development of Universalistic Hedonism considered merely as a type of ethical theory, while other names, almost forgotten in some instances, assume an unexpectedly commanding position.

But, even within the sphere of theoretical Ethics, an important distinction has often been made between so-called " Theological Utilitarianism " and non-Theological Utilitarianism. It will be well to pause for a little, in order to note just what this distinction reduces to. The term " Theological Utilitarianism " is itself rather misleading, as it almost inevitably suggests an affinity with certain early forms of ethical theory which regarded morality as depending upon the arbitrary will of God. J. S. Mill himself was guilty of serious confusion on this point in his early essay on Professor Sedgwick's *Discourse on the Studies of the University of Cambridge* (1835), though he tacitly corrected his error three years later in his well-known essay on Bentham. With less justification, Mr. Spencer made practically the same mistake more than forty years afterward, in the chapter on "Ways of Judging Conduct" in his *Data of Ethics.*

The true distinction may conveniently be indicated by briefly comparing Paley and Bentham in a single respect. The criterion of morality was the same for both. Actions were regarded by both as right or wrong, because they made for or against ' the greatest happiness of the greatest number ' ; and the ' greatest happiness ' was taken by both to mean the ' sum of pleasures,' with a consistent disregard of so-called ' qualitative distinctions '. So far they agreed ; but Paley, unlike Bentham, thought it necessary, not merely to mention, but to lay very special stress upon the doctrine of rewards and punishments after death, in order to prove that it is for the ultimate interest of the hypothetically egoistic moral agent to act for the common good. In so doing, he was merely taking what had long been the characteristic position of " Theological Utilitarianism ". More than half a century before, the Rev. John Gay, in his anonymous *Preliminary Dissertation* (1731) prefixed to Law's translation of King's

*Origin of Evil*, had aptly defined obligation, from this point of view, as "the necessity of doing or omitting any action in order to be happy"; and he had pertinently added that, therefore, complete obligation can come only from the authority of God, "because God only can in all cases make a man happy or miserable".

Now it is important to notice that this theory of obligation, however far it may fall short of satisfying the general moral and religious consciousness of the present day, was the logical result of hedonism working itself out on the principles of eighteenth century individualism. Bentham would have found himself in the same logical predicament as the "Theological Utilitarians," if he had worked the problem out to the end, instead of practically neglecting it. Certainly he would have recognised our complete obligation to do what is right and avoid what is wrong, and, since he was as much committed as the so-called "Theological Utilitarians" to the view that the moral agent could ultimately will only his own happiness, the very serious question would have arisen for him as for them, whether the selfish interest of the individual and the interest of society would coincide in each particular case, leaving the possibility of a future life out of consideration. It would have been no answer to say that, if it is not at present for the interest of the individual to do right in all cases, it ought to be made so by those very improvements in legislation in which Bentham himself was primarily interested, for even he could not have maintained that any general enactments would meet all special cases. The plain truth is, that if one begins by assuming an interest of the individual separate from that of society, in the sense of typical eighteenth century hedonism, one is logically driven to take refuge in the doctrine of rewards and punishments after death, in order to preserve the notion of our complete obligation to do what is right and avoid what is wrong, which all accredited moralists hold practically in common.

In so-called " Theological Utilitarianism," then, we find a theory of obligation based upon a theory of the moral motive which, so far from being peculiar to that school, was the conventional one during a large part of the eighteenth century. This form of ethical theory, whatever may be its other defects and shortcomings, does not gratuitously introduce theological considerations, but reserves them for the solution of a difficulty which could not otherwise be resolved—except by giving up the individualistic theory of the moral motive which had led to the theory of obligation itself. It thus represents the almost inevitable tendency of the earlier form of consistent Utilitarianism, *i.e.*, Utilitarianism basing upon the selfish theory of the moral motive. On the other hand, nineteenth century Utilitarianism represents a constant, though not uniformly successful, attempt to transcend this narrow theory of the moral motive, with the result that the Utilitarian theory of obligation has been profoundly modified, and brought into much closer relation to the highest concrete moral ideals. In truth, the degree of divergence between the spirit of typical eighteenth century and typical nineteenth century Utilitarianism can only be appreciated by those who have traced the development of the theory with considerable care.

One other problem should be kept in mind from the very beginning, that of the so-called ' qualitative distinctions ' between pleasures and pains. The frequent emphasis upon ' happiness,' or even ' pleasure,' in early systems of Ethics is not decisive, as indicating their hedonistic character, for some kinds of happiness may be put on an entirely different plane from others, being regarded as of greater intrinsic worth or dignity, quite apart from the matter of intensity and duration. It almost goes without saying that, in so far as such ' qualitative distinctions ' are consciously emphasised, the system in question departs from typical hedonism, and indeed, strictly speaking, becomes differentiated from hedonism altogether;

for an ethical system cannot logically begin by affirming that all moral values are to be computed in terms of pleasure, and then add that pleasures themselves are of greater or less value, not merely in terms of intensity and duration, but in proportion as they involve something else distinct from pleasure. At the same time, the explicit repudiation of 'qualitative distinctions' by hedonistic writers naturally came somewhat after they had practically adopted what was for them the only consistent position, and hardly dates back as far as the middle of the eighteenth century.

J. S. Mill's emphatic insistence upon 'qualitative distinctions,' which was too flagrant an inconsistency to exert much influence upon the further development of Utilitarianism, was, nevertheless, rather more than a mere reversion to the old confusion on the subject. It was one of those partly unconscious, but logically important, concessions to Intuitionism, which we shall find to characterise, in very different ways, the various forms of later Utilitarianism represented by the ethical writings of Mill himself, of Mr. Spencer, and of Professor Sidgwick. For it will appear, as we proceed with our investigation, that the history of Utilitarianism exhibits two fairly distinct phases: first, the gradual development of the theory in the direction of formal consistency down to about the beginning of the nineteenth century; and secondly, the later development, often at the expense of formal consistency, but always in the direction of doing justice to the concrete moral ideals which had been partly lost sight of in the earlier, more abstract form of the theory. This later and larger development of Utilitarianism, while particularly open to criticism in detail, since it was always in some danger of overstepping its own first principles, is nevertheless one of the most significant chapters in the History of Ethics, and contains much that is still worthy of the thoughtful consideration of those who are doing constructive work in Ethics at the present time.

# CHAPTER I.

## RICHARD CUMBERLAND.

WHILE the doctrine of Utilitarianism has played a most conspicuous part in English Ethics since the time of Paley and Bentham, it is not commonly realised that the essential features of the system were roughly stated and in part developed by a contemporary of the Cambridge Platonists. It is true that Bishop Cumberland's treatise, *De legibus naturae*, like most ethical works of the time, was largely controversial in character, having been written to refute Hobbes. Moreover, the jural aspect of the system, implied by the very title of the treatise, tends to obscure what for us is by far its most important feature. And even this is not all. The 'common good' which Cumberland regarded as the end of all truly moral action includes 'perfection' as well as 'happiness,' which leads to serious confusion in the working out of the system. But, making all allowances for what was incidental in the external form of the work, and for the confusion of two principles which have long since become clearly differentiated, it is well worth while to examine with some care the ablest, or at any rate the most successful, opponent of Hobbes and the true founder of English Utilitarianism.

It would be quite impossible adequately to treat of any important ethical system, without taking some account of the views of the author's contemporaries; but this is particularly necessary in the case of early writers. In their works we are almost sure to find in artificial combination principles which are now regarded as logically distinct, and the only possible explanation of the actual form of the system in question is often to be sought in contemporary influences. Sometimes, of course, an investigation of this sort is difficult, and, however

I

carefully prosecuted, yields no very certain results. Fortunately we are not thus hampered in the case of Cumberland. We shall find difficulty and uncertainty enough in certain aspects of his system, but there is little doubt with regard to the formative influences in his case. In his view of the nature of man, Cumberland stands in the closest and most obvious relation to Grotius and Hobbes—his relation to the former being that of substantial agreement; to the latter, that of opposition. We must, then, consider in the briefest possible way the ethical views of these two authors—particularly as regards the then current conception of Laws of Nature—and also notice the tendencies represented by the various opponents of Hobbes.

The idea of Laws of Nature was, of course, by no means original with Grotius. A Stoical conception at first, it had exercised a profound influence upon Roman Law, and had reappeared as an essential feature in the system of Thomas Aquinas. Here, however, as Professor Sidgwick points out, it "was rather the wider notion which belongs to Ethics than the narrower notion with which Jurisprudence or Politics is primarily concerned ".[1] It is one of the most important services of Grotius that he distinguished between the provinces of Ethics and Jurisprudence, the result being as fortunate for the former as for the latter.[2] However, as Professor Sidgwick remarks, while the distinction is clearly enough made in the body of his epoch-making work, *De jure belli et pacis*, still, in the general account which he gives of Natural Law, the wider ethical notion is retained. It will be important for the reader to keep this in mind.

In one of the earlier passages of the Prolegomena to his *De iure belli et pacis*, Grotius makes a significant statement regarding his view of the nature of man. Among the properties which are peculiar to man is a desire for society, and not only so, but for a life spent tranquilly and rationally.[3] The asser-

[1] *Hist. of Ethics*, p. 159.
[2] See Jodl, *Geschichte der Ethik*, vol. I., p. 102.
[3] Whewell's ed., vol. I., p. xli.

tion that by nature each seeks only his own advantage, cannot be conceded. Even animals manifest an altruistic instinct in caring for their young, while children show compassion at a very early age. In adult man, that which in the lower stages of development had manifested itself as instinctive altruistic conduct, becomes self-conscious and rational. And this tendency to the conservation of society is the source of 'Jus' or Natural Law, properly so called.[1] Natural Law would remain even if there were no God. But of the existence of God we are assured, partly by reason, partly by constant tradition. And here we are brought to another origin of 'Jus,' *i.e.*, the free will of God. But even Natural Law, though it proceed from the nature of man, may yet rightly be ascribed to God, because it was by His will that such principles came to exist in us.[2]

The relation between Natural Law and that which proceeds from the arbitrary will of God is of some importance. Apparently the latter is always in addition to the former, never in contradiction with it,[3] though it must be confessed that the author's treatment is wavering. As Professor Sidgwick says,[4] according to Grotius Natural Law may be overruled in any particular case by express revelation. It is to be noted, however, that this does not mean that Natural Law, as such, can be superseded by Divine Law, but rather that a special act which would ordinarily be a transgression of Natural Law may be right merely because God has commanded it. At best, however, this seems to contradict the fundamental principles of the system. But, apart from the question of a possible conflict between Natural and Divine Law, there is a further difficulty. Divine Law is what the name would indicate. In the case of such law, it may be said : God did not command the act because it was just, but it was just because God commanded it.[5] In the case of Natural Law, the reverse would seem to hold true ; but the language of Grotius on this point

---

[1] Whewell's ed., vol. I., p. xliv.
[2] See, *e.g.*, *ibid.*, p. lxxii.
[3] *Ibid.*, p. xlvii.
[4] *Hist. of Ethics*, p. 160.
[5] *De jure*, p. 20.

is somewhat ambiguous. For instance, we have seen that Natural Law may be ascribed to God, "because it was by His will that such principles came to exist in us"; but, on the other hand, Grotius holds that just as God cannot make twice two not be four, He cannot make that which is intrinsically bad not to be bad.[1] The undoubted confusion which one finds here suggests the difficulty of mediating between the views later represented by Descartes and by Cudworth: (1) that moral distinctions depend upon the arbitrary will of God; and (2) that they do not thus depend.

From the above it will be seen that Grotius insists upon the social and the rational nature of man. As to the proximate (not ultimate) origin of Natural Law, there seems to be a slight ambiguity. Now it appears to be founded upon the primitive altruistic instinct, and now upon the rational nature of man.[2] Probably it would be fair to say that, according to Grotius, the two are equally essential to human nature, which he regards as logically prior to Natural Law, just as that is logically prior to particular civil laws. The relation between Natural Law and Divine Law has just been considered. Logically, the latter should always be in addition to, never in conflict with, the former. When Grotius practically does allow such conflict, we must regard it as a natural, but not a necessary, concession to theology. Again, the relation of God to Natural Law is not quite clear. On the whole, however, Grotius would seem to hold that certain things are right, others wrong, in the nature of things, *i.e.*, apart from the will of God. Whether the nature of things be ultimately the same with the nature of God, we do not here need to ask. The question would hardly have occurred to Grotius.

When we turn to the writings of Hobbes, we are at once confronted with a very different, and much more original, system of thought; but it is to be carefully noted that his ethical and political philosophy is not so closely connected with his mechanical philosophy as he himself would have had us

[1] *De jure*, p. 12.
[2] *Cf.* Cumberland, who probably follows Grotius here, as so often.

believe. Certainly it is quite comprehensible by itself. Indeed, in the course of his expositions, Hobbes ordinarily refers to common experience rather than to his own first principles. The starting-point of his ethical speculation is probably to be found in the then current conception of Laws of Nature,[1] which we have just been considering. This will be assumed to be the case in what follows.

In order fully to understand Hobbes's view of the nature of man, we must distinguish (1) man's *need* of society ; (2) his *fitness* for society ; and (3) his *love* of society, for its own sake. (1) That man has need of society—in the sense of an organised commonwealth—Hobbes would have been the first to insist. Out of society, indeed, man cannot continue to exist at all. But (2) man's fitness for society does not by any means keep pace with his need of the same. Children and fools need society, if possible, more than others, and yet they " cannot enter into it," in Hobbes's sense of the words. Indeed, many, perhaps most, men remain throughout life ' unfit ' for society, either through defect of mind or want of education.[2] The main reason for this unfitness, however, is man's fundamental egoism. If it be asked : (3) Does man love society for its own sake ? Hobbes replies with a decided negative. " All society . . . is either for gain or for glory ; that is, not so much for love of our fellows as for the love of ourselves." [3] So much is plain, but it is not equally plain in what terms we are to express this primitive egoism. Sometimes pleasure as such would seem to be the end ; sometimes (probably more often) self-preservation.

Starting, then, with the assumption of man's original and ineradicable egoism ; and the further assumption that nature has made men essentially equal in faculties both of body and of mind,[4] so that all may aspire to everything—it is easy to see that the hypothetical ' state of nature ' must be a ' state of war,' with all the attendant evils which Hobbes so

[1] *Cf.* Sidgwick's *Hist. of Ethics*, p. 162.
[2] See *De cive*, Works, Molesworth's ed., vol. II., p. 2, note.
[3] *Ibid.*, p. 5.    [4] See *Leviathan*, vol. III., p. 110.

tersely, yet vividly describes.[1]   How are men to escape the
consequences of their own anti-social natures?   The possibility
of deliverance depends upon the fact that man is not merely a
bundle of selfish appetites, but, as Hobbes says: "True
Reason is . . . no less a part of human nature than any other
faculty or affection of the mind ".   Moreover, ' True Reason '
is " a certain law ".[2]

It is natural that one should ask just what is meant by
' True Reason,' and Hobbes has a note on the subject,[3] which,
however, is not particularly illuminating.   " By Right Reason
in the natural state of man," he says, " I understand not, as
many do, an infallible faculty, but the act of reasoning, that is,
the peculiar and true ratiocination of every man concerning
those actions of his which may either redound to the damage
or benefit of his neighbours."   He further explains that he calls
reason " true, that is, concluding from true principles, rightly
framed, because that the whole breach of the Laws of Nature
consists in the false reasoning, or rather folly, of those men
who do not see those duties they are necessarily to perform
towards others, in order to their own conservation ".[4]   In a
word, there is no infallible faculty of Right Reason that can be
implicitly trusted.   It can only be proved right by the event,
and the test is the conservation of the individual.

Right Reason, however, in the sense above explained, leads
us to formulate certain Laws of Nature.   Such a ' law ' is defined as " the dictate of Right Reason, conversant about those
things which are either to be done or omitted for the constant
preservation of life and members, as much as in us lies ".   The
first and fundamental Law of Nature is " that peace is to be
sought after, where it may be found; and where not, there

---

[1] See *Leviathan*, vol. III., p. 113.   For passages which seem to show that,
in his description of the ' state of nature,' Hobbes does not understand that he is
giving an *historical* account of the origin of human society, see, *e.g.*, *Leviathan*,
vol. III., p. 114, and particularly the last part of the interesting note in *De cive*,
vol. II., p. 10.

[2] *De cive*, vol. II., p. 16.                    [3] *Ibid.*

[4] See, also, *De corpore politico*, vol. IV., p. 225, where the author says: " But
this is certain, seeing Right Reason is not existent," etc.

to provide ourselves for helps of war ".[1]   From this law, all
the others—twenty in *De cive*, eighteen in *Leviathan*—are
derived.    " They direct the ways, either to peace or self-
defence."

We are not here concerned with the enumeration and deduction of the particular Laws of Nature, which will readily
be found by referring to *Leviathan*, *De cive*, or *De corpore
politico*.   The question as to their exact significance (*qua*
Laws of Nature), however, is of the greatest importance for
the system ; and it is just here that the expositions of Hobbes
are least helpful.   The philosopher himself says :  " The Laws
of Nature  are immutable and eternal :  what they forbid can
never be lawful ; what they command can never be unlawful ".[2]
At the same time it is important to observe that in a state
of nature it would be irrational for a man to obey these laws,
for he would have no assurance that others would do the same.
Such conduct would defeat the end which all these laws have
in mind, *i.e.*, the preservation of the individual.   Indeed, as
Hobbes reminds us, they are not ' laws ' at all in the ordinary
sense, " since they are nothing else but certain conclusions,
understood by reason, of things to be done and omitted " ;[3]
whereas the element of compulsion is essential to ' law ' in the
strict sense.

In order that there may be any security whatever, a government of some sort must be established.   The many conflicting
wills must be changed into *one*, not by a change in human
nature—which, of course, is impossible—but by the several
individuals submitting themselves either to a " council " or to
" one man ".   In this compact, the individual gives up all but
the right of defending himself against personal violence.   To
the governing power belong the " sword of justice " and the
" sword of war," and—what necessarily follows—judgment as
to the " right use " of each. But this is not all. Since differences
of opinion concerning "*meum* and *tuum*, just and unjust,

---

[1] *De cive*, vol. II., p. 16.   *Cf. Leviathan*, vol. III., p. 117.
[2] *De cive*, vol. II., p. 46.          [3] *Ibid.*, p. 49.

profitable and unprofitable, good and evil, honest and dis-
honest," [1] etc., are productive of discord, the civil power must
*define* the above. Also, the supreme power of the State is to
be judge of all theological doctrines, in so far as they tend
to practical results. In short, this power is "absolute," as
Hobbes himself frankly calls it.

We must now ask: What has become of the Laws of
Nature, with which we started? We have already seen that
Hobbes refers to them as "eternal and immutable". In the
latter part of *De cive* [2] he says, using words that Cudworth
himself could not have objected to: "Natural [Law] is that
which God hath declared to all men by His eternal word born
with them, to wit, their natural reason; and this is that law
which, in this whole book, I have endeavoured to unfold".
But suppose that civil laws should be in opposition to these
Laws of Nature? Hobbes meets the query with characteristic
boldness. "By the virtue of the natural law which forbids
breach of covenant, the Law of Nature commands us to keep
all the civil laws. For where we are tied to obedience before
we know what will be commanded us, there we are universally
tied to obey in all things. Whence it follows, that no civil
law whatsoever, which tends not to the reproach of the
deity [3] . . . can possibly be against the Law of Nature. For
though the Law of Nature forbid theft, adultery, &c.; yet,
if the civil law commands us to invade anything, that invasion
is not theft, adultery, &c." [4] The conclusion to which we are
brought by the philosopher himself is rather startling: Nothing in the civil laws can be against the Laws of Nature,
because not only is the civil power behind the Laws of
Nature that which makes them properly 'laws,' but also it is
that, and that alone, which gives them their content. It
makes comparatively little difference what the Laws of

---

[1] *De cive*, p. 77.—Note the heterogeneous items.     [2] See p. 186.

[3] This is only an apparent exception, for it would be precisely for the civil
power to decide, in any particular case, what was, or was not, " to the reproach
of the deity ".

[4] *De cive*, pp. 190, 191.

Nature command or forbid, so long as it lies wholly with the civil power to define the terms used.

Some pages back it was seen that there was ambiguity in Hobbes's use of ' Right Reason '.  In *De corpore politico* we are told :  " But this is certain, seeing Right Reason is not existent, the reason of some man or men must supply the place thereof ".[1]  In other words, the arbitrary use of civil power must make up for the lack of Right Reason in man.  Again, in *Leviathan :* " The unwritten Law of Nature . . . is now become, of all laws, the most obscure, and has consequently the greatest need of able interpreters ".[2]  But who should be the interpreter ?  Hobbes candidly remarks :  " The interpretation of the Laws of Nature, in a commonwealth, dependeth not on the books of moral philosophy. . . . That which I have written in this treatise concerning the moral virtues . . . though it be evident truth, is not therefore presently a law ; but because in all commonwealths in the world it is part of the civil law."  No amount of valid reasoning can vindicate the Laws of Nature.  Nothing but their presence in the statute-books of the commonwealths of the world can do that.  And the reason why they can be said to be so universally recognised is that the same power, in each particular case, that compels obedience to them, also practically furnishes them with their content.  It may also be noticed that Hobbes has proceeded deductively—in appearance, at least—in arriving at his Laws of Nature.  If presence in the statute-book be the only test, he should have proceeded inductively.  The utter confusion which we find here requires no comment.  The Laws of Nature, with which our philosopher began, have vanished into thin air.  We learn what is good for us as well as what is right, what is true as well as what is just, from the powers that be.  There would be no place for a theorist like Hobbes himself in his own ideal state.

It was inevitable that a theory of political absolutism like that of Hobbes—involving as it did a wholly egoistic system

[1] See vol. IV., p. 225.      [2] See vol. III., p. 262.

of Ethics, the unlovely character of which the philosopher was at no pains whatever to conceal—should excite the most violent opposition.  But while the ethical writers of his own time and country were practically unanimous in their opposition to Hobbes, their methods of attack were by no means the same.  Some were more incensed at the brutal egoism of the system, others at the arbitrary character which Hobbes had assigned to moral distinctions; though it is fair to suppose that all were a good deal disturbed by both sides of his doctrine.  A general statement like this, however, is apt to be misleading, as it does not suggest the complexity of the facts.  It is probable that in periods of controversy, quite as much as in periods of constructive work, the individualities of prominent writers play a determining part in shaping their productions.  Hence we must be on our guard against supposing that the conventional division of the opponents of Hobbes into 'schools' is wholly satisfactory.  For instance, Whewell classes together: (1) Sharrock, Henry More, and Cumberland, and (2) Cudworth and Clarke; while Professor Sidgwick, on the other hand, distinguishes between (1) the "Cambridge Moralists," including all the above but Sharrock, Cumberland, and Clarke, and (2) Cumberland.  This does not imply any essential difference in the way that Whewell and Professor Sidgwick interpret the doctrines of the authors named.  Any such classification is largely a matter of convenience and more or less arbitrary.  For our present purpose, three men may fairly be taken as typical of the tendencies represented by the opponents of Hobbes, *viz.*, Cudworth, More, and Cumberland.

Cudworth, of course, stands for Intellectualism.  He would reduce morality to a system of truths.  The result is that, in his unfinished *Treatise concerning Eternal and Immutable Morality*, we have a noteworthy system of Metaphysics, rather than a direct and explicit treatment of what are ordinarily regarded as the problems of Ethics.  Indeed, so much is Cudworth concerned to establish a system of "eternal and immutable" truths, *among* which are the truths of Ethics, that never once, in the course of the treatise just mentioned, does he take the trouble to combat the egoism of Hobbes. Obviously we are not concerned with his system here. Cumberland, on the other hand, is singularly devoid of metaphysical interests, and the passages in his treatise *De legibus naturae* which do incidentally treat of metaphysical questions, are certainly the least satisfactory part of his work. To the side of Hobbes's system which teaches the arbitrary character of moral distinctions, he replies by reproducing what we have already seen to be the views of Grotius regarding Natural Law; while, in opposition to the egoism of Hobbes, he teaches what practically amounts to the system of Universalistic Hedonism. As the first English writer standing for this principle, he has been taken as the subject of the first two chapters of the present volume.

More, whose *Enchiridion Ethicum* enjoyed an enormous popularity in its own generation,[1] is particularly hard to classify; but it is certainly safe to say that he occupies a position logically intermediate between the other two. The fact that he so nearly refrained from publishing his own work, owing to the supposed objections of Cudworth, is in itself a sufficient indication that the two authors concerned regarded their systems as standing for very much the same principles. On the other hand, however, while Cudworth had practically neglected the affective side of our nature in his own treatise, More makes the 'Boniform Faculty' (which is at once the touch-stone of virtue and that by which virtue in the moral agent is immediately and certainly rewarded) not only co-ordinate with Right Reason, but constantly suggests its primacy. It is difficult to express in a few words More's view of the relation in which these two faculties stand to each other. Sometimes he even seems to identify them; but, if one may venture upon a very concise statement, the case stands thus. In a 'state of grace,' the 'Boniform Faculty' (which plays much the same part as conscience) is all-sufficient.

---

[1] See Whewell's *Hist. of Mor. Phil. in England*, Lect. iii. In spite of its opularity, however, the *Enchiridion* has never been translated into English.

No appeal to Right Reason is necessary, or desirable. But, "since there are some men who have lost all sense of God and divine things, and recognised no fixed rule in their faculties," these "must be approached in another way," *i.e.*, by Right Reason.  The author therefore draws from this store "certain principles immediately true, and in need of no proof, but from which almost all moral reasoning (as mathematical demonstrations from common axioms) may be clearly and easily deduced".  These he calls 'Noemata'.

An examination of these 'Noemata' at once shows that we no longer have to do with the intellectualism of Cudworth. The first twelve 'Noemata' treat of our duty toward ourselves, and might fairly be termed 'maxims of prudence'.  The Good is here defined (not quite adequately for the system) as that "which to any perceptive life, or stage of such life, is grateful, pleasing, and suitable, and connected with the preservation of the percipient ".[1]  The remaining eleven 'Noemata' concern our duties to God and to other men.  Two of these might seem quite distinctly to point in the direction of Universalistic Hedonism.  "That good which you prefer for yourself in given circumstances, you ought to prefer for another in the same circumstances, so far as it is possible without injury to any third person." [2]  And again, "If it is good that one man should be supplied with means to live well and happily, it follows by a sure and wholly mathematical analogy that it is twice as good for two men to be supplied, three times for three, a thousand times for a thousand," etc.[3]

It might very well seem as if, in More, we had already found an exponent of the Utilitarian principle; but this is certainly not the case.  The system is one of the most perplexed in the whole history of English Ethics, but on the point just referred to, at least, the author does not leave us in doubt.  Even in the 'Scholia' appended to the chapter in which the 'Noemata' are treated, we find a significant statement of the author's position.  Referring to previous attempts

---

[1] Noema i., p. 25, of the fourth ed. of the *Enchiridion.*
[2] *Ibid.* xiv., p. 29.          [3] *Ibid.* xviii., p. 30.

to find some one principle, into which morality could be resolved, he shows that some have taken ' sociality ' as the first and simplest principle ; others, ' zeal for the public good '— " both parties supposing that there is no perfection or happiness pertaining to human nature which is not bound up with communion or society ".[1]  But " it is the internal life of the mind, and the pleasure which is derived from a sense of virtue," that is the proper object of Ethics.[2]  This would exist, if there were only one man in the world.[3]  It is not evident whom More has in mind here, and the criticisms which follow do not apply to Universalistic Hedonism (which had not yet been advanced as an ethical theory, at least in England [4]); but it is clear that More himself had no thought to develop what some would now recognise as a possible Intuitional basis of the Utilitarian principle.[5]  As a matter of fact, the system is a curious combination of Intuitionism and unconscious, undifferentiated Hedonism.  More says, in substance : A thing is simply and absolutely good which is pleasing, not to the animal appetite, which man has in common with the brutes, but to the Boniform Faculty, which distinguishes him as a man.[6]  He frequently admits, however, that this particular kind of pleasure is not sufficient in order to perfect happiness.  A certain amount of external goods is also necessary.[7]  The Good, then, is happiness, and happiness is pleasure—but pleasure of a particularly refined sort, such as only a person of developed moral sensibilities could enjoy.  The happiness considered is almost always that of the agent ; but it would be as unjust to call the system Egoistic as it would be misleading to call it Utilitarian.  In place of ' sociality,' or ' zeal for the public good,' More proposes, as the necessary unifying principle, " true and sincere

---

[1] See p. 33.          [2] See p. 35.          [3] See p. 36.

[4] The *Enchiridion* was published in 1667, and Cumberland's *De legibus naturae* did not appear till 1672.

[5] *Cf.* Sidgwick's *Methods of Ethics*, pp. 379 *et seq.*

[6] See p. 47.  Also the ' scholia ' appended to ch. ii., in which More attempts to distinguish his own view from ' Epicureanism '.

[7] See, *e.g.*, p. 2.

love of God," [1] and holds that all the 'Noemata' may be reduced to this.   In short, we have here a theological system of Ethics, unconsciously hedonistic, but never more than vaguely suggesting Utilitarianism.   If More had recognised the hedonistic side of his own system, it is not impossible that he might have made 'the greatest happiness of the greatest number' the end of moral action, but the important fact for us is that he did *not* develop his system in this direction.

We may now turn to a more careful examination of the first English moralist who can properly be termed a Utilitarian. We have not here, as often happens, the difficulty of keeping in mind two or more ethical works by the same author, possibly differing in point of view, when considering any particular problem arising in connection with the system.   In fact, the task might seem to be an easy one, as we have to depend, for our knowledge of Cumberland's Ethics, wholly upon the treatise entitled *De legibus naturae*,[2] which was first published in 1672.   This, however, is by no means the case.   While a thinker of no ordinary ability, and standing for a principle which has become clearly differentiated in the later development of English Ethics, Cumberland is so utterly lacking in a talent for exposition that the adequate presentation of his views is a matter of peculiar difficulty.   Indeed, even apart from its singular lack of method, the fact that the work is so largely controversial in character, increases the difficulty of extracting from it the author's own system.   The order of exposition is in many respects so unfortunate that one is tempted to disregard it altogether; but, even at the expense of some repetition, it seems desirable to begin by

---

[1] See p. 37.

[2] The whole title reads: *De legibus naturae: disquisitio philosophica, in qua earum forma, summa capita, ordo, promulgatio, et obligatio e rerum natura investigantur; quin etiam elementa philosophiae Hobbianae, cum moralis tum civilis, considerantur et refutantur.*   The passages cited in the following exposition will be from the English translation by John Maxwell, published in 1727, and all references will be to the pages of that edition.

noticing the principal points in the author's own somewhat elaborate Introduction. Here he was certainly writing with his whole system in view,[1] and it is well to let the somewhat heterogeneous elements that enter into it appear first in as close combination as they are capable of. After this general survey of the system, based upon the Introduction, we shall neglect the author's own order of exposition, and consider topically all the important problems which are discussed in the treatise.

Cumberland begins by asserting that the Laws of Nature are the foundation of all moral and civil knowledge. They may be deduced in two ways : (1) From the manifest 'effects' that flow from them ; (2) from the 'causes' whence they themselves arise. The author chooses to adopt the latter method, *i.e.*, that of 'arguing from cause to effect'. The former is practically the inductive, the latter the deductive method. Two objections are commonly made to the inductive method, as applied to the solution of the present problem. (1) It is said that we cannot infer from the writings of a few men, or even nations, what are the opinions or judgments of all men. (2) Even if the above objection did not hold, 'the authority of a known law-giver' is wanting to give these judgments the force of 'laws' to all men.[2] To neither of these objections does Cumberland himself attach much weight. The agreement of men is practically complete as to the things most essential, *e.g.*, worship of some deity, and a degree of humanity sufficient to prevent murder, theft, and adultery. Again, if the Laws of Nature be 'laws' at all, they need no new authority superadded to that originally belonging to them. However, to establish the existence of Natural Laws beyond the possibility of a doubt, Cumberland proposes to reverse the usual order of treatment. He says: "I have thought it proper to make a philosophical inquiry into their causes [*i.e.*, those of the Laws of Nature], as well internal

---

[1] It is to be noticed that he constantly uses the past tense, showing what *has been* the method of exposition in the following work.

[2] The reference here is plainly to Hobbes.

as external, the nearer and the more remote; for by this method we shall at last arrive at their first Author, or efficient Cause, from whose essential perfections, and internal sanction of them, by rewards and punishments, we have shown that their authority arises ".[1]

It will be seen that the method to be employed can hardly be described by the single word 'deductive'. First, we must work back to the First Cause; then, from the nature of the deity, as well as from human nature, which will have been considered on the way, certain results will follow. The 'Platonists,' to be sure, find an easy way out of the difficulty by assuming 'innate ideas'; but Cumberland is obliged to confess that he has "not been so happy as to learn the Laws of Nature in so short a way ".[2]    Not that he will oppose those who believe themselves more fortunate in this respect; but it seems ill-advised to base everything upon "an hypothesis which has been rejected by the generality of philosophers, as well heathen as Christian, and can never be proved against the Epicureans, with whom is our chief controversy ". The reference to the 'Epicureans' is significant. The author proposes to fight Hobbes with his own weapons. And, this being the case, he sets out to prove that "the Nature of Things, which subsists and is continually governed by its First Cause, does necessarily imprint on our minds some practical propositions . . . concerning the study of promoting the joint felicity of all rationals; and that the terms of these propositions do immediately and directly signify, that the First Cause, in his original constitution of things, has annexed the greatest rewards and punishments to the observance and neglect of these truths". Whence it manifestly follows that these are 'laws,' " Laws being nothing but practical propositions, with rewards or punishments annexed, promulg'd by competent authority ".[3]

The first point to be established, then, is that there *are* Laws of Nature, in the legitimate sense of the words. Having

[1] See p. 13.          [2] See p. 14.          [3] *Ibid.*

indicated his line of argument, which we shall consider later, Cumberland proceeds to the more characteristic and constructive part of his doctrine. From a consideration of the practical propositions which may fairly be ranked as Laws of Nature,[1] it appears that they may be reduced to one universal Law. This may be expressed as follows: "The endeavour, to the utmost of our power, of promoting the common good of the whole system of rational agents, conduces, as far as in us lies, to the good of every part, in which our own happiness, as that of a part, is contained. But contrary actions produce contrary effects, and consequently our own misery, among that of others."[2]

This reduction of the several Laws of Nature to a single ultimate one, regarding conduct on the part of the individual that shall conduce to the common weal, is shown by the author to be useful in a double way: (1) it is easier to remember [*sic*] one principle than many; and (2) "a certain rule or measure is afforded to the prudent man's judgment, by the help whereof he may ascertain that just measure in his actions and affections in which virtue consists".[3] This is eminently characteristic. The author's aim is practical throughout.[4] If he attempts to rationalise morality, to give a scientific explanation and justification of the existing moral code, it is in order that his work may prove an important help to right living. It is probable that Cumberland, like some contemporary writers, considerably exaggerates the 'practical' value of correct ethical theory.

The relation between Cumberland's Laws of Nature and Cudworth's Eternal Truths should be noticed. How shall we distinguish the so-called 'practical principles,' which we have been considering, from others equally ultimate, *e.g.*, those of mathematics? We say that the former 'oblige' us; the latter not—but why? Simply by reason of the nature of the effects, according to Cumberland. We can *afford* to disregard many, at least, of the truths of geometry; not so

---

[1] Cumberland nowhere attempts exhaustively to enumerate them.
[2] See p. 16.    [3] See p. 30.    [4] See p. 36.

the moral law, for our happiness—and, as the author shows later, even our preservation—depends upon our observance of it. The criterion, then, is frankly one of 'consequences' —a fact that must be borne in mind. But these 'consequences,' in part at least, are not arbitrary. " The happiness of each individual (from the prospect of enjoying which, or being deprived of it, the whole sanction is taken) is derived from the best state of the whole system, as the nourishment of each member of an animal depends upon the nourishment of the whole mass of blood diffused through the whole." [1] Now the actions which, by virtue of their own 'natural' force and efficacy, are calculated to promote the common good, are called 'naturally good'. Again, the common good being the end, " such actions as take the shortest way to this effect . . . are naturally [called] ' right,' because of their natural resemblance to a right line, which is the shortest that can be drawn between any two given points, . . . but the rule itself is called ' right,' as pointing out the shortest way to the end ".[2]

All this is characteristic and important, making allowance for the quaint use of language. The comparison of humanity to an organism is one to which the author frequently recurs.[3] That there is no ' categorical imperative ' for Cumberland is clear. The Laws of Nature themselves have, and need, a ' reason for being'. Conduct in accordance with them conduces to the common weal. It is with reference to this end that even they are ' right '.

The Introduction closes with a confession on the part of the author that his work is not altogether literary in style or method. The passage is itself, perhaps, calculated to emphasise this statement: " Its face is not painted with the florid colours of Rhetoric, nor are its eyes sparkling and sportive, the signs of a light wit; it wholly applies itself, as it were, with the composure and sedateness of an old man, to the study of natural knowledge, to gravity of manners, and to the cultivating of severer learning ".[4]

[1] See p. 21.    [2] See p. 22.    [3] See, *e.g.*, p. 115.    [4] See p. 36.

We shall now neglect the author's own order of exposition almost entirely, and endeavour to see the system as a whole, both in its strength and its weakness. It might seem as if we were logically bound to begin with a consideration of the Nature of Things, as Cumberland himself professes to do.[1] A very casual examination of the *De legibus naturae*, however, would be sufficient to show that the titles of the chapters give but a very indefinite idea of the nature of their contents. What Cumberland actually does, at the beginning of his treatise, is to explain at considerable length and with great care his notion of Laws of Nature. It is probable, however, that he was induced to do this largely for controversial reasons; and, as we are principally concerned with the constructive part of the work, we may neglect this order, although it is quite impossible to separate the constructive entirely from the controversial. It must always be remembered — the title of the treatise to the contrary notwithstanding—that the jural aspect of the system is *not* its most essential feature. Cumberland held the views that he did regarding Natural Laws in common with a great many of his contemporaries—perhaps the majority of those representing the conservative tendency.[2] His originality consisted in his attempt to discover an underlying principle from which all the special moral 'laws' or 'practical propositions' could be deduced.

It does not seem best, then, to begin, as Cumberland actually did, with an examination of the concept of Natural Law. Nor is one tempted to begin with the Nature of Things, ostensibly the first topic treated. Cumberland uses that expression throughout the treatise as if its meaning were perfectly clear and understood by everybody. His utterances on the subject, however, have all the confusion to which an author is liable whose interests are wholly practical, and who yet is obliged to speak in terms of an implicit metaphysic. At present we need notice only two passages. "The Nature

---

[1] See title of first chapter.
[2] Even Locke was influenced later by the current view.

of Things does not only signify this lower world, whereof
we are a part, but its Creator and Supreme Governor, God.
. . . It is certain that only true propositions, whether speculative or practical, are imprinted on our minds by the Nature
of Things, because a natural action points out that only
which exists, and is never the cause of any falsehood, which
proceeds wholly from a voluntary rashness, joining or separating notions which Nature has not joined or separated." [1]
Again, " We cannot doubt of the nature of created beings,
but that both things external, exciting thoughts in us, and
our mind comparing these thoughts, are the causes of Necessary Truths ".[2]   The vagueness and inconsequence of these
remarks speak for themselves, and show how unsatisfactory
Cumberland is when on metaphysical ground.   It is hardly
necessary to call attention to his agreement with Descartes
as to the origin of human error.

On the whole, it seems best to begin our examination of
the system by considering the author's view of the nature of
man and of society.   We have seen that Hobbes regarded
society as artificial.   According to his view, it was made up
of a certain number of mutually repellent atoms, each atom
being the radically and unalterably egoistic individual.   The
' contract ' was a device by which the antagonistic wills of an
indefinite number of self-seeking individuals gave place to
the ' one will ' of the sovereign.   Cumberland pronounces
emphatically against this view.   When Hobbes likens men
to ' wolves,' ' bears,' ' serpents,' [3] etc., he is guilty of libel
against human nature.   Referring to such remarks, our
author says :  " If they were true, it were evidently impossible
to reduce such beasts of prey, always thirsting after the blood
of their fellows, into a civil state ".[4]   The compact would
avail nothing, unless there were something in human nature
that would make men abide by their promises.   Cumberland
might have added that Hobbes is not at liberty to make any

[1] See p. 191.                          [2] See p. 192.
[3] *De homine*, vol. II. (Latin works, Molesworth's ed.), p. 91.
[4] See p. 295.

ultimate appeal to reason in the matter—even as showing
what is for the individual's selfish interest — for men learn
what is 'good' for them, as well as what is 'right,' from the
powers that be.

Hobbes had regarded the instinct of self-preservation, if
not the conscious seeking of one's own pleasure, as the
fundamental spring of human action. For Cumberland, on
the other hand, sympathy is as much an attribute of human
nature as a desire for one's own happiness. If this were not
so, as is suggested above, society itself could not exist. To
be sure, the author sometimes insists upon the pleasures of
(a not too expensive) benevolence in a way to lead one to
suspect that, after all, egoism may be at the basis of apparently disinterested conduct;[1] but such passages hardly need
detract from the force of distinct utterances, like the above,
regarding the impossibility of a society composed of absolutely egoistic individuals. The discussions regarding altruism *vs.* egoism which we meet with in the treatise, are
sometimes quite confusing on account of the author's naïve
certainty that the good of the individual and the good of
society are *always* (in the particular case as well as in the
long run) identical. We have seen that, in the Introduction,
society is already compared to an organism.[2] Such being
its nature, it is idle to speak of the good of one part as
*opposed* to the good of another ; for the good of any particular
part (*i.e.*, any individual) clearly must depend upon the
'health of the social organism,' as Mr. Stephen would say.
Cumberland does not go so far as some modern writers in
pushing this analogy, but it helps to bring out an important
side of his system.

So much in general regarding man's 'fitness' for society,
so far as an original tendency in the direction of altruistic, as
well as egoistic, conduct is concerned. Here man is regarded
from the standpoint of society, which is to be compared to
an organism rather than to a collection of mutually repellent

---

[1] See, *e.g.*, p. 211.  [2] See also p. 115.

atoms. When Cumberland has the individual more particularly in mind, he is apt to insist more upon the 'rational' nature of man. Before considering this question as to the meaning and scope of Right Reason, let us notice two definitions, and also the author's brief inventory of the powers of the mind. " By man," he says, at the beginning of Chap. ii., " I understand an animal endowed with a mind; and Hobbes himself, in his treatise of *Human Nature*, acknowledges the mind to be one of the principal parts of man ". By 'animal' is understood " what the philosophers agree is to be found in brutes: the powers of receiving increase by nourishment, of beginning motion, and of propagating their species ". It is not quite clear that Cumberland would allow sensation to brutes.[1] However, he sometimes refers to sub-human manifestations of sympathy. As regards the mind, he says: " To the mind we ascribe Understanding and Will; to the Understanding we reduce Apprehending, Comparing, Judging, Reasoning, a Methodical Disposition, and the Memory of all these things, and of the objects about which they are conversant. To the Will we ascribe both the simple acts of choosing and refusing, and that vehemence of those actions which discovers itself in the passions, over and above that emotion or disturbance of the body, which is visible in them." [2]

Such details are merely preliminary, and we shall now ask what is meant by 'Right Reason,' an expression which is constantly recurring in the treatise. Hobbes had practically denied that there was any such faculty in man. In Cumberland's system, on the other hand, Right Reason plays an important, if a somewhat Protean part. Here, as in the case of the Nature of Things, we find a degree of confusion that can only be explained by the fact that the author's interests are purely practical, and that he is speaking in terms of an incon-

---

[1] See, *e.g.*, p. 94.   Also *cf.* Dr. Frank E. Spaulding's *Richard Cumberland als Begründer der englischen Ethik*, p. 26.   There is an immense amount of physiological data in the treatise, and it is sometimes hard to tell whether Cumberland is speaking in terms of psychology or of physiology.

[2] See p. 94.

sistent metaphysic that he has never taken the trouble to think out. The following curious passage is perhaps the author's most explicit statement regarding the nature of Right Reason. He says: " I agree, however, with him [Hobbes], that by Right Reason is not to be understood an infallible Faculty (as he affirms many, but I know not who, to understand it); but yet by it is to be understood a faculty not false in these acts of judging. Nor is it properly understood to be an act of reasoning (as he too rashly asserts), but an effect of the Judgment; that is, true propositions treasured up in the memory, whether they be premises or conclusions, of which some that are practical are called ' laws,' for actions are compared with these in order to examine their goodness, not with those acts of reasoning which discover them; yet I willingly allow that these acts of reasoning are also included in the notion of Right Reason." [1] And then, as against Hobbes's view that, out of civil society, " every man's proper reason is to be esteemed, not only the standard of his own actions, which he does at his own peril, but also the measure of other men's reason with respect to his affairs," [2] Cumberland adds that this cannot be the case, " For, out of civil society, any one may distinguish Right Reason without making a comparison with his own. Because there is a common standard . . . the Nature of Things, as it lies before us, carefully to be observed and examined by all our faculties."

The first of the passages just quoted is one of the most perplexed in the whole treatise. Right Reason is not an " infallible faculty," yet " not false in these acts of judging "; it is not properly an " act of reasoning," but the resulting " true propositions "—yet these " acts of reasoning " are, after all, to be included under Right Reason. This seems hopeless, but perhaps we may find what Cumberland means by not expecting to find too much. First, with regard to that other expression so often used, ' The Nature of Things'. Cumberland is a

[1] See p. 103.
[2] This would apply, of course, only in the ' state of nature '.

wholly naïve realist. By the Nature of Things he seems to mean all that actually and objectively *is*—including God as well as His world. And it is needless to say that Cumberland's God is a 'transcendent' (as opposed to an 'immanent') deity. This Nature of Things being posited, we have a perfectly objective standard as regards not only theoretical truths but practical propositions. The Reason of man is such as to fit him to apprehend this Nature of Things exactly as it is, always provided that he does not, by a 'free' act of will, choose to assent to that which is not clear and distinct. Cumberland's test of truth and theory of error are the same as Descartes's; he differs from the founder of modern philosophy, of course, in his rejection of 'innate ideas'. For Cumberland, then, having no theory of cognition other than that of common-sense, and caring only for the *truth* of the deliverances of Right Reason, it is a matter of indifference whether we call the latter a 'faculty,' an 'act of reasoning,' or the resulting 'true propositions'. In the last resort, Cumberland, like Descartes, seems to depend upon the necessary truthfulness of God.

We now see what, in general, Cumberland holds regarding the nature of man. He is not without original altruistic instincts, and is, moreover, essentially a rational being. That his instinctive altruism tends to fit him for society goes without saying. But this alone is not sufficient. Alongside of the altruistic instincts, are others that must be recognised as egoistic. The relation in which the two stand to each other is not clearly indicated, but, at any rate, it is evident that they would be likely to conflict, if reason did not furnish a rule of conduct. Now man's rational character fits him for society in a double way.[1] (1) It enables him to see his own interests, not as something apart from, but in relation to, the common weal. (2) It enables him to apprehend and desire the Good, *qua* Good, quite independently of the question as to whose

---

[1] This will appear from what follows regarding the motive of the individual agent.

Good it may be.[1]   Thus, "whoever determines his Judgment and his Will by Right Reason, must *agree* with all others who judge according to Right Reason in the same matter".[2] Hence, to use Cumberland's own expression, "the fundamental cornerstone of the Temple of Concord is laid by Nature".

In any system of Ethics, it is of course necessary to distinguish between the (objective) ' end ' of moral action and the ' motive ' of the individual agent.   We have already seen, in the Introduction, what the ' end ' dictated by Right Reason is, and we shall have to consider it more at length later ; but it is important for us here to ask more particularly than we have yet done, regarding the motive of the individual agent, whether, and if so, how, he can directly will the ' common good '.   Here, again, Cumberland's utterances are confusing. For instance, in Chap. ii. he says : " Universal benevolence is the spring and source of every act of innocence and fidelity, of humanity and gratitude, and indeed of all the virtues by which property and commerce are maintained ".[3]   But when later, in the next chapter, he attempts to explain how man can will the common good, he rests the argument mainly upon the rational nature of man ; and proposes to demonstrate the possibility of altruistic conduct *a priori* to those who acknowledge the nature of the will to consist in " the consent of the mind with the judgment of the understanding, concerning things agreeing among themselves ".[4]   Since the understanding is able to judge what is ' good ' for others, as well as for the agent himself, there is no reason why one cannot act in a purely altruistic way.   Just what Cumberland means here will be seen more clearly by referring to what he says regarding Hobbes's contention that we first desire things, and then call them ' good '.   Cumberland holds, on the contrary, " that things are first judged to be good, and that they are afterwards desired only so far as they seem good ".[5]

[1] It will readily be seen that this second function of Right Reason is hardly consistent with the principles of the system.

[2] See p. 107.    [3] See pp. 114, 115.    [4] See p. 173.    [5] See p. 168.

All this, of course, is unsatisfactory. From a general statement of the universality of a certain degree of benevolence,
we have passed to a bit of more than questionable psychology, used to explain the possibility of altruistic conduct.
But Cumberland does not always attempt to rationalise the
matter in this way. Somewhat earlier in the treatise,[1] he
attempts to show how altruistic feelings would naturally
arise and be fostered, not only among men, but also among
the higher animals. We may omit as irrelevant the first two
considerations urged and pass to the third, which is, that " the
motion of the blood and heart, which is necessary to life, is
befriended by love, desire, hope, and joy, especially when conversant about a *great* good ". But a good known to extend
to the most possible will by that very fact be recognised as
the greatest. Hence benevolent affections will conduce to
the *preservation* of man or animal, as the case may be. A
fourth argument is " that animals are incited to endeavour the
propagation of their own species by the force of the same
causes which preserve the life of every individual, so that
these two are connected by [a] tie evidently natural ".[2] The
details of the argument are not particularly convincing. The
important point is: Cumberland argues that altruism first
appears as sexual love and the parental instinct to protect
offspring. Having once arisen, there is no reason why it
may not extend ever so much further.

But in the latter part of the treatise, there is an interesting
passage which should not be neglected. The author says:
" No one does truly observe the law unless he sincerely propose the same end with the legislator. But, if he directly and
constantly aim at this end, it is no diminution to the sincerity
of his obedience that, at the instigation of his own happiness,
he first perceived that his sovereign commanded him to respect a higher end." [3] There is a suggestion here that the
individual first comes to act in an (objectively) altruistic way,
because he finds that it conduces to his own happiness; but,

---

[1] See pp. 122 *et seq.*        [2] See p. 128.        [3] See p. 275.

this *habit* having been established, he comes to act for the common weal without any thought of self. This doctrine will be found clearly worked out in the case of two, at least, of Paley's predecessors, *i.e.*, Gay and Tucker.

From the above it will be seen that, while Cumberland's view of the nature of man is in striking contrast to that of Hobbes, and in substantial agreement with that of Grotius, his treatment of the motive of the individual is rather vague and unsatisfactory. It is difficult to say whether, according to Cumberland, moral action is ever prompted by purely disinterested benevolence or not. To be sure, all discussions of the kind are likely enough to end in misunderstanding, because the ' egoism ' and the ' altruism ' of which we speak with so much confidence are themselves more or less of the nature of abstractions. Granted that the good of the individual is inextricably connected with the good of society in many respects, why should we expect to find the ' self-regarding ' and the ' other-regarding ' affections clearly differentiated? If Cumberland had contented himself with showing that, in the case of beings endowed with sympathy, ' egoism ' and ' altruism ' must often coincide, we should have had no reason to complain of his treatment. But this he did not do. To what an extent he was capable of confusion on this point may be seen by referring to the more than paradoxical passage in the Introduction,[1] in which he attempts to prove that he who performs good actions in gratitude for benefits already received, shows less generosity than one who is moved to action " by the hope only of good ". The relation of Cumberland's biological proof of altruism to Evolutional theory is obvious. At the same time, it should be noted that his position here is not inconsistent with his own essentially static view of the Nature of Things.

[1] Not previously quoted. See p. 29.

# CHAPTER II.

HAVING considered somewhat at length Cumberland's view of the nature of man, we shall now turn to the second main division of our exposition, which depends essentially upon the above, *i.e.*, his doctrine of the Good. Although the author is particularly concerned to show the eternity and immutability of the Laws of Nature, this jural aspect of the system, which will be considered later, must not blind us to the fact that for Cumberland there is nothing corresponding to Kant's ' categorical imperative '. On this point he is quite explicit, as might be expected from the general character of the system. He says: " These propositions are called practical, nor is it necessary that they should be pronounced in the form of a gerund, 'this or that *ought* to be done,' as some school-men teach ; because that fitness which is expressed by a gerund wants explanation ".[1] The form of the propositions makes no particular difference, as the author goes on to show. They may be given : (1) as statements of fact, *i.e.*, that certain things necessarily conduce both to the ' common good ' and to that of the individual agent; or (2) as commands, *i.e.*, as Laws of Nature; or (3) as ' gerunds,' in the sense indicated above. Evidently we have here to do with an Ethics of the Good, and not with a Duty Ethics.

But what is the Good? Cumberland has much to say regarding the good of each and the good of all, ' natural ' good and ' moral ' good; but he nowhere tells us as definitely as we

---

[1] See p. 180.

could wish exactly what the Good is. It is a little curious that, just after remarking that "it is of the last consequence to establish a well-grounded and irrefragable notion of Good,"[1] he should make no serious attempt to do so, but indulge in a number of characteristic criticisms of Hobbes. Throughout the treatise Cumberland is concerned to oppose the two following related views of Hobbes regarding the Good: (1) that the [natural] Good for each man is merely what he wants; and (2) that, before the establishment of the State and the enacting of civil laws, there is no 'measure' of the Good.

We have already seen that, in opposition to Hobbes's doctrine that we call a thing good because we want it, Cumberland holds that we want it because first we believe it to be good.[2] As regards the view that in a 'state of nature' there is no 'common measure,' the author somewhat naïvely asserts that of course there is—the Nature of Things.[3] In the same paragraph, however, he explicitly says: "Whatsoever proposition points out the true cause of preservation does at the same time show what is true good". Later in the treatise, Good is defined as: "that which preserves, or enlarges and perfects, the faculties of any one thing or of several". And a few lines further on: "that is good to man which preserves or enlarges the powers of the mind and body, or of either, without prejudice to the other".[4]

The first passage quoted may sound like Hobbes; but of course what Cumberland has in mind, when he speaks of preservation, is the preservation, not primarily of the individual, but of society—the 'health of the social organism,' as Mr. Stephen would say. Another important difference is that Cum-

---

[1] See p. 169.

[2] Connected with this is the question regarding the permanence of the Good. Cumberland holds that "Hobbes's fiction that good and evil are changeable is perfectly inconsistent with the necessary and immutable causes, which he everywhere asserts, of the being and preservation of man" (p. 62). It is to be doubted if this is at all conclusive against Hobbes.

[3] See p. 62.  [4] See p. 165.

berland's idea of the Good, from this point of view, includes
perfection as well as preservation.  Indeed, the emphasis is
certainly to be laid upon perfection.  Man is not merely a
bundle of egoistic appetites, but a being essentially rational
—a personality to be developed.

But in Chap. v. we have an example of the other set of
passages, even more numerous, which might be cited as showing that Cumberland's ideal was that of ordinary Hedonism.
" I proceed more fully to explain the common, which also I
call the public good.  By these words I understand the aggregate or sum of all those good things which either we can
contribute towards, or are necessary to, the *happiness* of all
rational beings, considered as collected into one body, each
in his proper order." [1]  The ' rational ' beings referred to are
God and all men.  Animals are placed practically on the same
level with the vegetable world.  " The perfection [2] of these
things is not properly, at least not ultimately, sought after ;
their use and concurrence with our actions towards the good
of rational beings is the thing intended."

As it is not clear—thus far, at any rate—in what terms
Cumberland would have defined the Good, if he had been
forced to be more exact, it becomes important to consider his
treatment of happiness.  This is decidedly careless, and sometimes ' circular,' *i.e.*, the Good is frequently defined in terms
of happiness, while happiness is sometimes [3] defined as ' the
possession of good things '.  Indeed, Cumberland occasionally uses the words interchangeably even in the same sentence.  However, allowing for his careless use of language,
with which we are already familiar, his theory seems to be that
human happiness results largely from action, particularly from
the exercise of one's intellectual powers.  For instance, in
treating of the rewards that attend observance of the Laws
of Nature, he speaks of " that pleasure or part of our happiness which is necessarily contained in such natural employ-

---

[1] See p. 202.  The title of this long and important chapter is : " Of the Law
of Nature and its Obligation ".

[2] Note the use of the word.            [3] See, *e.g.*, p. 43.

ment of the human faculties as leads to the best end . . . for all exercise of natural powers, especially of the highest order, in which we neither miss our aim nor turn out of the direct road, is naturally pleasant ".[1] Now freedom from evil or uneasiness may depend upon external circumstances; no other pleasures than the so-called ' active ' ones take their rise from within ourselves. Hence this is the only happiness to which moral philosophy directs us.[2] But again, Cumberland says : " I have no inclination very curiously to inquire whether the happiness of man be an aggregate of the most vigorous actions, which can proceed from our faculties ; or rather a most grateful sense of them, joined with tranquillity and joy, which by some is called pleasure. These are inseparably connected, and both necessary to happiness." [3] This is one of the most ambiguous of the passages making for hedonism.[4] It will be noticed, however, that ' tranquillity ' is distinctly stated to be an essential constituent of happiness.

As regards the nature, or rather the cause, of this tranquillity, the author speaks earlier in the treatise of an ' essential part ' of happiness, *i.e.*, " that inward peace which arises from an uniform wisdom, always agreeing with itself ".[5] If we act differently toward others from what we do toward ourselves, we have the discomfort that attends any inconsistency. But, in addition, " that great joy is also wanting which arises in a benevolent mind from a sense of the felicity of others ". Of course, tranquillity does not depend entirely upon ' consistency ' in thought and action. We saw but a moment ago that it depended materially upon external things. It also depends largely, according to Cumberland, upon the con-

---

[1] See p. 100. *Cf.* p. 211, where Cumberland emphasises the pleasures of success in one's undertakings.

[2] This passage should not be too much insisted on. By itself, it is misleading.

[3] See p. 209.

[4] Strictly speaking, of course, it leaves open the question as to what terms we shall use (hedonistic or otherwise) in defining the Good.

[5] See p. 44.

sciousness of having deserved well of our fellows. But it is characteristic of our author to insist upon the partial dependence of tranquillity upon having acted consistently.

So far, then, happiness is seen to consist principally in (1) the pleasures attending our normal, particularly our intellectual, activities; (2) tranquillity, which depends partly upon (*a*) external circumstances, (*b*) the feeling that we have been 'consistent' in thought and action, (*c*) the consciousness that we have acted for the common weal; and (3) the pleasure which results from a knowledge of the happiness of others.

What shall be said, then, with regard to Cumberland's view of the Good in general? We have seen that he speaks, now in terms of 'preservation' and 'perfection,' now in terms of 'happiness'. In one passage, while maintaining the somewhat trite thesis that 'virtue is its own reward,' he says: " I care not in this argument to distinguish between the health of mind and the consciousness or enjoyment thereof by reflection, since nature has so intimately united these two, that the free exercise of the virtues and the perception or inward sense thereof are inseparable ".[1] A statement like this must put us on our guard against expecting too definite an answer to the question which we are considering. 'Happiness' always attends 'perfection'; 'perfection' is necessary in order that we may attain 'happiness'. Practically, then, it makes little difference which we say—and Cumberland's aim was preeminently a practical one, as we have seen. I do not believe that it is possible dogmatically to decide on either interpretation. We should be forcing a distinction, important for us, upon an author who regarded it with frank indifference. Indeed, it would be much truer to say that both happiness and perfection, in our understanding of the words, are included in the author's conception of the Good.

It should be noticed, however, that Cumberland's actual treatment of 'happiness' is a good deal clearer than his treatment of 'perfection'; and there is always the lurking possi-

---

[1] See p. 265.

bility that the latter may be regarded as of such importance, because it is a necessary means to the former. The general impression which the system gives one certainly is that, on the whole, it is hedonistic. At the same time, it would be sheer misrepresentation to hold that it is consistently so. It is much better to let the two principles, which we now regard as logically distinct, stand side by side, recognising, however, that greater emphasis is laid upon 'happiness' than upon 'perfection'.

This comparatively vague treatment of 'perfection' has led Professor Sidgwick to hold that Cumberland "does not even define perfection so as strictly to exclude from it the notion of moral perfection or virtue, and save his explanation of morality from an obvious logical circle".[1] I am inclined to think, however, that Professor Sidgwick exaggerates the ambiguity of Cumberland's notion of 'perfection'. As Dr. Spaulding has shown,[2] the 'perfection' referred to is a 'perfection of mind and body,'[3] which is explained as the 'development of their powers'.[4] This will be plain if we keep in mind what Cumberland says regarding 'naturally' good things. These are defined as (1) those which adorn and cheer the mind, and (2) those which preserve and increase the powers of the body.[5]

We shall now have to notice the distinction (just mentioned) which Cumberland makes between what is 'naturally' and what is 'morally' good. This has been ignored hitherto, because it is likely to lead to confusion. What things 'naturally' good are, we have just seen. On the other hand, "only voluntary actions conformable to some law, especially that of Nature," are 'morally' good. It is quite misleading, when Cumberland insists that 'natural' good is more extensive than 'moral' good. It is not a matter of more or less, but of what we may call, for convenience, the 'substantive' and the 'adjective' use of the word 'good'. Certain things, once for all, do, according to the eternal nature of things, conduce to

[1] See *Hist. of Ethics*, p. 173.
[2] See *Richard Cumberland*, pp. 55 *et seq.*     [3] See p. 305.
[4] See pp. 165 *et seq.*, already cited.     [5] See p. 203.

man's preservation, perfection, and happiness. These are 'naturally' good, or, as we now prefer to say, they constitute the Good. On the other hand, those 'voluntary actions' which conduce to the Good, and so fulfil the Laws of Nature, are called 'morally' good. This is a somewhat unfortunate use of language, for it looks at first as if Ethics had to do only with the 'morally' good. This is so far from being true that 'natural' good is the ultimate, not that which is 'morally' good; otherwise Cumberland would be involved in a manifest circle at the very outset. But while Ethics must needs begin with a consideration of 'natural good'—'the Good,' as we shall call it—it is not equally concerned with all that would ideally go to constitute the Good. Cumberland himself, in the first chapter of the treatise,[1] calls our attention to the usefulness of the Stoics' distinction between things in our power and things out of our power. Now Ethics, from the nature of the case, must be practically limited in its scope to a consideration of things in our power. At the same time, to limit the Good to things in our power would be obviously stultifying, whether we accept preservation, perfection, or happiness (in our sense of the word) as the criterion. The only type of Ethics which can do that is the 'duty Ethics,' the Ethics of the 'good will'; and, however heterogeneous the elements may be that enter into Cumberland's system, he surely is not logically affiliated to the Kantian school.

So far we have been considering the Good quite in general. As a matter of fact, of course, when the Laws of Nature are under consideration, Cumberland has in mind, not the good of any individual or class merely, but the good of all—or rather, to be more exact, the good of the greatest number. Indeed, that this good of the whole is greater than the (hypothetical) good of the isolated part, and therefore the 'greatest end' of human action, Cumberland practically puts among self-evident truths.[2] But, as he says, "the good of the collective body is no other than the greatest which accrues to all, or to the major

[1] See p. 63.        [2] See p. 97.

part of the whole ".[1]  Although he speaks of society as an organic whole—particularly when he is concerned to show that the good of each ultimately coincides with the good of all others—he never loses sight of the claims of the individual, as some modern theorists, standing on much the same ground, are inclined to do.

It is to be remembered that the 'greatest end' is nothing less than the 'joint felicity of *all* rationals,' so that the happiness or glory of God is included, as well as the happiness of all men.   If there be question as to the 'parts' of the 'greatest end,' and their 'order,' we are told : "that part of the end will be superior which is grateful to the nature of the more perfect being.   So that the glory of God is chief, then follows the happiness of many good men, and inferior to this is the happiness of any particular person."[2]

Thus far we have neglected what Cumberland himself may very well have regarded as most important, *i.e.*, the jural aspect of the system.   As we have already seen, he begins with an elaborate discussion concerning the Laws of Nature. It did not seem best to follow his order of exposition, because this appeared to have been dictated largely by controversial considerations.   Moreover, it is important to see that—from our present point of view, at least—the system stands alone, without the assistance of this scaffolding of Natural Laws.[3] At the same time, one would have but a very inadequate idea either of the external form of the system or of the author's actual application of his unifying principle, without a knowledge of the substance of what he says regarding the Laws of Nature.   To this subject, then, we shall proceed.   It will form the third, and last, main division of our exposition.

Hobbes himself had admitted Laws of Nature, but in a sense wholly different from that ordinarily attaching to the expression, as used by his contemporaries—indeed, in a sense not

---

[1] See p. 60.                              [2] See p. 280.
[3] Of course this is not intended to beg the question as to the ultimate validity of a Utilitarian system.

easy to define, as we have seen. Cumberland returns to the original conception of Natural Laws,[1] and is intensely in earnest in maintaining their existence.

It will be remembered that our author discards the doctrine of 'innate ideas'. We must, then, learn the Laws of Nature from experience. How does experience teach us? In early childhood, we act in a practically purposeless way until we come to recognise the different effects of different kinds of actions, not only upon ourselves, but upon others as well. "Hence," as Cumberland naïvely says, "we draw some conclusions concerning actions acceptable to God, but many more concerning such as are advantageous and disadvantageous to men."[2] When, in mature years, these conclusions come to be accurately expressed in a general form, they are called 'Practical Propositions'. We have already seen that the form of these propositions is immaterial. They may be expressed (1) as statements of fact, (2) as commands [laws], or (3) as 'gerunds'. Notwithstanding this, however, in the main body of the work, Cumberland almost always speaks of Practical Propositions as Laws, and is particularly concerned to show that they are technically such.

Hobbes had insisted that a Law must be *clearly* promulgated by a *competent* authority, *i.e.*, by one having power to enforce obedience; and had denied that the so-called Laws of Nature possessed either of these requisites. Cumberland, on the other hand, while accepting Hobbes's definition of a Law, attempts to show that the Laws of Nature are 'Laws' in precisely Hobbes's sense of the word. At the beginning of Chap. v., he defines the [general] Law of Nature as "a proposition proposed to the observation of, or impressed upon, the mind with sufficient clearness, by the Nature of Things, from the will of the First Cause, which points out that possible action of a rational agent, which will chiefly promote the common good, and by which only the entire happiness of particular persons can be obtained".[3] The former part of

---

[1] As held, *e.g.*, by Grotius.
[2] See p. 179.
[3] See p. 189.

the definition contains the 'precept,' the latter the 'sanction';
and the mind receives the 'impression' of both from the
Nature of Things. Neither words nor any arbitrary signs
whatever are essential to a Law. Given a knowledge of
actions and their consequences, we have all that is needed.

With regard to the *clearness* that is to be looked for in the
Laws of Nature, Cumberland says: "That proposition is proposed or imprinted by the objects with sufficient plainness,
whose terms and their natural connection are so exposed to
the senses and thoughts, by obvious and common experience,
that the mind of an adult person, not labouring under any
impediment, if it will attend or take notice, may easily observe
it".[1] There are such propositions. They are analogous to
the following: Men may be killed by a profuse loss of blood,
by suffocation, by want of food, etc.

These propositions, then, are given in human experience
with sufficient *clearness*. Is there any *power* behind them,
capable of enforcing obedience? The very fact that certain
consequences, good or bad, apparently always ensue upon certain classes of actions, would of itself suggest that this is the
case. But we can go further. The Law of Nature, as above
stated, points out the way to the common Good; God must
desire the common Good; therefore these [derived] propositions must be regarded as Laws of God—in which case there
can be no question as to the 'competent authority'. The
good or evil consequences which result from actions, must be
regarded as 'sanctions,' divinely ordained. In a word, these
Practical Propositions, derived from experience, are not only
Laws, but Laws in the completest possible sense.

We are now quite prepared to understand Cumberland's
notion of Obligation. He says: "Obligation is that act of a
legislator by which he declares that actions conformable to his
law are necessary to those for whom the law is made. An
action is then understood to be necessary to a rational agent,
when it is certainly one of the causes necessarily required to
that happiness which he naturally, and consequently neces-

[1] See p. 192.

sarily, desires." [1]  Obligation is regarded as perfectly immutable, for it could change only with the Nature of Things.[2] That anything in what is so vaguely termed the Nature of Things [3] could change, Cumberland did not for a moment suppose.

In treating of obligation, the author sometimes uses language which might suggest determinism.   It is to be remembered, however, that he is an uncompromising libertarian —so far, at least, as it is possible to define the position of one so little given to metaphysical speculation or the precise use of metaphysical language.   By the 'necessity' and 'immutability' of the Laws of Nature, he simply means that, if certain acts are performed, certain consequences will necessarily ensue, now and always.   That the acts themselves, in the particular case, are determined, he would deny.   We have already seen that human error is explained by Cumberland in the same way as by Descartes—*i.e.*, as resulting from a rash use of our Free Will, where we arbitrarily assent to that which is not clear and distinct.

It might seem highly improbable that so prominent and zealous a Churchman as Cumberland, in treating of the 'sanction' of the Law of Nature, would fail to insist upon rewards and punishments after death; yet such is the case.   In the Introduction, he states that he has abstained from 'theological questions,' and has attempted to prove his position from 'reason' and 'experience'.[4]   The treatise as a whole bears out this statement fairly well, it being understood that by 'theological questions' Cumberland means those pertaining to revelation.   In one passage, he says: "Among these rewards [attending obedience to the Laws of Nature] is that happy immortality which natural reason promises to attend

---

[1] See p. 233; *cf.* p. 206.          [2] See p. 226.

[3] This is a good case to illustrate the ambiguity of the expression 'Nature of Things'.   Does the 'immutable Nature of Things' mean certain physical and other laws which remain constant?   Or does the 'immutability' extend to the natures of particular classes of beings?

[4] See p. 34.

the minds of good men, when separated from the body ";[1] but this is almost the only instance in which he directly refers to the future life in connection with the ' sanction,' and it is significant, perhaps, that even here he does not refer to future punishments. Cumberland's reticence on this subject is by no means difficult to explain, and it argues nothing against his orthodoxy. In the first place, as we have seen, he wished to confute Hobbes on his own ground. Moreover, he doubt-less knew perfectly well that, for those who believed in im-mortality, rewards and punishments after death would be regarded as constituting by far the most important part of the sanction, whereas, to those who were sceptical in the matter, such considerations would not appeal at all.

But what Cumberland lost by confining himself to a con-sideration of the consequences of actions that might be ex-pected to ensue in this present life, he endeavoured to make up by distinguishing sharply between (1) ' immediate ' [inter-nal] and (2) ' mediate ' [external] consequences. The former are emphasised considerably at the expense of the latter, doubtless for the reason that here one might plausibly claim greater certainty. The wicked may, in particular cases, ap-pear to flourish in our own day, as they did in David's time ; but the ' external ' consequences of actions are by no means the only ones. By the ' internal ' consequences, Cumberland might seem to mean simply the approval or disapproval of conscience, but this is by no means the case. He says : " The immediate connection between every man's greatest happiness of mind, that is in his power, and the actions which he performs to promote most effectually the common good of God and men, consists in this : that these are the very actions, in the exercise and inward consciousness whereof every man's happiness (as far as it is in his own power) consists ". This is supposed to be " after the same manner as we perceive a connection between the health and unimpaired powers of the body and its actions ".[2] The case, then, is regarded as analo-gous to the connection between feeling well and being well

---

[1] See p. 267.  [2] See p. 207.

physically. If this seem like begging the question, it is to be observed further that man can find free scope for the varied activities (particularly mental) in which his happiness so largely consists, only by acting for the common weal.

As regards the 'mediate' effects, or external consequences of actions, Cumberland acknowledges that we have here to do, not with certainty, but with probability merely. Still it is a very high degree of probability. In the long run, actions tending to promote the common weal must lead to a maximum of possible happiness for the individual agent; actions against the common weal, to a maximum of possible unhappiness. If advantages are not to be procured in this way, *i.e.*, by acting for the common weal, they come under the head of 'things not in our power'. The Divine moral government of human affairs (here and now) is referred to as tending still further to justify the author's position.

The treatment of this subject is considerably perplexed, partly owing to the author's attempt to avoid the appearance of harbouring egoism in his system—an attempt, it should be added, which is not uniformly successful. From the controversial point of view, he doubtless had good reason to insist upon the greater importance of the internal sanction, and, indeed, his general position may very well be in accord with human experience; but it is to be doubted if the distinction will bear the weight which is actually put upon it in the treatise. For, by employing it, Cumberland attempted to prove the complete sufficiency of the 'sanction,' as given in the present life, for every moral agent whatsoever.

It will be seen that the whole account of 'obligation' brings out, in clear relief, the egoistic elements in the system. Cumberland's theory of obligation (so far as his explicit treatment is concerned) is not essentially different from Paley's, though it must be conceded that it is expressed in a much less offensive way. One may surmise that this appearance of egoism would have been more effectually guarded against, had it not been for the fact that the jural treatment of morality involving emphasis on reward and punishment, was made necessary by the author's desire to fight Hobbes on his own ground.

Cumberland's deduction of the particular Laws of Nature from the general Law, which we have thus far been considering, is by no means elaborate. It is contained in the three short chapters: vi., "Of Those Things which are Contained in the General Law of Nature"; vii., "Of the Original of Dominion and the Moral Virtues"; viii., "Of the Moral Virtues in Particular".[1] The last chapter, ix., "Corollaries," as the name might suggest, does not properly belong to the systematic part of the treatise. We shall now notice the principal points in the three chapters first mentioned.

Chapter vi., "Of Those Things which are Contained in the General Law of Nature," is very short, and even so contains a good deal that has been treated before. This is rather disappointing, for it is just here that we should naturally look for the most important part of the 'deduction'. Two questions are proposed by the author: (1) What things are comprehended in the common Good? and (2) What actions tend to promote it? The answer to the first question contains nothing new or to the present purpose. As regards actions tending to promote the common Good, Cumberland divides them into classes, each corresponding to the particular 'faculty' of the mind supposed to be principally involved. Hence we have (1) acts of the Understanding, (2) acts of the Will and Affections, or acts of the Body determined by the Will. Under the former head Cumberland treats of Prudence, which he divides into (*a*) Constancy, and (*b*) Moderation. Constancy, again, may manifest itself either as Fortitude or as Patience; while Moderation implies Integrity and Diligence, or Industry.

Passing to 'acts of the Will' enjoined by the Law of Nature, these are all found to be included in 'the most ex-

---

[1] The first five chapters are: i., "Of the Nature of Things"; ii., "Of Human Nature and Right Reason"; iii., "Of Natural Good"; iv., "Of the Practical Dictates of Reason"; v., "Of the Law of Nature and its Obligation". These titles, however, as already said, do not give a very definite idea of the nature of the contents of the several chapters.

tensive and operative benevolence'. The author says: "It belongs to the same benevolence to endeavour that nothing be done contrary to the common good, and to correct and amend it if there has; hence Equity [or Justice] is an essential branch of this virtue ".[1] This Universal Benevolence also includes Innocence, Gentleness, Repentance, Restitution, and Self-denial; and, further, Candour, Fidelity, and Gratitude. " In these few heads," says Cumberland, " are contained the primary special Laws of Nature and the fundamental principles of all virtues and societies ".[2]

In this connection, Cumberland asserts that some actions may be regarded as morally ' indifferent,' but the term is misleading. Those actions without which it is impossible to obtain the end proposed are ' necessary '; those to which there are others equivalent, *i.e.*, equally calculated to conduce to the common weal, are termed ' indifferent '. Every action, then, may very well have a moral character; and yet it may be no more efficacious in promoting the ' greatest end ' than certain other actions. Accordingly it may, in this sense only, be termed ' indifferent '. These cases, we are told, leave room for the greatest individual freedom; also for positive laws contracting such liberty within narrower bounds.

It will be seen that, however original and important may have been Cumberland's idea that the particular laws of moral action, or Laws of Nature, could be deduced from one principle, *viz.*, that requiring of all moral agents conduct that should conduce to the common Good, his ' deduction ' of these particular Laws thus far contains little or nothing calling for remark, unless it be the naïve application of a more than usually crude ' faculty psychology,' where he distinguishes between acts of the Understanding and those of the Will and Affections. This, however, is not relevant to the present discussion.

The two remaining chapters, vii., " Of the Original of Dominion and the Moral Virtues," and viii., " Of the Moral Virtues in Particular," treat incidentally of a great variety of

[1] See p. 309.     [2] See p. 311.

topics, but are principally concerned with the Laws of Nature which have to do with the distribution and tenure of property.

It will be remembered that Hobbes had maintained, though not in so many words, that ' self-preservation is the first law of nature'; and also, as regards property, that in a state of nature each had a ' right' to all—which, of course, means only that each had a ' right' to all that he could get and keep.[1] Otherwise stated, self-preservation (or the conscious seeking of one's own happiness) was regarded not only as a ' right,' but as the only original spring of action, while brute force was regarded as the only criterion. Possession was *ten*-tenths of the law; though, of course, this possession on the part of the strongest could be only of the most temporary character, owing to the (approximate) ' original equality' of men.

Now, as regards the former, self-preservation, Cumberland does not admit either that men have a primary and inalienable right to preserve themselves, or that the desire of self-preservation is naturally their ruling motive. He had already said, in Chapter i., " Of the Nature of Things " : " It cannot be known that any one has a right to preserve himself, unless it be known that this will contribute to the common good, or that it is at least consistent with it. . . . A right even to self-defence cannot be understood without respect had to the concessions of the Law of Nature which consults the good of all." [2] This is nothing if not explicit; but it is to be noticed that we are here concerned only with the question as to what is to be regarded as the ultimate ethical principle. As regards our mode of action, this very ' good of all,' which is the ethical ultimate, demands that (in all ordinary circumstances) " every one should study his own preservation, and further perfection ".[3] The degree to which one should subordinate one's own interests to the common Good, depends, of course, upon circumstances. That it may extend even to the sacrifice of one's life, Cumberland would have been the last to deny. In such a case he

---

[1] As a matter of fact, this hypothetical ' right to all things' extended not only to the material good things of life, but to everything whatever.

[2] See p. 67.            [3] See p. 69.

would have maintained his general thesis, that the good of all and the good of each coincide, by insisting upon the benefits already received by the individual at the hands of society.[1] We have already seen that this does not really prove his point.

Passing then to Cumberland's deduction of the right to personal property, we must remember that he was confronted with Hobbes's doctrine that, in a state of nature, each had a 'right' to all. His argument, which practically is, that society could not exist without proprietorship in the case of at least some things, however sound it may be in itself, can hardly be called the conclusive answer to Hobbes that he himself supposed it to be. The difference between the two was primarily regarding the nature of man, and not so much regarding the conditions under which society could exist. For it was just Hobbes's contention that society could *not* exist in what he chose to call a 'state of nature'; hence the absolute need of founding the State, and such a state as the 'Leviathan' that he described. The irrelevance of a good many of the author's particular criticisms of Hobbes cannot but strike the reader.

The controversial part of the treatise, however, is not that with which we are mainly concerned, so we pass on to Cumberland's own deduction of the right to property. It is somewhat important to notice the exact form of the argument. "It has been proved," he says, "that in the common happiness are contained both the highest honour of God, and the perfections both of the minds and bodies of men; moreover, it is well known from the Nature of Things that, in order to these ends, are necessarily required both many actions of men, and uses of things which cannot, at the same time, be subservient to other uses. From whence it follows that men, who are obliged to promote the common good, are likewise necessarily obliged to consent that the use of things and labour of persons, so far as they are necessary to particular men to enable them to promote the public good, should be so granted them, that they may not

---

[1] See, *e.g.*, p. 27.

lawfully be taken from them, whilst the aforesaid necessity continues ; that is, that those things should, at least during such time, become their property and be called their own. But such necessity continuing, by reason of the continuance of like times and circumstances, a perpetual property, or right to the use of things, and to the assistance of persons necessary, will follow to each person during life." [1]

It is to be noticed that there are two parts of this deduction : (1) the argument for the original partition of goods ; (2) the argument for the permanence of that partition.[2] These should be carefully distinguished. It is precisely in the confusion of the two that the obscurity of Cumberland's treatment of property lies.

(1) As regards the (original) *temporary* right to the use of things and the services of other people, there seems to be no difficulty. Without some external things, the individual cannot exist, still less be of any service to his fellow-men. Moreover, as the author says, " the same nourishment and necessary clothing which preserves the life of one man cannot at the same time perform the same office for any other ". Hence, in practice, some of the things essential to the maintenance of life must be divided in order to be used at all. This applies absolutely, however, only to food and clothing. Cumberland certainly has a great deal more than these in mind. Indeed, he shows that in a state of nature, preceding the complete division of things, frequent disputes would arise " where it was not very evident what was necessary to each ".[3] These, and also the sloth of those ' neglecting to cultivate the common fields,' would inevitably, he thinks, lead to the further division.

(2) But this division, having once been made, is *final*, owing to the assumed continuance of ' like times and circumstances '. The too easy transition from (1) to (2) is the weak point in the deduction. Some division had to be made ; a certain division has actually been made ; and the complete and abid-

---

[1] See p. 313. *Cf.* pp. 64 *et seq.* This is put in the form of a Law on p. 315, which, of course, involves nothing but a purely verbal change.

[2] Involving inheritance, of course.     [3] See p. 321.

ing justice of this division Cumberland accepts as a matter of course. We need not discuss the division, he says, " because we all find it ready made to our hands, in a manner plainly sufficient to procure the best end, the honour of God and the happiness of all men, if they be not wanting to themselves ".[1] That there is any way radically to remove the hardships of the present distribution (which certainly is not worse than it was in Cumberland's time), it would perhaps be difficult to maintain ; but the author's breezy optimism with regard to the felicity resulting from the existing distribution, is a little amusing, in the light of the economic problems of the present day. The choice, according to his view, would seem to be between the present system and " violating and overturning all settled rights, divine and human, and endeavouring to introduce a new division of all property, according to the judgment or affections of [some] one man ".[2]

Indeed, Cumberland's argument for the existing distribution of wealth is curiously analogous to that of Hobbes for the absolute character of the then existing government. Hobbes had practically said : Any government is better than none ; choose between an absolute government (the only stable one) and none at all. Cumberland, as we have seen, practically says : Some division of property had to be made ; this actually was made ; choose between this and " violating and overturning *all* settled rights ". In this connection, he remarks that, with Grotius, he highly approves of that saying of Thucydides : " It is just for every one to preserve that form of government in the state, which has been delivered down to him ".

According to Cumberland, then, our ultimate right to that which we legally possess, under the existing order of things, depends upon the fact that a recognition of the sanctity of property is essential to the stability of society ; not so much upon the fact that our property enables us to promote the common good. If the latter were really the criterion, a partial

[1] See p. 322, particularly the passage at the foot of the page.
[2] See p. 323.

redistribution of property every now and again might seem to be the inevitable consequence. My only object in referring to this is to call attention to the fact—somewhat important, as it seems to me—that Cumberland's criterion for the distribution of property applies only, or mainly, to the (hypothetical) original partition of the same; not to the actual distribution as we now find it. And the (actual) 'original partition,' surely, was made upon anything but ethical principles.

With the last chapter, viii., "Of the Moral Virtues in Particular," we are not here specially concerned, as the fundamental principles have already been considered. The mode of treatment is sufficiently indicated by the following passage : "The special laws of the moral virtues may, after this manner, be deduced from the law of Universal Justice. There being a law given which fixes and preserves the rights of particular persons, for this end only, that the common good of all be promoted by every one, all will be laid under these two obligations, in order to that end : (1) To contribute to others such a share of those things which are committed to their trust, as may not destroy that part which is necessary to themselves for the same end ; (2) to reserve to themselves that use of what is their own, as may be most advantageous to, or at least consistent with, the good of others." [1] Thus abstractly stated, the principles may seem commonplace enough ; but it is characteristic of the best side of Cumberland's ethical theory that, in carrying them out, he preserves so true a balance between duties of 'giving' and duties of 'receiving'. He himself says that, if confusion be attributed to him by reason of his recognition of the two classes of duties, the confusion must be attributed to Nature herself. Here, again, as so often, he illustrates his position by reference to what we know to be the conditions necessary to the preservation and health of any organism. His deduction of the particular virtues under each class, we need not stop to consider.

Although Cumberland's ethical system has been treated

[1] See p. 329.

topically throughout, in these two chapters, it seems desirable
to restate, as briefly as may be, the principal results of our
investigation. This is the more necessary on account of the
somewhat heterogeneous elements that enter into the system

I. Hobbes had regarded man as a bundle of egoistic instincts,
and had practically denied the existence of Right Reason.
Cumberland insists, on the other hand, that the non-rational
side of human nature manifests altruistic as well as egoistic
tendencies; and also that man is essentially a rational being.
Our sympathetic feelings are emphasised more when the author
is thinking of society as an organic whole, while the rationality
of man is usually brought out into strong relief when the discussion is regarding the individual. That the existence of
sympathetic feeling ' fits ' us for society is evident, of course.
Our rationality, on the other hand, ' fits ' us for society in a
double way: (1) It enables us to see our own good as indis-
solubly connected with the good of society, and so leads to
objectively moral conduct from ultimately egoistic motives;
(2) it enables us to recognise and desire the Good in and for
itself—irrespective of the question as to whose good it may be.
The difference between these two parts which Reason plays
is important. The second is, perhaps, hardly consistent with
the general tendency of the system. Cumberland's view, that
benevolent feeling first came into human life as sexual love
and the parental instinct to protect the young, has been sufficiently noticed; as also his view that the kindly affections (regarded physiologically) tend toward the conservation of the
individual, while the contrary is true of the malevolent affections. It should also be kept in mind that, when opposing the
egoism of Hobbes, the author always attempts to prove, not
simply that man *is*, to a certain degree, benevolent; but that
he *must* be so, from the nature of the human organism and its
relation to that greater organism, society, of which it is a
constituent part. Cumberland's treatment of the benevolent
feelings inevitably suggests the Evolutional view, but it is easy
to see that it is consistent with his own static view of things.
On the whole, we are left somewhat in doubt as to whether

the motive of the moral agent is ever wholly altruistic. At the same time, as we have already seen, perhaps this is not one of the things which we should criticise in the system, as the question is a somewhat abstract one, which naturally did not trouble Cumberland, whose aim throughout was eminently practical. It was enough for him that we are practically altruistic in many of our actions, *i.e.*, free from selfish calculations regarding a probable reward.

II. Turning to the problem of the Good, we were obliged to conclude that the Good is described, now in terms of 'preservation' or 'perfection,' now in terms of 'happiness'. As regards the first set of passages, Professor Sidgwick probably exaggerates the ambiguity of Cumberland's notion of 'perfection'. From this point of view, the Good is that which preserves and perfects both mind and body. As regards the passages which seem to make 'happiness' the end, we were obliged to ask what was meant by 'happiness,' for the term is very vaguely used by early ethical writers. It was found to be *pleasure* depending upon (1) the unimpeded (and effective) normal activities of mind and body; (2) a tranquil frame of mind, which, in turn, depends upon (*a*) external circumstances, (*b*) the feeling that we have acted 'consistently,' (*c*) the consciousness that we have acted for the common weal; and (3) a knowledge that others around us are happy. It will also be remembered that Cumberland distinguishes between what is 'naturally' and what is 'morally' good. 'Natural' good is the ultimate for Ethics. On the other hand, only voluntary actions which tend to that which is 'naturally' good, are 'morally' good. So much for the Good in general. Of course, what Cumberland sets up as the (objective) end of all truly moral action is the Good of all, or of as many as possible.

III. As regards the Laws of Nature, we saw that the system did not really need such a scaffolding, and, indeed, that it was rather hampered than helped by it. At the same time, we had to recognise that the external form of the system was practically determined by this conception; also that it was here that we must look for Cumberland's application of his unifying principle, *i.e.*, his deduction of the particular virtues. Hobbes had demanded that a Law should be 'clearly promulgated by a competent authority'; and had denied that, in this sense, the Laws of Nature were Laws at all. Cumberland, on the other hand, is concerned to show that they are technically such. They are 'clearly promulgated,' for the effects of actions are uniform; and we cannot doubt of the 'competent authority' in this case, for it is none less than the First Cause, the Author of Nature. The effects of actions were found to be treated only in so far as they belonged to the present life; but a sharp distinction was made between the 'immediate' [internal] and the 'mediate' [external] effects, for the confessed reason that 'mediate' effects were somewhat uncertain. The deduction of the particular Laws of Nature was found to be hardly adequate, but, on the whole, consistent.

What shall be said of the system which we have been examining? Cumberland's philosophical style is radically bad, his order of exposition almost uniformly unfortunate. Moreover, a good many of his very numerous criticisms of Hobbes are somewhat wide of the mark. It might seem as if there were little use in attempting to revive interest in this practically forgotten moralist. Yet the curious fact is, that Cumberland alone, of the English ethical writers of his time, sounds modern, as we read him to-day. Hobbes and Cudworth were greater men; More had a more charming personality; but when we read their works, we feel that Absolutism, Intellectualism, and theological Mysticism, as foundations of ethical theory, belong essentially to the past. Cumberland, on the other hand, 'builded better than he knew'. He was the first exponent, in England, at least, of a tendency which for a long time practically dominated English Ethics. And even this is not all. Though writing nearly two centuries before Darwin, he viewed society as an organic whole. Perhaps no single phrase would express his ideal so completely as 'the health of the social organism'; and yet we regard that formula as the peculiar property of the present generation. Moreover, if he recognises 'preservation' and 'perfection,' on the one hand, and 'happiness,' on the other, as parallel principles, we must concede that neither of these principles has definitely supplanted the other even yet. Indeed—if one may venture to attribute anything like unanimity to the constructive ethical literature of the last few years—it may be said that what is now being sought, more than anything else, is some principle at once comprehensive enough to combine these two seemingly antagonistic notions in a higher synthesis, and definite enough to serve as the basis of a coherent system of Ethics.

# CHAPTER III.

## SHAFTESBURY AND FRANCIS HUTCHESON: THEIR RELATION TO UTILITARIANISM.

WHILE we are certainly bound to recognise in Cumberland's *De legibus naturae*, published in 1672, the first statement by an English writer of the Utilitarian principle, it would be idle to claim that the system of the Bishop of Peterborough is free from ambiguity, or even internal contradictions. Indeed, throughout the treatise 'perfection' (in the sense of highest development of the powers of mind and body) is regarded as a principle parallel to that of 'the greatest happiness of all'. It is only by noting the greater emphasis laid upon the Utilitarian principle, the greater actual use made of it in rationalising morality, that we are able confidently to place Cumberland, where he belongs, at the head of the distinguished list of English Utilitarian moralists.

We shall now attempt to trace the further development of the 'greatest happiness' principle. The first step might seem to be an obvious one; for Locke—whose *Essay*, it will be remembered, was first published in 1689-90—is popularly regarded not only as a Utilitarian, but as the founder of English Utilitarianism. One can hardly understand the prevalence of this mistaken view, particularly as no recognised authority on the history of English Ethics seems really to have committed himself to such an interpretation of Locke.[1]

[1] It is to be admitted that Whewell's treatment of Locke's system, at once careless and somewhat partisan, would be almost sure to mislead the ordinary reader. He takes no pains to distinguish between the supposed tendency of the system of thought as a whole and what Locke actually set forth as his own views on ethical subjects. At the same time, he does mention, toward the end

The fact is that Locke, while he devoted the first book of the *Essay* to controverting the doctrine of 'innate ideas' (as he understood it), is by no means opposed to Intuitional Ethics in its more moderate form. To be sure, he holds that " good and evil . . . are nothing but pleasure or pain, or that which occasions or procures pleasure or pain to us ".[1] If he had actually worked out his ethical theory on this basis, we should, of course, find him standing for acknowledged Hedonism; but this he did not do. One has to gather his views on the subject from works devoted to other matters, mainly from the *Essay* and the *Reasonableness of Christianity*. If the result is not altogether satisfactory, we must be particularly careful not to read into the philosopher's views on Ethics a consistency not to be found there. On the one hand, he was not a little influenced by the then almost universal conception of Laws of Nature; and, on the other, he seems to hold the contradictory theses (1) that human reason is not able to arrive at proper notions of morality, apart from revelation;[2] and (2) that moral, like mathematical, truths are capable of rigorous and complete demonstration.[3] Often, indeed, Locke is concerned to show that the practice of virtue is conducive to happiness; but this, in itself, proves nothing. Nearly all his contemporaries, of whatever ethical school, did the same. It is wholly characteristic, when he speaks of Divine Law as " the eternal, immutable, standard of right ".[4] In fact, apart from certain more or less doubtful corollaries from his philosophical system —like his position that the truths of Ethics are capable of quasi-mathematical demonstration — his ethical speculations were mainly on the theological plane. In so far as this was true, he did not, of course, definitely commit himself to any particular ethical theory. It would thus hardly be too much

of his exposition, certain features of the ethical system proper which ought to keep one from regarding it as standing for the 'greatest happiness' principle.— See *Hist. of Mor. Phil. in England*, Lect. v.

[1] *Essay*, Bk. II., ch. xxviii., § 5.
[2] See, *e.g.*, *Reas. of Chr.*, Works, vol. VII., p. 141.
[3] See, *e.g.*, *Essay*, Bk. III., ch. xi., § 16.
[4] *Reas. of Chr.*, Works, vol. VII., p. 133.

to say that Locke had no ethical *system* at all, in the strict sense of the word. This implies nothing whatever in disparagement of the philosopher, but simply that he never gave to Ethics a sufficient amount of consecutive attention to develop a coherent system of his own. There is, of course, no doubt that Empiricism, which Locke did so much to inaugurate, had most important consequences for Ethics; but these will best be considered when we come to examine the earlier form of Associationist-Utilitarianism.

The case of two other important English philosophers, whose interests were pre-eminently ethical, *viz.*, Shaftesbury and Hutcheson, presents much more difficulty. While it is quite unusual, and, as it seems to the present writer, equally unjustifiable, to class them as Utilitarians,[1] their systems do stand in a relation to Utilitarianism sufficiently close to require careful examination. And, unfortunately, it is quite impossible adequately to treat this matter without devoting to it more space than would be proper in a History of English Utilitarianism. To do so, would mean to exhibit in detail all sides of these complex systems, and then to show the subordinate importance of their Utilitarian aspect. We must therefore confine ourselves here to a brief, if not somewhat dogmatic, presentation of what is, in itself, worthy of much more elaborate treatment.

Two questions, in particular, occupied the ethical writers of the period which we are considering: (1) What is the 'end' of moral action? (2) What is the nature of man, and in what relation does this stand to the 'end'? But it might very well happen—did constantly happen, in fact—that different writers would give a very different emphasis to these two questions, fundamentally related as they are. Thus Shaftesbury[2] was so concerned with the question regarding

[1] The relation of Hutcheson to Utilitarianism is much closer than that of Shaftesbury, as we shall presently see.

[2] The first edition of the *Characteristics of Men, Manners, Opinions, Times*, was published in three volumes, in 1711. The following references are to the second edition, published in 1714.

the nature of man, and with his idea that virtue is 'natural, and consists in a proper 'balance' of the affections, that he practically failed to give the first question, that regarding the 'end' of moral action, explicit treatment. As a result, while we find in his system by far the best refutation of Hobbes which had appeared up to his time, it is particularly hard to say exactly how he would have defined the Good.

But first, with regard to the nature of man. Nothing is more absurdly fictitious, according to Shaftesbury's view, than Hobbes's 'state of nature'. In the first place, we can find no true starting-point for Ethics in the individual. Try as we may, we still find him forming part of a system.[1] But, keeping to the individual for the sake of the argument, "the creature must have endured many changes; and each change, whilst he was thus growing up, was as *natural,* one as another. So that either there must be reckoned a hundred different states of nature; or, if one, it can be only that in which nature was *perfect*, and her growth *complete*."[2] Again, nothing is so natural as that which conduces to preservation, whether the creature in question be man or animal. Then, "if eating and drinking be natural, herding is so too. If any appetite or sense be natural, the sense of fellowship is the same."[3]

We are thus prepared to see that the popular antithesis between egoism and altruism—upon which any theory of absolute egoism, like that of Hobbes, must be based—is largely artificial. We may very well distinguish the 'natural' [social, benevolent] affections from the 'self' affections [love of life, bodily appetites, etc.], and both of these from the 'unnatural' affections [malevolence, etc.];[4] but only the last are really bad. 'Self' affections are not only permissible, but necessary, while the 'natural' affections may exist in excess, and thus defeat themselves. Virtue, then, consists not so much in a triumph of the one set of impulses over the other as

---

[1] *Inquiry concerning Virtue,* "Characteristics," vol. II., pp. 16 *et seq.*

[2] *The Moralists,* vol. II., p. 316.

[3] *Freedom of Wit and Humour,* vol. I., p. 110.

[4] *Inquiry,* vol. II., pp. 86 *et seq.*

in a proper 'balance' between the two. As we have seen, man finds himself part of a system from the very first. Since he is originally a social being, he derives his greatest happiness from that which makes for the existence of society and the common weal. Hence the good of all tends to become realised through the enlightened endeavours of each to attain his own *true* happiness; for vice, according to Shaftesbury, ultimately springs from ignorance. Therefore " the question would not be, Who loved himself, or Who not? but Who loved and served himself the rightest, and after the truest manner?" [1]

Virtue, then, consists in the harmony of the first two classes of affections. But the necessary concomitant of virtue is happiness, just as pleasure attends the right state of the physical organism. The good man is his own best friend, the bad man his own worst enemy; for every good act tends to harmonise the affections, every bad act to derange them.[2] Whether happiness itself be the Good, we shall have to ask almost immediately. Here we are only concerned with its relation to virtue, as the necessary concomitant of the latter.

Before leaving Shaftesbury's treatment of the nature of man, it will be necessary to consider his doctrine of a ' moral sense '. The importance of this doctrine for the system is, of course, variously estimated; [3] but certainly it cannot by any means be ignored. As the name would imply, the 'moral sense' is original. It is analogous to the faculty by virtue of which, as Shaftesbury assumes, we are able in some measure to appreciate the beautiful from the very first. But it is to be noted that both these faculties require cultivation. Thus the ' moral sense ' is hardly the infallible guide which Butler thought he found in Conscience. It also differs from the latter in that it seems to belong almost wholly to the affective side of our nature. But though it acts, in a way, independently of reason,

---

[1] *Freedom of Wit and Humour*, vol. I., p. 121.

[2] *Inquiry*, vol. II., p. 85.

[3] Professor Sidgwick very justly says: " This doctrine, though characteristic and important, is not exactly necessary to his main argument; it is the crown rather than the keystone of his ethical structure ".—See *Hist. of Ethics*, p. 187.

it is never in contradiction with the latter. On the contrary, its deliverances may be vindicated by reference to reason and experience. When it is perverted, this is through habitual wrong action (which deranges the affections), or through superstition.

Turning now to the author's account of the 'end' of moral action, we are prepared for some ambiguity. Of course the good of *all* must be the end, or must be implied by the end,[1] since the author begins with the conception of man as a social being. But what is the Good? Shaftesbury's frequent use of the word 'happiness' is not in itself decisive. Happiness, as we have just seen, is the necessary concomitant of the right state of the being in question. This latter seems generally to be regarded as the thing most important;[2] at the same time, it is impossible to deny that the author's interpretation of the Good often seems clearly enough to be hedonistic.[3] In Cumberland we found 'happiness' and 'perfection' as distinct, but parallel principles. In Shaftesbury, on the other hand, we do not find them thus in mechanical juxtaposition, but wrought together, so that they appear as different aspects of the same fact of moral health or harmony. Therefore, we have here a system more difficult than even that of Cumberland to place under one of the conventional modern rubrics. The good of society is the test, indeed, but what this good is, Shaftesbury nowhere quite clearly states. The system would seem to bear at least a closer relation to the modern doctrine of 'Self-realisation' than to Utilitarianism, and this, in spite of the author's habitual emphasis of the affective side of our nature, at the expense of the cognitive and volitional sides.[4] It will be remembered that he constantly insists upon the importance of an harmonious development of the truly human nature, even

---

[1] See, *e.g.*, *Inquiry*, vol. II., p. 78.

[2] See, *e.g.*, *ibid.*, pp. 14 *et seq. Cf.* Sidgwick, *Hist. of Ethics*, p. 184, note.

[3] See, *e.g.*, *Inquiry*, vol. II., pp. 99 *et seq.*

[4] This one-sidedness of Shaftesbury's system doubtless arose in part from the fact that he was contending explicitly against Hobbes and implicitly against the Intellectualists.

where he is concerned to show that the practice of virtue is conducive to the agent's own happiness, and seldom, if ever, suggests definite hedonistic calculations as determining the morality of a given action or class of actions.   In what has just been said, the complication arising from Shaftesbury's theory of a 'moral sense' has been purposely neglected.   For many this would at once determine the non-Utilitarian character of the system; but it should be remembered that the importance of this theory for the system as a whole is variously estimated.

It is customary to regard Hutcheson's system [1] as the logical development of Shaftesbury's; but, while true in a sense, this view requires important modification.   Though we have already found in Shaftesbury's system practically all the elements that enter into Hutcheson's, the different emphasis which is given to two of these in the latter system should be carefully noted.   Shaftesbury, in his explicit opposition to Hobbes and his implicit opposition to the Intellectualists, had tended to identify virtue with benevolence.   At the same time, his fundamental thought seems to have been that virtue consists in the harmony of the 'natural' and 'self' affections.   With Hutcheson, on the other hand, benevolence becomes much more prominent, and is practically regarded as the beginning and the end of virtue.   Again, Shaftesbury had assumed the existence of a 'moral sense,' but his system is quite intelligible without it.   On the other hand, it would hardly be too much to say that Hutcheson's main object was to prove the existence of a 'moral sense,' distinct from self-interest.

Let us consider the 'moral sense' first.   This is defined as " that determination to be pleased with the contemplation of those affections, actions, or characters of rational agents, which

---

[1] The *Inquiry concerning Beauty, Order, Harmony, Design* and the *Inquiry concerning Moral Good and Evil* appeared in 1725; the *Essay on the Nature and Conduct of the Passions and Affections*, and *Illustrations upon the Moral Sense*, in 1728.   The *System of Moral Philosophy* was published posthumously in 1755.

we call virtuous ". It is universal in distribution, immediate in action, and original in character. We are obliged to assume such a faculty, mainly because it is impossible to reduce our moral judgments to considerations of self-interest. This doctrine of a ' moral sense ' is not to be confused with that of ' innate ideas,' to which it bears " no relation ".[1] The ' moral sense ' requires education and development, like our other faculties. In respect of importance, it appears to be designed for regulating and controlling all our powers.[2] It is to be observed that this faculty approves always, and only, of benevolence in the moral agent ;[3] also that " it gives us more pleasure and pain than all our other faculties ".[4]

As we have just seen, benevolence, in this system, is the very essence of virtue ; and (as with Shaftesbury) it is in the truest sense 'natural,' not a subtle refinement of egoism. Indeed, Hutcheson's extreme insistence on benevolence results in a one-sidedness which cannot be overlooked. Yet the author admits that the want of some degree of self-love would be " universally pernicious," [5] and even holds that one may treat oneself as one would a third person " who was a competitor of equal merit ".[6] He attempts to avoid the difficulty —a real one for a system identifying virtue with benevolence— by showing that we may moralise our naïve tendency to pursue our own happiness by remembering always that a due regard for it is necessary for the good of all. Again, he does not claim, of course, that the benevolence in which virtue practically consists is felt equally for all men ; but rather likens it to gravitation, which " increases as the distance is diminished ".[7]

The relation between benevolence and the ' moral sense ' in the system is now tolerably plain. The fact that we approve benevolence, and nothing but benevolence, as virtuous, proves the existence of the ' moral sense '. If we had no such faculty,

---

[1] *Inquiry into the Original of our Ideas of Beauty and Virtue*, second ed., p. xvi. Of course this is only Hutcheson's view of the matter.

[2] *System of Moral Philosophy*, vol. I., p. 61.

[3] *Inquiry*, pp. 196 *et seq.*          [4] *Ibid.*, p. 242.

[5] *Ibid.*, p. 172.          [6] *Ibid.*, p. 174.          [7] *Ibid.*, p. 220.

we should approve only what was advantageous to ourselves. On the other hand, it is our 'moral sense' that proves the essence of virtue to consist in benevolence. We must avoid confusion on one point, however: benevolence, as an impulse to virtue, is quite distinct from the 'moral sense,' as a disposition to receive pleasure from the contemplation of virtue. We do not act benevolently for the pleasure which we may thus obtain. That would be a contradiction in terms.[1]

So much, then, for benevolence and the 'moral sense,' as the two most important aspects of man's moral nature. Taken alone, however, they are not sufficient. Our natural benevolence is a merely general tendency impelling us to conduct for the good of our fellows, particularly those standing to us in the closest relations of life. As such, it needs guidance. And again, the 'moral sense'—so far, at least, as we have yet seen—simply approves of actions performed from benevolent motives. Thus it approves of what is 'formally' good,[2] the good intention. But when we are electing what course of action we shall pursue, we are to aim at that which is 'materially' good. Here it is still, perhaps, the 'moral sense' that gives us the clue, but for practical guidance we must depend largely upon our cognitive powers, as employed with reference to an external criterion.

It will be best to let the author give his own account of this very important matter. "In comparing the moral qualities of actions, in order to regulate our election among various actions proposed, or to find which of them has the greatest moral excellency, we are led by our moral sense of virtue to judge thus: that in equal degrees of happiness, expected to proceed from the action, the virtue is in proportion to the number of persons to whom the happiness shall extend; (and here the *dignity* or *moral importance* of persons may compensate numbers) and, in equal numbers, the virtue is as the quantity of the happiness, or natural good; or that the virtue is in a compound ratio of the quantity of good and number of enjoyers.

[1] *Inquiry*, p. 116.
[2] The distinction is made by Hutcheson himself. See *System*, vol. I., p. 252.

In the same manner, the moral evil, or vice, is as the degree
of misery, and number of sufferers ; so that, that action is best
which procures the greatest happiness for the greatest numbers ; and that worst which, in like manner, occasions misery." [1]

This looks at first like Utilitarianism pure and simple ; but
Hutcheson is mainly interested in that which is *formally* good,
the benevolent intention, and he develops a calculus, the object
of which is to show the degree of morality of a given action in
terms of the *net* benevolence of the agent, *i.e.*, excess of
benevolence over self-interest.   He begins with five ' axioms '.
For example : Let $M$ = moment of good ; $B$ = benevolence ;
and  $A$ = ability.   Then $M = B \times A$.[2]   These apparently
simple ' axioms ' lend themselves to decidedly elaborate computations, the ultimate object of which, in each case, is to
ascertain the value of $B$.   It must always be remembered,
however, that $M$ (the amount of happiness produced by the
action) is assumed in these computations as a known quantity.
Now $M$ must be learned from experience, and the ' hedonistic
calculus ' of the Utilitarian must be employed to find it.   Thus
the calculus referred to supplements, but does not supplant,
the ' hedonistic calculus '.   In spite of the ' moral sense,' the
actual content of the moral laws would have to be largely
determined by Utilitarian methods.[3]

It may still seem as if the system were Utilitarianism in
disguise — and Hutcheson does actually stand in a much
closer relation to the ' greatest happiness ' theory than does
Shaftesbury—but the matter is not so simple as would at first
appear.   That which makes for happiness is the ' materially '
Good, to be sure ; but we have seen that " the dignity or moral
importance of persons may compensate numbers ".   Moreover,
as might be expected, when the happiness of only one person
is under consideration, the qualitative distinction between pleasures is regarded as absolute.   The author says : " We have
an immediate sense of a dignity, a perfection, or beatific quality
in some kinds, which no intenseness of the lower kinds can

---

[1] *Inquiry*, p. 177.  [2] *Ibid.*, pp. 183-188.
[3] Such is actually Hutcheson's procedure in many of his deductions.

equal, were they also as lasting as we could wish ".[1]      And this feeling of human dignity, we are told, is something which we have quite independently of the 'moral sense'.[2]

It is further to be noted that, while Hutcheson came a good deal nearer than Shaftesbury to stating the Utilitarian principle (and was apparently the first English writer to hit upon the exact Utilitarian formula), he also emphasised the doctrine of a 'moral sense' much more strongly than Shaftesbury had done. This results in a very considerable complication.   The 'moral sense' is by hypothesis ultimate.   Now, not only is it, according to Hutcheson, the touchstone of virtue ; but from it, either directly or indirectly, are derived the major part of our pleasures and pains.   Obviously this has an important bearing upon the 'hedonistic calculus,' which we found to be logically implied by the system.   In computing the 'material' goodness of an action, we must take into account, not merely the natural effects of the action, but these complicated with the much more important effects of the 'moral sense' itself.   The result is that the 'hedonistic calculus,' as ordinarily understood, is pushed into the background.   Indeed, as we have had occasion to notice, when Hutcheson actually develops a 'calculus,' it is to ascertain the amount of benevolence implied by a given action, not the amount of happiness which may be expected to result from it, this latter, curiously enough, being assumed as a known quantity.

From what has been said, it will be seen that the system which we have been examining is not properly Utilitarian.   Of course, if the author had been as predominantly interested in the 'materially' good as he actually was in the 'formally' good, and had avoided certain minor inconsistencies, his system would have closely resembled that of J. S. Mill; but, on the one hand, we are not at liberty to neglect the emphasis which he actually gave to the different sides of his system, and, on the other, it is now generally admitted that J. S. Mill was not a consistent exponent of Utilitarianism.   In short, Hutche-

[1] *System*, vol. I., p. 117.           [2] *Ibid.*, p. 27.

son is the 'Moral Sense' philosopher *par excellence*. To lose sight of this, is to misinterpret his system. The general drift of his argument is plain. If we approve or disapprove of actions, we must do so from motives of self-interest or from motives independent of self-interest. The author's first step is to prove the disinterestedness of our moral judgments. This, he thinks, shows conclusively the existence of a 'moral sense,' and so vindicates his characteristic position.

It hardly need be said, that the two very suggestive systems which we have been examining necessarily appear at a disadvantage in being compared with a type of ethical theory to which they do not properly belong. Most certainly they are not to be criticised merely for teaching more than can be comprehended within the bounds of the Utilitarian formula. Subsequent ethical theory for a long time represented an increasing degree of differentiation, which could only end in one-sidedness all round. In our own generation, there is a marked tendency to return to that more comprehensive view of man which Shaftesbury, in particular, did so much to work out, and to attempt a synthesis which shall do justice to our human nature as a whole.

# CHAPTER IV.

## GEORGE BERKELEY, JOHN GAY, AND JOHN BROWN.

THOSE who are inclined to regard Utilitarianism as necessarily irreligious in its tendency, would do well to examine somewhat carefully the numerous 'replies,' explicit and implicit, called forth by the writings of Shaftesbury and Hutcheson. These 'replies' naturally represented various points of view, but they were more similar in spirit than the reader of our own day would be likely to expect. The almost universal verdict of those who opposed the 'Moral Sense' ethics was, that it claimed too much for human nature, *i.e.*, that it assumed a degree of unselfishness and a natural inclination toward virtue on the part of the moral agent, which by no means corresponded with the hard facts. Now it is highly important to notice from what quarter these attacks for the most part came. Mandeville, indeed, whose *Fable of the Bees, or Private Vices Public Benefits* (1714), represented the extreme form of this view that Shaftesbury had paid too high a compliment to human nature, was as far as possible from being a theologian, though he cynically suggested that, by proving the utter selfishness and insincerity of man (in his unregenerate state), he had put himself on the side of orthodox belief. But, as a matter of fact, by far the greater number of such protests came from the theologians themselves. They thought, and were right in thinking, that the 'Moral Sense' ethics, in its attempt to prove the perfect naturalness of virtue, had done something to obscure the notion of moral obligation. In fact, they commonly went to the extreme of believing that the 'æsthetic' view of morality involved consequences dangerous

(64)

to religion itself. For if the ultimate ground of obligation lay in a refined sensitiveness to differences between right and wrong actions, what should be said to a man who might affirm that, just as he had no very good ear for music, he was unable to perceive the ethical differences commonly recognised? Moreover, if the 'moral sense' were sufficient, why did we need religion at all?

In short, a very large proportion of the earlier theological opponents of the 'Moral Sense' philosophers agreed in believing that self-interest was the ruling principle of human nature. This being the case, all depended upon showing that it was for the agent's interest to be moral. Now no amount of argument could prove that this would always hold true, if we should leave out of account the supernatural sanctions of morality. Hence what we would now term 'Theological Utilitarianism' seemed the only natural position for orthodox Christianity. It may seem a little strange to those who know Bishop Berkeley only, or mainly, as the enthusiastic exponent of 'immaterialism' and the champion of orthodoxy against the free-thinkers, that he should have been one of the very first of the opponents of Shaftesbury to put this doctrine of so-called 'Theological Utilitarianism' into definite form. But one has only to examine his sermon on "Passive Obedience" (1712) to see that this is the case. His principal object here, as the full title of the sermon would indicate, was to emphasise the duty of complete submission to recognised civil authority; but he gives, near the beginning of the sermon, the most definite statement to be found in his works of his theory of the ultimate ground of moral obligation.[1]

The argument is as follows. Since self-love is the ruling principle of human action, we naturally term things that make for or against our happiness 'good' or 'evil,' as the case may be. "It is the whole business of our lives to endeavour, by a proper application of our faculties, to procure the one and avoid the other." At first, pleasures and pains of sense are all that appeal to us; but even on this plane experience

---

[1] See Works (Fraser's ed.), vol. III., pp. 110 *et seq.*

soon shows that we must often forego a present pleasure, if we would avoid a greater future pain. " Besides, as the nobler faculties of the human soul begin to display themselves, they discover to us goods far more excellent than those which affect the senses." This naturally impresses upon us still further the lesson of self-control. But since all that is temporal is 'less than nothing' in comparison with that which is eternal, and since we further learn by the 'light of nature' that there is a Divine Being who alone can make us either eternally happy or eternally miserable, it clearly follows that we should implicitly obey the will of God. But what is the will of God? Since He is a Being of infinite goodness, He can will nothing but that which is good. Further, since He cannot Himself be conceived as standing in need of anything, He must will the good of His creatures, and that alone. But this we have seen to be happiness. And " as nothing in a natural state can entitle one man more than another to the favour of God, except only moral goodness . . . it follows that, antecedent to the end proposed by God, no distinction can be conceived between men. . . . It is not therefore the private good of this or that man, nation, or age, but the general well-being of all men, of all nations, of all ages of the world, which God designs should be procured by the concurring actions of each individual."

How shall this 'great end' of all human action be attained? Only two methods of divine moral government would seem possible. (1) We might be left to do that which, in the particular case, should seem likely to conduce to the public good; or (2) the Divine Being might enjoin " the observation of some determinate, established laws, which, if universally practised, have, from the nature of things, an essential fitness to procure the well-being of mankind; though, in their particular application, they are sometimes, through untoward accidents, and the perverse irregularity of human wills, the occasions of great sufferings and misfortunes, it may be, to very many good men". Against the first possible method, Berkeley makes two objections. First, it is impossible accurately to foresee the consequences of our action in any particular case ; and even if it were possible, such calculation " would yet take up too much time to be of use in the affairs of life ". And secondly, we should in this case be without an infallible standard of conduct.

General rules, then, are absolutely necessary. How shall they be ascertained ? Here Berkeley seems to follow Cumberland closely. " Whatsoever practical proposition doth to right reason evidently appear to have a necessary connection with the universal well-being included in it, is to be looked upon as enjoined by the will of God." These propositions, he goes on to show, may be called Laws of Nature, " because they are universal, and do not derive their obligation from any civil sanction, but immediately from the Author of nature Himself ". Or again, they may be termed Eternal Rules of Reason, " because they necessarily result from the nature of things, and may be demonstrated by the infallible deductions of reason ". Here Berkeley pauses to insist in the strongest terms that these laws are to be observed in all cases whatever, and at the expense of no matter what real or apparent hardship to oneself or others. No exhaustive enumeration of the Laws of Nature (or Laws of Reason) is attempted, but those mentioned correspond to the commands of the Decalogue.

It will readily be surmised that this sermon would hardly have been noticed at such length, but for a special reason. While the argument is clear and tolerably consistent, it does not represent any real advance upon Cumberland's treatment, unless perhaps we may regard as such the tacit omission of ' perfection ' (of mind and body) as a principle parallel to that of ' the greatest happiness of all '. The real significance of the sermon lies in the fact that it expresses, with clearness and precision, the view that almost inevitably commended itself to those orthodox theologians of the day who thought they detected dangerous tendencies in the ' Moral Sense ' ethics. It will be necessary to examine Berkeley's ethical theory a little further, in order that we may be able to distinguish from it a theory stated anonymously nineteen years later, which was destined to exert a very marked influence upon the further development of ethical speculation in England.

In the first place, it will be noticed that Berkeley accepts, without any attempt at further analysis, the then current conception of Laws of Nature. His treatment here, as already indicated, is a pretty close reproduction of that of Cumberland. This does not of itself make against the general Utilitarian character of his doctrine, but it plainly tends to emphasise the eternal and absolute character of particular moral laws in a way that would hardly result from the mere consideration of consequences. So long as the Laws of Nature were taken with absolute seriousness, the belief in them tended to retard the development of ethical theory; and this quite apart from the particular 'method' of Ethics in question.

We have seen that Berkeley starts from the assumption that self-interest is the universal spring of human action, and this would seem to differentiate his view from that of Cumberland; but Berkeley's writings are not quite free from ambiguity on this point. He sometimes assumes the social nature of man, without, however, attempting an *a priori* demonstration of the necessity of altruism, as Cumberland had done. In this connection, the question naturally arises, whether he recognised qualitative differences between pleasures, and here again we are left in uncertainty. This is rather curious, for a large part of the Second Dialogue in *Alciphron, or the Minute Philosopher* (1732), is devoted to a consideration of the question as to what pleasures are most desirable. Sometimes he seems to insist upon the dignity of human nature;[1] but after all the general drift of the argument is to show that the 'pleasures of imagination' and 'pleasures of reason' are *greater*, or at any rate more permanently satisfactory, than the 'pleasures of sense'. It would not do to insist too much upon his treatment here, however, for it might reasonably be held that Berkeley is using an *argumentum ad hominem*, since the argument is directed, for the most part, against those

---

[1] See Works, vol. II., p. 80. *Cf.* an important passage on p. 89.

who are gratuitously assumed to hold a particularly unworthy view of what things are desirable for man.

Two other points may properly be noticed. In the first place, Berkeley frankly depended upon the doctrine of future rewards and punishments in a way that Cumberland had, presumably from controversial considerations, refrained from doing. Henceforth this was to be the most characteristic feature of the doctrine of the so-called 'Theological Utilitarians'. Secondly, Berkeley states with admirable clearness two of the three main reasons against depending upon the computation of consequences in the particular case, *viz.:* (1) that it is impossible to predict the consequences of any particular action, and (2) that at the moment of action there would be no time for deliberate computations, even if such computations were capable of yielding exact results. The other obvious reason is, that at the moment of action self-interest is likely to be, more than ever, a complicating factor in our moral judgments. These three arguments were destined to play an important part in Utilitarian discussions during the rest of the eighteenth century. To those who favoured the Utilitarian doctrine, they were regarded as a sufficient demonstration of the necessity of 'general rules,' while to many of the opponents of Utilitarianism, they seemed conclusive against the doctrine itself.

It might seem highly improbable that an anonymous dissertation of only about thirty pages, prefixed to a translation, actually by another hand, of a third writer's Latin work, should be one of the most interesting and important contributions to the early development of the 'greatest happiness' principle. Yet such undoubtedly is the *Preliminary Dissertation : concerning the Fundamental Principle of Virtue or Morality*, now known to have been written by the Rev. John Gay, prefixed to Law's translation of King's *Origin of Evil*. The first edition (of the translation and the *Dissertation*) was published in 1731 ; the second, " revised and enlarged "—an almost exact reprint, so far as the *Dissertation* is concerned—in 1732.

A few dates should be kept in mind here. The first edition of Shaftesbury's *Inquiry concerning Virtue and Merit* was published in 1699 ; that of Hutcheson's *Inquiry into the Original of our Ideas of Beauty and Virtue* in 1725. Hume's ethical system first appeared in 1740, as the third book of the *Treatise of Human Nature*, the other two books having been published the year before. Gay's *Dissertation*, therefore, appeared six years after Hutcheson's first ethical work, and nine years before the corresponding work of Hume. It is interesting to note that Gay's true successors, Tucker and Paley—for Hume does not seem to have been influenced by him—belong to a later generation. The *Light of Nature Pursued* was first published in 1768-77, and the *Moral and Political Philosophy* in 1785.

We shall now turn to the *Preliminary Dissertation* itself, and give it the very careful examination which its importance justifies. The author's own order of exposition, which is not uniformly fortunate, will be followed substantially, except where notice is given to the contrary. This is possible on account of the brevity of the *Dissertation*, and desirable, on the whole, as it will facilitate a comparison of the substance of this remarkable essay—which is not, for most, readily accessible [1]— with the other ethical works named above.

Gay begins by remarking that, though all writers on morality have practically agreed as to what particular classes of actions are virtuous or the reverse, they have at least seemed to differ in their answers to the related questions : (1) What is the ' criterion ' of virtue ? and (2) What is the motive by which men are induced to pursue it ? Both of these questions must be considered, of course, in any treatment of Ethics, and the author's own view is that the same principle, or the same set of principles, will be found to solve both.

It is therefore indifferent which side of the moral problem we consider first. But, before attempting anything constructive,

---

[1] Since the above was written, the *Dissertation* has been reprinted in Mr. Selby-Bigge's *British Moralists* (vol. II., §§ 849-887), but the text there followed is that of the fifth edition (1781).

Gay stops to notice a current view. Some hold that a rational creature will choose only that which, on the whole, is calculated to bring him most happiness; further, that virtue does bring the agent most happiness; and that therefore it will be chosen just in proportion as one is rational.[1] Moreover, they hold that whatever is an 'object of choice' is 'approved of'. Gay seems to object to this view mainly because it implies too great a degree of self-consciousness on the part of the agent. He admits that Hutcheson [2] has made abundantly plain: (1) that most men do actually approve virtue without knowing why; and (2) that some pursue it even in opposition to their own apparent advantage. But Hutcheson was not content with emphasising the facts; he had recourse to a 'moral sense' to explain moral approval, and a 'public or benevolent affection' to explain apparently disinterested conduct. This, however, is cutting the knot instead of untying it. We may very well be practically benevolent and capable of forming what seem like ultimate moral judgments, and yet these phenomena of our moral life may be perfectly explicable without assuming unknown 'faculties' or 'principles'.

So much for the point of departure. We are now ready to follow the author's own attempt at a solution of the problems of Ethics. At the very beginning, unfortunately, he entangles himself and his readers in a fruitless discussion regarding the meaning of the term 'criterion,' which we may safely omit.[3] In this discussion, however, he has occasion to define virtue, and the definition—which he wrongly supposes would be accepted by all, despite differences in ethical theory—is important for his own treatment of Ethics. He says: "Virtue is the conformity to a rule of life, directing the actions of all rational creatures with respect to each other's happiness; to which conformity every one in all cases is obliged: and every

---

[1] Here Gay carelessly speaks of virtue as being "always an object of choice".

[2] Referred to as "the ingenious author of the *Inquiry into the Original of our Idea of Virtue*".

[3] Gay's own use of 'criterion' is not quite exact, as will be seen later; but the omitted discussion throws practically no light on his use of the word.

one that does so conform is, or ought to be, approved of, esteemed, and loved for so doing ".[1] In justification of this definition, Gay observes that virtue always implies some relation to others. "Where self is only concerned, a man is called 'prudent' (not virtuous), and an action which relates immediately to God is styled 'religious'." Again, as we have already seen, whatever men may believe virtue to consist in, they always assume that it implies 'obligation,' and that it deserves 'approbation'.

Before treating directly of the 'criterion' of virtue, the author chooses to consider 'obligation'. This section [2] of the *Dissertation* is so important—particularly with a view to subsequent ethical theory, as represented by Tucker, Paley, and Bentham—that the first two paragraphs may be quoted in full.

"*Obligation is the necessity of doing or omitting any action in order to be happy*: *i.e.*, when there is such a relation between an agent and an action that the agent cannot be happy without doing or omitting that action, then the agent is said to be *obliged* to do or omit that action. So that obligation is evidently founded upon the prospect of *happiness*, and arises from that necessary influence which any action has upon present or future happiness or misery. And no greater obligation can be supposed to be laid upon any *free agent* without an express contradiction.[3]

"This obligation may be considered four ways, according to the four different manners in which it is induced: First, that obligation which ariseth from perceiving the natural consequences of things, *i.e.*, the consequences of things acting according to the fixed laws of nature, may be called *natural*. Secondly, that arising from merit or demerit, as producing the esteem and favour of our fellow-creatures, or the contrary, is usually styled *virtuous*.[4] Thirdly, that arising from the

---

[1] See p. xxxvi. (second ed.).          [2] *I.e.*, § ii.
[3] *Cf.* Paley's *Principles of Moral and Political Philosophy*, Bk. II., ch. ii.
[4] The confusion here is only in the form of expression.

authority of the civil magistrate, *civil.* Fourthly, that from the authority of God, *religious.*"[1]

Gay proceeds to show that *complete* obligation can come only from the authority of God, "because God only can in all cases make a man happy or miserable". A few paragraphs further on the author is as explicit as one could wish on this point—a very important one, as hardly need be remarked, for the early Utilitarians, who, with the exception of Cumberland, Hartley, and Hume, agree in regarding the motive of the moral agent as ultimately egoistic. He says : " Thus those who either expressly exclude, or don't mention the will of God, making the immediate criterion of virtue to be the good of mankind, must either allow that virtue is not in all cases *obligatory* (contrary to the idea which all or most men have of it) or they must say that the good of mankind is a sufficient obligation. But how can the good of mankind be any obligation to *me*, when perhaps in particular cases, such as laying down my life, or the like, it is contrary to my happiness ? "[2]

We are now prepared to return to the question regarding the ' criterion ' of virtue. Since complete obligation can come only from God, the will of God is the immediate rule or criterion,[3] though not the ' whole will of God,' since virtue was defined as ' the conformity to a rule directing my behaviour with respect to my fellow-creatures '. But, as regards my fellows, what does God will that I do? From the infinite goodness of God it follows that He must desire the happiness of men. Hence He must will such conduct on my part as is calculated to conduce to their happiness. Thus, the will of God is the ' immediate criterion ' of virtue, but the happiness of mankind is the ' criterion ' of the will of God. Hence we must consider the consequences of actions, and from these deduce all particular virtues and vices.

[1] *Cf.* Bentham's *Principles of Morals and Legislation*, ch. iii., particularly §§ ii.-vi.

[2] See p. xli. (In the second edition one must look out for errors in paging· The correct paging is given here.)

[3] Observe the ambiguity in the use of ' criterion,' referred to in note above.

We now have in outline all the essential principles of Gay's ethical system proper.   The remainder of the *Dissertation* consists in an attempt to furnish an adequate psychological foundation for the principles above set forth.   It will be noticed that this second part [1] was as important for the development of the Associationist Psychology as both parts were for the development of early Utilitarian theory.

The author begins by remarking that man is a being capable, not only of passively experiencing pleasure and pain, but of foreseeing the causes of these and governing himself accordingly.   The 'end' of action—that pursued for its own sake— is pleasure.   That which man finds calculated to produce pleasure, he calls the 'Good,' and approves of it; while his attitude is precisely the contrary in the case of that which is known to have painful consequences.   Now Good or Evil, when thought of, give rise to a proportionate present pleasure or pain.   This is called 'passion,' and the attending desire, 'affection'.   Hence, by reflecting upon Good and Evil, desires and aversions are excited which are (roughly) distinguished as Love and Hatred.   From these, variously modified, arise all the other 'passions' and 'affections'.   It is a mistake to suppose that these latter are implanted in our nature originally, like our capacity for experiencing pleasure or pain.

When directed toward inanimate objects, the passions and affections [2] are Hope, Fear, Despair, and its unnamed opposite. As a matter of fact, however, our pleasures and pains depend quite as much upon other conscious agents as upon inanimate objects.   Hence, as Gay says : "As I perceive that my happiness is dependent on others, I cannot but judge whatever I apprehend to be proper to excite them to endeavour to promote my happiness, to be a means of happiness, *i.e.*, I cannot but *approve it*".   Moreover, since others can be induced to act for my happiness only by the prospect of their own future happiness, I cannot but approve of "the annexing pleasure to such

---

[1] This division of the *Dissertation* into two parts is not explicitly made by Gay.   At the same time his order of exposition inevitably suggests it.

[2] Gay makes no serious attempt to keep the two separate.

actions of theirs as are undertaken upon my account ". And, since we desire what we approve of,[1] we desire the happiness of those who have done us good. That in the agent (a voluntary action or series of such actions) which constitutes the ground for the approbation and love just accounted for, is called the 'merit' of the agent; the contrary, 'demerit'.

But here a difficulty arises. How can there be 'merit' in the action of another, when that action is performed (ultimately) for the agent's own happiness? The main reason why this seems paradoxical, or worse, to common-sense is that common-sense does not distinguish between an 'inferior' and an 'ultimate' end. In by far the greater part of human actions, it is an 'inferior' end that the agent has in mind. Thus, though the happiness of the agent is always the 'ultimate' end, all that the beau *immediately* desires is to please by his dress, and all that the student *immediately* desires is knowledge. For any such 'particular' end, we may, of course, inquire the reason; but to expect a reason for the 'ultimate' end is absurd. "To ask why I pursue happiness, will admit of no other answer than an explanation of the terms."

But, to proceed, when the 'particular' end of any action is the happiness of another, that action is 'meritorious'. On the other hand, "when an agent has a view in any particular action distinct from my happiness, and that view is his *only motive* to that action, tho' that action promote my happiness to never so great a degree, yet that agent acquires no *merit*; *i.e.*, he is not thereby entitled to any favour and esteem". It makes a great difference, indeed, whether another aims at my favour in general, or only at some particular end which he has in view. "I am under less obligation (*caeteris paribus*) the more *particular* his expectations from me are; but under obligation I am."[2]

Gay concludes by noticing a possible "grand objection" to his theory. It is this. The reason or end of action must always be known to the agent; otherwise, it would not actu-

---

[1] The apparent logical inversion here is Gay's.　　[2] See p. xlviii.

ally be his motive. The problem here is not why one should
be grateful, but why one is so. As Hutcheson has shown,
the majority of mankind approve of virtue immediately, and
apparently without regard to their own interest. Must we not,
then, after all, assume that author's 'moral sense' and 'public
affections'?

The reply given to this supposed objection is substantially
as follows. The matter of fact here appealed to has already
been admitted, and it is perfectly consistent with our theory.
" As, in the pursuit of truth, we don't always trace every proposition whose truth we are examining, to a first principle or
axiom, but acquiesce as soon as we perceive it deducible from
some known or presumed truth ; so in our conduct we do not
always travel to the ultimate end of our actions, *happiness :*
but rest contented as soon as we perceive any action subservient to a known or presumed *means* of happiness. . . . And
these RESTING PLACES [1] are so often used as principles,
that at last, letting that slip out of our minds which first
inclined us to embrace them, we are apt to imagine them not,
as they really are, the *substitutes* of principles, but principles
themselves." Hence people have imagined 'innate ideas,'
'instincts,' and the like ; and the author adds : " I cannot but
wonder why the *pecuniary* sense, a sense of *power* and *party*,
&c., were not mentioned, as well as the *moral*,—that of *honour*,
*order*, and some others".[2]

More exactly, the true explanation is this. " We first
perceive or imagine some real good, *i.e.*, fitness to promote
our happiness, in those things which we love and approve of."
Hence we annex pleasure to the idea of the same, with the
result that the idea and the attendant pleasure become indis-
solubly associated. Gay's first example is the one which has
since become so well known in this connection, *i.e.*, the love of
money. It is matter of experience that money, first desired
merely for what it will procure, sometimes itself becomes the
exclusive object of pursuit. In the same way knowledge,

---

[1] The large capitals are Gay's, and they occur here only.
[2] See pp. lii., liii.

fame, etc., come to be regarded as ends in themselves. Now this principle is quite sufficient, he holds, to explain our disinterested practice of virtue, as well as certain perverted tendencies of human nature.

As regards these latter, Gay treats in particular of envy, emphasising the fact that we never envy those who are very much above or below us, but rather those who may fairly be regarded as in some sense competitors. The teleology is plain, he thinks: the success of those with whom we either directly or indirectly compete means less chance for ourselves. "This," as he quaintly adds, "may possibly cast some light upon the black designs and envious purposes of the fallen angels. For why might not they have formerly had some competition with their fellows? And why may not such associations be as strong in them as [in] us?"

At the very close of the *Dissertation* the author barely refers—though what he says is perfectly clear and to the point—to another consideration which does much to make his general (hedonistic) position plausible. It is not necessary, he says, that we should form associations like those above described for ourselves. We may very well take them from others, *i.e.*, "annex pleasure or pain to certain things or actions because we see others do it, and acquire principles of action by imitating those whom we admire, or whose esteem we would procure. Hence the son too often inherits both the vices and the party of his father, as well as his estate." In this way we can account for national virtues and vices, dispositions and opinions, as well as for what is generally called 'prejudice of education'.

We should now probably agree that, even from the empirical point of view, the phenomena to which Gay refers would have to be explained, not merely by 'association,' but partly by heredity and partly by what we can hardly avoid calling the 'instinct of imitation'. Such considerations at once add plausibility to the hedonistic aspect of Gay's system, and suggest the important limitations of the principle of 'association,' which he inclines to regard as all-sufficient. Perhaps it was from a certain paternal tenderness for the infant principle of ' association ' that Gay neglected to press an argument which might have threatened to prove a two-edged sword.

The *Dissertation* was so distinctly a new departure that it is difficult to avoid remarking at once upon Gay's relation to subsequent ethical theory. How completely his position was adopted by Tucker and Paley, will be evident to any one acquainted with those writers who has carefully followed the above. Here, however, we must rather attempt to show the relation of the author of the *Dissertation* to those of his predecessors who had been either directly or indirectly concerned with the development of the Utilitarian principle.

Cumberland had seemed to make both ' the greatest happiness of all ' and ' the perfection of body and mind ' the moral end, and this without suspecting any difficulty in so doing; while Locke, though deeply interested in Ethics on the theological and practical side, and, in the general sense of the word, a hedonist, could hardly be said to have a coherent ethical system of his own. Shaftesbury and Hutcheson, on the other hand, had done much for the development of English ethical theory, but their relation to hedonism was only indirect. In Gay's *Dissertation* we have, in its complete and unmistakable form, what we later shall have to recognise as the first characteristic phase of English Utilitarianism.[1]

---

[1] It is important to remember that, while Hume, who published his ethical system in its first form only nine years after the *Dissertation*, was incomparably superior to Gay, both as a thinker and as a writer, he did not happen to state the Utilitarian doctrine in the form which was destined first to be developed. Indeed, it may be doubted if this was a matter of chance. Hume's system, much more complex than Gay's, and, one may add, on a distinctly higher plane, was not calculated to appeal to writers like Tucker, Paley, and Bentham, whose single aim appears to have been simplicity of theory. All the writers just named form a perfectly definite school (Bentham and most historians of Ethics to the contrary notwithstanding), while the phase of Utilitarianism which Hume represents was not further developed until comparatively recent times. Historically, then, Hume stands outside the direct line of development, though he doubtless represents the Utilitarian position, as we now understand it, much more adequately than any one else who wrote in his own, or even in the succeeding, generation.

Evidently the more particular comparison must be between Gay and Cumberland, for these authors alone, up to this time, had really stated the 'greatest happiness' principle in fairly scientific form. Cumberland, as we have just seen, defined the Good, now in terms of 'happiness,' now in terms of 'perfection,' though the emphasis, on the whole, seems clearly enough to be on the hedonistic aspect of the system. Gay, on the other hand, consistently defined the Good as Happiness, and Happiness as 'the sum of pleasures'. Moreover, though he does not discuss the question of possible 'qualitative distinctions' between pleasures, it is evident that for him such distinctions would have no meaning. This, again, is an advance upon Cumberland, for though the latter author by no means commits himself to the theory of 'qualitative distinctions,' and sometimes appears to hold the opposite view, there is a serious ambiguity in his treatment which was almost inevitable, considering that he practically carries through Happiness and Perfection as co-ordinate principles.

As regards the motive of the moral agent, there is in Gay no trace whatever of the confusion which is so striking in Cumberland. It is true that Cumberland had held, what Shaftesbury later made evident, that man is essentially a social being and that the true Good must be a common good. His actual treatment, however, is quite confusing; generally the agent's motive in moral action seems to be regarded as altruistic, but sometimes the language used seems to imply at least a very considerable admixture of egoism. In Gay, on the contrary, we find even a fictitious simplicity. All the phenomena of moral action, as we have seen, are explained by the 'association of ideas' and what has more recently been termed the 'law of obliviscence'. We begin as egoists, and, indeed, throughout our lives we uniformly seek our own pleasures, avoid our own pains. But it amounts to much the same thing as if we were originally altruistic to a certain degree. For, although our own happiness is always our 'ultimate' end, it is by no means always our 'proximate' end. The system theoretically allows for cases of extreme self-sacrifice.

Whether it really affords a satisfactory explanation of these, is a question which we hardly need enter upon here. The present generation is not likely to make, or allow, extraordinary claims for the unaided principle of 'association'.

So much for the treatment of the 'criterion' of moral action and of the motive of the moral agent by the two authors whom we are comparing. Closely related to the latter question is that of the ultimate meaning of 'obligation'. It will be remembered that Cumberland's treatment of obligation was not altogether consistent with his system as a whole. Instead of basing upon the essentially social nature of man and claiming here, as generally elsewhere, a certain degree of altruism for the moral agent, he merely tries to show that it is greatly for the selfish advantage of any given individual to lead the moral life, even when extreme sacrifices are demanded. This was doubtless done in order to meet Hobbes on his own ground, but the same reason led Cumberland to confine his arguments to consequences that might be expected in this present life. For obvious reasons, he does not make out a perfectly clear case.

Gay was not hampered with any such controversial considerations. His treatment is only too clear and consistent throughout. "Obligation is the necessity of doing or omitting any action in order to be happy. . . . And no greater obligation can be supposed to be laid upon any free agent without an express contradiction." This, of course, is the logical consequence of his theory of the moral motive ; and he immediately goes on to enumerate "the four different manners in which [obligation] is induced". These are precisely what appear later as Bentham's four "sanctions". But how can *complete* obligation (which common-sense demands) be vindicated, if we define obligation as has just been done? Gay sees very clearly that we must here depend upon the power and wisdom of the Divine Being, "because God only can in all cases make a man happy or miserable". And there is no restriction to rewards and punishments as given in this present life. This position was, of course, adopted by Tucker and Paley, the only difference being that Paley particularly insists upon rewards and punishments after death. This whole question as to the meaning of ' complete obligation ' for Utilitarianism in its earlier form, would have to be discussed at some length, if we were comparing Paley and Bentham with Gay and with each other. Here it is enough to notice that, if we assume the necessarily egoistic nature of the motive of the moral agent, and at the same time attempt to preserve the absolute character of obligation, Gay's position is the only logical one.

In Cumberland we found some confusion in the use of the expression ' Right Reason '. The author had evidently been somewhat influenced by the intuitionists and intellectualists, though he opposed most of their characteristic doctrines, and this without really having worked out his own position in detail. Nothing corresponding to this confusion is to be found in Gay. He does, indeed, in one passage seem to distinguish between Experience and Reason, but this is misleading, for he immediately adds : " You either perceive the inconveniences of some things and actions, when they happen, or you *foresee* them by contemplating the nature of the things and actions ". Reason here is evidently nothing but the faculty of predicting upon the basis of past experience.

Again, in Cumberland we are constantly confronted with the then almost universally current conception of Laws of Nature. It is easy to show that the system does not really depend upon this scaffolding, but that, on the contrary, it is rather cumbered than helped by it. At the same time, this conception of Natural Laws not only gives its name to Cumberland's treatise, but almost wholly determines its external form. The reader hardly needs to be reminded that Gay's remarkable essay is entirely free from such superfluities. One point, however, should be noticed in this connection. Gay refers, of course, to the Will of God as the ' immediate criterion ' of morality ; but the Divine Will itself is determined to that which will bring the greatest happiness to mankind, or, as the author himself expresses it, " The happiness of mankind is the criterion of the Will of God ". The Utilitarian principle, then, is clearly regarded as ultimate. It would be a gross misunderstanding of Gay to class him with those who make morality depend upon the *arbitrary* will of God.

It will be noticed that neither Cumberland nor Gay discusses the possibility of the 'hedonistic calculus'. Neither of them seems to suspect any difficulty in the matter, and apparently this had never been distinctly raised as an objection to hedonism up to the time that we are considering. Perhaps this was to be expected, for such refinements are likely to belong to a later stage of ethical discussion; but it does at first seem rather strange that, while Gay was the earliest consistent exponent of the Utilitarian principle, he did not anywhere use the formula, 'the greatest happiness of the greatest number'. Hutcheson, it will be remembered, had used this very formula, though it does not for him express the whole essence of morality, as it would have done for Gay; and Gay must have been familiar with Hutcheson's writings, for he controverts them intelligently.

It would be quite too ingenious to suggest that Gay refrained from using the expression precisely because Hutcheson had happened to use it. He seems to have been willing to avail himself of all that he considered true in the *Inquiry*. The only importance which really can be attached to the omission is this: Gay and his immediate successors [1] held clearly and definitely to the view that, in the last resort, all human motives are selfish. From this standpoint, the now accepted formula is by no means so inevitable as it would be, if one admitted the existence of disinterested sympathy and insisted that this latter must be present in the case of all truly moral action.

In taking leave of this remarkable essay, we should not forget that its full significance can be appreciated only after one has taken the trouble to trace back many of what are commonly regarded as characteristic doctrines of Tucker and

---

[1] With the exception of Hartley and Hume (whose treatment of 'sympathy' is ambiguous in Book III. of the *Treatise*, but who admits a certain degree of native altruism in the *Inquiry concerning the Principles of Morals*).

Paley to this their undoubted source. However much these authors did to fill in the outline—and Tucker, at least, did a very great deal—it must be granted that the whole outline of Utilitarianism, in its first complete and unencumbered form, is to be found in Gay's *Preliminary Dissertation*.

It will readily be seen that Gay's importance for Ethics was due, not merely to the fact that he stated the Utilitarian doctrine for the first time in perfectly clear and unambiguous form, but quite as much to the fact that he provided the doctrine with at least the essentials of a psychological foundation. This first appearance of what we may call 'scientific method' in the literature of Utilitarianism, was destined to have most important consequences. In truth, it is only when we take these consequences into consideration, that we are able fully to appreciate the very great difference between a production like the sermon on "Passive Obedience" and the *Dissertation*. But, before we proceed further in the direct line of our investigation, it will be well to pause for a little, and, neglecting the strict chronological order, notice a belated criticism of Shaftesbury which appeared about twenty years after Gay's remarkable essay. The propriety of noticing this here will be apparent from the fact, that the part of the *Essays on the Characteristics* which we shall examine consists almost wholly in the careful development of Gay's theory of the moral motive.

It may be doubted whether this book, published in 1751 by the Rev. John Brown, has been at all generally appreciated in recent years, though J. S. Mill and Professor Fowler have spoken of it in the highest terms.[1] Indeed, it is one of the very few controversial books of this period that can still be read with satisfaction. Even the Bishop of Cloyne was by no means always just or courteous to his opponents,[2] but Brown

---

[1] It must have been popular at the time when it was published, for the third edition was printed the year after the first.

[2] See, *e.g.*, the Third Dialogue of *Alciphron*, where Shaftesbury's views are criticised—particularly the passage in which Shaftesbury himself is described under the name Cratylus.—Works, Fraser's ed., vol. II., p. 128.

is almost uniformly so.   Nor did this prevent him from being
one of the most effective critics of his generation.   It will be
remembered that the Essays were three in number, the first
being on " Ridicule, considered as a Test of Truth "; the
second, on " The Obligations of Man to Virtue, and the Necessity of Religious Principle "; and the third, on " Revealed
Religion and Christianity ".   The second alone is to the
present purpose.

The author begins by remarking that, just as the rainbow
seems to the uninstructed to possess an ' original ' beauty, but
yet is as capable of scientific explanation as the more commonplace phenomena of nature, so virtue must not hastily be regarded as an ultimate, since it may be explained by reference
to the end to which all good actions conduce.   He then proceeds to argue in a rather ingenious way that, while Wollaston,
Clarke, and Shaftesbury, each from his own point of view,
professed to vindicate the absolute character of virtue, they all
really introduced hedonistic considerations at the crucial point.
Moreover, he holds that " if we appeal to the common-sense
of mankind, we shall see that the idea of virtue hath never been
universally affixed to any action or affection of the mind,
unless where this tendency to produce happiness was at least
*apparent* ".[1]   The two following arguments for happiness
as the criterion of morality seem to the author particularly
convincing.   (1) " Those very affections and actions which, in
the ordinary course of things, are approved as virtuous, do
change their nature, and become vicious in the strictest sense,
when they contradict this fundamental law of the greatest
public happiness.'   (2) " With such uncontrolled authority
does this great principle command us, that actions which are
in their own nature most shocking to every humane affection
lose at once their moral deformity, when they become subservient to the general welfare, and assume both the name and
the nature of virtue."   An example of the first would be an
act of dishonesty committed for the sake of one's own child ;
of the second, the execution of a notorious criminal by due

[1] Essay II., § iii., p. 133 (first ed.).

process of law. Thus virtue is found to be nothing else than " the conformity of our affections with the public good : or the voluntary production of the greatest happiness ".[1]

There follows a rather severe criticism of Mandeville, which, as a whole, does not concern us. One passage, however, is interesting. Mandeville had insisted upon the extreme variability of moral ideas in different countries and in different ages of the world. Without by any means denying all the alleged facts, Brown argues that a sound critic would discriminate. " If from the variety of opinions among mankind as to *some* virtues or vices, he concluded these were *variable ;* then from the universal agreement of mankind with regard to *other* virtues and vices, he would conclude these were *fixed* and *invariable.*" This, of course, is the natural reply ; but Brown very pertinently adds : " And 'tis evident that both their consent and disagreement arise from the same principle " (*i.e.,* regard for the common weal under existing circumstances). In short, Shaftesbury and Mandeville, though representing quite opposite points of view as regards the nature of virtue— the one assigning to it an intrinsic, the other a wholly conventional character—made the same fatal mistake of neglecting the objective end of virtuous action, the recognition of which alone can put morality on a safe foundation.

Having thus obtained a tolerably clear notion of what virtue itself is, we are at once confronted with the question : What are the motives by which mankind can be induced to the practice of it ? Here, as before, we must avoid sentimentality. It will appear upon examination that " the only reason or motive, by which individuals can possibly be induced or obliged to the practice of virtue, must be the feeling immediate, or the prospect of future private happiness ".[2] To the followers of Shaftesbury, this will doubtless seem like an

---

[1] See § iii., p. 136. The author here definitely refers to "the *Preliminary Dissertation* to Dr. Law's translation of King's *Origin of Evil,*" and advises the reader who is curious to examine further into this subject to consult both that and certain of the translator's notes.

[2] See § vi., p. 159.

unworthy account of the matter; but it is to be remarked
that the words ' selfishness ' and ' disinterestedness ' have been
used in a very loose and indeterminate manner. " In one
sense a motive is called disinterested, when it consists in a
pure benevolent affection, or a regard to the moral sense.
In another, no motive is disinterested; for even in acting
according to these impulses of benevolence and conscience,
we gratify an inclination, and act upon the principle or immediate feeling of private happiness." This becomes evident
from the fact that " a motive, from its very nature, must be
something that affects *ourself*. . . . Now what can possibly
affect *ourself*, or determine us to action, but either the feeling
or prospect of pleasure or pain, happiness or misery ? " Indeed, if we push the argument further, " 'tis evident, even to
demonstration, that no affection can, in the strict sense, be
more or less selfish or disinterested than another; because,
whatever be its object, the affection itself is still no more
than a mode either of pleasure or of pain, and is therefore
equally to be referred to the mind or feeling of the patient,
whatever be its external occasion ".[1] But, while all this is
true, the followers of Shaftesbury are perfectly right in holding
that, as sources of happiness, the benevolent affections clearly
have the advantage over those ordinarily termed selfish. The
preceding argument, which appears to have retained its co-
gency for many even to the present day, is open to the most
serious objection. It will call for special discussion, when we
come to consider the second form of Hume's ethical theory.
Here it has seemed to merit the explicit treatment that has
been accorded to it, for this is probably the most definite
statement that we have (up to the date of the publication of
Brown's book) of the view held practically in common by the
earlier Utilitarians.

We have now seen what virtue is, and what is the universal
character of human motives. There remains the crucial
question : " How far, and upon what foundation, the uniform
practice of virtue is *really* and *clearly* connected with the

[1] See § vi., p. 163.

happiness of every individual?" And just here it is to be noted that moralists have made the serious mistake of discussing the 'sources of happiness' too much in the abstract. These are three: sense, imagination, and the passions. The slightest observation will convince us, however, that they are of varying importance for different temperaments. "In some, the pleasures and pains of sense predominate; imagination is dull, the passions inactive. In others, a more delicate frame awakens all the powers of the imagination; the passions are refined, the senses disregarded. A third constitution is carried away by the strength of passion; the calls of sense are contemned, and imagination becomes no more than the necessary instrument of some further gratification." [1] The differences between moralists, with regard to their theory of the moral motive, are thus susceptible of a psychological explanation. Each has unconsciously appealed, and appealed only, to those of like mental constitution with himself. And while this is an important commentary on the majority of the ethical systems that have come down to us, it shows in a rather startling light their essential weakness. Morality is a very serious matter, and it is important to the last degree that the motives to right action presented shall be such as to appeal to *all* men.

If we revert to the classification of temperaments just adopted, it will be evident that those susceptible only, or mainly, to pleasures and pains of sense will be quite oblivious to æsthetic or benevolent considerations. Private interest is all that can possibly appeal to them. In the case of the second class, those of a distinctly æsthetic temperament, it is to be remembered that a pronounced taste for the fine arts argues little or nothing for sound moral perceptions. Sometimes, indeed, we are tempted to believe that the two are hardly compatible. And even of the third class, for whom the passions are the chief sources of pleasure, it must be said that, if we find here the best of men, we also find the worst. We must not avoid the difficulty by terming the baser affections 'un-

[1] See § vii., p. 169.

natural,' as Shaftesbury has done. Whether 'unnatural' or
' natural,' they seem to be thoroughly rooted in far too many
cases, and it is not so certain as one would like to believe
that they are "a source of constant misery" to the agent, as
Shaftesbury claimed.    There are, to be sure, rare cases,
"where the senses are weak, the imagination refined, and the
public affections strongly predominant".[1]    In such cases,
virtue is indeed its own reward ; all right actions are then
spontaneous in the strictest sense.    But how few these cases
are !

One touch alone was needed to complete the gloomy picture, and the author adds this with cool precision.    Shaftesbury
had allowed himself to emphasise the external consequences
which naturally follow upon good and bad actions, though
this looks like deserting his characteristic position, that happiness is essential to virtue and inseparable from it, while unhappiness is equally bound up with vice.    Waiving the matter
of consistency, however, this raises a general and very serious
question : Are moralists right in holding, as many of them
seem to do, that virtue is the parent of external happiness just as vice undoubtedly is of external misery, and this
in the natural course of things ?    The fact seems to be that
the happy consequences which are commonly attributed to
virtue, belong not so much to positive virtue as to ' innocence '.
The man who indulges in no vices, and who never disregards
the rights of others, undoubtedly reaps a certain reward,
though it can hardly be claimed that this is proportionate to
the corresponding punishments which naturally attend vice
and crime.    But this is as far as the argument holds.    "If
we rigorously examine the external consequences of an *active*
virtue in such a world as this, we shall find, it must be often
maintained at the expense both of health, ease, and fortune ;
often the loss of friends, and increase of enemies ; not to
mention the unwearied diligence of envy, which is ever watch-
ful and prepared to blast distinguished merit.    In the meantime, the *innoxious* man sits unmolested and tranquil ; loves

[1] See § vii., p. 186.

virtue, and praiseth it; avoids the miseries of vice, and the fatigues of active virtue; offends no man, and therefore is beloved by all." [1]

Let us return, then, to the question how private and public happiness may be shown to coincide. This agreement is necessary in order to the realisation of the moral end, but impossible in the natural course of things—except for the favoured few, as we have seen. One thing alone can achieve for humanity this all-important result: "the lively and active belief of an all-seeing and all-powerful God, who will hereafter make them happy or miserable, according as they designedly promote or violate the happiness of their fellow creatures". "And this," adds the author, "is the essence of religion." [2] Here we find Theological Utilitarianism stated in its most impressive form. We are no longer, as when dealing with Berkeley, confronted with Laws of Nature or of Reason, the ultimate ground of which, to be sure, is Utilitarian, but which are to be accepted as absolute and obeyed without any thought of further analysis. The Good is the happiness of mankind; and to this we must actively contribute, according to our best knowledge and ability, at all times and under all circumstances. There is no suggestion of difficulty in ascertaining what does contribute to the common weal; the real problem for Brown is: How can we will what we perfectly well know to be for the good of mankind, when this does not happen to coincide with our private interest?

It is to be noted that he does not base his argument upon any theological dogma like that of the 'total depravity' of man in his natural condition. There are some, he admits, who have a moral endowment such that they seem hardly to need even the internal sanctions of religion, much less its external sanctions. But these are very few. And what shall be said of the vast majority, to whom neither the beauty of holiness nor considerations of disinterested benevolence directly appeal? Morality is a matter of awful consequence, not merely to the few, but to all men absolutely without exception. Must

[1] See § viii., p. 198.    [2] See § ix., p. 210.

not the motives, then, be such as will appeal to all? And if so, nothing but religion, with its doctrine of rewards and punishments after death—the rewards, in particular, being insufficient in this life—can reclaim the world from the lamentable condition in which we find it. This argument, that the sanctions of morality must be such as to appeal to *all* men, may provoke a sneer, for the implication would seem to be that the motives presented must be low enough to appeal to all; but Theological Utilitarianism has at least something to say for itself on this point. In the case of those who have made little or no progress in the moral life, the motive will doubtless be low enough, if one please to call it so, since it will amount to little or nothing more than a desire to ' flee the wrath to come '; but it may be said of the stern law, not merely of the old dispensation, but of the new as well, that it is ' a school-master to lead us ' to something far better.

No comparison has been made between Brown's treatment of Ethics and that of Gay, for this has not seemed necessary. The most characteristic feature of the *Dissertation*, *i.e.*, the psychological foundation of the system, and, in particular, the explanation of the genesis of practical altruism, is not treated at all, but for this we are directly referred by the author to the *Dissertation* itself. The importance of Brown's work arises from the fact that it is, in some respects, the best statement we have of the Utilitarian doctrine, from the distinctly theological point of view. Paley afterward presented the theory in a much more clear-cut and systematic form; but it may be doubted whether his clever formulas (often adapted from Gay) do not on the whole detract from, rather than add to, the real impressiveness of the position. It seems fair to assume that Theological Utilitarianism will never regain its former importance; but it represents a very significant, and perhaps necessary, stage in the development of moral theory. Until the student has brought himself to appreciate its force, such as it is, he will find a difficulty in understanding much of what is most characteristic in the English Ethics of the eighteenth century.

# CHAPTER V.

## DAVID HUME.

WE must not look for perfect continuity in the development of Utilitarianism, even after the doctrine had once been clearly enunciated. Two of the most prominent writers of the Utilitarian school, Tucker and Paley, were destined to carry out, almost to the letter, the scheme of moral theory which Gay had outlined in his *Preliminary Dissertation* of 1731; but the next writer standing for the ' greatest happiness' principle appears to owe nothing to Gay. On the contrary, so far as formative influences are concerned, Hume seems to have taken his starting-point in Ethics from those who, like Shaftesbury and Hutcheson, had maintained the existence of a ' moral sense'.

This is by no means to say that Hume was himself a ' Moral Sense' philosopher. Quite as much as anything else, his object was to show that what the ' Moral Sense' writers had professed to explain by merely referring to a supposed ' faculty,' could really be explained in a scientific way, according to the most general principles of human nature. Still, his primary contention was that morality was founded, not on ' reason,' as he expressed it, but on ' sentiment'; that our starting-point in ethical discussions must always be the fact of our approval of moral actions—a fact which could not, by any possibility, be explained on purely rational principles. In emphasising ' feeling' at the expense of ' reason,' Hume was clearly with the ' Moral Sense' writers, and it is fair to assume that he was historically, as well as logically, related to them in this respect.

Although Hume's writings are so much better known at first hand than those of Cumberland and Gay — the most prominent of his Utilitarian predecessors—it is more difficult than might be supposed to present his views on Ethics in a way to leave no room for misunderstanding. In the first place, one has to keep in mind Hume's relation to the ' Moral Sense ' school, and avoid attributing either too much or too little importance to this relation ; and, in the second place—what is much more important—one has to decide, after the most careful examination and comparison, whether one shall accept his earlier or his later treatment of Ethics as the more adequately representing his system.

As regards Hume's relation to the ' Moral Sense ' philosophers, little need be said at present. It is worth noticing, however, that the apparently complex character of his ethical system has led some to believe that its general drift is somewhat ambiguous, and that to the end it holds a rather close relation to the ' Moral Sense ' school.[1] This view is, in my opinion, by no means correct ; but as the mistake is a natural one, a comparison may prove helpful. In the case of Hutcheson, we found a moralist whose doctrine could hardly be understood without comparing it carefully with the ' greatest happiness ' principle. At the same time, we found that, in its general tendency, it was radically distinct from that principle. Exactly the opposite, it seems to me, is true in the case of Hume. While he certainly was influenced by the ' Moral Sense ' writers, ' utility ' is with him by no means a subsidiary principle, as with Hutcheson, but incontestably the basis of his whole ethical system. This is a dogmatic statement ; but its truth will, I think, become abundantly plain as we proceed with our examination of Hume's treatment of the subject.

The second difficulty which we noticed, that regarding the two forms in which Hume has left us his ethical theory,

---

[1] See, *e.g.*, Professor Hyslop's *Elements of Ethics*, p. 84 ; also, for a much more guarded statement, referring only to the later form of Hume's ethical theory, see Mr. Selby-Bigge's Introduction to his edition of Hume's *Inquiries* p. xxvi.

requires more immediate and altogether more serious attention. It will be remembered that his first treatment of Ethics appeared as Book III. of the *Treatise of Human Nature* in 1740, the year after the publication of the other two books. The *Inquiry concerning the Principles of Morals* did not appear till 1751, three years after he had published the *Inquiry concerning Human Understanding*, in which he had presented, in a more popular form, the substance of Book I. of the *Treatise*. The story of Hume's chagrin at the poor reception which his juvenile work met with, and of his explicit repudiation of the *Treatise* in after years, as not giving his mature views on philosophical subjects, is too familiar to admit of repetition. Critics are now perfectly agreed that the *Inquiry concerning Human Understanding*, however superior in style to the first book of the *Treatise*, is an inadequate statement of the author's views on metaphysics; and, since one is bound to disregard Hume's own judgment concerning the relative merits of Book I. of the *Treatise* and the corresponding *Inquiry*, it is natural that the *Inquiry concerning the Principles of Morals* should have been estimated in much the same way, in spite of the fact that Hume himself considered the second *Inquiry* as "of all [his] writings, historical, philosophical, or literary, incomparably the best". The present tendency plainly is either (1) to regard the two statements of his ethical theory as practically equivalent, and therefore to prefer Book III. of the *Treatise* merely as historically prior; or (2) to hold that, in the *Inquiry concerning the Principles of Morals*, as well as in the *Inquiry concerning Human Understanding*, there is an observable falling off in thoroughness of treatment which is by no means compensated for by the undoubted improvement in style.

I cannot believe that either of these views is correct. It must never be forgotten that, in his later years, Hume was perfectly right in regarding the *Treatise of Human Nature* as a work abounding in serious defects, mainly such as betray the youth of the author. It is in spite of these defects that the book takes its place as perhaps the most remarkable single work in English philosophical literature. The common statement that Book I. of the *Treatise* is to be preferred to the first *Inquiry* because it is 'more thorough'—while perfectly true — might be misleading to one not equally acquainted with both works. A great many of the perversely subtle discussions in the *Treatise*, which Hume ruthlessly pruned away in revising it, were not only mere digressions, tending seriously to confuse the reader, but they were, in themselves, by no means uniformly convincing. To do away with many of these discussions was in itself a real advantage ; but, unfortunately, Hume was not so much trying to improve the book as trying to make it more acceptable. The result is that, along with what was at once irrelevant and of doubtful validity, he omitted much that was really essential to the adequate statement of his peculiar views on metaphysics.

One would naturally expect to find much the same thing true in the case of the *Inquiry concerning the Principles of Morals*. As a matter of fact, however, in spite of what is apparently the current view, I am strongly of the opinion that the *Inquiry* is not only a clearer, but a better statement of Hume's ethical theory than the third book of the *Treatise*. Here the elimination has nearly always conduced to that really consecutive treatment which is so important in any philosophical work, and nothing in the least essential to the system as a whole seems to have been left out. Much more important for us, however, is the fact that, in the second *Inquiry*, Hume does away with the one exasperating ambiguity of his earlier work, *i.e.*, his treatment of 'sympathy '. Other comparisons between the *Inquiry* and the corresponding book of the *Treatise* will be made, as it becomes necessary. This, however, is so important that we must take account of it at the very beginning.

In both the *Treatise* and the *Inquiry*—though the order of exposition in the two works differs otherwise, in certain respects—Hume begins with the fact of moral approbation. He first shows—in the *Treatise* at considerable length ; in the *Inquiry* more briefly, but perhaps as convincingly—that moral approbation cannot ultimately be founded upon principles of mere reason. After thus clearing the ground, he attempts to explain our approbation of moral conduct by referring, not to a supposed 'moral sense,' but to what he assumes to be the springs of human action and the determining effects of human experience.

Now the important difference between the standpoint of the *Treatise* and that of the *Inquiry*, just referred to, consists in the radically different answers given in the two works to the question: What are the springs of action—the fundamental tendencies of human nature? In the *Treatise*, these are held to be (1) egoism, (2) limited altruism, and (3) 'sympathy'. The relation between them is difficult to state in a few words—indeed, so far as 'sympathy' is concerned, difficult to state at all—but Hume's position in the *Treatise* apparently is that human nature is essentially egoistic. As regards altruism, he holds distinctly that we have no particular love for our fellow-beings as such.[1] Our limited altruism manifests itself only in the case of those standing to us in the closest relations of life, and in a way which does not permit us to suppose that it is an original principle of human nature, strictly co-ordinate with the self-regarding tendency.

At this point Hume employs the rather mysterious principle of 'sympathy'. For him, in his earlier work, as for many of the later empiricists, 'sympathy' is produced through the 'association of ideas'. His peculiar mode of explanation is as follows—the point being to show that in this case an 'idea' is practically converted into an 'impression'. The 'impression of ourselves' is particularly vivid, and by 'association' it happens that a corresponding (though of course not equal) vividness is imparted to that which relates to ourselves. But other human beings are *similar* to ourselves. This relation of 'similarity' makes us vividly conceive what concerns them, the other relations of 'contiguity' and 'causation' [*i.e.*, kinship here] assisting in the matter. Thus our idea of another's emotion

---

[1] *Treatise*, Bk. III., Pt. II., § i.

may become so vivid as to give rise to the same emotion in ourselves.[1]  In spite of its obvious ingenuity, this explanation of 'sympathy' is far from being satisfactory.  One readily sees that for Hume, as for the Associationist school in general, 'sympathy' is left in a condition of unstable equilibrium, liable at a touch to be precipitated into egoism pure and simple.

This aspect of Hume's system, in its earlier form, is the more confusing for the reason that he never seriously attempts to state the relation between our derived 'sympathy' and our fundamental self-regarding tendency.  The result is a degree of theoretical confusion that can only be appreciated by those who have read the *Treatise* with considerable care.  It should be observed that one does not here refer to the inevitable ambiguity of the words 'egoism' and 'altruism,' as ordinarily used,[2] but rather to the fact that Hume professes to explain— almost in the sense of explaining away—what we ordinarily understand by (general) 'sympathy,' without anywhere telling us exactly what he claims to have reduced it to.

If Hume's treatment of 'sympathy' were the same in the *Inquiry concerning the Principles of Morals* as in Book III. of the *Treatise*—which is apparently the careless assumption of those who regard his position in the two works as identical— we should need to examine the mysterious principle consider- ably in detail.  As a matter of fact, however, Hume seems to have been keenly aware that his earlier treatment of 'sym- pathy' was a mistake, and a bad one ; and he gives us what he would probably have regarded as the best possible antidote in what he says on the same subject in the *Inquiry*.[3]  There he means by the word 'sympathy' nothing essentially different from the general benevolent tendency, the degree of which he shows his good judgment in not attempting to define, but

[1] See *Treatise*, Bk. II., Pt. I., § xi.

[2] This ambiguity, of course, depends upon the unwarranted abstraction made by those who speak as if ' egoism ' and ' altruism ' stood for two absolutely dis- tinct tendencies of human nature.

[3] See, *e.g.*, § V., pt. ii., *et seq.*; also Appendix ii.

which he regards as the foundation of the historical development of morality.

The significance of this change can hardly be overrated. It does away at once with an almost indefinite amount of theoretical confusion, and puts Hume on the right track just where his historical, but not logical, successors—Tucker, Paley, and Bentham—were destined to go astray. Nor must it for a moment be supposed that Hume is here going to the other extreme, and contending for the existence of a perfectly differentiated 'altruism' in our human nature, as opposed to an equally differentiated 'egoism'—as Hutcheson, for example, had mistakenly done. He rather shows that, in the last resort, this distinction resolves itself into an abstraction, and holds, in language which Butler himself would have had to commend: " Whatever contradiction may vulgarly be supposed between the *selfish* and *social* sentiments or dispositions, they are really no more opposite than selfish and ambitious, selfish and revengeful, selfish and vain ". And one is almost startled at the agreement with Butler, when he immediately adds: " It is requisite that there be an original propensity of some kind, in order to be a basis to self-love, by giving a relish to the objects of its pursuit; and none more fit for this purpose than benevolence or humanity ".[1]

To conclude, then: in place of the three quasi-distinct (but by no means co-ordinate) principles—egoism, limited altruism,[2] and 'sympathy'—which had been assumed in the *Treatise*, we have 'sympathy,' in the ambiguous sense first explained, struck out in the *Inquiry*, and a human nature there assumed which, as Hume sometimes has occasion to show, necessarily implies at least a certain degree of the benevolent tendency, alongside of the equally essential self-regarding tendency— the two becoming differentiated, in so far as they do become differentiated at all, only in the course of human experience.

[1] See *Inquiry*, § IX., pt. ii. Butler's *Sermons upon Human Nature* had been published in 1726.

[2] Our limited altruism is mentioned here as a quasi-distinct principle, because it implies another kind of association, *i.e.*, by 'causation,' besides association by 'similarity' and by 'contiguity,' which are involved in our general sympathy.

While I am inclined to lay a great deal of stress upon this change of position on the part of Hume, I cannot at all agree with Mr. Selby-Bigge, when he says (in the brief, but mainly admirable introduction to his edition of Hume's two *Inquiries*): " In the *Enquiry* [*concerning the Principles of Morals*] there is little to distinguish his [Hume's] theory from the ordinary ' moral sense ' theory, except perhaps a more .destructive use of ' utility ' ".[1] For, as Mr. Selby-Bigge himself points out, even freer use is made of the principle of ' utility ' in the *Inquiry* than in the *Treatise*. And I cannot at all follow him when he adds : " It would be easy to draw consequences from this principle which would neutralise the concessions made to benevolence, but he [Hume] is content himself to leave it without development, and to say in effect that utility pleases simply because it does please ". Why the admission of a certain undefined degree of native altruism and the use of the principle of ' utility ' should be regarded as necessarily conflicting, I have never been able to understand. As in most discussions where abstract ' egoism ' and abstract ' altruism ' figure, the supposed difficulty resolves itself into an ambiguity in the use of words. Even if the hedonist, in order to be consistent, is obliged to hold that one is always determined to act for one's own pleasure,[2] he is not therefore committed to egoism in any offensive sense. If one derive pleasure from the pleasure of others, one is just so far altruistic. Whether or not one does derive pleasure from the pleasure of others, is solely a question of fact; and the inevitable answer cannot properly be used

---

[1] See p. xxvi.

[2] The expression ' determined to act for one's own pleasure ' is in itself seriously misleading. Even when we are acting with a direct view to our own future pleasure, it is, of course, the *present* pleasure attaching to the idea of our future pleasure, not the future pleasure itself, which determines our action. And to assume that no idea but that of our own future pleasure can attract us, manifestly begs the whole question. In the text, however, I have attempted to show that, even if the hedonist admit that, in his view, we always act for our own pleasure, he is not committed to ' egoism,' in the derogatory sense.—All this, of course, has nothing to do with the ultimate validity of hedonism, which the present writer would by no means admit.

against 'Universalistic Hedonism' or any other recognised type of ethical theory.

Having considered the relation between the standpoint of Book III. of the *Treatise* and that of the *Inquiry concerning the Principles of Morals*, as regards the springs of human action, we shall now proceed to an examination of Hume's ethical system as a whole. In order to understand his mode of procedure, either in the *Treatise* or in the *Inquiry*, one should keep in mind the distinction, explicit in the former work, implicit in the latter, between what he calls the 'natural' and the 'artificial' virtues. For instance, in the *Treatise* Hume contends that justice is an 'artificial' virtue, while he regards benevolence, in its various forms, as 'natural'.[1] By 'artificial' he does not mean, as he explains, that which is a superfluity in organised society; on the contrary, he holds that a recognition of justice is basal to all social life whatever. He simply means that the utility which, as he is going to show, all virtues have in common, is *indirect* in the case of justice and other 'artificial' virtues, while *direct* in the case of all the so-called 'natural' virtues.[2] More particularly, he means—what, to be sure, is not strictly true—that the effect of the so-called 'natural' virtues is immediately and always an increase of happiness, while, in the case of justice, etc., this is manifestly true only in the long run.

This at first looks like one of the many fine distinctions which Hume draws in the *Treatise* only to practically neglect them in the *Inquiry*, and that to the manifest advantage of his exposition. As a matter of fact, however, the position, though unsound, is characteristic. While Hume does not directly speak of 'artificial' as opposed to 'natural' virtues in the *Inquiry*, he does not seem really to appreciate his mistake and

---

[1] It will be seen that the term 'natural,' as here applied, is rather misleading, since Hume does not admit native altruism in the *Treatise*.

[2] The other virtues beside justice which Hume designates as 'artificial' are allegiance, modesty, and good manners. The 'natural' virtues specified are meekness, beneficence, charity, generosity, clemency, moderation, and equity.— See *Treatise*, Bk. III., Pt. III., § i.

give up the distinction altogether. In both works he is primarily concerned to show the relation of the several virtues to what he recognises as the springs of human action, the fundamental impulsive tendencies of human nature. Now he holds with much truth that, in the case of justice, for example, we have no mere native impulses which of themselves are sufficient to explain either the fact that we approve justice, or the fact that we ourselves practise this virtue. But when he comes to treat the so-called ' natural ' virtues, he seems to assume—in the later as well as in the earlier work—that the virtues in question are, on the one hand, the direct result of our natural springs of action, and, on the other hand, that their effects are immediately and always fortunate.

Keeping in mind, then, this distinction, which, though not consistently carried out, really determines in a general way the form of exposition in both the *Treatise* and the *Inquiry*, we are now prepared to notice Hume's more specific treatment of the problems of Ethics. As will readily be seen, it is not without significance that in the *Treatise* he considers justice before benevolence, while in the *Inquiry* he does the contrary : for in the *Treatise* he is concerned to prove, not only the general utilitarian character of justice, but that it is ultimately based on (practically) egoistic principles ; while in the *Inquiry* he begins with the assumption that the measure of benevolence is the measure of virtue, and that benevolence is good because it results in the increase of human happiness. As I regard the position taken in the *Inquiry* as more consistent and more characteristic, for reasons sufficiently given above, I shall mainly follow that work rather than the *Treatise*, in the present account of Hume's proof of the utilitarian principle.[1]

Hume's treatment of benevolence in the *Inquiry* is very brief. In fact, after he had given up his peculiar view of ' sympathy,' as worked out in the *Treatise*, he probably thought that little remained to be said on the subject. The possibility of such a virtue could hardly have seemed to him to need proof, for in

---

[1] Important differences of treatment in the two works will of course be noted.

this later work he had once for all assumed a certain degree of altruism, as belonging to human nature; and it must be remembered that he did not seriously consider, or even distinctly recognise, the question how, given altruistic as well as egoistic tendencies, the developed virtue of benevolence (as distinguished from mere impulsive kindliness) was to be explained.

Beginning, as he nearly always does, with our actual approval of moral actions, Hume remarks that the very words we use to describe " the benevolent or softer affections " indicate the universal attitude toward them.   He says: " The epithets *sociable, good-natured, humane, merciful, grateful, friendly, generous, beneficent,* or their equivalents, are known in all languages, and universally express the highest merit which human nature is capable of attaining ".[1]  But Hume further points out that, when we praise the benevolent man, there is one circumstance which we always insist upon, *i.e.,* the happiness of others which inevitably results from his habitual mode of action.   Now, since benevolence does have this universal tendency to make for happiness, it seems fair to assume that utility forms at least a part of the merit of benevolent actions. But the further we examine into the matter, the more utility is found to be an adequate explanation of our approbation of such actions, while other modes of explanation in a corresponding degree lose their plausibility.  The practically inevitable presumption, then, is that utility is the sole ground of our approbation of benevolent actions.  It remains to be seen, of course, whether it will prove sufficient to explain the other great social virtue, justice, as well as a number of self-regarding virtues which will be mentioned later.

Before leaving this present subject of benevolence, however, it will be well to see how Hume's treatment of the virtue accords with his mature view regarding the springs of human action.  It has been said that benevolent actions please on account of their utility, meaning by this their tendency to

---

[1] See *Inquiry,* § II., pt. i.

produce pleasure, either in particular individuals or in mankind at large. Why does utility please, even when we have no private interest at stake? In Hume's earlier treatment of Ethics, it was just here that he had been obliged to have recourse to the principle of (derived) 'sympathy,' thus reducing our apparent altruism to terms of something very like egoism. In the present work, he expressly states that the selfish principle is inadequate, and that the use of it by philosophers to explain the phenomena of our moral life results from a love of fictitious simplicity.[1] Man does have an original altruistic, as well as egoistic, tendency, the one being just as 'natural' as the other. But this is not all. Hume further points out that sensibility to the happiness and unhappiness of others and moral discrimination keep pace with each other. It will thus be seen that he makes the former, *i.e.*, 'sympathy' in its ordinary sense, the foundation of moral development.

Now there is a difficulty here, already mentioned, which Hume quite forgets to take account of in his treatment of benevolence. How do we pass from the mere *impulse* to benevolent action, whether strong or weak, to a *virtue* of benevolence, which latter, of course, implies an objective standard? It must be admitted that, when Hume incidentally tries to answer this question, somewhat later in the *Inquiry*, his account of the matter, though interesting, is hardly adequate. His view seems to be that human intercourse involves meeting our fellows half-way; that language is formed, not for expressing that which is merely subjective, but that which may, in a sense, be regarded as objective. He says: "The intercourse of sentiments, therefore, in society and conversation, makes us form some general unalterable standard, by which we may approve or disapprove of characters and manners".[2] Here, apparently, we have the germ of Adam Smith's characteristic notion of the 'ideal impartial spectator'.

After having argued that benevolence, as a virtue, is actually approved on account of its utility, Hume proceeds to the

---

[1] See *Inquiry*, Appendix ii.        [2] *Ibid.*, § V., pt. ii.

consideration of justice. His treatment of this virtue in the *Inquiry* substantially corresponds to his previous treatment in the third book of the *Treatise*, so far as his attempt is merely to show its general utilitarian origin. Minor differences in the two expositions need not detain us, but it may be well to note in passing that here, as in the case of benevolence, we ultimately are confronted with the question as to ' why utility pleases,' and that the question would have to be answered somewhat differently in the two works, in a way to correspond to the different springs of action recognised. What has been said regarding this question in the case of benevolence will, of course, apply in all essential respects in the present case of justice.

At the beginning of his treatment of justice, Hume properly enough remarks that all are so completely agreed as to the utility of this virtue that nothing need be said on that score. His object, of course, is to show, not merely that justice is useful, but that its character as a virtue is determined wholly by its usefulness. It should be noted that here, as in the third book of the *Treatise*, Hume writes of justice as if the virtue had a bearing only upon cases where external goods are in question. Later we shall find reason seriously to object to this view. Granting, however, for the present, that justice is to be taken in this restricted sense, Hume's line of argument is at least plausible. He says, as every one will remember, that justice would have no meaning if there were either (1) an unlimited supply of the goods in question, or (2) perfect generosity in human nature. As a matter of fact, of course, most external goods are limited in quantity; and here, as in the *Treatise*, Hume holds that the egoistic impulses predominate, although he forsakes his former position to the extent of admitting a certain degree of original altruism. Our natural tendency, then, would be in the direction of appropriating more than belonged to us. But, since the same tendency is present in all others, society can only exist in a permanent form where property rights are to some extent recognised.

Since justice has no meaning for Hume, apart from the insufficient supply of external goods and the predominant selfishness of man, it might seem as if he would have us look for a thorough-going utility in all the particular rules of justice. As a matter of fact, however, he suggests that we do not need to carry our analysis very far to see that these rules are sometimes, in the last resort, more or less arbitrary. Such cases Hume attributes to the natural processes of the 'imagination,' as determined by the all-important principle of the 'association of ideas'.[1] It must not be supposed that we really have two principles operating here, utility and some arbitrary principle—the two standing to each other in an unknown relation. The *all*-important thing is that principles of some sort should be recognised, where the ownership of property is concerned. Beyond a certain point, Hume would seem to say, it makes no very great difference how goods are apportioned, at least in the hypothetical first instance—and it is there, mainly, that the 'imagination' is conceived to come in as a complicating factor.[2]

Such, then, is Hume's actual treatment of justice reduced to its lowest terms. Up to this point, we have admitted his assumption that justice concerns only our pecuniary dealings with others. But is this really true? In order not to misin-

---

[1] "Sometimes the interests of society may require a rule of justice in a particular case; but may not determine any particular rule, among several, which are all equally beneficial. In that case, the slightest *analogies* are laid hold of, in order to prevent that indifference and ambiguity, which would be the source of perpetual dissension. Thus possession alone, and first possession, is supposed to convey property, where nobody else has any preceding claim and pretension. Many of the reasonings of lawyers are of this analogical nature, and depend on very slight connexions of the imagination."—See *Inquiry*, § III., pt. ii.

[2] It is interesting to see how English ethical writers, from the time of Hobbes to that of Paley, were unable to free themselves entirely from the conception of a 'state of nature' and a 'compact' made when men entered into society. With those who accepted the doctrine, wholly or in part, we are not here concerned; but it will be found that those who expressly repudiate this view (*e.g.*, Hume and Paley) often lapse into a mode of speech which seems to imply it. An interesting case will be found in Paley's *Moral and Political Philosophy*, Bk. III., Pt. II., ch. v.

terpret Hume's position, we must keep in mind that he treats the obligation of promises in connection with justice, and as necessarily arising from it. But the ultimate reference is always to external goods, and the two complications always are the insufficiency of such goods and the excess of human egoism. It will hardly be denied that, while justice should always be differentiated as clearly as possible from benevolence, its scope is inevitably much greater than Hume seems prepared to admit. Let us suppose, for the moment, that there were an unlimited supply of the good things of life, and that, at the same time, human nature were as predominantly altruistic as it often seems to be egoistic. Even in this doubly millennial condition of things, it would still be absolutely necessary, in order that society might exist at all, that men should be able in some measure to depend upon each other. It is only upon the basis of some definite expectations that one can live with one's fellows from day to day. Even in the family, justice of a sort would seem to be as necessary as anywhere else—a necessary foundation for enlightened benevolence.

We may now examine the remaining part of Hume's systematic treatment of Ethics. In considering this somewhat briefly, we shall merely be following the author's own example. And first we must notice Hume's general classification of the virtues. In the *Inquiry*,[1] as well as in the third book of the *Treatise*,[2] he distinguishes between virtues which are (1) 'useful to oneself,' *e.g.*, prudence, constancy, good judgment, etc.; (2) 'immediately agreeable to oneself,' *e.g.*, magnanimity; (3) 'useful to others,' *e.g.*, justice and benevolence; and (4) 'immediately agreeable to others,' *e.g.*, politeness, wit, and cleanliness. Even a somewhat casual examination of this classification will reveal its artificial character. At the same time, before criticising Hume, it is important to see exactly what he means. For instance, let us take the first class of virtues, those 'useful to oneself'—prudence, constancy, etc.

---

[1] See §§ VI., VII., VIII., IX.
[2] See Bk. III., Pt. III., § i. (end).

Hume does not by any means set himself the gratuitous task
of showing that these virtues are, as a matter of fact, useful to
oneself. The question really is: Why do I commend prudence, etc., in another? The value to the community of
prudence in the individual, even when exercised in his own
affairs, is not what is here emphasised, though that would
seem to be the most natural line of argument. Hume is
rather concerned to show, in his later work, that it cannot be
from motives of self-love that one commends prudence in
others. Indeed, he holds that it is more clearly impossible to
resolve moral approbation into self-love here than in the case
of justice. In his somewhat obscure account of this matter in
the third book of the *Treatise*, Hume had seemed to hold that
we unconsciously put ourselves in the place of the person sympathised with, and, in a sense, feel for ourselves, rather than
strictly feel for him. On the other hand, in the *Inquiry*,
which we are here following, he explicitly abandons all such
speculations, and not only accepts, but emphasises, the fact
that an original altruistic tendency in human nature must be
admitted.

In distinguishing the virtues which are ' immediately agreeable ' to oneself from those which are merely ' useful,' Hume
carelessly adopts a terminology which, in a writer less clear
than himself, might lead to confusion. Pleasure is the ultimate test, of course, in one case as much as in the other—
the only difference being that in the second class of virtues,
as the name would imply, the pleasure is experienced immediately, while in the first class it results rather in the long run.
As a matter of fact, however, when all allowances are made,
one can hardly defend Hume in adopting a classification which
seems to explain magnanimity as a virtue, on the ground that
we approve it because it is immediately agreeable to its fortunate possessor! Virtues of the third class, justice and benevolence, are perhaps naturally enough termed ' useful to others,'
though ultimately the distinction between the first two classes
of virtues (self-regarding) and the last two classes (other-
regarding) breaks down, even under Hume's own handling.

The fourth class of virtues, those 'immediately agreeable to others'—politeness, wit, cleanliness—are apparently not all on the same plane, and further illustrate the difficulty of making the distinction just noted.

In fact, this whole classification and treatment of the particular virtues, first adopted in the *Treatise*, and retained without important revision in the *Inquiry*, seems out of place in the latter work, since there Hume once for all admits an original sympathetic tendency in human nature. It would have been much more consistent for him to show that both the self-regarding and the other-regarding virtues are ultimately to be recognised as virtues, because they conduce to the common weal, or—if we may use the phrase now so hackneyed, which had already, in Hume's time, been employed by Hutcheson—'the greatest happiness of the greatest number'.

No account of Hume's ethical system, however brief, can afford to neglect the admirable Conclusion to the *Inquiry*, in which he takes a comprehensive view of the issues which have been raised and met separately, and makes a final plea for the validity of his general position.[1] Like most of the preceding chapters, or 'sections,' the Conclusion is divided into two parts. The first and more important part of the argument attempts in outline a sort of natural history of morals, while the second part gives an account of the ground of moral obligation. It will be found that the second part is too much of the nature of an *argumentum ad hominem*, and fails to do justice to the spirit of the first part, to which latter we shall principally direct our attention.

Hume begins by arguing that, whatever philosophers may teach, we never actually continue to approve of any quality in

[1] See § IX. A less satisfactory form of the same argument may be found at the end of Book III. of the *Treatise* (see §§ v. and vi.); but this may be safely neglected here, not only because the whole argument is put in a more convincing form in the later work, but also, and particularly, because the principle of sympathy, or humanity, upon which the recognition of moral distinctions is supposed ultimately to depend, is developed here, as throughout the *Inquiry*, in a much more satisfactory manner than in the *Treatise*.

human nature, which does not at least appear to be either useful or agreeable to ourselves or others.   The apparent approval of celibacy, fasting, penance, etc., is to be attributed to superstition and false religion, and it is important to notice that, in the course of a healthy intellectual and moral development, such fictitious virtues are gradually transferred to the opposite column, and placed in the catalogue of vices. So far we have little but a reaffirmation of the author's general position, marred somewhat by his continued use of the artificial division, just criticised, of moral actions into those which give pleasure either directly or indirectly to oneself or others. But now Hume pertinently points out that he has avoided becoming entangled in the wearisome dispute concerning the degrees of benevolence or self-love which prevail in human nature.   "It is sufficient for our present purpose," he says, "if it be allowed, what surely, without the greatest absurdity cannot be disputed, that there is some benevolence, however small, infused into our bosom."   No matter how faint these generous sentiments may be thought to be, they must at any rate direct the determinations of our mind where everything else is equal, and "produce a cool preference of what is useful and serviceable to mankind, above what is pernicious and dangerous".

The result is most important : " A *moral distinction*, therefore, immediately arises; a general sentiment of blame and approbation; a tendency, however faint, to the objects of the one, and a proportionable aversion to those of the other ". Avarice, ambition, vanity, and all the other passions which are commonly, though improperly, comprised under the general head of ' self-love,' are to be ruled out as wholly inadequate to explain our original recognition of moral distinctions, not because they are too weak, but because they have not a ' proper direction ' for that purpose.   They wholly fail to explain that principle of objectivity which we demand and recognise in moral judgments.   This implies some sentiment which is at once common to all mankind, and so comprehensive as to extend to all mankind, no matter how remote from ourselves in space or time. Nothing but the sentiment of humanity, here insisted upon, can reasonably be regarded as the ultimate cause of the all-important phenomenon which we are attempting to explain. An important auxiliary sentiment, however, which does much to re-enforce our strictly moral sentiments, is to be found in that very love of fame, which has so often been regarded as a merely selfish passion. This tends to make us regard our own conduct objectively, and to keep alive in us the highest ideals ; and it further begets in noble natures that habit of self-reverence which is the surest guardian of every virtue.[1]

As already indicated, the second part of the Conclusion, concerning the ground of moral obligation, is hardly in the spirit of the first part. There the common feeling of humanity had been treated as the ultimate ground of our recognition of moral distinctions; here one would naturally expect Hume to take the same principle as a starting-point, from which to revise the conception of moral obligation. As a matter of fact, however, he mainly contents himself with commending his system to those who hold the selfish theory of the moral motive rather than his own. The principal question considered, then, is how far morality is for the interest of the individual, abstractly considered, although in the course of this very argument he makes the highly significant remark, already quoted, that " whatever contradiction may vulgarly be supposed between the *selfish* and *social* sentiments or dispositions, they are really no more opposite than selfish and ambitious, selfish and revengeful, selfish and vain ".

Returning still again to his artificial classification of the virtues, he does not, of course, have to prove that the virtues which are such because they conduce either directly or indirectly to the pleasure of the individual agent are for the

---

[1] The last paragraph of part i. of this section, in which Hume reverts to his characteristic sceptical position, on the ground that " an hypothesis, so obvious, had it been a true one, would, long ere now, have been received by the unanimous suffrage and consent of mankind," can hardly be regarded as significant here, except, perhaps, as indicating the author's personal attitude.

individual's selfish interest, for that follows from the definitions themselves. And he points out that it is really superfluous to prove that the 'companionable virtues,' *i.e.*, those 'immediately agreeable to others,' like good manners and wit, decency and genteelness, are more desirable than the contrary qualities. The only real problem arises in the case of justice, the typical virtue of the remaining class, *i.e.*, the class of virtues 'useful to others'. That 'honesty is the best policy' is a good general rule; but how about the possible exceptions, where a man may seem to be the loser by his integrity? Hume practically admits that he has no arguments of a strictly logical kind with which to meet this real or supposed difficulty, but rather lays stress upon the inward peace of mind, consciousness of integrity, etc., which, as he says, "are circumstances very requisite to happiness, and will be cherished and cultivated by every honest man, who feels the importance of them". It will readily be seen that this appeal to our moral consciousness hardly meets the theoretical difficulty—the self-imposed difficulty of eighteenth century individualism—which was to show that morality was for the advantage of the moral agent, not as a social being, with no interests wholly separate from those of society, but rather as an isolated centre of self-interest. The only logical solution, from that point of view, was that of the so-called 'Theological Utilitarians,' who frankly depended upon the doctrine of rewards and punishments after death.

Such was Hume's system as actually worked out by himself. When we come to compare it with that of Gay—his only predecessor who had stated the Utilitarian principle in a perfectly unambiguous form—we see at once what an important advance had been made in the development of ethical theory. Gay's system had been as frankly individualistic, in its way, as that of Hobbes; but, at the same time, it had avoided those offensive paradoxes of the earlier doctrine, which had undoubtedly kept many from appreciating the plausibility of the egoistic position. Indeed, it would be quite unfair to put Gay and his successors (*i.e.*, those Utilitarian writers who maintained the egoistic character of the motive of the moral agent) in the same category with Hobbes. Gay and the others never employed egoism as a means by which to vilify human nature, but rather seem to have regarded it as a tempting device for simplifying ethical theory. Moreover, they partly succeeded in disguising its essentially unlovely character by supposing the development of a derived ' sympathy' through the ' association of ideas '. Hume had at first allowed himself to use ' association' in much the same way; but the very fact that his explanations in the *Treatise* are so much less clear than those of Gay in the *Dissertation*, suggests a lack of certainty in his own mind as to the validity of the method; and, as we have seen, he entirely gave up, in his later work, any attempt to reduce the altruistic tendencies of human nature to terms of something else.

Taken by itself, Hume's recognition and defence of original altruism could not be regarded as an important contribution to English Ethics. From the time of Cumberland to that of Shaftesbury and Hutcheson, there had never been wanting those who, from one point of view or another, opposed the egoistic position of Hobbes. But of all those moralists, Cumberland alone can properly be termed a Utilitarian, and even he, it will be remembered, had carried through ' the perfection of mind and body' as a principle parallel to that of ' the greatest happiness of all '. Hume, then, was the first to hold the Utilitarian doctrine in its unmistakable form and at the same time to admit, and defend, the altruistic tendencies of human nature.

Gay had vigorously, and more or less successfully, opposed the ' Moral Sense' theory, as held by Shaftesbury and Hutcheson. While, however, he was greatly in advance of those writers in clearness and simplicity of ethical theory, he by no means equalled them in his grasp of the fundamental facts of our moral experience. Hume was as sure as Gay had been that we must not explain the phenomena of our moral life by referring them, or any part of them, to a special faculty like the ' moral sense'; but he took a much broader view of human nature than Gay had done, and, from first to last, attributed more importance to the part played by the affective side of our nature in the formation of moral judgments. In fact, he has sometimes been misjudged on account of this very catholicity of treatment. As we have had occasion to note, there are even those who hold that he never quite departed from the ' Moral Sense ' theory. I can only regard this view as a serious mistake. We have seen again and again, that, while he always begins with the fact of moral approbation, as applying to a particular class of actions, it is his special endeavour to show how this approbation arises, according to the recognised principles of human nature. With all his faults as a philosopher and as a moralist, Hume was far too scientific, both in his ideals and his methods, to be guilty of any flagrant form of ' faculty psychology '.

We can only speculate as to just what Hume's system might have become, if the author had given up his artificial and somewhat misleading classification of the virtues. It is fair to remark, however, that, if he had been more thorough in his revision of the third book of the *Treatise*, and had definitely shown, what certainly was implicit in his system, that all the virtues are such because they conduce to ' the greatest happiness of the greatest number,' he would have stated the Utilitarian principle practically in its modern form. As it was, he freed the doctrine from the unfortunate dogma that the motive of the moral agent is always, in the last resort, egoistic. This was a distinct advance upon Gay, which, however, was wasted upon Tucker, Paley, and Bentham, all of whom reproduce the position of the *Dissertation*. Even as stated to-day, the ' greatest happiness ' theory does seem likely to be accepted as the final word of Ethics ; but it would hardly be too much to claim that the *Inquiry concerning the Principles of Morals*, with all its defects and shortcomings, is the classic statement of English Utilitarianism.

# CHAPTER VI.

## DAVID HARTLEY.

THE first writer who made the attempt systematically to develop the theory of the Association of Ideas, as outlined by Gay, and to show, more in detail, the consequences of this theory for Ethics, was the physician David Hartley. He did this in his well-known *Observations on Man, his Frame, his Duty, and his Expectations*, which was first published in 1749. Probably no writer on philosophical subjects has gained more from mere priority of publication. Even at the present day, the Associationist theory is often called by his name, although he was confessedly not the originator of the theory, and developed it with a clumsiness which can only be appreciated by those who know his book at first hand. Ten years before the publication of the *Observations*, Hume had published the first two books of the *Treatise of Human Nature*, in which, while apparently working in independence of Gay, he had not indeed treated the principle of Association directly and at length, but had presupposed it throughout, and with a perfect understanding of its implications. By the time Hartley published, the theory seems to have become, in a sense, public property; and it was probably this fact, almost as much as the undoubted dulness of Hartley's style and the crudeness of his general treatment, that caused the book to make so slight an impression at the time of publication. Although the Associationist Psychology was so important for the further development of English Utilitarianism that the early form of the theory will soon have to be considered at some length, it will be more helpful to take Tucker, who published only nineteen years later, as its exponent. At the same time, Hartley cannot with propriety be neglected: first, because of his traditional position in the history of the principle which we are considering; and, secondly, because he was not, as constantly assumed, the typical early Associationist.

This misapprehension as to Hartley's real originality and importance, however, is something for which he himself was not at all responsible. If his manner is dry and uninteresting, the tone of his treatise is modest and unassuming throughout. For instance, in the Preface to his *Observations*, he says: "About eighteen years ago I was informed that the Rev. Mr. Gay, then living, asserted the possibility of deducing all our intellectual pleasures and pains from association. This put me upon considering the power of association. Mr. Gay published his sentiments on this matter, about the same time, in a *Dissertation on the Fundamental Principle of Virtue* prefixed to Mr. Archdeacon Law's translation of Archbishop King's *Origin of Evil.*" Such a statement might seem natural and almost inevitable, under the circumstances, but Hartley's frankness in acknowledging his obligations to Gay is in shining contrast to the strange reticence of some of his more gifted successors.

The Introduction to Part I. of the *Observations* is perfectly clear and business-like—a very necessary guide, in fact, through the arid tracts that are to follow. We shall do well to note a few of the distinctions at once. Sensations and ideas are clearly distinguished, and defined in what we would now regard as the conventional way, except that they are made to include pleasures and pains. The ideas which resemble sensations are called 'ideas of sensation'; all the rest are called 'intellectual ideas'. As will appear later, ideas of sensation are the elements of which all the rest are compounded. The faculties of the mind recognised are memory, imagination (or fancy), understanding, affection, and will. Only two of the definitions require further notice. "The *affections* have the pleasures and pains for their objects;

as the understanding has the mere sensations and ideas. By the affections we are excited to pursue happiness, and all its means, and to fly from misery, and all its apparent causes. The *will* is that state of mind which is immediately previous to, and causes, those express acts of memory, fancy, and bodily motion, which are termed voluntary."

Now it must always be remembered that Hartley is concerned to prove, not merely the association of ideas, but his peculiar 'doctrine of vibrations,' by which he explains all neural phenomena. The former is to explain our mental life down to its smallest details; the latter is to explain the necessary physiological accompaniments of all mental life. While this frank recognition of, and insistence upon, the physiological concomitants of our mental life must be regarded as an indication of the scientific spirit of Hartley, his recklessness in elaborating his theory of vibrations far beyond what neurological science in his own day (or, of course, later) would justify, could only result in disaster. Wherever he thinks he finds a mental law, he provides it with a parallel hypothetical physiological law, until the reader holds his breath at the audacity of this plodding and seemingly unimaginative scientist. In our brief examination of Hartley's psychological system, we shall, of course, neglect this ' deadly parallel' mythological neurology; but, in so doing, we must not forget that a part of the great crudeness which we shall have to notice, was not improbably due to this fanciful attempt to keep the mental and the physical series exactly parallel.

A few words, however, regarding the 'theory of vibrations' before we dismiss it altogether. We are told that " the white medullary substance of the brain, spinal marrow, and the nerves proceeding from them, is the immediate instrument of sensation and motion ".[1] In the case of simple sensations, we must suppose a simple vibration in this substance; in the case of complex sensations, associated vibrations. But " sensory vibrations, by being often repeated,

[1] See Pt. I., prop. i., p. 5 (of "sixth edition, corrected," 1834).

beget, in the medullary substance of the brain, a disposition
to diminutive vibrations, which may also be called vibratiuncles, and miniatures, corresponding to themselves respectively ".[1]     To the vibratiuncles, correspond simple ideas;
to associated vibratiuncles, complex ideas.   There are also
' motory vibrations,' which contract the muscles and so cause
automatic movements; while voluntary and semi-voluntary
movements must be explained by corresponding ' motory
vibratiuncles '.     One might, perhaps, expect some theory
regarding the relation of mind and body from Hartley, since
he attempts so minutely to trace out the psycho-physical
parallelism.   The nearest approach to such a theory seems
to be the following : " If we suppose an infinitesimal elementary body to be intermediate between the soul and gross
body, which appears to be no improbable supposition, then
the changes in our sensations, ideas, and motions, may correspond to the changes made in the medullary substance, only
as far as these correspond to the changes made in the elementary body ".[2]   It was probably well that Hartley did not carry
his speculations further in this direction.

Leaving, then, this very debatable territory, let us examine
the essentials of Hartley's psychology proper.   Sensations,
by being often repeated, leave certain vestiges, types, or
images, of themselves, which may be called ' simple ideas of
sensation '.     But " any sensations, A, B, C, &c., by being
associated with one another a sufficient number of times, get
such a power over the corresponding ideas, a, b, c, &c., that any
one of the sensations, A, when impressed alone, shall be able to
excite in the mind b, c, &c., the ideas of the rest ".[3]   After
this very clear statement of the general principle of association,
Hartley goes on to show, in the usual way, how simple ideas
go to form complex ones by means of association.   That this
is true in very many cases, seems to him certain.   The presumption, therefore, is that the same principle will hold
throughout our mental life, and that all our complex ideas

[1] See Pt. I., prop. ix., p. 37.
[2] *Ibid.*, v., p. 22.          [3] *Ibid.*, x., p. 41.

may finally be resolved into their constituent parts, *i.e.*, simple ideas of sensation.

When we pass beyond mere sensation, and come to consider our intellectual life, we are confronted, at the very outset, with a conspicuous example of association. " Words and. phrases must excite ideas in us by association, and they excite ideas in us by no other means." [1] After making certain obvious remarks on this score, the indefatigable writer launches out into elaborate speculations regarding the origin of language, not omitting to consider what language may have been before and after the Fall of Man. The language of Paradise was presumably monosyllabic, as man's intellectual nature had hardly yet been awakened. In this connection, the author remarks that " to set a value upon knowledge considered in itself, and exclusively of its tendency to carry us to God, is a most pernicious error, derived originally from Adam's having eaten of the tree of knowledge ".[2] Rational assent and dissent are explained by the author by means of association. He says: " Rational assent then to any proposition, may be defined, a readiness to affirm it to be true, proceeding from a close association of the ideas suggested by the proposition, with the idea, or internal feeling, belonging to the word truth ".[3] ' Practical' assent is nothing but " the natural and necessary consequence of rational, when sufficiently impressed". It hardly need be pointed out that association, as here invoked, explains nothing, since the ' idea, or internal feeling, belonging to the word truth ' is taken for granted. Of course a single passage is likely to caricature a writer's solution of a difficult problem; but that can hardly be claimed in the present case. The following passage is perhaps the clearest and most plausible of many to the same general purpose. " Now the cause that a person affirms the truth of the proposition *twice two is four*, is the entire coincidence of the visible or tangible idea of twice two with that of four, as impressed upon the mind by various

---

[1] See Pt. I., prop. lxxix., p. 169.
[2] *Ibid.*, lxxxiii., p. 188.  [3] *Ibid.*, lxxxvi., p. 204.

objects. We see everywhere that twice two and four are only different names for the same impression. And it is mere association which appropriates the word truth, its definition, or its internal feeling, to this coincidence." [1]

So much, in brief, concerning our purely intellectual life; but, according to Hartley, " our passions or affections can be no more than aggregates of simple ideas united by association ". [2]   This was, of course, the natural consequence of regarding pleasures and pains as ' ideas '.   It would be quite hypercritical to raise the difficulty which modern psychology might find here, as to whether feeling, as such, is capable of revival in memory, like sense-perception, and so capable of association.   None of the early Associationists dreamed of any such difficulty.   Certainly no part of Hartley's treatise is better known than his chapters on " The Six Classes of Intellectual Pleasures and Pains ". [3]   These are the pleasures and pains (1) of imagination, (2) of ambition, (3) of self-interest, (4) of sympathy, (5) of theopathy, and (6) of the moral sense.   Before considering these, however, and the order in which they are developed, it will be best to notice briefly Hartley's general account of the passions, which will be found really to include his treatment of the will.   Since all the passions arise from pleasure and pain, the first and most natural division is into ' love ' and ' hatred,' the former arising from the thought of what gives us pleasure, the latter from the thought of what gives us pain.   But we are so constituted that pleasure and pain impel us to action.   Thus ' active ' love becomes ' desire,' and ' active ' hatred ' aversion '.   These are the moving forces in man.   Action is first automatic : the child originally grasps at the attractive plaything or withdraws his hand from the fire that burns him ' from the mechanism of his nature '; but in time he learns, partly by repetition of this mechanical process, and partly as a result of imitating others or being instructed by them, to

---

[1] See Pt. I., prop. lxxxvi., p. 204.
[2] *Ibid.*, lxxxix., p. 231.      [3] *Ibid.*, xciv., pp. 262 *et seq.*

pursue whatever he loves and desires, and to flee from everything which he hates.[1]

Now the logic of this might seem to be, that man must always do what he likes and refrain from doing what he dislikes—in other words, act always for the increase of his own happiness or the diminution of his own pain. Hartley recognises that this was a very common, perhaps the most common, theory in his own day. But against this view he declares unequivocally, though recognising no *original* principle of sympathy. And this is what principally distinguishes him from all the other Associationists who attempted to derive sympathy from something else. He holds that the complicated phenomena of human action in no way countenance "the notion of an essential, original, perpetual desire of happiness, and endeavour to attain it".[2] Is sympathy factitious? Well, so are several of the other principles on which adults habitually act. This is his general position ; the arguments by which he sustains it will be noticed immediately. After the preceding, little remains to be said concerning the will. In a single passage, the author says practically all he has to say about that faculty. "The will appears to be nothing but a desire or aversion sufficiently strong to produce an action that is not automatic primarily or secondarily. At least it appears to me, that the substitution of these words for the word *will* may be justified by the common usage of language. The will is therefore that desire or aversion which is strongest for the then present time."[3]

In order to understand human volition, then, we must investigate the genesis of our 'intellectual affections,' for these are much more important in determining us to action than mere pleasures or pains of sense. Hartley outlines his whole treatment in a long paragraph which it is necessary to quote, since it not only throws the strongest light upon his view of what actually determines the will in adult life, but explains

---

[1] See Pt. I., prop. lxxxix., p. 232.
[2] See *ibid.*, p. 233.     [3] See *ibid.*

his peculiar position, just mentioned, regarding sympathy, and, in truth, suggests his whole ethical theory. He says: "As sensation is the common foundation of all these, so each in its turn, when sufficiently generated, contributes to generate and model all the rest. We may conceive this to be done in the following manner. Let sensation generate imagination; then will sensation and imagination together generate ambition; sensation, imagination, and ambition, self-interest; sensation, imagination, ambition, and self-interest, sympathy; sensation, imagination, ambition, self-interest, and sympathy, theopathy; sensation, imagination, ambition, self-interest, sympathy, and theopathy, the moral sense: and, in an inverted order, imagination will new model sensation; ambition, sensation and imagination; self-interest, sensation, imagination, and ambition; sympathy, sensation, imagination, ambition, and self-interest; theopathy, sensation, imagination, ambition, self-interest, and sympathy; and the moral sense, sensation, imagination, ambition, self-interest, sympathy, and theopathy: till at last, by the numerous reciprocal influences of all these upon each other, the passions arrive at that degree of complexness, which is observed in fact, and which makes them so difficult to be analysed." [1]

This quaint passage can hardly fail to provoke a smile; but, as already suggested, it is very significant in several ways. (1) It throws light upon Hartley's otherwise inexplicable classification of the 'intellectual affections'. A mere glance would show that the classification was not psychological, but developed with a view to Ethics. This passage, showing the supposed genesis of the 'intellectual affections,' explains the peculiar order in which the various classes of those affections appear in Hartley's list. Since all except pleasures and pains of sensation were to be proved factitious, and since sympathy was to be vindicated as no more factitious than the others, this was the order corresponding to the supposed order of development. (2) That the development itself, as here explained, is problematical in the ex-

---

[1] See Pt. I., prop. lxxxix., p. 232.

treme hardly need be pointed out. The reader feels as if he were being treated to a not over-skilful exhibition of psychological sleight of hand. At least this remark applies to the first part of the explanation, where the ascent from pleasures and pains of sensation to those of theopathy and moral sense is explained. And it may be added that the author's more extended treatment of the same subject makes the details of his theory hardly, if at all, more plausible. But (3) the last part of the explanation, where the author shows how the 'higher' affections (however generated) are bound to react upon the 'lower,' and make them essentially different in the civilised adult from what they would otherwise be, is calculated to make the discerning reader somewhat lenient; for it was just this very important reciprocal influence which the Associationists, particularly those of early date, were accustomed to neglect. But, unfortunately, what Hartley gains in our estimation here, in one respect, he loses in another. It was most important to call attention to this reciprocal influence between one part or side of our nature and all the rest; but the resulting complication is greater than Associationism had the apparatus to cope with. That was doubtless why this idea of Hartley's was not carried further.

The 'rule of life' which Hartley lays down, has been so completely foreshadowed by his psychological explanation of our 'intellectual affections,' that there can be little doubt that his ethical theory, in outline at least, anticipated this part of his psychology. The two, in fact, as we find them, are inseparable. The classification and explanation of our 'intellectual affections' furnishes the outline for his unsystematic and decidedly clumsy treatment of Ethics proper. Beginning with sensation, he shows, as might be expected, that the pleasures of sensation ought not to be made a primary pursuit.[1] The reasons given for this are largely of the obvious prudential kind; but he also resorts to a kind of *a priori* reasoning from analogy, which is to become more

---

[1] See Pt. II., prop. I., pp. 454 *et seq.*

and more prominent as he proceeds with his treatment of
Ethics.   That which is prior in nature is always less perfect
than that which is posterior; but we have seen that pleasures
and pains of sensation are prior to the 'intellectual affections'; therefore they "cannot be supposed of equal value
and dignity with the intellectual, to the generation of which
they are made subservient".   Hartley is always true to this
belief in the qualitative distinctions between pleasures, which
forms an essential feature of his ethical system.    Just as
sympathy, though factitious as regards its origin, is practically
co-ordinate with egoism, as a principle of human action, and
should be more than that; so the distinction between 'higher'
and 'lower,' though explained in terms of development, is
to all intents and purposes an ultimate distinction, one of
kind and not of degree.   Those who speak of Hartley in
general terms as the typical Associationist-Utilitarian, should
be very careful to recall these cases where his interpretation
of the logical consequences of his method was precisely the
reverse of that of his successors of whatever ethical school.

But if the pleasures of sense should not be made a primary
pursuit, neither should those of the imagination.[1]   Our regard for these, as for the pleasures of sensation, should
be regulated by the precepts of benevolence, piety, and the
moral sense.   The arguments advanced here are very
similar to those advanced with reference to sensible pleasures.
For instance, as sensible pleasures were presumably of less
worth than the intellectual, because prior, so here we have
to do with the earliest, and therefore presumably the lowest,
intellectual pleasures.   And when the author comes to treat
of the pleasures and pains of ambition, much the same arguments, adapted as the case requires (since we are one step
higher in the series), have to do service again.   The prudential
arguments, also, are repeated with considerable emphasis in
each case.

If the remainder of Hartley's treatment of the 'rule of
life' consisted merely in repeating, as he is bound to do,

---

[1] See Pt. II., prop. lv., pp. 473 *et seq.*

almost the same arguments at each successive step, as showing that the 'lower' pleasures must be subordinated to the
'higher,' it would hardly be necessary to proceed with our
exposition, since the reader could readily anticipate the course
of the argument for himself. But a glance at the list of
'intellectual affections,' which Hartley takes as the outline
for his treatment of Ethics, will show that we still have to
deal with the relative value of the pleasures and pains of
'self-interest,' 'sympathy,' 'theopathy,' and the 'moral sense'.
Evidently we come here to the very core of his ethical system.
Neglecting the form of exposition, which, as just said, can
readily be surmised from the preceding, let us first examine
the position of self-interest in Hartley's system. Three kinds
of self-interest are recognised: (1) 'gross' self-interest, or
the pursuit of the means for obtaining the pleasures of sensation, imagination, and ambition; (2) 'refined' self-interest, or
the pursuit of the means for obtaining the pleasures of sympathy, theopathy, and the moral sense; and (3) 'rational
self-interest, or the pursuit of such things as are believed
to be the means for obtaining our greatest possible happiness,
"at the same time that we are ignorant, or do not consider,
from what particular species of pleasure this our greatest
possible happiness will arise ".[1]

Now, apart from the general criticism that the classification
as a whole is on a questionable principle, this very analysis
shows that to make one class of 'intellectual affections'
pleasures and pains of 'self-interest,' was absurd. There is
nothing in self-interest, by itself considered, to afford the
basis for a particular class of affections. 'Gross' self-interest,
according to Hartley, is satisfied by the three 'lower' classes
of pleasures, in the ascending order of sensation, imagination,
and ambition; 'refined' self-interest, by the three 'higher'
classes of pleasures, in the order of sympathy, theopathy, and
moral sense. It might be assumed, as a matter of course,
that Hartley would put 'refined' self-interest upon a higher
plane than 'gross' self-interest, since it must look for its

[1] See Pt. II., prop. lxv., p. 491.

satisfaction to the 'higher' pleasures, just mentioned. He does, indeed, show that 'gross' self-interest being incompatible with the pleasures of theopathy and the moral sense, is "an insuperable objection to its being made our primary pursuit," —this quite apart from the fact, strongly urged, that it tends to defeat itself. But when he comes to show that neither should 'refined' self-interest be made our primary pursuit, he says: "Refined self-interest, when indulged, is a much deeper and more dangerous error than the gross, because it shelters itself under sympathy, theopathy, and the moral sense, so as to grow through their protection". Moreover, "the pride attending on refined self-interest, when carried to a certain height, is of an incorrigible, and, as it were, diabolical nature ".[1]

What, then, one is moved to ask, can 'rational' self-interest (the third kind) mean, according to Hartley's system? Earlier in the book, he says of 'rational' self-interest: "This is the same thing with the abstract desire of happiness, and aversion to misery, which is supposed to attend every intelligent being during the whole course of his existence ".[2] Now this 'abstract desire of happiness' must be for the pleasures within the reach of the agent, and there are no such pleasures, except those already enumerated. There can be no doubt that on this point Hartley is, even more than ordinarily, confused. His clearest statement is the following: "Rational self-interest may therefore be said to lie between the impure motives of sensation, imagination, ambition, gross self-interest, and refined self-interest, on the one hand, and the pure ones of sympathy, theopathy, and the moral sense, on the other; so that when it restrains the impure ones, or cherishes the pure, it may be reckoned a virtue; when it cherishes the impure, or damps the pure, a vice ".[3]

This, of course, is hopeless. We only begin to understand the author, when, in the course of his practical observations, he says, *e.g.:* "However the gross or refined self-interest

---

[1] See Pt. II., prop. lxv., p. 494.
[2] See Pt. I., prop. xcvi., p. 291.
[3] See Pt. II., prop. lxv., p. 495.

may, upon certain occasions, be disappointed, the rational one never can, whilst we act upon a principle of duty ". The statement is confused, but Hartley probably means to say that we must never act from considerations of purely personal interest at all; if we do our whole duty, our higher interest will take care of itself. This comes out most clearly, when Hartley explains his characteristic doctrine of ' self-annihilation'. He proposes to mediate between the egoistic and altruistic theories regarding the motive in moral action; but, as will be seen, he really declares for one side in the controversy. His conclusion is as follows: " The virtuous dispositions of benevolence, piety, and the moral sense, and particularly that of the love of God, check all the foregoing ones, and seem sufficient utterly to extinguish them at last. This would be perfect self-annihilation, and resting in God as our centre. And upon the whole, we may conclude, that though it be impossible to begin without sensuality, and sensual selfishness, or to proceed without the other intermediate principles, and particularly that of rational self-interest; yet we ought never to be satisfied with ourselves, till we arrive at perfect self-annihilation, and the pure love of God." [1]

We are now in possession of all that is really essential to Hartley's system. We need not be thrown off the track, even when, in treating of the pleasures of sympathy, the author shows that these, on the one hand, increase those of sensation, imagination, ambition, and self-interest, and, on the other hand, unite with those of theopathy and the moral sense; and when he adds: " They are self-consistent, and admit of an unlimited extent: they may therefore be our primary pursuit ".[2] Of course, this is not what Hartley really means to say, for he has just urged that ' refined' self-interest is even more dangerous (because more insidious) than ' gross' self-interest. Hence, of course, the *pleasures* of sympathy are by no means to be indulged in (*qua* pleasures) without restriction. What he doubtless means is, that the principle of sympathy is to be allowed perfectly free play.

[1] See Pt. II., prop. lxvii., p. 497.       [2] *Ibid.*, lxviii., p. 498.

The confusion results from Hartley's inveterate habit of appealing constantly to egoistic motives, while holding all the time that, not egoism, but self-annihilation is the true principle of human action. Indeed, he says : " Since benevolence is now proved to be a primary pursuit, it follows, that we are to direct every action so as to produce the greatest happiness, and the least misery, in our power. This is that rule of social behaviour, which universal unlimited benevolence inculcates." [1]

It might seem as if, after all Hartley's logical inconsistencies, he had ended by stating Utilitarianism in its modern form : the 'greatest happiness of the greatest number' the end of moral action, and the motive of the agent, in very considerable degree, at least, unselfish. But in the application of his principles, Hartley halts far behind Gay and Hume. He says : " It is impossible for the most sagacious and experienced persons to make any accurate estimate of the future consequences of particular actions, so as, in all the variety of circumstances which occur, to determine justly, which action would contribute most to augment happiness and lessen misery ". Then, instead of showing, as Tucker and Paley did later, that, owing to such difficulties, we must act, not from computations in the particular case, but with a view to the general consequences of given classes of actions, he lays down ten rules, which amount really to shirking the consideration of external consequences almost altogether. The first rule is, that we follow the Scriptural precepts in the natural, obvious, and popular meaning of them ; the second, that we have great regard for our own moral sense, and that of others. Hartley says : " This rule coincides remarkably with the foregoing. They are together the chief supports of all that is good, even in the most refined and philosophical, as well as in the vulgar ; and therefore must not be weakened, or explained away." The third rule, indeed, is that we are to take account of consequences, and let such considerations have some influence with us, but never in opposition to the

first two rules. The other rules mentioned are purely practical precepts, and need not be considered here.

With characteristic infelicity, Hartley confuses his treatment of the relation of Ethics to Religion by urging that the
love of God procures a pleasure superior in kind and degree
to all the rest, and that this is one important reason why it
should be our primary pursuit and ultimate end. Neglecting
this inconsistency, we may find Hartley's real meaning in the
first part of the same proposition, where he shows that " the
love of God regulates, improves, and perfects all the other
parts of our nature ".[1] A very commonplace statement this,
it may be thought, and the following reflections are, on the
whole, far from intellectually illuminating ; but their dulness
should not blind us to one very important fact, *viz.*, that
according to Hartley we need religion, not primarily because
we need to remain in constant fear of a God who has it in
His power to inflict unlimited punishments, or to bribe us with
rewards beyond computation, but because self-annihilation
and communion with God presuppose each other, are two
essential phases of our growth in moral perfection, so that at
the last fear is lost in love. An examination of the text would
perhaps show that Hartley is even less of a theologian than a
moral philosopher, in the sense of technical proficiency ; but
we can forgive much in the man who saw 'through a glass
darkly' what was beyond the vision of so many of the accredited theologians of his own and later times.

Inseparably connected with Hartley's view of the relation
of Ethics to Religion, is his theory of the moral sense. As we
have just seen, he holds that we cannot determine the morality
of actions primarily with respect to consequences ; but that
we must act always with a view to Scriptural precepts, taking
very particular pains to do nothing that shall blunt the moral
sense, either in ourselves or in others. When he comes to
consider the moral sense directly, he says that this " ought
to be made the immediate guide of our actions on all sudden
emergencies ; and therefore its pleasures may be considered

---

[1] See Pt. II., prop. lxxi., p. 514.

as making part of our primary pursuit ".[1] Since this confusion is of the same kind that we have repeatedly noticed,
and since the author's real meaning is sufficiently plain, we
may properly neglect it.

For Hartley's clearest account of the genesis of the moral
sense, we must look to his earlier analysis of the pleasures
and pains pertaining to that faculty. After some rather
scattering observations, he concludes: " And thus we may
perceive, that all the pleasures and pains of sensation,
imagination, ambition, self-interest, sympathy, and theopathy,
as far as they are consistent with one another, with the frame
of our natures, and with the course of the world, beget in us
a moral sense, and lead us to the love and approbation of
virtue, and to the fear, hatred, and abhorrence of vice ".[2] The
meaning seems to be, that the harmony of our other affections
in some way produces the moral sense; but for Hartley, as
for others, the moral sense, when once it exists, exercises a
regulative function, one very important object of which is
to produce a harmony of all the other affections. We are
not reassured, when he immediately adds: " This moral sense
therefore carries its own authority with it, inasmuch as it
is the sum total of all the rest, and the ultimate result from
them; and employs the force and authority of the whole
nature of man against any particular part of it, that rebels
against the determinations and commands of the conscience
or moral judgment ". Later in the book, Hartley says:
" The moral sense is generated chiefly by piety, benevolence,
and rational self-interest; all of which are explicit guides of
life in deliberate actions ";[3] but this only makes the confusion worse. These vague and partly conflicting accounts of
the genesis of the moral sense are hardly calculated to give us
a firm conviction of its authoritative character. The difficulty
is not so much that it has in some way been developed in the
course of human experience, as that we are left so largely in
the dark as to how it was developed, and exactly what it is.

[1] See Pt. II., prop. lxxiv., p. 531.
[2] See Pt. I., prop. xcix., p. 311.        [3] See Pt. II., prop. lxxiv., p. 532.

The preceding exposition will probably convince the reader that Hartley's system is principally important, as being the first elaborate attempt to work out the Associationist theory, with reference both to Psychology and to Ethics. Of the value of his contribution to Psychology, we shall be able better to judge when we have examined Tucker's system. Until then, indeed, we can hardly be said to have anything with which to compare it. On the other hand, it is perfectly clear that this first attempt systematically to develop Associationism produced very little of permanent value for Ethics. We have but to compare Hartley's treatment of Ethics with the outline sketched by Gay, in order to see how greatly inferior it is both in consistency and originality ; while it goes without saying that Hartley contributed nothing to ethical literature at all comparable in value with even the first (and, in the present writer's opinion, inferior) version of Hume's theory, which had been published as Book III. of the *Treatise* nine years before the *Observations*. But, more particularly, we must notice that Hartley was not the typical Associationist-Utilitarian, as is frequently assumed. Unlike any of that school who immediately followed, he held (1) that there are qualitative differences between pleasures ; (2) that ' derived ' sympathy, and not the pursuit of one's own ultimate happiness, must be regarded as the true motive in moral action ; and (3) that the consideration of consequences should play a very subordinate part in determining the rightness or wrongness of actions. This last feature of Hartley's system, indeed, nearly excludes him from the Utilitarian school altogether. Hutcheson actually conceded almost, if not quite, as much to the importance of the consequences of actions as did Hartley. The ethical part of the *Observations* remains an instructive example of a truth with which one is often impressed in the History of Philosophy : that those who are the first to employ a new ' method ' are often more blind even than their own contemporaries as to its logical consequences.

# CHAPTER VII.

## ABRAHAM TUCKER.

GAY'S *Preliminary Dissertation*—which, as we have seen, appeared in 1731 as an essay prefixed to Law's translation of King's *Origin of Evil*—had a most peculiar fate. Published anonymously, it seems never to have been claimed by the author, whose first name, even, is not generally known.[1] Though this remarkable essay was the first statement of Utilitarianism in its completely differentiated form, Hume does not mention it, or show that he was acquainted with it, either in Book III. of the *Treatise of Human Nature* (1740) or in the *Inquiry concerning the Principles of Morals* (1751). Hartley, indeed, with a scrupulousness which the more gifted writers of his own and the succeeding generation might well have imitated, did mention "the Rev. Mr. Gay" as having suggested to him, through his reported views and his published *Dissertation*, "the possibility of deducing all our intellectual pleasures and pains from association". This was in the preface to the well-known *Observations on Man*, published in 1749. Hartley's actual treatment of 'association,' however, was quite different from that suggested by Gay, while his particular applications of the principle to the solution of ethical problems differed still more from those to be found in the *Preliminary Dissertation*.

---

[1] Whewell was probably right in thinking that he had identified him with "John Gay, who took the degree of B.A. at Sidney College in 1721, and was afterwards Fellow of the College". See *Lectures on the History of Moral Philosophy in England*, Lect. x. Other writers commonly follow Hartley's example, and refer to him as "the Rev. Mr. Gay".

But nineteen years after the publication of Hartley's book—thirty-seven years after the publication of the *Dissertation* itself—the first four volumes appeared of a work entitled *The Light of Nature Pursued* (1768), published under the obvious pseudonym of "Edward Search". Here, to be sure, we have no direct mention of Gay; but the work consists largely in the complete and systematic development of the fundamental ideas of the *Dissertation*, as regards both Psychology and Ethics. It would be difficult to mention two ethical writers standing for almost exactly the same general principles, who differ so much in style and method of treatment as do Gay and Abraham Tucker. Not only was the *Preliminary Dissertation* severely compressed and published anonymously, but it was, in itself, a singularly impersonal essay. Regarding the author, one can only infer that he was a remarkably clear, logical, and original thinker, though with hardly a realising sense of the complexity of the phenomena of our moral life. In the case of Tucker, on the other hand, in spite of his employment of a whimsical pseudonym, the personality of the author is always before us. Indeed, for purposes of illustration, he does not hesitate to refer to his own courtship. We see him in his book for what he actually was in life, an English gentleman of the old school, full of humanity and good sense, and possessed of an infinite leisure which one envies him far more than his wealth: setting about his task each day with the consciousness that he may devote the rest of his life to it, if he will; now displaying great keenness of insight in his treatment of psychological and ethical problems; now indulging in fantastical speculations like that regarding the 'vehicular soul'; now concerned with the revision of theology according to the dictates not of the head but of the heart; and now discussing current metaphysical problems with unbounded good nature, it is true, but with an utter failure to comprehend their import which reminds one of Dr. Johnson's classic refutation of idealism.

In a word, we find in Tucker the almost perfect embodiment of old-fashioned English good-nature and good sense, so long as he is concerned with the concrete realities of human experience; but when he ventures upon distinctly metaphysical ground, we find this charming old gentleman alternating between the complacent obstinacy of common-sense and the wildest vagaries of a metaphysical dreamer. His style is as diffuse as well could be, but is uniformly clear, and his illustrations have sometimes been mentioned as about the best in English ethical literature. It will readily be seen that the portentous bulk of Tucker's work — the conclusion was published posthumously in three volumes in 1777—would alone make it impossible to follow the author exactly, as regards order of treatment, even if one desired to do so. But the lack of methodical arrangement in the *Light of Nature* would make this undesirable in any case. We shall, however, attempt to follow the main thread of the argument which knits together the mass of material contained in the first three or four of the seven octavo volumes.[1]

In order to understand Tucker's ethical system, with which alone we are here primarily concerned, we must first examine its psychological foundation. Moreover, it will be well to do this in some detail, for the *Light of Nature* probably contains a better account than any other single work of the psychological views held practically in common by the older school of Utilitarians. Tucker begins by once for all, and confessedly, adopting Locke's psychology as the basis for his own. He is fond of emphasising small differences on occasion, but he never pretends to depart materially from his master where fundamentals are concerned. And yet, it would be grossly inaccurate to describe Tucker's psychology as merely a reproduction of Locke's. The principle of the Association of Ideas — hardly more than indicated by his

---

[1] The whole work is divided into three Parts (not so called, however) of quite unequal length. These are (1) " Human Nature," (2) " Theology," (3) " Lights of Nature and Gospel Blended ". The first two Parts are important, while the third, though constituting almost exactly half the work, is of very minor consequence. For brevity, these main divisions will be designated in future references as Parts I., II., and III.

master,[1] and employed only to explain the vagaries of our mental life—plays in Tucker's system the all-important part. This makes it the more strange that he should omit all mention of Gay, and speak of Hartley—whose *Observations on Man* had long been published—very seldom, and then almost always to criticise him adversely. But if Tucker fails to confess his obligations to these two writers, as modern literary courtesy would seem to require, he does something to make up for it by his constant references to Locke, for whom he seems to have entertained an extravagant admiration. All of Hume's philosophical works had, of course, appeared some time before the publication of the first four volumes of the *Light of Nature;* but his influence is difficult, if not impossible, to trace.[2] As might be expected, moreover, Butler's *Sermons upon Human Nature* (1726), with their very suggestive treatment of the psychology of desire, etc., were wasted on Tucker, as, indeed, they were on all the earlier Utilitarians.

Having thus noticed Tucker's general relation to his predecessors, we may profitably turn at once to his own treatment of Psychology. The question of mental 'faculties' he disposes of, not very satisfactorily, in a few words. " Hence we may reasonably gather that the mind possesses two faculties; one by which we perform whatever we do, and another by which we discern whatever presents itself to our apprehension. The former has usually been styled the Will, and the latter the Understanding." [3] The author immediately goes on to explain that he regards will as 'active' and understanding as 'passive'. As we shall have occasion to notice later, however, this 'activity' of the will is vaguely

---

[1] This refers, of course, to Locke's explicit treatment of Association.

[2] We fail to detect Hume's influence just where it might be expected to show itself. It would be anticipating to go into details, but one point will perhaps serve to illustrate. In his treatment of the for him all-important principle of Association, Tucker does not recognise the (at least apparent) difference between 'association by contiguity' and 'association by similarity'. This had been clearly done by Hume in the *Treatise* (1739; see Bk. I., Pt. I., § iv.), and later in the *Inquiry concerning Human Understanding* (1748 ; see § III.).

[3] See Pt. I., ch. i., § 2 (second ed.).

conceived by him. Though Tucker theoretically recognises only the two faculties above named, he puts pleasure and pain on an entirely different footing from other 'sensations' and 'ideas'. The former always tend to make us do, or cease from doing, something ; the latter cannot by themselves even be conceived as having such an influence. We shall therefore be justified in treating separately pleasure and pain, as well as 'satisfaction' and 'dissatisfaction,' which are employed merely as more general terms. This will conduce to clearness of exposition and do no violence to Tucker's own views.[1]

And, first, let us consider his account of the cognitive side of our experience. What is said concerning 'sensation' and 'reflection' [2] amounts to little more than a reassertion of the general Lockean position with regard to the origin of our knowledge. Hartley's influence, however, may also be detected here, as, for instance, in the following peculiar passage : " I **have** before declared that by the term ideas, I do not understand the very perceptions of the mind, but the figure, motion, or other modification, of some interior fibres, animal spirits, or other substances, immediately causing perception ; which substances I have since called the mental organs ".[3] This is rather worse than Hartley himself—to whom, by the way, no allusion is here made—but it is only fair to Tucker to say that he does not follow up this attempt to translate the mental into imaginary physiological terms, which so greatly detracts from the value of Hartley's own work.

Tucker's account of 'association' is more characteristic. When ideas, originally obtained through 'sensation' or 'reflection,' have co-existed in the mind a sufficient number of times, they may combine in either of two ways : (1) by 'composition,' when they fuse, so as to form one single complex idea ; (2) by 'association' proper, " when they appear in couples, strongly adhering to each other ". The most obvious case of association is that between words and their meanings. In fact, all the examples given are of what would

---

[1] See, particularly, Pt. I., chs. v., vi.
[2] See Pt. I., chs. vii., viii.  　　[3] *Ibid.*, ch. viii., § 3.

now be called ' association by contiguity,' as opposed to ' association by similarity '. Here Tucker seems to follow Hartley (1749) and neglect Hume (1739).[1] Of course it was later held by certain Associationists, that all cases of so-called ' association by similarity ' could be reduced to terms of what they assumed to be the more fundamental form, ' association by contiguity '; but—even apart from the apparently insuperable difficulties in the way of such simplification —this is a refinement of the Associationist doctrine with which we are not concerned at present. If Tucker had left the theory of ' association ' here, his treatment could not have been regarded as really important. It would have been little more than a popular version of what Hume had expressed both more briefly and more exactly, and of what Hartley had worked out in almost wearisome detail. But the author seems to have in mind a teacher more suggestive, from his point of view, than either of the others—the writer of the *Dissertation*. For he immediately goes on to consider what he calls ' trains '. Associations are by no means exhausted by the cases where two ideas only go together. As a rule, several ideas follow in succession, all having reference to some general topic, and these Tucker calls a ' train '. The fact that such ' trains ' are the rule, and not the exception, is sufficiently evident. As to their origin, he says: " Desire, curiosity, amusement, voluntary attention, or whatever else carries the notice frequently through a number of ideas always in the same series, links them into a train ".[2] Incidentally, the author commits himself to the view, that we must recognise cases where the connecting links are physiological rather than mental, in other words to what, in comparatively recent times, has become familiarly known as the theory of ' unconscious cerebration '.

But even this is only preliminary to Tucker's main purpose, though many rambling discussions intervene before he again takes up what is really the thread of the present

[1] Hume had, of course, clearly recognised both kinds of association.
[2] See Pt. I., ch. x., § 3.

argument.   At length he says, following Gay almost exactly,
so far as the principle is concerned : " But daily experience
testifies that conviction will often remain after the grounds
of it have slipped out of our thought : whenever we reflect on
the thing proved, there occurs a judgment of its being true,
united in the same assemblage without aid of any proof to
support it ; and this many times after the proofs are so far
gone out of our memory that we cannot possibly recall them.
By this channel we are supplied with many truths, commonly
reputed self-evident, because though we know them assuredly
for truths, we cannot discover how we came by that knowledge.   In like manner we have store of propensities, generally esteemed natural, because we cannot readily trace them
to any other origin than that quality of affecting us, assigned
by nature to certain ideas.   But having shown how translation
prevails in satisfaction, as well as assent, there will appear
reason to conclude, that we derive our inclinations and moral
senses through the same channel as our knowledge, without
having them interwoven originally into our constitution." [1]

I have chosen to quote Tucker's own language here—
though it may require a few words of explanation, and though
the last passage carries us beyond his treatment of mere
cognition—for it shows at once what his position is, as regards Intuitionism and the Moral Sense doctrine, and also
how exactly he follows Gay at this, the crucial point of his
whole argument.   What Tucker means here, and what he
sufficiently explains elsewhere, though hardly in the proper
context, is practically as follows.   Our thought proceeds, as
we have seen, not ordinarily by isolated ' associations,' but in
continuous ' trains '.   Now, these ' trains ' may be, and frequently are, repeated.   And the more they are repeated, the
more two things tend to happen : (1) some part of the ' train '
comes more and more to absorb our attention, while (2)—
what is equally important—the remaining parts gradually
drop out of consciousness.   Thus, $a$, $b$, $c$, etc., may be the
original steps by which we reached some important truth, $M$.

[1] See Pt. I., ch. xviii., § 1.

It might seem at first as if habit would tend to make indelible the series as a whole. As a matter of fact, however, it does nothing of the kind; and this because the really interesting thing is *M*, and not the antecedent steps, which latter fall more and more into the background until they may become wholly forgotten. This, of course, will make *M* stand out as a fictitious ultimate, *e.g.*, as a particular 'intuitive' truth. Now this theoretically deceptive, but practically economical, principle is what Tucker means by 'translation'. It applies constantly, not only to the development of our cognitions, but to that of our emotions and passions as well; and in this latter function, particularly, it becomes for Tucker the universal solvent of the difficulties of Ethics.

Let us now turn to the author's treatment of the affective and volitional side of our nature. As we have already noted, he recognises only two 'faculties,' Understanding and Will. At the same time, his treatment of pleasure and pain could hardly have been more distinct from his treatment of our other perceptions, if he had assigned them to a third 'faculty,' as was later done by members of the Associationist school. So far, then, there is no difficulty; but for Tucker, as for other determinist Associationists, the will is little more than the resultant of a psychic parallelogram of forces — the 'forces' in the case being, of course, pleasurable or painful perceptions. Thus, in treating of pleasure and pain, 'satisfaction' and 'dissatisfaction,' as constituting motives, we shall necessarily be considering, at the same time, the more important part of what he has to say regarding the will.

We may profitably begin by raising Tucker's own question: What is it that gives 'weight' to our motives? Certain things attract us, others repel us. Why? The obvious answer is, that the former suggest what we call 'pleasurable,' the latter what we call 'painful' experiences—for surely ideas, merely as such, do not lead to action. But we must be more careful in the use of language, if we would express the exact truth. The author says: "Pleasure in vulgar estimation stands opposed to business, duty, works of use and necessity: yet in all these we feel some engagement, self-approbation or complacence of mind, that carries us through with them. Pleasures, usually so called, often lose their gust, they satiate and cloy upon repetition, and nauseate instead of inviting. Therefore Mr. Locke has fixed upon the term Satisfaction, as being more extensive, comprehending all that complacence we feel as well in business as diversion, as well in the works of prudence as in the starts of fancy." [1] This term 'satisfaction' is adopted by Tucker, and there he practically lets the matter rest, though he says a good deal more by way of popular explanation and illustration.

It must not be supposed, however, that he is attempting to evade a difficulty which he sees by the use of an ambiguous term. For him, there is no other difficulty in the case than this, that positive and unmistakable pleasures and pains are less numerous than we are apt to suppose, and therefore not sufficient to determine all our actions. It never seems to occur to him as a possibility, that we can desire anything qualitatively different from our own greater pleasure or less pain. 'Satisfaction' and 'dissatisfaction,' therefore, are merely more general terms than pleasure and pain, in the sense that they include even the lowest possible stages of these latter, such as we habitually disregard in our ordinary experience. There is nothing to indicate that Tucker was even acquainted with Butler's view, that the major part of our desires, even those of sense, 'terminate in the object'. From the latter point of view, so familiar at the present time, the word 'satisfaction' would of course take on an entirely different meaning from that just explained.

But, while Tucker never doubts that 'satisfaction' and 'dissatisfaction' alone can constitute a motive, he is not quite clear as to how we are induced to seek our own future satisfaction, avoid our own future dissatisfaction—and yet this, according to his view, is precisely that in which all deliberate action ultimately consists. He points out that " it is not very satis-

[1] See Pt. I., ch. vi., § 1.

faction, but the prospect or idea of it" that leads to action.
Indeed, he says: "Since, then, expectation is not the same
with the thing expected, it follows that we may pursue satisfaction without being in a state of enjoyment, and fly uneasiness without being in a state of suffering".[1]  But if the idea of
satisfaction, not satisfaction itself, is what moves one, why
may not other ideas conceivably have the same effect?  Or,
if one adopt the altogether safer position, that it is the
'satisfaction' attaching to some idea and not the idea attaching to 'satisfaction' that constitutes the motive, the question
immediately arises: Why may not 'satisfaction' attach to
other ideas besides that of one's own future pleasure?  But
Tucker did not follow up this question, so fraught with danger
for one holding, as he does, that one can ultimately desire
nothing but one's own satisfaction.[2]

But if Tucker is somewhat confused on the question as to
what, exactly, constitutes a motive, he is not only consistent,
but perfectly explicit in the statement of his general hedonistic position.  He will hear nothing of 'qualitative distinctions,' as applying to pleasures and pains.  He says:
"Satisfaction is always one and the same in kind, how much
soever it may vary in degree, for it is that state the mind is
thrown into upon the application of things agreeable; and
whatever possesses that quality in equal degree, whether
meats and drinks, or diversion, or gain, or acquisition of power,
or reflection on past performances, fills it with the same content and complacence: wherefore the various species of
motives must be distinguished by the variety of vehicles

[1] See Pt. I., ch. vi., § 5.
[2] In one passage, Tucker seems to be on the point of at least partially ex-
tricating himself from his confusion on this matter.  He says that, in one
sense, "present satisfaction is the end we have constantly in view on proceeding
to action" (Pt. I., ch. vi., § 6).  But he immediately explains that "the satisfaction we propose in every exertion of our activity is that of the moment next
immediately ensuing, and this may be called present satisfaction without any
impropriety of speech".  Clearly this does not enable the author to escape
from the theoretical difficulty mentioned above, though it does probably show
that he vaguely felt the difficulty.

containing satisfaction ".[1]   These 'vehicles' the author quite
arbitrarily, and rather inconsistently, reduces to 'pleasure,'
'use,' 'honour,' and 'necessity'—terms which might prove
misleading, if his meaning were not otherwise clear.   This
denial of 'qualitative distinctions' between different classes
of pleasures and pains, sounds commonplace enough now
for we are all agreed that it is the only consistent view for
hedonism; but, while other English writers (*e.g.*, Gay) had
held views from which this position alone was logically deducible, Tucker was the first, so far as I am aware, to state
it in so many words.[2]

In his account of the 'genesis of pleasures,' Tucker is
true to his universally convenient principle of 'translation'.[3]
Nature gives us at first only the pleasures of 'sensation' and
'appetite'; but soon 'reflection' comes upon the scene, and
supplies us with the many and various pleasures which we call
'mental,' as distinguished from those which depend entirely
upon the condition of the body.   These 'mental,' or so-called
'higher,' pleasures constitute by far the greater part of our
enjoyments in adult life, as any one will readily see from
his own experience.   But they differ from 'pleasures of sense,'
not by any means qualitatively, but merely by virtue of the
complexity of the associations which they involve, and the
dropping out of the intermediate links which would otherwise
betray their lowly origin.   In short, the 'higher' pleasures are,
as a class, more 'translated' than the 'lower' ones; and the
'higher' any individual pleasure is, the more 'translated' it
will always on inspection prove to be.

But, while we can desire nothing but our own 'satisfaction,'
according to Tucker, we are often thwarted in our attempt to
secure that which we desire; and hence arise the 'passions'.
We cannot follow the author through his explanation of the
genesis and development of the particular passions.   Often,
perhaps usually, he is perversely ingenious.   For example,

---

[1] See Pt. I., ch. xvi., § 1.
[2] Others, of course—*e.g.*, Hutcheson—had explicitly maintained the contrary.
[3] See Pt. I., ch. xxii.

he says of revenge : " The desire of revenge is not a natural but a translated desire : we first look upon it as a means of procuring ease to ourselves, and security from injury ; but having often beheld it in this light, the end at length drops out of sight, and desire, according to the usual process of translation, rests upon the means, which thenceforward become an end whereon our views will terminate ".[1]   In other words, revenge, so far from being an original tendency of human nature, is to be regarded as a highly ' translated ' passion.   And, as regards the other ' passions ' and ' affections '— the ' affections ' differing from the ' passions ' only in their less degree of intensity—not only is the love of money derived, as Gay had shown, but also that of liberty and power ; nay, even the so-called ' instinct of self-preservation '!   Surely this must be regarded as the *reductio ad absurdum* of the conception of mind as a *tabula rasa*, helped out by the principles of ' association ' and ' translation '.

Such explanations hardly do Tucker justice, and may best be viewed as curiosities of his psychology ; but there is another explanation, analogous to the above, which can by no means be neglected, *viz.*, the author's derivation of ' sympathy ' by means of ' translation '.   He says : " We are not long in the world from our first entrance before we perceive that our pleasures and pains depend much upon the actions of those about us : on a little further progress, we discover that their actions follow their disposition of mind, and afterwards learn to distinguish those dispositions by certain marks of them in their looks and gestures.   This makes children perpetually attentive to the motions and countenance of persons into whose hands they fall : nor does there want another cause to render them more so, for having but few stores in their own imagination, they catch the ideas of other people to supply themselves with employment.   And in our advanced years we cannot well carry on any business or argument, or enjoy the pleasures of conversation, without entering into the thoughts and notions of one another.   When

[1] See Pt. I., ch. xxi., § 6.

we arrive at the use of understanding, the judgment of others
weighs with us as a just and natural evidence, inducing us to
judge accordingly ; but we have seen how the judgment of
expedience, frequently reiterated, transfers satisfaction upon
the measures so conceived expedient : and we purposely
imitate the ways and manners of our teachers, or other persons whom we esteem more expert and knowing in any
matter than ourselves.    Thus we acquire much of our sympathy by inadvertent notice, and add more by design and
industry ; until custom in both ways has worked out trains
wherein imagination learns to run involuntarily and mechanically.    This appears most evident in compassion, for we cannot help sympathising with distress, though we feel it painful
to ourselves, and know it can afford no relief to the party
suffering." [1]

It has seemed best to quote this long passage in full, not
only because of the great importance of the matter in question
for Tucker's ethical theory, but also because the explanation
itself is by no means as simple and unambiguous as it seems
to be at first.    In fact, this is a good example of the way in
which the author occasionally makes a number of fairly just
observations, without trying sharply to distinguish the principles involved.    As it stands, the explanation is open to
serious criticism.    All is ostensibly due to habit and the
principle of ' translation ' ; but an original curiosity and imi-
tative tendency have also been tacitly assumed, and, what is
much more important, the chasm between feeling *like* others
and feeling *for* them has apparently not been bridged over
at all.    But it would be unjust to criticise this attempt to explain the derivation of ' sympathy,' without giving in the same
connection the author's explanation of the origin and growth
of ' love ' (in the most general sense).    This explanation,
practically identical with Gay's, is a good deal more plausible
than the other, though not, perhaps, in the last resort much
more convincing.    We first care for people because they give

[1] See Pt. I., ch. xix., § 2.

us pleasure ; and so, as Tucker observes, " a child's first love is his nurse ". But when the association becomes fixed, the person is loved ' disinterestedly,' as we say, that is, quite independently of pleasure then afforded.[1] Here, again, the statements contain a certain modicum of truth. But why is it that certain people do originally please us, while others do not? And, in general, why do we differ so much from each other in our original likes and dislikes? Precisely because we are each a bundle of tendencies and predispositions, instead of the receptive waxen tablet that Tucker, following Locke, assumes.

As already indicated, Tucker has not much of a strictly psychological character to say about the Will, except what has necessarily been involved in the preceding. Will is the ' active ' side of mind, as opposed to Understanding, the ' passive ' side ; but he nowhere gives a clear account of what is to be understood by mental activity. All the mechanism of thought and feeling are explained by the principles of ' association ' and ' translation,' and nothing practically is left for the will to do but to follow the strongest motives thus supplied. The efficient force seems to be in the ' emotions ' and ' passions,' and also in the feelings of lesser intensity. Particular passages might prove misleading. For instance, in one of the earlier chapters of his work, Tucker criticises Hartley for maintaining the essential ' passivity ' of the mind. He says : " Thus the mind remains totally inactive, reduced to one faculty alone, for the Will, which he terms expressly a certain state of the vibratiuncles, belongs to the ether, not to her : she sits a spectator only, and not an agent of all we perform ; she may indeed discern what is doing, but has no share in what is done : like the fly upon the chariot wheel, she fancies herself raising a cloud of dust, but contributes nothing towards increasing it ".[2] This, however, is merely the protest of common sense against reducing the mind to what our more modern theorists would call an ' epi-

---

[1] See Pt. I., ch. xxi., § 10.    [2] *Ibid.*, ch. iii., § 2.

phenomenon'; it implies no theory at all as to what the mental activity contended for really is, or how this is related to the 'passive' side of the mind, which alone is treated in detail or with any attempt at scientific precision.

Another passage, which occurs somewhat later in the book, may properly be noted in this connection. The author says: " To prevent mistakes, when I speak of the efficacy of motives and of their moving the mind to exert herself, I desire it may be understood that these are figurative expressions; and I do not mean thereby to deny the efficacy of the mind, or to assert any motion, force, or impulse imparted to her from the motives, as there is to one billiard ball from another upon their striking: but only to observe that motives give occasion to the mind to exert her endeavours in attaining whatever they invite her to, which she does by her own inherent activity, not by any power derived from them ".[1] Taken by itself, this passage might seem to make seriously against the interpretation of Tucker's theory of the will here given. Read in the light of his general treatment, however—in the course of which he never even attempts to give an intelligible account of the nature of mental 'activity'—it will be found to be of significance only as showing how difficult it sometimes is to make our author give an account of himself, when he employs the terminology of a 'faculty' psychology.

Indeed, there is little to detain us here, for nearly all that Tucker says directly about the will refers to the metaphysical, rather than psychological, question regarding the so-called 'freedom of the will'. Into this wearisome controversy, we need not follow him. It is enough to remark that he is an out-and-out determinist, and that he defends his position not only with great vigour, but with very considerable skill.[2] One should remember, however, that the arguments employed here by Tucker were by no means so trite then as, in many cases, they are now. In fact, owing to the great popularity of his book, Tucker was probably not an unimportant factor

---

[1] See Pt. I., ch. v., § 3.

[2] See, *e.g.*, the whole of ch. v. (Pt. I.), on " Motives ".

in reducing the arguments for determinism to what we would now regard as their traditional form.

Such, in brief, is the psychological basis of Tucker's ethical system. Any attempt to give in a few pages the substance of what in the original occupies several hundred, must necessarily be somewhat unsatisfactory. At the same time, if much has been lost, something at least has been gained. One must remember that Tucker's style is almost unpardonably diffuse—the chapter on " Satisfaction," for instance, occupies nearly a hundred pages—and also that he makes little pretence to methodical arrangement, so that the book itself is likely to leave a rather vague impression, unless it has been read with considerable care. But at any rate, we have been able to see, in sufficient detail, how Tucker followed up the fruitful suggestions of Gay, whom he does not mention at all; and we have probably been led to suspect that, though he seldom mentions Hartley except to criticise him adversely, he had by no means failed to profit by the fact that he published the first instalment of his own work nineteen years after the appearance of the *Observations on Man*. Still, his definite obligations to Hartley are not easy to make out, while there is little or nothing in his treatment of psychological problems to suggest Hume's influence. Even his direct obligations to Gay, though more than probable, could hardly be proved. The fact is that Tucker was a writer of very considerable originality in Psychology as well as in Ethics ; and that the first part of his *Light of Nature*, though far from corresponding to one's ideal of a scientific treatise, was decidedly the best account of the Associationist Psychology, which had appeared up to his time. Indeed, it might reasonably be held that the later Associationists were a good deal more successful in concealing, than in actually removing, the defects of method which we have had to notice in this part of Tucker's work.

# CHAPTER VIII.

## ABRAHAM TUCKER (*continued*).

As was almost inevitable, considering its psychological foundation, Tucker's ethical system, to which we must now turn, was radically opposed to Rationalism, Intuitionism, and the 'Moral Sense' theory. Locke, indeed, as we have had occasion to notice, did not actually construct a system of Ethics upon the basis of his own philosophy; Tucker's system, on the other hand, was the legitimate result of thoroughgoing Empiricism. Before taking up the constructive side of his treatment of Ethics, it may be well to consider, in a general way, his attitude toward the three types of ethical theory just mentioned. Tucker has little to say in direct criticism of the Rationalists. We can readily surmise, however, what form his objections to that ethical school would have taken, if he had been more explicit. First, according to his own theory of knowledge, he would have had to deny the existence of any abstract faculty of ' reason,' capable of discerning ultimate and absolute truth. In one characteristic passage, he does say in so many words that we must be content with ' moral certainty '. Secondly, he always held, of course, that our recognition of moral distinctions could be adequately explained by experience. Thirdly, he was as sure as Hume had been that what we call ' reason ' can never itself directly lead to action. It may discover the means by which to attain some end; but the end itself must be otherwise supplied, *viz.*, by the affective side of our nature. This would plainly make a rationalistic system valueless, even if it could be logically constructed.

As regards Intuitionism in general, Tucker's whole system

was intended largely as a confutation of those who refused
to go behind the mere facts of our moral experience, and who
would not even attempt to find a scientific explanation for
them. The 'Moral Sense' theory, on the other hand, as the
particular form of Intuitionism which was most in evidence
among philosophical writers of this period, comes in for more
specific notice. Tucker criticises this theory much as Gay
had done in the *Dissertation*. He regards it as a mere
substitute for ethical theories based upon ' innate ideas,' the
existence of which latter Locke had once for all disproved
in the first book of his *Essay*. All the supposed phenomena
of the ' moral sense' may be explained by experience, as
showing the expediency or inexpediency of particular classes
of actions. And the author holds consistently that we obtain
our first notions of moral good and evil, rather by observing
the conduct of others, than by reflecting upon our own.[1] It
must not be supposed, however, that our so-called ' moral
sense' is less valuable because acquired. Tucker is always
ready to emphasise the truth, sometimes forgotten in ethical
discussions, that as moralists we all begin, or should begin,
with the same facts of moral experience, and that to explain
these facts, when such a thing can be done, is by no means
necessarily to explain them away.

Let us now examine the author's attempt to place Ethics
upon what he regarded as the only sure foundation, *viz.*,
that of human experience. He begins by raising the traditional question : What are we to regard, not merely as good,
but as the Ultimate Good? And he indicates the general
character of his own solution as follows : " Upon perusal of
the chapter of satisfaction and those of the four classes of
motives, whoever shall happen to think they contain a just
representation of human nature, need not be long in seeking
for this *summum bonum* : for he will perceive it to be none
other than pleasure or satisfaction, which is pleasure taken
in the largest sense, as comprising every complacence of

[1] See Pt. I., ch. xxiv., § 13.

mind together with the avoidance of pain or uneasiness ".[1] As we have already seen, Tucker emphasises the so-called 'higher' or 'intellectual' pleasures at the expense of the so-called 'lower' ones. In this he agrees with Hartley ; but, unlike Hartley, he holds that 'satisfaction' is one, and that concrete satisfactions differ only in degree. The sum total of these concrete satisfactions is what we mean by 'happiness'. If any one would after all deny that happiness is the Good, Tucker thinks he may be silenced by being reminded that, as a matter of fact, it is the one thing universally sought.

But while Tucker is an uncompromising hedonist, he fully appreciates the importance of acting according to 'general rules,' and not seeking particular pleasures too eagerly, as if ends in themselves. He thus describes the proper task of the moralist : " As we cannot upon every occasion see to the end of our proceedings, he will establish certain rules to serve as landmarks for guiding us on the way. These rules, when he has leisure and opportunity for mature consideration, he will build on one another, erecting the whole fabric upon the basis of *summum bonum* before described. But because their reference to the ultimate end cannot be continually kept in mind, he will inure himself and everybody within his reach, by such methods as he shall find feasible, to look upon them as good in themselves, that they may become influencing principles of action." [2] This is wholly characteristic, and more important than might appear. It should always be remembered that early Utilitarianism was not a 'calculating' ethics, in the offensive and obviously impracticable sense of the words. Neither Tucker nor Paley, for example, taught that we are to determine the morality of a particular action by computing its probable effects in the individual case. On the contrary, they both insisted that we must act on general principles of expediency, not merely because we are intellectually finite beings, but because we are largely creatures of habit. Bentham later seemed to hold,

---

[1] See Pt. I., ch. xxvii., § 2.   [2] See *ibid.*, § 8.

not only that we may, but that we must, thus compute in the individual case — instead of acting according to 'general rules' of utility—but, if this was really his view, it was merely one of that arrogant writer's improvements in Utilitarianism which did so much to bring the doctrine into needless discredit.

We have seen that Hutcheson, though not really a hedonist himself, assumes without question the possibility of computing with sufficient exactness the effects of different kinds of actions, as regards their tendency to make for the general happiness or unhappiness, and of thus determining their 'objective' goodness or badness. In fact, up to this time the difficulty regarding the 'hedonistic calculus' seems hardly to have been raised, except by Hartley.[1] It is characteristic of Tucker's perfect frankness and honesty, that he should emphasise, if not over-emphasise, this difficulty. For instance, he says: "Our tastes, varying as much as our faces, make us very bad judges of one another's enjoyments. . . . Nor do we judge much better of our own pleasures, for want of being well aware of their aptness to cloy upon repetition, and to change their relish perpetually according to our disposition of body or mind, or the circumstances we happen to stand in: neither can we trust even experience itself in this case, for because a thing has pleased us once, we cannot always be sure it will do so again. . . . But if we make mistakes in estimating pleasures singly, we commit more in computing the value of a series of them taken collectively. . . . Therefore we are forced to take our pleasures in the lump, and estimate them upon view; as a man who guesses at a flock of sheep by the ground they cover, without being able to count them, and who will do it very imperfectly, until he has gotten an expertness by long and careful practice. For absent enjoyments, whether past or future, being not actually existent, we cannot hold them as it were in our hand to weigh them, but must judge by the representative idea we have of them in our imagination; and we ordinarily determine their value

---

[1] Berkeley also had suggested the difficulty, but only in a very general way.

by the degree of desire we feel in ourselves towards them." [1]
This is decidedly interesting, for it shows that, while Tucker
himself was a thoroughgoing hedonist, he anticipated nearly
all the objections which anti-hedonists have so long been
accustomed to raise against the possibility of the 'hedonistic
calculus'.[2]   But it never seems to have occurred to the author
that computations of this sort, being so difficult, may be
impossible.

One point should be carefully noted in this connection.
When considering Hutcheson's relation to hedonism, we saw
that for him the 'hedonistic calculus' would be considerably
complicated by the fact that the 'moral sense,' by hypothesis
ultimate, was itself, according to his view, the source of a
very great part of our pleasures and pains.   Evidently there
is no corresponding complication for Tucker, since all of our
pleasures and pains are held by him to be derived from the
primary ones of 'sensation' and 'reflection,' through the
agency of 'association' and 'translation'.

There are two questions, obviously very closely related,
which every moralist must face : (1) What is the [objective]
Good?   (2) How is this calculated to appeal to the individual
agent?   To decide either of these questions without reference
to the other—or, indeed, to give either undue emphasis—is
to make a mistake which is sure to be serious, and which
very well may prove fatal.   The conspicuous weakness of the
early rationalistic systems is, that they give no intelligible
account of how that which is ideally right can be willed by
the agent.   On the other hand, the early hedonists were so
deeply interested in this very question, that they were somewhat hampered in their treatment of the Good.   Tucker is
no exception to the general rule.   In fact, he sometimes
allows himself to use language which would seem to indicate

---

[1] See Pt. I., ch. xxii., §§ 11, 12.

[2] Except the very important one, which was not clearly recognised and
urged until a good deal later, that hedonistic values vary with the development
of moral character.   Spencer makes effective use of this objection in his early
criticism of the Expediency Philosophy in *Social Statics* (1851).

that the Good is one's own happiness, without much reference to that of others. He says, for example, " nor would I advise a man ever to deny himself, unless in order to please himself better another time ".[1] It is probably needless to say that passages like this do Tucker injustice. He incidentally points out—in other passages too numerous to quote, or even definitely to refer to—that we find our greatest ' satisfaction ' in the most intimate relations of life, where, of course, a good deal of what we are apt to call ' self-sacrifice ' is necessarily involved. But the theoretical question regarding the motive of the moral agent cannot be disposed of by merely referring to such passages, in however amiable a light they may exhibit the author.

Tucker's explicit treatment of this question seems always to imply that real disinterestedness must not be looked for anywhere. In what one is bound to recognise as a characteristic passage, he says, in effect : Honesty is the best policy, and if men were omniscient, a sense of honour would be needless.[2] Understanding, of course, that the author here indulges in some rhetorical exaggeration, let us attempt to see exactly what he means. In the first place, it should be stated that, throughout the First Part of the treatise, on " Human Nature "—which might very well be supposed to contain his final view of the matter—he confines himself to the consideration of consequences which may be expected to ensue in the present life and according to the natural course of events. For the moment, let us assume this to be his ultimate view. What, then, does the passage just referred to mean ? Hardly what it seems to say ; for an omniscient rogue, surely, would be able to do much that was wrong without suffering the consequences, while, on the other hand, cases are not far to seek where perfect honesty has led to disaster, even death itself.

Indeed, the case of Regulus is brought up early in the First Part of the *Light of Nature*, and throughout the greater portion of the Second Part that unhappy hero is kept on

[1] See Pt. I., ch. xxvii., § 6.       [2] *Ibid.*, xxiv., § 8.

trial for ' imprudence '!    Now, obviously no approximation
to omniscience on the part of Regulus would show that,
under the peculiar circumstances in which he was placed, it
was 'good policy' for him to be 'honest,' *if* this present
life be all, and *if* ' good policy' be equivalent to one's selfish
interest.  As Gay had pertinently remarked : " God alone can
in all cases make a man happy or miserable " ; and obviously
He does not always, or perhaps usually, bestow adequate
rewards or inflict adequate punishments in this life—particularly if by these we are to understand ' external' rewards and
punishments.  Such perfect distributive justice, which alone
can constitute ' complete obligation,' according to this view
of the moral motive, must be looked for in the life to come.

The reader may be relieved to know that Regulus is finally
acquitted on this ground.    In the interesting chapter on
" Re-enlargement of Virtue," with which Part II. on " Theology" ends, Tucker says that he has refrained before from
referring to rewards and punishments after death merely to
show that, in the last resort, we cannot afford to leave them
out of consideration.    Concerning the particular case of
Regulus, he says : " Therefore now we may do ample justice
to Regulus, whom we left under a sentence of folly for throw-
ing away life with all its enjoyments for a phantom of
honour. . . . For he will now plead that it was not a phantastic
joy in the transports of rectitude, nor the stoical rhodo-
montade of a day spent in virtue containing more enjoyment
than an age of bodily delights, nor his inability to bear a
life of general odium and contempt, had his duty so required,
which fixed him in his resolution : but the prudence of the
thing upon a full and calm deliberation.  Because he considered himself as a citizen of the universe, whose interests
are promoted and maintained by the particular members
contributing their endeavours towards increasing the quantity
of happiness, wherever possible, among others with whom
they have connection and intercourse. . . . He was persuaded
likewise that all the good a man does, stands placed to his
account, to be repaid him in full value when it will be most

useful to him : so that whoever works for another, works for himself ; and by working for numbers, earns more than he could possibly do by working for himself alone." [1]

The passage just quoted might give a wrong impression, if no reference were made to Tucker's peculiar theory regarding ' equality,' set forth in a preceding chapter.[2] Hitherto this has been neglected, because it is one of the eccentricities of his system, which has had no appreciable effect upon subsequent ethical theory, and which the author does not succeed in making even plausible. He holds that, of all the attributes of God, ' equity ' is the one of which we have the clearest conception. But from the ' equity ' of God, he claims, " it follows unavoidably that there must be an exact equality of fortunes among us, and the value of each person's existence, computed throughout the whole extent of his Being, precisely the same ". And this, for him, means even more than might appear. Not only are the inequalities of external fortune to be made up in the future life : but the evils resulting from our own wickedness are by no means to have an indefinite duration. In some way, not sufficiently explained, our natures are to be purified and our individual accounts of happiness made to balance in the end. " After Favour has had her course, and Justice been satisfied, it remains that Equity should be satisfied too." [3] And equity means an equal amount of happiness for each, apparently regardless of the question of deserts. Probably Tucker would say that, in the strict sense, we have no ' deserts,' since our good or bad characters must be regarded as results of the preceding course of events, which God has ordered for some good purpose.[4] For the apparent evils in the world, God Himself is in the last resort responsible ; and it must be that He has ordained a final equality of happiness for all. This rather crude form of Theological Universalism might be neglected, but for the fact that Tucker tries partly to

[1] See Pt. II., ch. xxxi., § 5.
[2] *Ibid.*, ch. xxvii.     [3] *Ibid.*, §§ 2, 4.
[4] He does say practically this in *ibid.*, § 3.

base upon it his argument for the reasonableness of altruistic action. Since the value of every one's existence is the same, we must esteem every one alike, harbour no hatred, work for the general fund of happiness, etc. " Hence follows a general connection of interests throughout the universe, a partnership in one common stock, which cannot be increased or diminished in any individual without proportionably affecting the share of every other." [1] It is hardly necessary to point out that such an attempt as this to bridge over the chasm between egoism and altruism is foredoomed to failure. The difficulty remains precisely where it was before.

Is Tucker's system, then, a ' selfish ' theory of morality? To a large and quite unnecessary extent, yes; and yet I think that both Tucker and Paley have often been misunderstood in this respect. The fact that nearly all men are practically ' sympathetic,' practically capable of some degree of self-sacrifice, is fully recognised by both of them; and they further agree that, in the present life at least, our greatest pleasures are derived from the exercise of the ' social affections '. Their view of concrete human nature, therefore, is radically different from that of Hobbes, and not so very unlike our own. What we are bound to object to, is their futile attempt to explain ' sympathy ' as a mere product of ' translation '. Here they both followed Gay exactly, and did not profit by the later form of Hume's ethical theory, as found in the *Inquiry concerning the Principles of Morals.* Now their choice in this matter was of the greatest importance, for it determined the type of Utilitarian theory to which they must always be assigned; it identified them with the old order, not the new. Tucker developed Gay's theory; Paley reduced Tucker's to concise and manageable form; Bentham, in fancied (or, at any rate, professed) independence of them both, and of Hume as well, tacitly neglected the theological [2] sanction—which, as we shall see later, he was not

---

[1] See Pt. III., ch. xxxviii. (the concluding chapter of the work), § 3.

[2] The theological sanction is mentioned in all three of his slightly differing lists of the sanctions, but does not play any part in his actual treatment.

in a position logically to do—and also introduced certain refinements into the 'hedonistic calculus'. But all this development and modification was external; the theory was one and the same at the core. It remained so until there was a general return to Hume's later position, that a certain degree of original altruism must be conceded to human nature. Not until then could 'the greatest happiness of the greatest number' be regarded as (in part, at least) the motive as well as the objective 'end' of all truly moral action.

We have now examined all the fundamental principles of Tucker's ethical system, and have attempted to see them in their proper relation to each other. We may therefore pass on immediately to his treatment of the particular virtues. Here he is for once comparatively brief, and we may profitably follow his example, for we are only concerned with his consistency or inconsistency in the handling of his own first principles, and his success or failure in deducing from these what we all recognise as the rules of concrete morality. Tucker, whose undoubted originality never shows itself in felicitous order of exposition, begins by adopting the conventional list of four 'cardinal virtues'—Prudence, Fortitude, Temperance, and Justice—and by translating the distinctions thus made into terms of his own system. It is natural that he should regard Prudence as the chief virtue, and as practically comprehending the others, which, as he says, "relate to the removing three certain obstacles in our nature most apt to disturb and stop us in the exercise of prudence".[1] 'Moral prudence,' which is here meant, should be distinguished from 'physical prudence'. The latter depends upon sagacity, experience, etc.; the former, on the other hand, consists in "making the best use of the lights we have". In most cases where moral action is concerned, it is easy enough to see what should be done; what we most need to cultivate in ourselves is a disposition actually to follow our own best judgment.

[1] See Pt. I., ch. xxx., §§ 1 *et seq.*

As a matter of fact, Tucker does not succeed very well in differentiating 'moral' from 'physical' prudence; and his general treatment of Fortitude (moral, rather than physical, courage) and Temperance (self-control, in the most general sense) contains little that is worthy of note. Incidentally, however, when showing that by Fortitude he does not mean mere physical courage, Tucker makes a remark which affords an interesting commentary on his system. He says: "Now we must acknowledge this insensibility a very useful quality to the public, for without it, perhaps, we could not properly man our fleets nor recruit our armies: yet is it so far from deserving the name of virtue, that it seems scarce compatible with the principal of them, I mean prudence, which grows out of caution".[1] Two things must be noted with regard to this interesting passage. First, it shows how completely Tucker was committed to the view that virtue must make not only for happiness, but for the happiness of the individual moral agent. In fact, a possible conflict between public and private interest is here suggested; and the implication seems to be that in such a case the latter must prevail, if we would be truly virtuous! But, secondly—what is quite as important —the passage quoted suggests a theory which Tucker elsewhere [2] sets forth regarding the teleology of moral approbation, as actually bestowed. According to his view, we do not by any means approve conduct in exact proportion to its intrinsic rightness—*i.e.*, tendency to promote happiness. For the conduct that is absolutely necessary, both for the individual and for society, largely takes care of itself—for example, the mother may in all ordinary cases be depended upon to care for her child. If she does this, we do not think of approving her action; but if she wholly neglects her child, we are horrified. In a word, there is an *economy* of moral approbation: we approve of actions necessary for the common good largely in proportion as this very approval is itself necessary in order to get them done. Let us return to the case of mere physical courage, which Tucker has said is not

<hr>

[1] See Pt. I., ch. xxxi., § 1.      [2] *Ibid.*, xxxiv., § 6.

a virtue; but yet is apparently necessary for the public good. It is easy to see what he would have to say of this, in order to be consistent. We do not call physical courage (by itself) a virtue, because we do not have to do so; because the supply is equal to the demand. But if, for any reason, the supply should fall short, we might be driven into calling brute courage even the chief of all the virtues—as our barbarous ancestors actually did.[1]

The treatment of Justice is much more satisfactory than that of the three other 'cardinal virtues'. This more or less resembles Hume's account of the same matter, but there is nothing to prove a real dependence of Tucker's work upon Hume's. Indeed, as regards mere form, Tucker's treatment resembles Cumberland's rather more closely than it does Hume's; though here, again, there is nothing to prove direct imitation. As the arguments here given for the Utilitarian origin of the notion of justice are wholly the now familiar ones, we may pass over them somewhat rapidly. Men have to depend for their very existence, not to say comfort, upon certain products of the earth. These, however, cannot be used in common without constant disputes arising; and, moreover, the natural products of the earth will not suffice, unless improved by human labour, and no one will work unless he knows that he is going to receive the benefits himself. Certain rules, implying a mutual recognition of rights, would insensibly arise, and lay the foundation for the institution of private property. The obligation of truth and fidelity may readily be explained in the same way, for without these human intercourse and co-operation would be impossible.

The above arguments for the Utilitarian origin of justice and veracity seem to Tucker so obvious that he does not dwell upon them. It must not be supposed, however, that the author regards the notion of justice as something which

---

[1] There is doubtless a limited amount of grim truth in Tucker's view; but I do not think that what must be conceded on this point will be found to make for any great degree of relativity in our moral judgments, or for Utilitarianism, as against other systems.

has to be developed anew in the experience of each individual. Our particular notions regarding what is just, are
almost always learned, or adopted, from the community in
which we live, so that the explanation given above refers
only to the ultimate origin of the notion under consideration.
But precisely because we do, to so large an extent, take our
ideas of justice on trust, our obligation to practice this virtue
appears to be the ultimate thing which common sense regards
it; hence justice and 'interest' are popularly contrasted.
But if we could see to the end, and know our true interest,
we should need no other guide. As it is, we have need
enough of the restraints of justice, and should never allow
ourselves to act against the general principles which men, on
the basis of an unconscious induction from experience, have
agreed in calling 'just'.

It is interesting to note that Tucker holds what we would
now agree in regarding as the consistent Utilitarian theory
of punishment. Indeed, he seems to believe, not only that
punishment should be applied according to Utilitarian principles, but that it actually is so applied, at least in the great
majority of cases. To quote his own expression: "The
law carries always a prospect forwards".[1] The logically
primary form of punishment, according to his view, is the
payment of damages for the injury done, whatever that may
be. But since, in many instances, reparation is impossible
from the nature of the case, punishment would naturally be
inflicted in order to prevent the repetition of the offence;
and this (logically) derived form of punishment may be regarded as normal in the complicated relations of civilised
society. It follows, of course, from this point of view, that
punishment should not be more severe than the given case
requires, for that would mean so much gratuitous suffering
in the world; but Tucker does not mention the reformation
of the criminal as an end to be held in view by the legislator
or judge. While he fails to recognise the hold which the
notion of 'retributive justice' still retains even in the common

---

[1] See Pt. I., ch. xxxiii., § 5.

law, he has a ready explanation for this notion, which he regards as a manifest perversion of true, *i.e.*, Utilitarian, justice. If we regard the law as a personality, as is sometimes done for convenience, we may bring the idea of punishment under the idea of reparation, not to the party injured, but to the law itself. But here the principle of ' translation ' comes in : we forget that we are merely employing a figure of speech, when we speak of injury as being done to the law itself, and regard this as a statement of the actual fact. The obviously Utilitarian links in the chain of association drop out of consciousness, and we come to regard the relation between the infringement of law and punishment as logically necessary, and not merely as extremely desirable, provided that the punishment inflicted be just and humane.

So far, the author believes he has shown that the general rules of justice are founded upon utility, and upon that alone ; and here, as always, he holds that the interested individual is not a good judge as to the desirability of an infringement of a general rule. But suppose it could be shown, in some particular case, that unjust conduct was certainly for the general advantage ? Then we should have to consider the undoubted mischief of a bad example. But suppose, further, that the act in question could be concealed from all the world ? Still we should have to take into account the bad influence upon the agent's own character. The result, then, is merely to bring out what Tucker consistently holds throughout his treatise, that moral actions must, on strictly Utilitarian principles, be according to general rules, and not according to any attempted computation in the particular case.

When the author comes to treat of Benevolence, he is somewhat hampered by the fact that this virtue is not really provided for by the old Greek scheme of the virtues which he had happened to adopt. He tries to show that, strictly speaking, benevolence would come under justice, since we must put under the latter head " whatever we do for the benefit or pleasure of others without [immediate] regard to our own ". At the same time, he practically breaks loose from his classifi-

cation, and treats benevolence as a fifth ' cardinal ' virtue.
Indeed, he later suggests that benevolence may ultimately
be regarded as the root, and justice as the branch, although
it will be remembered that his actual treatment of justice
would not seem to corroborate this view.   Of course, Tucker
does not here mean that benevolence itself is ' original,'
though he holds with Gay that, at the moment of action, one
must forget that one is determined by motives of self-interest.
The explanation is evidently to be found in the all-cogent
principle of ' translation '.   What was previously said regarding the author's derivation of ' sympathy ' and ' love,'
will apply here, at least sufficiently for the present purpose.
In this connection, Tucker again refers to his theory of moral
approbation.   He says: " As commendation and a return of
good offices tend to encourage benevolence, therefore it deserves them : for we have seen in a former place, that honour
and reward belong properly to where they will do most
service.   But the reward must not constantly follow too close
upon the action, for then it will be apt to catch the eye, and
become the end expected at every performance, which will
render it selfish." [1]

Tucker naturally has much to say in praise of benevolence,
but his treatment of this virtue after all rather tends to bring
out the egoistic elements in his system.   It is needless to go
into details here, particularly as we have already discussed,
somewhat at length, the author's view regarding the motive
of the moral agent.   It may be noted that—while he carelessly allows himself to say that, if benevolence were universal,
it would bring back the Golden Age—he is, nevertheless,
quite inclined to question the sentimental view that all would
be happy, if everyone were only good.   In one characteristic
passage, he says: " Were all our artisans and professors to
barter their knowledge and dexterity for a proportionable
degree of virtue, the world would suffer greatly by the exchange : we should all be ready, indeed, to help one another,

[1] See Pt. I., ch. xxxiv., § 6.

but could do no good for want of knowing how to go about it ".[1]

We have already somewhat carefully compared Gay's outline of an ethical system, as given in the *Dissertation*, with Cumberland's extended treatment of Ethics in his *De legibus naturae*. We noticed in the *Dissertation* an unmistakable departure from the position of Cumberland in various important respects. It is needless to recapitulate here. What is important to observe in the present connection, is the fact that Tucker follows Gay as against Cumberland in every case where we have had occasion to notice an important difference in theory between those two authors. On the other hand, it is hardly necessary for our present purpose to compare Tucker's ethical theory at all minutely either with that of Hartley or with that of Hume. One thing, however, should always be remembered. We have seen that the earlier form of (completely differentiated) Utilitarianism is mainly distinguished from the later form by its different treatment of the motive of the moral agent. It is interesting to compare Gay, Hume, Hartley, and Tucker, in this very important respect. Gay, of course, was the first to explain apparent altruism as a development from egoism, by means of the 'association of ideas' and the further process which Tucker afterward called 'translation'. According to his view, we begin and end as egoists, though not in the sense of Hobbes. Hume, in apparent independence of Gay, developed in succession two quite different views of human nature, as regards the origin of 'sympathy'. In the *Treatise* he explains 'sympathy' by the 'association of ideas,' and, though his method of explanation is somewhat different from that of Gay, the result at which he arrives is much the same, for it amounts to treating egoism as the original, ineradicable tendency of human nature, and apparent altruism as little more than a development from egoism. But in the *Inquiry* he entirely gives up any such attempt to reduce the one

[1] See Pt. I., ch. xxxv., § 8.

principle to terms of the other. Egoism and altruism are there regarded as co-ordinate tendencies of human nature; not, apparently, in the sense that they are absolutely distinct from each other, but rather in the sense that they are parallel differentiations of something in our nature more aboriginal than either. In taking up this later position, he anticipated what we may call the later, as opposed to the earlier, Utilitarianism.

We have seen that Hartley interpreted the results of ' association' and 'translation' quite differently from his successors. For in his view it is possible to forget oneself more and more until one finally loses oneself in love for one's fellow men, still more in love for God; and in a similar way, while our 'higher' pleasures are regarded by him as developed from our 'lower' ones, by increasingly elaborate combinations at each step, he is unlike the others in regarding the 'higher' pleasures as differing from the 'lower' ones, not only in degree, but in kind. All this, of course, would make Hartley difficult to classify, according to the principle which we have adopted, if we should regard his conclusions as the logical result of his own first principles and of the method which he employs. But this we can by no means do. In short, we find in Hartley what we often find in pioneers of any new tendency of philosophical thought, a writer who hardly appreciates the full significance of the principles with which he deals. Tucker, on the other hand, represents the return to Gay, which was to characterise all the writers standing for what we here call the earlier form of Utilitarianism. According to this view, there are no qualitative distinctions between pleasures, and altruism is merely a more highly developed (*i.e.*, a more many-sided) egoism.

But if we must say that Tucker only filled in the outline of ethical theory which Gay [1] had already supplied—and this,

---

[1] Tucker's *direct* dependence upon Gay could hardly be proved. It should be remembered that he published thirty-seven years later.

curiously, without giving credit for it, as we should have expected—we are making a statement which, though true, is by itself seriously misleading. If it be thought that little skill or originality was required to follow out the line of argument which the author of the *Dissertation* had suggested, one has only to examine Hartley's well-known work to be convinced of the contrary ; for though the *Observations on Man* is so largely a failure, from the point of view both of psychological and of ethical theory, we have no right to assume that the author was altogether a mediocre man. In fact, it probably takes quite as much originality consistently to develop a theory on the basis of a few suggestions, as to provide the original scheme itself. The path was really untried to a very large extent even after Hartley had done his imperfect work.

Tucker is a writer whose actual ability and discrimination we are apt greatly to underrate. His faults are almost fatally calculated to obscure his merits. Not only was he recklessly diffuse, but he was so utterly lacking in metaphysical talent and training that the considerable part of his treatise which he devotes to theological discussions is practically valueless. But his skill and originality in the treatment of psychological and ethical problems is in the most striking contrast to his weakness as a theologian. Many passages in the *Light of Nature*, which are likely to impress one as being rather commonplace, are actually the first tolerably satisfactory treatment of the topics in question from the Associationist point of view ; so that, if Tucker was careless in not giving credit to others, he is probably himself to be regarded as ' more sinned against than sinning '. Indeed, the defects in his treatment of psychological and ethical problems will quite commonly be found to be defects inherent in the Associationist theory itself, and not due to any individual weakness or superficiality on his part. Moreover, while his far too bulky treatise will doubtless continue unread by the general student, it is to this that one must look for the first full statement of the theory which Paley practically adopted entire, and made almost universally popular in his own generation by his singular felicity as an expositor ; which Bentham and his followers, on the other hand, chose to disregard, though their own ethical theory is reducible to substantially the same principles.

# CHAPTER IX.

## WILLIAM PALEY AND JEREMY BENTHAM.

IT is customary to regard Bentham as the typical exponent of Utilitarianism in its earlier form, while Paley, though frequently given more credit than he deserves on the score of originality, is generally classed as a 'theological' moralist, and therefore put on quite a different plane. For reasons which will appear in the course of this chapter, the present writer is obliged partly to dissent from this traditional estimate of the two authors—and, in particular, from the opinion that Bentham contributed anything essentially new to ethical theory. Whether or not these reasons are sufficient, the reader must, of course, decide for himself. But, in any case, it will certainly be well for him to abstract as far as possible from the popular verdict regarding the theologian and the legislative reformer, in order that he may be able to form an independent judgment as to the true position of each in the history of English Ethics. The two are as different as possible from each other in their attitude toward their predecessors. In a well-known passage in the preface to his only ethical work, Paley expresses with perfect frankness his very great indebtedness to Tucker.[1] Bentham, on the

[1] " There is, however, one work to which I owe so much, that it would be ungrateful not to confess the obligation : I mean the writings of the late Abraham Tucker, Esq. . . . I have found in this writer more original thinking and observation upon the several subjects that he has taken in hand, than in any other, not to say, than in all others put together. His talent also for illustration is unrivalled. But his thoughts are diffused through a long, various, and irregular work. I shall account it no mean praise, if I have been sometimes able to dis-

other hand, always writes as if he were the first propounder of the Utilitarian principle.  Indeed, in a conversation recorded by his disciple Bowring, he is made to speak as if his only indebtedness to others consisted in the fact that he had been deeply impressed by Dr. Priestley's incidental use of the expression, ' the greatest happiness of the greatest number,' in his *Treatise on Government* (1768).[1]

The use which Paley made of the works of previous writers can, for the most part, be easily determined, and may be described sufficiently for our present purpose in a few words. He reduced the unwieldy bulk of Tucker's hopelessly diffuse *Light of Nature* to clear, definite, and—to his contemporaries —convincing form.  And, as we have just seen, he makes no secret of his obligations to Tucker.  By what seems a curious fatality, however, he failed to mention Gay, exactly as Tucker had done, though he, at any rate, evidently had the *Preliminary Dissertation* constantly in mind.  In fact, of all the writers whom we have thus far considered, Hartley is the only one, except the Rev. John Brown, who admits definitely his obligations to Gay.  But Paley's silence regarding the *Dissertation* can hardly be interpreted as indicating disingenuousness on his part, for his order of exposition, totally different from that of Tucker—if, indeed, Tucker can be said to have followed any definite order at all—is obviously an adaptation of Gay's, and he sometimes reproduces passages from the *Dissertation* almost word for word.  Moreover, as the *Dissertation* was always published as introductory to the translation of King's *Origin of Evil* by Paley's own patron, Bishop Law, his acquaintance with the book could not possibly have been denied, and seems to have been tacitly admitted.

On the other hand, it would be difficult, if not impossible, to determine exactly Bentham's indebtedness to previous

pose into method, to collect into heads and articles, or to exhibit in more compact and tangible masses, what, in that otherwise excellent performance, is spread over too much surface."—See *Moral and Political Philosophy*, p. xix. (1816 ed.).          [1] See *Deontology*, vol. I, (appendix), p. 300.

ethical writers. Like the school which he inaugurated, he was singularly lacking in the historical spirit. Many of his references to non-Utilitarian systems seem to imply an almost startling ignorance of their true character, while he never for a moment appears to admit, in his published works, that others besides himself had stated the Utilitarian principle. One is willing to believe that he was as nearly unacquainted with the previous development of English Ethics as it was possible for an intelligent writer on kindred subjects to be ; but Utilitarianism had been so distinctly in the air for more than a generation before he published his *Principles of Morals and Legislation* that he could not possibly have failed very substantially to profit by the fact.

Probably Bentham and his immediate followers alike believed that he was making an entirely new departure in his attempt to treat Ethics without reference to theological considerations.[1] Indeed, this seems to have been the verdict of most writers on English Ethics. It would be anticipating to discuss the question of Bentham's originality at length here, but it will be remembered that both Gay and Tucker had avoided the theological reference, except where their systems logically required it. For example, Gay had held that complete obligation can come only from God, " because God only can in all cases make a man happy or miserable ".[2] Bentham found himself face to face with the same difficulty in working out the Utilitarian doctrine. Perfect obligation to follow the fundamental principles of morality was tacitly conceded by him, as it is by practically all moralists ; and obligation for Bentham, as for Gay, Tucker, and Paley, could mean only that it must ultimately be for the agent's own interest to be virtuous. The main difference, then, between his procedure and theirs, lies in the fact that he practically shirked the difficulty that the ' sanctions ' are not sufficient in this present life, and implied, rather than directly argued, that if

---

[1] The 'theological sanction' appears in Bentham's list, but he practically neglects it in his treatment of Ethics.

[2] See *Dissertation*, § ii.

it is not for the individual's interest to be virtuous, as things are now, it ought to be made so, and this by the very improvements in legislation in which he was primarily interested. But clearly his position as a reformer does not help him to escape the very grave difficulty which besets every Utilitarian system that assumes the selfish motive of the agent in moral action. It therefore seems to the present writer that Bentham's non-theological treatment of Ethics merely indicates his individual attitude, and does not, in itself, represent an advance in ethical theory.[1]

Paley's direct treatment of Ethics is contained in his well-known *Principles of Moral and Political Philosophy*, published in 1785. This book is fatally easy to caricature, and certainly it is not based upon the loftiest conception of human nature; but one must lay aside one's prejudices, as far as possible, if only to understand the significant fact that it was immediately adopted as a text-book in Cambridge University, and that it held undisputed sway there for a very considerable time. And it must not be supposed that Cambridge University was peculiar in its attitude toward the question as to the foundation of morality. It merely happened to represent, more exactly than Oxford, the prevailing tendency of the time and country. Moreover, Paley's treatise is by no means as disagreeable in tone as one might be led to expect from the classic passages which are so sure to be quoted by adverse critics. The author wrote with great clearness and force, as well as with much good sense and unruffled good temper. Indeed, his tone throughout the *Principles* is really admirable, as compared with that of Bentham in his corresponding works.

Paley's aim, like that of most writers on Ethics in his own

---

[1] Of course, the mere fact that he treated the Utilitarian doctrine from the non-theological point of view, was an important influence in the direction of completely secularising the doctrine; but he nowhere shows how one can dispense with the theological sanction in a system of Ethics where the motive of the agent is assumed to be necessarily egoistic. This, in fact, is impossible, if the notion of complete obligation is to be retained.

time, was eminently practical. Ethics was of importance for
him, not primarily as a philosophical discipline, but as a help
toward right conduct. His treatment, therefore, is concrete
from the very beginning. After showing the insufficiency of
such codes as the 'Law of Honour' and the 'Law of the
Land,' he raises the question : Do we find in the Scriptures
a complete rule of life? His answer, it will be remembered,
is, that the Scriptures were designed, not so much to bring
to our notice new rules of morality, as to enforce by *sufficient
sanctions* those already evident through natural reason.
This, of course, is characteristic, though not of the best
side of Paley's system. One is disappointed that he does
not call attention to the fact—important, if somewhat obvious
—that the Scriptures do not, of themselves, commit us to any
particular type of ethical theory.

Upon what, then, are we to depend, in directing our conduct in the complex relations of ordinary life? Paley will
not listen to the 'Moral Sense' philosophers, whose characteristic position he regards, not only as theoretically unsound, but as practically objectionable. His arguments
against the existence of a 'moral sense' are what had already
become the familiar ones. In the main, he merely reproduces
what Gay and Tucker had said more clearly, because more
at length; but he does justice to the importance of the almost
universal tendency to imitate which, in the case of young
children, he is inclined to call an instinct'. This neither
of the others can really be said to have done. But, apart from
its theoretical unsoundness, Paley regards the 'Moral Sense'
doctrine as pernicious in its tendency, because it leads to
arbitrariness in moral judgments. "Nothing is so soon
made as a maxim." [1] It is evident that he would have
objected equally to the position, that all we have to do is to
'follow conscience'; for he insists that what we really need
is some objective standard in Ethics, and that this can be
found only when we come to consider carefully the conse-

* See Bk. I., ch. v., p. 14 (1816 ed.).

quences of our different classes of actions. For Paley, as for nearly all writers on Ethics, the consequences of actions are equivalent to their results expressed in hedonistic terms.[1] And he is perfectly explicit in his use of the word 'happiness'. For him, as for both Gay and Tucker, happiness is merely a 'sum of pleasures'; and he also follows Tucker almost verbally in his denial of qualitative differences between pleasures and pains.[2]   Like Tucker, again, he emphasises the much greater importance of the so-called 'higher' pleasures, and holds that the greatest permanent satisfaction is to be found in the exercise of the 'social affections'.

The Good, then, is 'happiness,' in the sense of a 'sum of pleasures,' or the decided preponderance of pleasures over pains in a sufficiently long succession of human experiences. Hence, in defining Virtue as "the doing good to mankind, in obedience to the will of God, and for the sake of everlasting happiness," [3] the author states in epitome all that is absolutely essential to his system.   His familiar and rather unsavoury treatment of Obligation, as the being "urged by a violent motive resulting from the command of another" [4]— which, of course, is implied in the definition of virtue, just quoted—will be found, upon examination, to be an almost literal reproduction of the corresponding passage in Gay's *Dissertation*.   Indeed, in this case, he certainly has not improved upon the author whom he has imitated.

The only difference between 'prudence' and 'duty,' according to this theory of obligation, is that in the one case we consider what we shall gain or lose in the present world,

---

[1] It is rather curious that non-hedonistic writers should so generally look askance at all theoretical discussion regarding the good and bad consequences of actions, as if to admit the importance of consequences were to play into the hands of Hedonism.   These consequences, of course, may be important to any degree whatever; only they may be explained as good or bad, not merely in terms of Hedonism, but in terms of any other recognised form of ethical theory, with the single exception, perhaps, of Intuitionism—and this would be an exception only when held in its naïve form.

[2] See Bk. I., ch. vi., p. 17.

[3] *Ibid.*, vii., p. 32.                    [4] See Bk. II., ch. ii., p. 44.

while in the other case we consider also, and particularly, what we shall gain or lose in the world to come.[1] We have seen that Gay and Tucker, starting with the same view that human nature is essentially egoistic—mitigated, of course, by the use of the principle of 'translation'—had found it impossible to vindicate objectively altruistic conduct without taking the future life into consideration. Paley frankly rests his whole system upon the theological doctrine of rewards and punishments after death. What had been kept more or less in the background by the other two writers, becomes in his case most unpleasantly explicit. But while one is sure to be repelled by this side of Paley's system, one must be very careful not to confound the egoism of Paley with the egoism of Hobbes. According to Hobbes, men are essentially anti-social beings : in their 'natural' state, they desire only the gratification of their passions and the subjugation of their fellows. Paley, on the other hand, emphasises the fact, already made prominent by Tucker, that we find our most lasting satisfaction precisely in the exercise of the 'social affections'.[2] Indeed, if one read between the lines in a work like Paley's, one cannot help seeing how obscure, upon examination, the apparently evident distinction between theoretical egoism and theoretical altruism becomes —always supposing, of course, that man is regarded as originally a social being.[3]

The author's transition from his general definition of virtue to his method of arriving at the rules of concrete morality, is closely imitated from Gay.[4] It is hardly necessary to trace the successive steps, as they are so generally familiar. The rules of action must, according to the formula adopted, result from the will of God. But what is the will of God? From the very conception of God as a being of infinite

[1] See Bk. II., ch. iii., p. 47.     [2] See Bk. I., ch. vi., p. 25.

[3] The egoism of Paley's system becomes offensive only by reason of his constant reference to the theological sanction, as making it for the agent's selfish interest to be moral. Tucker was much more careful in this respect.

[4] See Bk. II., chs. iv., v., and vi.

goodness, it follows that He must desire the happiness of men ; and what we should thus *a priori* deduce from the necessary character of God, is borne out by the numberless beneficent contrivances in which nature abounds. The obvious conclusion is, that the method of learning the will of God concerning any action, by the 'light of nature,' is to inquire into the general tendency of such actions to promote or diminish the common happiness. Paley takes no pains to use language that might be expected to conciliate his opponents. He says: "Whatever is expedient is right. It is the utility of any moral rule alone which constitutes the obligation of it." [1]

Paley shows his good judgment in following Gay and Tucker with regard to the necessity of acting according to general rules,[2] instead of attempting to show that we may, at least roughly, compute the consequences in each particular case. He does not, to be sure, treat the matter at length and adequately, as Tucker had done ; but he puts it even more concretely when he says, *e.g.:* "The particular consequence of coining [counterfeiting] is, the loss of a guinea, or of half a guinea, to the person who receives the counterfeit money : the general consequence (by which I mean the consequence that would ensue, if the same practice were generally permitted) is, to abolish the use of money ".[3]   In this connection, he is able to show that the principle of 'doing evil that good may come' is as obviously fallacious according to Utilitarianism as according to non-Utilitarian systems.

It is needless, for our present purpose, to follow Paley through his somewhat artificial classification of duties and his deduction of the particular virtues.[4]  Some of his deductions are rather more satisfactory than those of Tucker ;

---

[1] See Bk. II., ch. vi., p. 53.

[2] *Ibid.*, chs. vii. and viii.          [3] *Ibid.*, ch. viii., p. 60.

[4] Paley recognises three classes of 'relative' duties (*i.e.*, duties to others) : (1) 'determinate' (*e.g.*, property, promises, etc.) ; (2) 'indeterminate' (*e.g.*, charity, resentment, anger, etc.) ; and (3) those 'which result from the constitution of the sexes '.  Besides these, he considers : (4) duties to ourselves (*e.g.*, self-defence) ; and (5) duties toward God (*e.g.*, worship).

but this is merely on account of his greater skill as an expositor. On the whole, they are less adequate than those of his predecessor. For the most part, he keeps clear of theories which are incongruous with his own fundamental principle of utility. But in one case, at least, he allows himself to base his treatment upon the conception of 'natural rights' in a way that Tucker, apparently, had always carefully avoided doing. When treating of the duty of charity, he says: "All things were originally common. No one being able to produce a charter from Heaven, had any better title to a particular possession than his next neighbour. There were reasons for mankind's agreeing upon a separation of this common fund; and God for these reasons is presumed to have ratified it. But this separation was made and consented to, upon the expectation and condition that every one should have left a sufficiency for his subsistence, or the means of procuring it: and as no fixed laws for the regulation of property can be so contrived, as to provide for the relief of every case and distress which may arise, these cases and distresses . . . were supposed to be left to the voluntary bounty of those who might be acquainted with the exigencies of their situation, and in the way of affording assistance." [1]

This would seem to imply an actual original compact, the idea of which is expressly repudiated by Paley himself in the latter part of his book. Examples like this are interesting, as showing what a strong hold the related notions of 'natural rights' and 'natural laws' still had at the time that we are considering, even upon an author like Paley. It should be admitted, however, that such inconsistencies mean less in Paley's case than they would in that of the average ethical writer, for his interests were almost wholly practical, and, where it was possible, he seems purposely to have avoided all controversy with regard to current and generally accepted theories, as being beside his purpose.

Brief as our review of Paley's system has been, it has probably shown that the author was essentially a great ex-

[1] See Bk. III., Pt. II., ch. v., p. 179.

positor, and not the originator of anything really new in
ethical theory. There was, of course, the greatest difference
between the originality which Tucker displayed in working
out a fairly coherent ethical system upon the basis of the
outline suggested in Gay's *Dissertation*, and that which
enabled Paley to make almost universally popular for the
time what had been thus completely developed. At the
same time, here, as so frequently in the history of thought,
the clearest exponent of the principle in question receives
the popular credit, at the expense of those who had actually
originated the principle and worked it out.

We have confined ourselves entirely to an examination of
Paley's ethical treatise, and it is not at all necessary, for our
present purpose, that we should consider his other works,
which are not only very well known, but not in the least
calculated to modify one's impression of his system. But,
before leaving the author of the *Moral and Political Philosophy*, it may be well to recall what manner of man he was.
Paley may have been rather too liberal in some of his views,
particularly on political subjects, to obtain the preferment
in the Church to which his very considerable talents seem to
have entitled him; but, on the whole, he was a man pre-
eminently in touch with his time, for better and for worse.
He seems to have been free from strong feeling of any sort.
If one has to regret the lack of spirituality in his writings,
one must at least give him credit for abstaining from violent
polemics, and for writing in a straightforward and manly
way. Moreover, he made no extreme claims to originality.
It is true that he desired to be thought " something more than
a mere compiler," as he certainly was; but even when he did
not explicitly acknowledge his indebtedness to others, he took
no pains to conceal it. He was not at all the type of man
who wastes energy in pushing personal claims of priority.

When we turn to Bentham, we soon find that we have to
do with a very different personality. Though brought up a
Tory, he was by temperament ' of the opposition '—in all

respects a Radical. He generally writes clearly, and not without force; but he constantly loses his temper, and even goes out of his way to vilify those whom he opposes by imputing to them interested motives.[1] The result is that, however much the reader may happen to sympathise with the general tenor of his thought, he is almost sure to find his works irritating in style and method. Yet it was this very fervour of the reformer that commended Bentham so strongly to certain young men of radical tendencies in his own day. While Paley's *Moral and Political Philosophy* met with extraordinary success as a text-book, the author could not properly be said to have founded a 'school'. His work rather made explicit what had long been implicit in the ethical teaching of his own University. Bentham, on the other hand, was regarded, both by himself and by his immediate followers, as the inaugurator of a perfectly new régime. The statement of Whewell, that "The school of Bentham, for a time, afforded as near a resemblance as modern times can show, of the ancient schools of Philosophy, which were formed and held together by an almost unbounded veneration for their master, and in which the disciples were content to place their glory in understanding and extending the master's principles,"[2] is doubtless an exaggeration, but hardly so misleading as Mill would have us believe.[3]

In considering Bentham's ethical system, it is important to decide, once for all, what works we should be prepared to recognise as authoritatively representing his doctrine. Three only need come under consideration: his *Fragment on Government* (1776), his *Principles of Morals and Legislation* (printed in 1780, but not published till 1789), and his posthumous work, *Deontology* (edited by his literary executor, Bowring, and published in 1834).[4] Of these, the *Fragment*

---

[1] See, *e.g.*, *Principles of Morals and Legislation*, ch. i., § xiii., note.

[2] See *Lectures on the History of Moral Philosophy in England*, Lect. xiii.

[3] See *Autobiography*, p. 101.

[4] A useful epitome of his ethical doctrine will be found in the *Principles of Legislation* prefixed to the *Theory of Legislation*, first published by Dumont in France.

*on Government*, which deals only very incidentally with ethical problems, is of importance for us only as indicating the author's attitude at the time when it was published. It is sufficient to note that, as early as 1776, he had adopted the general position with which his name later became identified, and also that the tendency toward violent polemics, which later became so disagreeable a feature of his works, was already clearly apparent. *The Principles of Morals and Legislation* is by far the best known of the three works mentioned, and it is upon this that expositions of Bentham's ethical system are commonly based. But, while one can clearly enough gather the author's general views on Ethics from the first few chapters of this book, one should always remember that it is primarily of Jurisprudence, and not of theoretical Ethics, that Bentham is here treating. In the case of a writer representing a really new principle in Ethics, or one more difficult to expound in comparatively summary fashion, this might lead to serious confusion, seeing that the relation between Ethics and Jurisprudence must itself be regarded as a vexed question.[1]

The *Deontology*, then, is the only work which Bentham wrote on Ethics proper. But here we are confronted with a difficulty quite as serious as that just noted in the case of his *Principles of Morals and Legislation ;* for the *Deontology*, which was a posthumous publication, was not merely 'edited,' in the ordinary sense, but (in part, at least) arranged from Bentham's papers by his enthusiastic friend and admirer, John Bowring, whom he had made his literary executor.[2] The general impression seems to be, that Bowring took un-

---

[1] For Bentham's distinction between the two, see *Deontology*, vol. I., ch. ii., p. 27. He says, in substance: "Where legal rewards and punishments cease to interfere with human actions, there precepts of morality come in with their influences. . . . In a word, Deontology, or Private Ethics, may be considered the science by which happiness is created out of motives extra-legislational—while Jurisprudence is the science by which law is applied to the production of felicity."

[2] It appeared in 1834, two years after Bentham's death, and, so far as I am aware, only one edition was printed.

warranted liberties with the manuscripts, many of which had been handed over to him during Bentham's lifetime. But, while it would be rash to assert the contrary, I am not aware that any conclusive evidence to this effect has ever been produced.[1] Indeed, most of the blemishes which are found in the book, and which would make one willing to believe that it had been changed here and there by another hand, can be almost exactly duplicated from those of Bentham's works which were published during his lifetime, and about whose authenticity there has never been the shadow of a doubt. Moreover, the style in many of the more important passages, including some of the most disagreeable, is unmistakably Bentham's. It should be further noted that, although there are two volumes of the *Deontology*—(1) "Theory of Virtue" and (2) "Practice of Virtue"—the first volume alone is of theoretical importance; and it is mainly with regard to the second volume, as it seems to the present writer, that the question of authenticity arises.[2]

If the *Deontology* represented any material departure in theory, or even in treatment, from the *Principles of Morals and Legislation*, this question of authenticity would become one of capital importance. This, however, is not the case; and, as the expositions in this book are by far the most complete treatment of ethical problems to be found in Bentham's works, it cannot properly be neglected. In fact, it will be largely followed in the present exposition, because the book is out of print and very rare, while an excellent reprint of the *Principles of Morals and Legislation* is readily obtainable. At the same time, no distinctive opinion will here be attributed to Bentham, for which warrant is not to be found in his other works, and parallel references will be given in all cases of importance.

[1] It is probable that J. S. Mill was largely responsible for this general opinion.

[2] The difference in style between the first volume and much of the second volume is unmistakable. If Bowring was responsible for the literary form of the second volume, as seems probable, since the style often resembles that which he ordinarily uses, it is difficult to believe that he tampered much with the first volume, which certainly reads like Bentham from beginning to end.

Gay had remarked, at the beginning of the *Dissertation*, that the theoretical differences between moralists were less than might appear. Indeed, he suspects " that they only talk a different language, and that all of them have the same criterion in reality, only they have expressed it in different words ". The suggestion doubtless is, that we must look for latent Utilitarianism in non-Utilitarian systems. Paley — apparently following the *Dissertation* — expresses himself in a similar way, but is more explicit. He says: " ' The fitness of things,' means their fitness to produce happiness; ' the nature of things,' means that actual constitution of the world, by which some things, as such and such actions, for example, produce happiness, and others misery; ' reason ' is the principle by which we discover or judge of this constitution; ' truth ' is this judgment expressed or drawn out into propositions ". And, again, Paley follows Gay in the doubtful thesis that " This is the reason that moralists, from whatever different principles they set out, commonly meet in their conclusions ".[1]

Bentham, on the other hand, never mentions non-hedonistic systems, except in terms of contempt. The following passages—taken almost at random from the *Principles* and the *Deontology*—speak for themselves. " The various systems that have been formed concerning the standard of right and wrong, may all be reduced to the principle of sympathy and antipathy. . . . They consist all of them in so many contrivances for avoiding the obligation of appealing to any external standard, and for prevailing upon the reader to accept of the author's sentiment or opinion as a reason for itself." [2] " He who, on any other occasion, should say, ' It is as I say, because I say it is so,' would not be thought to have said any great matter: but on the question concerning

---

[1] See Bk. II., ch. i., pp. 42, 43. The rather obvious reason why moralists ' meet in their conclusions' is, that they begin by (at least provisionally) assuming the same concrete moral principles, *i.e.*, the prevailing ones of their own age and country.

[2] See *Principles*, ch. ii., § xiv.

the standard of morality, men have written great books, wherein from beginning to end they are employed in saying this and nothing else." [1] " The *summum bonum*—the sovereign good—what is it? . . . It is this thing, and that thing, and the other thing—it is anything but pleasure—it is the Irishman's apple-pie made of nothing but quinces. . . . While Xenophon was writing history, and Euclid giving instruction in geometry, Socrates and Plato were talking nonsense under pretence of teaching wisdom and morality." [2] ' Moral sense,' ' common sense,' ' understanding,' ' reason,' ' right reason,' ' nature,' and ' nature's law,' ' natural justice,' natural equity,' ' good order,' ' truth '—" all these are but the dogmas of men who insist on implicit obedience to their decrees ".[3]

Unlike his Utilitarian predecessors, then, Bentham becomes nervous, and often violent, at the mere mention of the term ' *summum bonum* '; but his own treatment of the question as to the fundamental ground of morality is in all essential respects identical with theirs. Not only does he, of course, regard happiness as the true Good, but his arguments to substantiate this view are those which had long been familiar before he wrote. Indeed, in the *Principles of Morals and Legislation*, he can hardly be said to argue the matter at all ; but rather assumes dogmatically the Utilitarian criterion of morality. The Good is ' happiness' and ' happiness ' is merely the ' sum of pleasures,' as Gay and Tucker had held. Moreover, there are no ' qualitative distinctions' between pleasures, as Tucker had explicitly taught — all concrete differences being reducible to differences of intensity and permanence. Not only does each seek his own happiness, but each is incomparably the best judge of what will make for his own happiness, as Tucker had been at pains to point out. Like Tucker, again, Bentham remarks that the words ' pleasure ' and ' pain ' are likely to prove misleading in ethical discussions, because they seem to imply too much, and suggests ' well-being ' and its contrary as convenient substitutes,

---

[1] See *Deontology*, vol. I., ch. i., p. 9.
[2] *Ibid.*, ch. iii., pp. 39, 40.  [3] *Ibid.*, ch. iv., p. 71.

more general in meaning—just as Tucker had suggested the terms 'satisfaction' and 'dissatisfaction'.[1]

Of course Bentham is not to be blamed for not developing the hedonistic conception of the Good beyond what had been done, *e.g.*, by Paley—for the simple reason that Paley and his predecessors had already stated Hedonism in perfectly unmistakable terms. But even in 1834, Bentham's ardent disciple, Bowring, was able to write: "It was in 1785 that Paley published his *Elements of Moral and Political Philosophy.* He mentions the principle of utility, but seems to have no idea of its bearing upon happiness. And if he had any such idea, he was the last man to give expression to it." [2] Then follows a passage of personal abuse which it is the more unnecessary to quote, as Whewell has already done so in his *Lectures.*

But it might seem at first as if there were a difference between Bentham, on the one hand, and Gay, Tucker, and Paley, on the other, inasmuch as Bentham once for all adopted the formula, 'the greatest happiness of the greatest number,' as the corner-stone of his system. In other words, the previous Utilitarian systems — except Cumberland's, Hume's (in its later form), and Hartley's [3]—had assumed that all motives were ultimately selfish, while Bentham's, by virtue of its very formula, suggested devotion to one's fellow men. It cannot be too strongly insisted, however, that there is no theoretical difference between the four authors on this question regarding the motive of the moral agent. Bentham used the 'greatest happiness' formula because he was a reformer—obviously a fortuitous circumstance from the point of view of theoretical Ethics. Certainly none of the authors just mentioned had emphasised more strongly than Bentham does the necessary egoism of the individual. For instance,

---

[1] See *Deontology*, vol. I., chs. iv. and v.

[2] See appendix on "History of the Greatest Happiness Principle," by Bowring, *Deontology*, vol. I., p. 310.

[3] Which, however, is so peculiar that its Utilitarian character might, with some show of justice, be denied.

he says : " A man, a moralist, gets into an elbow-chair, and pours forth pompous dogmatisms about *duty*—and *duties.* Why is he not listened to ? Because every man is thinking about *interests*." And again : " To prove that the immoral action is a miscalculation of self-interest — to show how erroneous an estimate the vicious man makes of pains and pleasures, is the purpose of the intelligent moralist ".[1] Indeed, Bentham is at a disadvantage here, as compared with the others, because he is nowhere quite explicit with regard to the origin of sympathy and its place in his system. It may be well to note, in this connection, that he consistently holds that " the good produced by effective benevolence is small in proportion to that produced by the personal motives ".

Not only, then, is the Good pleasure, according to Bentham's view ; but the good immediately sought is not the pleasure of 'the greatest number,' but rather one's own. How may the good of each and the good of all be shown to coincide ? For clearly they must coincide, if a multitude of self-seeking individuals are capable of working out a common good. This is a question which had been discussed, not only by the earlier Utilitarians, but by writers like Shaftesbury and Hutcheson, who could not properly be classed with them. Indeed, up to this time, the non-Utilitarian writers seem to have had better succes; than the Utilitarians in their attempts to reconcile public and private interest. It is unnecessary to recapitulate here what has been discussed at length in the proper connection. For our present purpose, it is enough to notice that Bentham did not profit by the suggestions of those who, like Cumberland and Shaftesbury, had attempted to demonstrate the necessarily organic character of society. Though adopting the 'greatest happiness' formula, his logical position is distinctly that of eighteenth century Individualism.

From this point of view, rewards and (more particularly)

---

[1] See *Deontology,* vol. I., p. 12.

punishments, or, as Bentham chooses to call them, ' sanctions,' must be looked to, in order to effect this reconciliation. Bentham's list of these ' sanctions ' differs somewhat, as regards their number, in his various works bearing upon Ethics. In the *Fragment on Government*, three are mentioned: (1) the ' political,' (2) the ' religious,' and (3) the ' moral '. In the *Principles of Morals and Legislation*, four are recognised: (1) the ' physical,' (2) the ' political,' (3) the ' moral ' or ' popular,' and (4) the ' religious '.[1] In the *Deontology*, Bentham succeeds in distinguishing five ' sanctions ': (1) the ' physical ' (*i.e.*, natural consequences, abstracting from one's relations to other human beings); (2) the ' social ' or ' sympathetic ' (*i.e.*, consequences which result from one's personal or domestic relations); (3) the ' moral ' or ' popular ' (*i.e.*, public opinion); (4) the ' political ' or ' legal '; and (5) the ' religious ' or ' superhuman '.[2] It is to be doubted if he improved matters by trying to distinguish sharply between (2) and (3); indeed, he himself hardly insists upon the separation. If we neglect this rather fine distinction, and regard the list of ' sanctions ' in the *Principles of Morals and Legislation* as his complete list, an interesting comparison suggests itself. For this list of ' sanctions '—often regarded as particularly characteristic of Bentham — is identical with that given by Gay in the *Dissertation*.

It might be imagined by one who knew the early Utilitarians only at second hand, that Bentham's treatment of the particular virtues, as following from the Utilitarian principle, must be more definite and consistent than that of his predecessors; but, if anything, the contrary is true. Indeed, if we go so far as to rule out the *Deontology* altogether as unreliable—as I am not myself prepared to do—we must admit that Bentham never even attempted to give a systematic treatment of the particular virtues. The *Fragment on Government*, of course, contains nothing of the kind; and, in the *Principles of Morals and Legislation*, where he was

---

[1] See ch. iii.        [2] See vol. I., ch. vii.

writing mainly from the point of view of Jurisprudence, he very properly omitted any such treatment of the virtues. In the latter work, when writing of the distinction between Ethics and Jurisprudence, he merely remarks that the virtues may conveniently be divided into those of (1) 'prudence,' (2) 'probity' [justice], and (3) 'beneficence'.[1]

In the *Deontology*, then, upon which we must here depend, Bentham begins by dividing virtue into two branches: (1) 'prudence,' and (2) 'effective benevolence'. Quite after the manner of Cumberland, 'prudence' is regarded as having its seat in the understanding; 'effective benevolence,' principally in the affections. 'Prudence,' in turn, is divided into (*a*) 'self-regarding,' and (*b*) 'extra-regarding'; while 'effective benevolence,' again, is either (*a*) 'positive' (*i.e.*, productive of positive pleasure) or (*b*) 'negative' (*i.e.*, calculated to diminish pain).[2] The latent confusion here, which Bentham might easily have avoided by retaining his earlier classification, hardly needs to be pointed out; indeed, the distinctions thus made are practically unmanageable. In his actual treatment of the virtues, he seems to use the term 'prudence' only in the first sense. This was, perhaps, almost inevitable; but the result is, that he is at a very serious disadvantage, not only as compared with Hume, but as compared with Tucker and Paley, in his treatment of what was for them all the fundamental virtue—Justice. In fact, Bentham's deduction of the particular virtues, so far as he considers them at all, is so manifestly weak, that one must charitably conclude that this part of the *Deontology* was—by him, at least—unfinished. If our knowledge of Ethics were confined to what is contained in the *Deontology*, we would have to agree most emphatically with Bentham, when he says: "Though the Linnæus of Natural History has appeared in the world, and restored its chaos into order and harmony, the Linnæus of Ethics is yet to come ".[3]

[1] See ch. xvii., § 6.
[2] See vol. I., ch. i., pp. 15, 16; also chs. xi., xii., xiii., and xiv.
[3] See *Deontology*, vol. I., ch. xv., p. 202.

One important topic—Bentham's treatment of the hedonistic calculus—remains to be considered. Here, if anywhere, we must look for originality in Bentham's treatment of ethical problems. We have seen that both Tucker and Paley taught, not only that we could not predict consequences in any particular case exactly enough thus to determine the rightness or wrongness of the proposed action; but also that there are obvious reasons, from the Utilitarian point of view, why we should not attempt to do anything of the kind. In other words, we must confine ourselves, in the main, to a consideration of the 'general' consequences of different classes of actions, and thus act upon a basis of 'general rules'. We further saw that both authors were willing enough that, at the time of action, the agent should regard the moral law as an end in itself.

To Bentham, on the other hand, this probably would have seemed a pitiful subterfuge. He apparently holds that we not only may, but must compute in the particular case, and be largely determined by such computations. And, if there be virtue in terminology, he elaborated a formidable instrument for the hedonistic calculus.[1] The value of pleasures and pains must be estimated in terms of their 'intensity,' 'duration,' 'certainty,' 'proximity,' and 'extent'. But this is not all. A pleasure or pain may be 'fruitful' or 'barren,' 'pure' or 'impure'. Of the distinctions thus made, the first five hardly require explanation. 'Extent' may properly be put by itself, as it refers merely to the number of individuals concerned. It is the multiplier, and not the multiplicand. 'Certainty' and 'proximity,' as the words would imply, refer only to the probability or improbability of the pleasures or pains being experienced, so that in the last resort 'intensity' and 'duration' are all that have to be considered. So far, Bentham's treatment of the hedonistic calculus in the *Deontology* corresponds exactly to his treatment in the *Principles of Morals and Legislation.* We have to be more careful,

---

[1] See, in particular, *Deontology*, vol. I., ch. iv.

however, in the case of 'fecundity' and 'purity'. In the *Principles*, the 'fecundity' of a pleasure or pain is defined as "the chance it has of being followed by sensations of the *same* kind : that is, pleasures, if it be a pleasure : pains, if it be a pain ".[1] Its 'purity,' on the other hand, is defined as "the chance it has of *not* being followed by sensations of the *opposite* kind : that is, pains, if it be a pleasure : pleasures, if it be a pain ". In the *Deontology*, the author says : " A pleasure or a pain may be fruitful or barren. A pleasure may be fruitful in pleasures, or fruitful in pains, or fruitful in both ; and a pain, on the contrary, may be fruitful in pleasures or pains, or both." [2] As regards 'purity,' he says in the same work : " A pleasure is considered pure, in the degree in which it is unaccompanied by counterbalancing pains—a pain is pure, in the proportion in which it is unaccompanied by counterbalancing pleasures ".[3]

It will readily be seen that, as used in the *Principles*, 'fecundity' and 'purity' both refer to the future. Given a pleasure or a pain, we call it 'fruitful,' if it is likely to be followed by other affections of the *same* kind ; 'pure,' if it is *not* likely to be followed by other affections of the *opposite* kind. In the *Deontology*, as will be noted, the same terms are used, but with a somewhat different signification. The 'fruitfulness' or 'barrenness' of the particular pleasure or pain is here regarded as its productiveness or unproductiveness of future affections — whether of the same or of the opposite kind, or of both. 'Purity' and 'impurity,' on the other hand, apparently refer merely to the unmixed or mixed character of our affections, *i.e.*, pleasure without pain, or pain without pleasure. I do not understand that Bentham necessarily commits himself to the dubious position that we have states of consciousness which are at the same time pleasurable and painful. It is enough that, in some cases, circumstances are such that our consciousness vibrates back

[1] See ch. iv., § iii.
[2] See vol. I., ch. iv., p. 62.     [3] See *ibid.*, p. 76.

and forth between pleasure and pain with rapid alternation. Roughly speaking, we might say that pleasures and pains experienced under such conditions were 'impure,' in Bentham's sense. Perhaps it may seem finical to criticise Bentham's choice of technical terms; but it will be seen that the word 'fecundity,' as here applied, is rather misleading, as it almost inevitably suggests a causal relation between pleasures and pains themselves, which the author could not have intended.

After thus considering the general aspects of pleasure-pain, Bentham gives an elaborate classification of pleasures and pains in both the *Principles* and the *Deontology*. In the *Deontology*, the list is as follows: (1) pleasures and pains of sense, (2) pleasures of wealth, with the corresponding pains of privation, (3) pleasures of skill and pains of awkwardness, (4) pleasures of amity and pains of enmity, (5) pleasures of good reputation and pains of ill-repute, (6) pleasures of power, (7) pleasures of piety, with their contrasted pains, (8) pleasures and pains of sympathy or benevolence, (9) those of malevolence, (10) those of memory, (11) those of imagination, (12) those of expectation, and (13) those of association. The list given in the *Principles* is practically the same, except that still another class of pleasures is added, *i.e.*, those of relief. Such minor differences may be neglected; but Bentham himself pertinently points out that " Of the whole list of pains and pleasures, two classes only regard others—they are those of benevolence and malevolence. All the rest are self-regarding." [1] It goes without saying that this list is a purely arbitrary one, having no warrant in Psychology, and that it is hardly, if at all, calculated to assist us in the actual computation of pleasures and pains. In fact, the list is mainly interesting, because it illustrates particularly well a limitation of Bentham's which has often been pointed out, *viz.*, his narrow and mechanical view of human nature.

Such, then, was Bentham's treatment of the hedonistic

---

[1] See vol. I., ch. iv., p. 66.

calculus. Without entering on any more general criticism of Bentham's Utilitarianism, we are now prepared to ask two questions : (1) Were the refinements which he introduced of practical importance? (2) Was he right in holding, as he at least seemed to do, that we should largely depend upon such computations as we can make in the individual case? The first question need not detain us long. The distinctions which we have just been examining seem, on the whole, to be helpful, though the particular words used to designate them do not always appear to be the best that might have been chosen. Any such related technical terms, which tend to abbreviate discussion, are likely to have considerable currency ; and this has undeniably been true of those under consideration. At the same time, I fail to see that anything essentially new was contributed by Bentham even here, except the terms themselves ; for all the distinctions are rather obvious, and apparently they had all been (at least, implicitly) recognised before.

The second question, *viz.*, whether Bentham was right in holding, as he at least seemed to do, that we may, and must, compute the probable consequences (including, of course, the remote consequences) in the particular case, and act accordingly—is in itself more important ; but it hardly seems to admit of serious debate. For the question, of course, is not whether the moral agent is to take the probable consequences of his contemplated act into consideration—every sane man, whatever his ethical creed, is likely to do that—but whether such particular computations are to take precedence of general rules. Since we are not omniscient, we cannot predict with certainty the consequences of any action taken by itself. Moreover, it is important that we should not make the attempt : first, because we have not sufficient time for elaborate computations in a particular moral exigency ; and secondly, because we are in no proper frame of mind to judge impartially in those cases where our own interests are to any important extent at stake.

In truth, all this is so evident that one might be tempted to

believe that Bentham has commonly been misunderstood on
the point in question; but to the present writer this seems
hardly possible.    There is no doubt, of course, that in the
*Principles of Morals and Legislation* the hedonistic calculus
is employed in the interest of 'general rules,' since the laws
which the author has in mind would necessarily, *qua* laws,
be general in their application.    In the *Deontology*, however,
where the object is to guide the individual agent in his moral
life, computations in the particular case seem, not merely
often, but generally, to be suggested, while there is no
single passage in the book which insists upon the importance
of general rules, as opposed to such particular computations.
The passages illustrating this general drift of the argument
are far too numerous to quote.    The following, which may
fairly be regarded as typical, will probably suffice.    Bentham
says:  "The province of Deontology is to teach him [the
moral agent] a proper arithmetic, is to lay before him a fit
estimate of pain and pleasure—a budget of receipt and dis-
bursement, out of every operation of which he is to draw a
balance of good ".[1]    And again the author says:  "Vice may
be defined to be a miscalculation of chances: a mistake in
estimating the value of pleasures and pains.    It is false moral
arithmetic; and there is the consolation of knowing that, by
the application of a right standard, there are few moral
questions which may not be resolved with an accuracy and a
certainty not far removed from mathematical demonstration." [2]

It is evident, however, that Bentham's attempt to reduce
our moral judgments to a series of problems in 'moral
arithmetic' was not a success, and tended to put the Utilitarian doctrine itself in a false light.    In fact, it would hardly
be too much to say that Bentham blundered into an untenable position here, which his Utilitarian predecessors had
had the good judgment to avoid.    Of course, it is sometimes

[1] See vol. I., ch. xiv., p. 192.
[2] See vol. I., p. 131.    For other passages illustrating this general line of
argument, see, *e.g.*, *ibid.*, pp. 60, 68, 79, 84, 118, 156, 168, 190, 269.

held that, since such particular computations are, on the one hand, impossible, and, on the other hand, dangerous to attempt, Utilitarianism as a system falls to the ground. The argument, however, does not seem at all conclusive. To say that we must act according to 'general rules,' is merely to recognise that we are finite beings; and surely this evident fact does not make for or against any particular form of ethical theory. Indeed, we must be very careful not to cite the concrete difficulties of our moral experience, as if they disproved the validity of ethical theories different from our own. No ethical theory can help us in such cases; we must rather depend upon what may fairly be called 'moral tact'. As Kant long ago pointed out in another connection, there can be no rules for the application of rules.

We have now examined with some care all that seems really essential in Bentham's ethical system. The results of our examination may be summed up in a few words. Bentham's conception of the Good was in all respects identical with that of his Utilitarian predecessors; and his adoption of the 'greatest happiness' formula did not imply a departure from what had become the traditional view of the Utilitarians, that the motive of the agent is uniformly egoistic. Moreover, he did not go beyond the others in showing how, in the natural order of things, public and private interest coincide; but depended wholly upon the four 'sanctions' which Gay had already distinguished. The 'theological sanction,' indeed, though named by him in each of his three lists, is practically disregarded in his treatment of Ethics. His actual procedure in this respect was doubtless an important influence in secularising Utilitarianism, but this was mainly due to his reputation as a writer on Jurisprudence. It is always to be remembered that, with his selfish theory of the moral motive, he was not himself in a position to explain complete obligation without reference to rewards and punishments after death. His deduction of the particular virtues, again, was clearly inferior to that which we find in the works of Tucker and Paley—not to mention Hume, whose work was, of course, on a very different and altogether higher plane. This, however, was at least partly due to the fact that he was treating primarily of Jurisprudence in his completed works. Indeed, the one important respect in which Bentham departs from his predecessors is in his dubious attempt to reduce Ethics to 'moral arithmetic,' in the grimly literal sense. This, however, cannot be regarded as a real advance in ethical theory, but quite the contrary. The inevitable conclusion, then, seems to be that Bentham contributed almost nothing of importance to Ethics, considered strictly as such, though he unquestionably did more than any of his contemporaries to bring the Utilitarian theory into popular ethical discussions. In fact, there were very special reasons why he was constitutionally unfitted to transform the older Utilitarianism, which, as a mere theory, had already been completely developed before he wrote, into anything like the modern form of the doctrine. These fatal limitations would have to be considered here, but for the fact that J. S. Mill has performed the task once for all in his classic essay on Bentham (1838), to be duly examined hereafter, which perhaps may itself, without exaggeration, be said to mark the transition from the eighteenth century Utilitarianism to that of the present time.

# CHAPTER X.

IN the last chapter, Paley and Bentham were considered together, in order that it might be evident how essentially similar their distinctively ethical views really were. It is, however, equally certain that to their own generation, and quite as much to themselves, they must have seemed to stand for very different, if not antithetical, tendencies. Paley, indeed, had held somewhat liberal, though by no means radical, views on politics, which probably stood in the way of his rapid advancement in the Church; but this was purely accidental. Berkeley, as will be remembered, had expressed similar ethical views in his sermon on " Passive Obedience," although his main purpose was to urge upon his hearers an attitude toward the powers that be, very different from that which Paley later advocated in his *Political Philosophy*. And it is not easy to say that one was more consistent than the other. There was nothing in the doctrine of so-called ' Theological Utilitarianism,' either in its earlier or in its later form, which logically demanded of its adherents either a conservative or a liberal attitude toward the State. This must have been partly recognised by Paley's contemporaries, as otherwise his *Moral and Political Philosophy* would never have enjoyed such almost universal popularity.

Bentham, on the other hand, was first, last, and always a reformer and a radical. This was the light in which he was regarded both by his contemporaries and by himself. Such being the case, it was perfectly natural that he should develop anti-theological tendencies, for the influence of the Church,

on the whole, was strongly in the direction of conservatism.
Here again, however, the relation between political attitude,
on the one hand, and religious and ethical theory, on the other,
was largely a fortuitous one.      Religious orthodoxy easily
may, and often does, go with political heterodoxy, while the
contrary combination is still more frequent.   So far as the
anti-theological (or at least non-theological) side of Bentham's
doctrine is concerned, there can be no serious question.    But
it certainly seemed to Bentham himself and to most of those
immediately associated with him in the reform movement,
that the principle of ' the greatest happiness of the greatest
number,' in the technical sense of the formula, was the necessary foundation  of their schemes of practical reform.   They
hardly realised that those holding ethical theories radically
different from their own might consistently enough admit
that ' the greatest happiness of the greatest number ' is, under
all ordinary circumstances, the true end of co-operative social
action.

In truth, we should now probably agree in holding, not only
that our attitude toward religion does not necessarily commit
us for or against radicalism, liberalism, or conservatism, but
also that any political attitude consistent with the ordinary
notions of ' good morals,' which we all hold practically in
common, is logically compatible with any recognised form of
ethical theory.   We agree that the common good should be
the end of all governmental action ; and we further agree, in
the main, as to what concrete things are good.   There are
two respects, however, in which we may differ to almost any
extent.   First, we may differ as to how the concrete good of
society is practically to be attained (in other words, in political
' opinions ') ; and secondly, we may differ as to the abstract
terms in which the concrete ' good ' is to be defined (difference
in ethical and political theory).   The mistake of Bentham
and his followers was in assuming a logical relation between
theoretical Ethics proper and practical methods of government.

It would be quite outside our present purpose to trace
the fortunes of the so-called ' Bentham school '.   None of

the writers thus designated, whether properly or improperly, can be said to have really contributed to theoretical Ethics, with the very important exception of J. S. Mill; and all of Mill's more important writings on Ethics were published after the well-known essay on Bentham (1838), which shows in the most unmistakable way that he was thus early very far from being a mere disciple of the older moralist. In truth, it will be remembered that, in an often-quoted passage in the *Autobiography*, Mill denies outright that there was any 'Bentham school,' in the sense ordinarily understood. His contention is that the purely personal influence of his father, James Mill, was greater than that of Bentham, though he acknowledges that his father's total influence was very considerably less. He says: "The influence which Bentham exercised was by his writings. Through them he has produced, and is producing, effects on the condition of mankind, wider and deeper, no doubt, than any which can be attributed to my father. He is a much greater name in history. But my father exercised a far greater personal ascendency." [1] He then goes on to indicate circumstantially the various channels of his father's influence. The first impression might be that Mill considerably overrated this influence; but the facts, so far as they are generally accessible, seem on the whole to bear out his statement of the case. One has only to read any of the authoritative accounts of the elder Mill's life [2] to see how closely and continuously he was in touch with the men who were most prominently engaged in this liberal propagandism, and how he was regarded by them. But all this is really a digression, and we shall best proceed at once to an examination of the ethical doctrine of J. S. Mill himself, after giving necessary attention to the formative influences of his childhood and early youth.

The strange experiment which James Mill tried in the

---

[1] See pp. 101 *et seq.*

[2] See, in particular, the valuable life of James Mill by Professor Bain; also the second volume of Mr. Leslie Stephen's admirable work on the Utilitarians.

education of his eldest son has been described so often, and from such different points of view, that it would be almost an impertinence to speak of it here at any length. It will be remembered that James Mill, himself one of the busiest of men, irritable and somewhat harsh by nature, constantly engaged in literary work (which, perhaps, less than any other admits readily of systematic interruption), undertook to be his son's only schoolmaster from the very beginning. That he accomplished the seemingly impossible, is doubtless an interesting fact, for it exhibits in a most striking light the remarkable intellectual endowments of both father and son. But this was, perhaps, the most costly education of which we have definite record, not less for student than for teacher. If the victim had been one whit less than he was, he very well might have been ruined for life by the forcing process that he was put through. We do not refer merely to the fact that he began the study of Greek at three, and other similar studies, ordinarily considered to belong to a secondary, rather than to a strictly primary education, at a correspondingly early age. It is, we believe, reported of Mill's gifted contemporary, Thirwall, that he began to read Latin at three and Greek at four. But the future Bishop and historian of Greece was doubtless most fortunate in being permitted the conventional education of his class, after this startling exhibition of infant precocity. Mill, on the contrary, utterly lost his boyhood, with all the humanising effects of normal early associations. As a natural result, in after years he never quite found his fellowmen.

The particular studies to which J. S. Mill devoted himself in his early years, were not essentially different from those which formed the staple of higher education at that time— except that he was made to give some attention to Political Economy, which was then still an infant science. The peculiarity in his case lay in the fact that the ground covered was unusually large, and that these studies were pursued under the private tuition of his father and, for the most part, at an extremely early age. But in another aspect, much more important for us, his early training was, as he himself points out in the *Autobiography*, for the time and country in which he lived, almost unique. He was brought up from the first without any religious belief, in the ordinary acceptation of the term. James Mill had, indeed, begun his career with a theological training; but he soon found it impossible to retain his early religious views. His son points out that his difficulties had been "moral, still more than intellectual". "He found it impossible to believe that a world so full of evil was the work of an Author combining infinite power with perfect goodness and righteousness."[1] Moreover, he seems to have held that positive religion was distinctly detrimental to good morals, on the ground that it was a fatally convenient pretext by which to justify the existing order of things, involving, as this does, so many evils that may be remedied. Morality, he believed, must cease to be a matter of mere tradition and be founded upon some definite objective principle.

The glimpse of James Mill's private views on Ethics and Religion that is afforded in this part of the *Autobiography* is decidedly interesting. The following passage is particularly significant. "In his views of life he partook of the character of the Stoic, the Epicurean, and the Cynic, not in the modern, but the ancient sense of the word. In his personal qualities the Stoic predominated. His standard of morals was Epicurean, inasmuch as it was Utilitarian, taking as the exclusive test of right and wrong, the tendency of actions to produce pleasure or pain. But he had (and this was the Cynic element) scarcely any belief in pleasure. . . . He thought human life a poor thing at best, after the freshness of youth and of unsatisfied curiosity had gone by. . . . He would sometimes say, that if life were made what it might be, by good government and good education, it would be worth having: but he never spoke with anything like enthusiasm even of that possibility."[2]

---

[1] See p. 39.      [2] See pp. 47 *et seq.*

We are so constantly reminded of the complex character of J. S. Mill's ethical system, that it is most interesting to find sentiments like these attributed by him to his father. The sentences quoted are even more significant in their proper context. Almost as interesting as this (at first sight) paradoxical combination of theoretical hedonism with practical asceticism, is the sense of irremediable evil in the world which we find here. Both of the Mills were inclined to regard not unfavourably the Manichaean doctrine. J. S. Mill took a much less despondent view than his father of the possibilities of the race; but he never, at least in his mature years, entertained anything like Bentham's breezy, if somewhat shallow, optimism.

The influence of Bentham himself upon J. S. Mill was, of course, partly personal and partly philosophical. The elder Mill was already a friend of Bentham, when his son was but three years of age, and the precocious child and youth met the reformer frequently and on familiar terms. It was principally through his writings, however, that Bentham influenced Mill. There is an interesting passage in the *Autobiography*, in which the author tells how, when reading in the direction of law as a boy of fifteen or sixteen, he became acquainted for the first time with Bentham's doctrine in its technical form, as interpreted by Dumont in the *Traité de Législation*.[1] Unfortunately, however, it seems to have been the worst in Bentham, as well as the best, that attracted his early admiration; for he cites in particular the chapter in which Bentham impatiently dismisses all non-hedonistic theories as dogmatism in disguise. If Mill had at this time been better read in ethical literature, it might have occurred to him that, in the very chapter cited, Bentham shows himself a good deal more of a dogmatist than the men whom he criticises; and that his cheerful ignorance of nearly all systems opposed to his own, as shown here and elsewhere, is perhaps the most amazing phenomenon of the ethical literature of his day. But one

[1] See p. 64.

must remember that Mill had read no modern philosophy at this time. It was after this, according to his own account, that he became acquainted even with English writers like Locke, Berkeley, Hume, Hartley, and Brown.[1] This being the case, one is rather puzzled to understand why, when he wrote the *Autobiography*, Mill should have taken his juvenile impressions of Bentham so seriously. He says, *e.g.*: " I now had opinions ; a creed, a doctrine, a philosophy ; in one among the best senses of the word, a religion ; the inculcation and diffusion of which could be made the principal outward purpose of a life ".[2]

For several years Mill seems to have remained almost wholly under the influence of Bentham's writings and his father's personality, and, in the enthusiasm of youth, he doubtless developed much of that spirit of partisanship which in after years he so much deprecated. The first step in the direction of what he calls his 'youthful propagandism' was the foundation of the " Utilitarian Society ". This was in the year following that in which he first became acquainted with Bentham's writings. The fact is of interest merely because this was the first time that the word 'Utilitarian' had been used by hedonists themselves, as representing their doctrine. In a passage often quoted, Mill says: " I did not invent the word, but found it in one of Galt's novels, the *Annals of the Parish*, in which the Scotch clergyman, of whom the book is a supposed autobiography, is represented as warning his parishioners not to leave the Gospel and become utilitarians. With a boy's fondness for a name and a banner I seized on the word, and for some years called myself and others by it as a sectarian appellation. . . . As those opinions attracted more notice, the term was repeated by strangers and opponents, and got into rather common use just about the time when those who had originally assumed it, laid down that along with other sectarian characteristics." [3]

Passing over Mill's very circumstantial account of his early

---

[1] See p. 69.          [2] See p. 67.
[3] See pp. 79 *et seq.*: *cf. Utilitarianism*, p. 9, note.

achievements as a writer, during the two years following the foundation of the first *Westminster Review* in 1824—which, as a mere *tour de force* on the part of a youth who had not yet attained majority, are perhaps the most striking feature of his whole literary career—we shall pause to notice only one more stage of his mental history, as given in the *Auto-biography*. At length, in the autumn of 1826, the young writer had to pay the penalty for his abnormal education and life experience up to that time. His own account of what he calls "A Crisis in my Mental History" is perhaps the best known chapter in the *Autobiography*, and so calls for no re-production here. For some months all sources of satisfaction seemed for ever dried up for this 'disquisitive young man,' as Peacock had called him soon after he made his appearance at the India House—this martyr, one would be inclined to add, of a monstrous training. With capacities of almost the highest order, and living among those who, of all Englishmen at that time, had the word 'freedom' oftenest on their lips, J. S. Mill had in reality lived under quite as narrow and tyrannical a régime as fell to the lot of the average young school-man of the Middle Ages. It was, perhaps, not alto-gether to his discredit that he had serious doubts, at the time of which we speak, as to whether life was worth living. With considerable confidence we may answer for him, that such a life as his own had been up to this time was scarcely to be reckoned so. This period of unrest and inner conflict was of some months' duration ; but in the end it was decided that the world should lose a singularly perfect calculating-machine and gain another human philosopher.

We may now take leave of the *Autobiography* (1873), and trace the development of Mill's views on Ethics from his earlier published writings. Unfortunately he never wrote a detailed treatise on the subject. Apart from the well-known *Utilitarianism* (1863), we have to depend upon miscellaneous essays or upon chapters in his various works, where the ex-pression of his own views on Ethics is incidental rather than the main purpose. This is in itself a serious disadvantage, but the difficulty is greater than this alone would indicate. After his early course in rigorous Benthamism, and the crisis in his mental life which we have just considered, he drifted insensibly away from many of his earlier tenets, without by any means realising the extent of the divergence of his later from his earlier views. This being the case, it will be necessary to consider his various writings which bear upon Ethics separately, in spite of the obvious inconvenience of this method.

And first, it will be desirable to see how, after he became an independent ethical writer, he chose to define his position toward Paley and Bentham. Unfortunately, we have to depend, for his estimate of Paley, upon his not very satisfactory essay on Professor Sedgwick's *Discourse on the Studies of the University of Cambridge* (1835).[1] This does not by any means exhibit Mill at his best; for the most part, the essay reads like a mere apology for the position of Bentham. It will be remembered that the *Discourse* itself attracted a very great deal of attention at the time, and had a most important influence toward modifying the whole scheme of philosophical studies at Cambridge. Most students of Ethics at the present day, having heard so much of the *Discourse* before reading it, are probably at a loss to understand why it should have exerted such a considerable influence. It makes no philosophical pretensions whatever, being written more in the form of a sermon than that of even a popular lecture on philosophy. But it was an earnest and most effective protest, from the point of view of an English churchman of this period, against the tendencies of English Empiricism, as represented by Locke; and, in particular, against the ethical system of Paley. It is rather startling to find that Locke was being taught at this time without any special notice being taken of his lineal successors of the English Empirical school. Moreover, the criticism of Paley, to which

[1] *London Review*, April, 1835.

by far the most important part of the *Discourse* is devoted, is anything but fair, and certainly does not show that Professor Sedgwick appreciated the strength (such as it was) of Paley's position. But, after all abatements, the *Discourse* brings out with a good deal of force the fact, which must long have been more or less definitely appreciated, that Paley's system did not really do justice to the higher, more ideal side of the Christian doctrine. In this connection, Professor Sedgwick undertakes to criticise the hedonistic position in general ; although it must be admitted that this part of the *Discourse* is far from being either clear or convincing.

Now, in the essay which we are considering, Mill does an unconscious injustice to Professor Sedgwick, albeit we must confess that the latter's friends were largely to blame for the misunderstanding. In short, he seems to assume throughout that the *Discourse* is a philosophical disquisition, and that it is to be criticised accordingly. This will perhaps partly account for the unfortunate tone of the essay, even of the part which directly refers to Paley, and with which alone we are here concerned. Mill says : " Of Paley's work, though it possesses in a high degree some minor merits, we think, on the whole, meanly ".[1] One reason for this, perhaps, is, that Mill appreciates Paley's position as little, or almost as little, as Professor Sedgwick himself had done. For instance, he says : " In the first place, he does not consider utility as itself the source of moral obligation, but as a mere index to the will of God, which he regards as the ultimate groundwork of all morality, and the origin of its binding force. . . . The only view of the connection between religion and morality which does not annihilate the very idea of the latter, is that which considers the Deity as not making, but recognising and sanctioning, moral obligation." [2]

The first sentence quoted would seem to indicate that, according to Paley, morality is essentially arbitrary in its character—depending ultimately upon the mere will of God.

---

[1] See *Dissertations and Discussions* (first ed.), vol. I., p. 114.
[2] See *ibid.*, p. 125.

This is a point which we have already discussed in connection with Gay's *Dissertation*, which Paley follows here exactly. According to the selfish theory of moral action, complete obligation could indeed come only from the will of God, because God alone has it in His power to provide adequate rewards and punishments. But it was precisely the point of the argument of both Gay and Paley, to show that the will of God was *not* arbitrary in this case, but rather that the Divine Being was necessarily determined to will that human beings should perform such actions as would be conducive to the greatest happiness of all—which alone, according to their view, could be regarded as the true Good. Their idea of the objective end of all moral action was precisely the same as that of Mill himself,[1] the difference between their position and his being, of course, that they depended to a large extent upon supernatural sanctions, the belief in which seemed to Mill, on the other hand, worse than useless. In the last chapter, we saw that Bentham, at any rate, had no logical objection to urge against the Theological Utilitarians on this point. Mill, on the contrary, seems already to assert the existence of a certain degree of altruism as the necessary foundation of morality. What is implicit here, becomes perfectly explicit in his later teaching.

Mill further objects to Paley that throughout his conclusions are the starting-point of his premises. " His book is one of a class which has since become very numerous, and is likely to become still more so—an apology for commonplace. . . . He took the doctrines of practical morals which he found current." [2] A little further on, Mill adds : " If he had started from any other principle, we have as little doubt that he would have arrived at the very same conclusions ". This arraignment is by no means so serious as the writer seems to suppose. If Paley began by accepting the notions of morality which were almost universally current in his time, and attempted to rationalise them, he did what any moralist in a

---

[1] Mill saw his mistake later.  *Cf. ibid.*, pp. 345, 346 ; also vol. II., p. 455.
[2] See p. 128.

similar position should do. The corrective use of Ethics must
come later. Whether or not one is a reformer by nature and
education, it is dangerous to begin with an eccentric morality
of one's own. It may very well be true that, if Paley had
'started from any other principle,' he would have reached
the 'same conclusions'. We have no reason to assume, however, that the 'conclusions' were not his honest convictions
with regard to what things were right and what wrong. If
our concrete notions of right and wrong were as likely to
waver or to change as our purely theoretical views concerning
a possible science of Ethics, the case would be a serious one
indeed. In short, as we saw at the beginning of this chapter,
the acceptance of Hedonism, whether theological or non-theological, does not by any means commit one for or against any
of the radical views with regard to government and society
which appealed to Mill so strongly at this time.

We have allowed ourselves to say of this essay that it reads,
for the most part, 'like a mere apology for the position of
Bentham'. To Mill himself such a characterisation would
doubtless have seemed unjust. In the *Autobiography* he says:
" And here, I imagined, was an opportunity of at the same
time repelling an unjust attack, and inserting into my defence
of Hartleianism and Utilitarianism a number of the opinions
which constituted my view of those subjects, as distinguished
from that of my old associates. In this I partially succeeded,
though my relation to my father would have made it painful
to me in any case, and impossible in a Review for which he
wrote, to speak out my whole mind on the subject at this
time." [1] The last sentence quoted is particularly significant.
Though nearly thirty years of age, and a writer for serious
periodicals during almost half of this time, Mill was not yet
in a position to say quite what he thought, or all that he
believed, for fear of calling down upon his head the paternal
wrath. This is not said in any spirit of ridicule. On the
whole, the younger Mill was right, even apart from his filial
feelings. He was obliged constantly to co-operate with his

[1] See p. 201.

father, not only in the daily work of the India Office, but in the reform movement which they both had so much at heart. Any breach between them would have been a serious matter, from a public no less than a private point of view. How great this restraining influence really was, may be surmised by those who will take the trouble to compare this essay with the one on Bentham (1838), which was published two years after James Mill's death, and to which we shall almost immediately proceed.

But, before leaving this essay on the *Discourse*, it is fair to ask: Where are we to look for those 'new opinions' of Mill, which distinguished him from his former associates? The mere fact that the young writer, with his wider interests and sympathies, now and again expressed himself as neither Bentham nor James Mill would have done, is not to the point, for we are here concerned merely with abstract ethical theory. There is, however, one divergence from the older 'greatest happiness' theory which is of real, and even considerable, importance. This is with regard to the motive of the moral agent. Unfortunately, Mill is not quite fair to Professor Sedgwick here. He says: "The remainder of Mr. Sedgwick's argument — if argument it can be called — is a perpetual *ignoratio elenchi*. He lumps up the principle of utility—which is a theory of right and wrong—with the theory, if there be such a theory, of the universal selfishness of mankind. We never know, for many sentences together, which of the two he is arguing against; he never seems to know it himself. He begins a sentence on the one, and ends it on the other. In his mind they seem to be one and the same." [1]

As against many anti-Utilitarian writers of the present day, this would be perfectly legitimate and most damaging criticism; but Professor Sedgwick was hardly to be blamed for connecting the Utilitarian doctrine with the selfish theory of moral action, for this latter had been as strongly insisted upon by Bentham as by Paley, and, indeed, in quite as offensive

[1] See *Dissertations*, vol. I., p. 154.

terms.   Mill was quite right in refusing to follow his immediate predecessors in this matter, but at any rate he ought to have given due notice of the fact.   It must have been rather provoking to Professor Sedgwick and his friends, that Mill should blame him for not making a distinction which—except by Hume (in the second form of his theory) and by Hartley (whose treatment of Ethics had been too confused to influence his immediate successors)—had never been clearly made up to this time by prominent writers on the Utilitarian side.

The essay on Bentham (1838) [1] is, in every way, far more important than that which we have just been considering. For one at all acquainted with the history of English Ethics, and, in particular, with Bentham's writings, it is perhaps the very best introduction to Mill's own system.   With all its remarkable qualities, however, this essay is rather a strange production.   One is not surprised that it should have puzzled and irritated both friends and enemies.   While professing, and doubtless intending, to put Bentham on a very high pedestal, Mill in reality proved himself a most dangerous idol-breaker.   He begins by characterising Bentham as " the great *subversive*, or, in the language of continental philosophers, the great *critical*, thinker of his age and country," —' the great questioner of things established '.   But Bentham's positive qualities, according to Mill, were even more important.    Though not a ' great philosopher,' he was a ' great reformer in philosophy,' one of the ' great teachers and permanent intellectual ornaments of the human race '. This is a very large claim.   How is it established?   It seems that Bentham " introduced into morals and politics those habits of thought and modes of investigation, which are essential to the idea of science ; and the absence of which made those departments of inquiry, as physics had been before Bacon [*sic*], a field of interminable discussion, leading to no result ".[2]   But more particularly : " Bentham's method may

[1] *London and Westminster Review*, August, 1838.
[2] See *Dissertations*, vol. I., pp. 339 *et seq.*

be shortly described as the method of detail; of treating wholes by separating them into their parts," etc.   If it be asked whether this method was after all so very original, Mill replies : " Whatever originality there was in the method—in the subjects he applied it to, and in the rigidity with which he adhered to it, there was the greatest.   Hence his interminable classifications.   Hence his elaborate demonstrations of the most acknowledged truths."   Those who are at all familiar with Bentham's ' interminable classifications ' (often enough on no apparent logical or psychological principle) and his ' elaborate demonstrations ' of the commonplace, will hardly agree that it is here that we must look for the secret of his strength.

In truth, as Mill admits : " The generalities of his philosophy itself have little or no novelty : to ascribe any to the doctrine that general utility is the foundation of morality, would imply great ignorance of the history of philosophy, of general literature, and of Bentham's own writings.   He derived the idea, as he says himself, from Helvetius ; and it was the doctrine no less, of the religious philosophers of that age, prior to Reid and Beattie.   We never saw an abler defence of the doctrine of utility than in a book written in refutation of Shaftesbury, and now little read — Brown's *Essays on the Characteristics.* . . .   In all ages of philosophy, one of its schools has been utilitarian—not only from the time of Epicurus, but long before.   It was by mere accident that this opinion became connected in Bentham with his peculiar method." [1]   But, as if to bewilder the reader completely, Mill adds two or three pages further on : " This [peculiar method of Bentham's], which he calls the exhaustive method, is as old as philosophy itself.   Plato owes everything to it, and does everything by it ; " etc.   In short, this ' great re-

---

[1] See *ibid.*, pp. 345, 346.   *Cf.* with Mill's previous remarks on Paley, whose system is practically the same as that of Brown.   See also a passage in the essay on Whewell (*Dissertations*, vol. II., p. 455), where Mill speaks of several writers, " all of whom, as explicitly as Bentham, laid down the doctrine that utility is the foundation of morals ".

former of philosophy' was such, not because he had anything
in Ethics really new to impart, for hedonism is as old as
philosophy; but rather by virtue of his peculiar method, that
of ' detail '—which, in turn, is acknowledged to be as old as
philosophy, or at least as old as Plato. The novelty, apparently, consisted merely in applying this ' exhaustive method '
to the problems of morals and legislation as they appeared
to the hedonist. Apart from rhetoric, this apparently means
that Bentham insisted upon a more definite treatment of particular legal or ethical problems than was common among his
contemporaries. So far he was undoubtedly in the right, and,
as Mill points out, exercised a salutary influence upon his
opponents as well as upon his followers. But can we agree
that this constitutes him a ' great reformer' in moral philosophy? In truth, method has been a sort of fetish throughout a large part of the development of modern, as well as of
ancient, philosophy. The really important question with regard to any particular philosopher is not : What method has
he followed? but : What has he actually accomplished, or put
others in the way of accomplishing, by virtue of his method?

When Mill tries to answer the question, as to what Bentham
did thus actually accomplish, he concedes almost everything
that Bentham's bitterest opponents would need to claim. He
very properly remarks that the success of one who attempts
the adequate treatment of Ethics " will be proportional to two
things : the degree in which his own nature and circumstances
furnish him with a correct and complete picture of man's
nature and circumstances; and his capacity of deriving light
from other minds ".[1] In the last respect, he admits that Bentham was lamentably deficient. " His writings contain few
traces of the accurate knowledge of any schools of thinking
but his own; and many proofs of his entire conviction that
they could teach him nothing worth knowing. For some of
the most illustrious of previous thinkers, his contempt was
unmeasured." All ethical theories differing from his own,
he dismissed as ' vague generalities '. Mill very suggestively

---

[1] See pp. 350 *et seq.*

emarks : " He did not heed, or rather the nature of his mind prevented it from occurring to him, that these generalities contained the whole unanalysed experience of the human race ". And then Mill proceeds to show, in an admirable passage too long to be quoted, that he who thus neglects, not only the speculations of previous moralists, but 'the general opinion of mankind' on moral subjects, cannot take even the first necessary step toward a truly objective treatment of Ethics.

One of the two most important qualifications for a moral philosopher, then, Bentham utterly lacked, according to his former disciple. Did he possess the other qualification? Was he able, from the completeness of his own experience and from sympathy with the many sides of human nature, to make up what he lost by this ignorant contempt for previous thinkers? No, we are told : " In many of the most natural and strongest feelings of human nature he had no sympathy ; from many of its graver experiences he was altogether cut off ; and the faculty by which one mind understands a mind different from itself, and throws itself into the feelings of that other mind, was denied him by his deficiency of imagination ".[1] His knowledge of human nature was not only wholly empirical, but with " the empiricism of one who has had little experience. . . . Other ages and other nations were a blank to him for purposes of instruction. . . . His own lot was cast in a generation of the leanest and barrenest men whom England had yet produced ; and he was an old man when a better race came in with the present century. He saw accordingly in man little but what the vulgarest eye can see ; recognised no diversities of character but such as he who runs may read." And again : " Nothing is more curious than the absence of recognition in any of his writings of the existence of conscience, as a thing distinct from philanthropy, from affection for God or man, and from self-interest in this world or in the next ". But even this is not all. Not only does he overlook the moral part of man's nature, in the strict sense of the term, the desire of perfection or the feeling of an accusing

[1] See pp. 353 *et seq.*

conscience; "he but faintly recognises, as a fact of human nature, the pursuit of any other ideal end for its own sake". The 'sense of honour,' 'love of beauty,' 'love of order,' 'love of power,' 'love of action'—"none of these powerful constituents of human nature are thought worthy of a place among the 'Springs of Action'".

Such was Bentham's theory of the world. What will it accomplish for Ethics? Mill says: "It will do nothing for the conduct of the individual, beyond prescribing some of the more obvious dictates of worldly prudence, and outward probity and beneficence".[1] That very important part of Ethics, moral 'self-education,' is left out entirely. As regards one's attitude toward society, "a moralist on Bentham's principles may get as far as this, that he ought not to slay, burn, or steal"; but, apparently, not much further. Such a doctrine "will enable a society which has attained a certain state of spiritual development, and the maintenance of which in that state is otherwise provided for, to prescribe the rules by which it may protect its material interests. It will do nothing (except sometimes as an instrument in the hands of a higher doctrine) for the spiritual interests of society; nor does it suffice of itself even for the material interests." In short, Bentham's philosophy can only "teach the means of organising and regulating the merely *business* part of the social arrangements. . . . He committed the mistake of supposing that the business part of human affairs was the whole of them; all at least that the legislator and the moralist had to do with." Bentham's services in the field of Jurisprudence and of practical reform are spoken of in the last part of the essay at considerable length and with (at least partly) deserved appreciation; but Mill has already allowed himself to say what is manifestly true, and what takes away much from the force of his eulogium. "A philosophy of laws and institutions, not founded on a philosophy of national character, is an absurdity. But what could Bentham's opinion be worth on national character? How could he, whose mind contained so few and

[1] See pp. 363 *et seq.*

so poor types of individual character, rise to that higher generalisation?" [1]

This essay has been noticed at such length, and, as far as possible, reproduced in Mill's own words, for two reasons. First, in spite of its simple, though partly unconscious, severity, it is in the main a perfectly just criticism. At the present day, two generations after this essay was published, many of the criticisms are such as would be almost sure to occur to a writer on ethical theory ; but it has seemed best not to weaken the force of the criticisms by putting them in terms of the commonplace of current ethical discussion. What Mill has done once for all, does not need to be done again in a necessarily far less satisfactory manner. Secondly, as already said, this essay is perhaps the very best introduction to Mill's own system, seeing that some of the most important of Mill's own contributions to Ethics may be directly deduced from it. One might even say that, just as Mill here cuts himself loose from the narrow and partisan traditions of Benthamism proper, so the hedonism of the nineteenth century here takes final leave of much that was most characteristic of the hedonism of the eighteenth century. This is not to say that Mill himself founded a new school. From beginning to end, he met with serious, and (from the point of view of logical consistency) sometimes well-grounded, opposition from the Utilitarians of his own generation. But he did something far better than found a new school ; he raised the whole plane of ethical discussion, and did much to show what the points at issue really were. The hedonists, on the one hand, finally took the trouble to try to understand their opponents, while, on the other hand, it gradually dawned upon the opponents of hedonism, that the stock arguments against Paley and Bentham would not suffice against Utilitarianism in its regenerated form.

Mill's essay on Coleridge (1840) [2] should always be read in connection with the one on Bentham, though greatly in-

---

[1] See p. 366.
[2] *London and Westminster Review*, March, 1840.

ferior to that in most respects. The weakness of the essay
may be described in a word: it is an external criticism from
beginning to end, by one who regarded Coleridge merely as
the typical conservative, as opposed to Bentham, the typical
progressive philosopher. This conveniently shows how
dangerous it is to estimate a philosophical method by its real
or supposed practical consequences. In respect to practical
reforms, Bentham was indeed for, as Coleridge was against,
many innovations; but when we consider how the two stand
with regard to the development of speculation in England,
we find that Mill's estimate is almost the exact contrary of
what we would now probably agree in regarding as the truth.
Though neither was strictly an original philosopher—though,
in fact, there is very little propriety in calling Bentham a
philosopher at all—the type of Utilitarianism for which Bentham stood was certainly the logical result of the whole previous development of English Empiricism; while Coleridge, if
he originated little, did much to bring his countrymen to
understand and appreciate those German modes of thought
which, for better or for worse, were destined to change the
whole face of English philosophy in little less than two
generations. In short, if Coleridge was a reactionary in his
views on Church and State, he was to some extent a prophet
of the future in his rejection of the traditional English Empiricism and his (not always critical) acceptance of German
methods in philosophy; while Bentham's treatment of Ethics
(in which alone he enters the field of philosophy proper) may
almost be regarded as the *reductio ad absurdum* of English
Empiricism working, not only in opposition to, but in practical ignorance of, the principles of the Critical Philosophy.

But if Mill's criticism of Coleridge is unsatisfactory,[1] in
that he failed to appreciate the real significance of Coleridge's

---

[1] In the last part of the essay, Mill makes the rather peculiar confession that,
"of Coleridge as a moral and religious philosopher (the character which he
presents most prominently in his principal works), there is neither room, nor
would it be expedient for us to speak more than generally ". (See *Dissertations*,
vol. I., p. 458.)

position in the English philosophy of the day, one can find no fault whatever with the tone of the essay which we are examining. It is more than courteous throughout, and, so far as the writer's intentions are concerned, appreciative. Indeed, there are passages which almost surprise one by what is conceded to the opposite school. This may have been partly due to Mill's early, and somewhat intimate, acquaintance with Frederick Maurice and John Sterling, both of whom were, of course, very decidedly under the influence of Coleridge. In the *Autobiography*, Mill admits that both of these young men had been of ' considerable use ' to his development, while he says of the latter : " With Sterling I soon became very intimate, and was more attached to him than I have ever been to any other man ".[1] For Mill, then, Coleridge was the great awakener of the spirit of philosophy " within the bounds of traditional opinions ".[2] Bentham had asked of every doctrine : Is it true ? Coleridge asks : What does it mean ? Both types of mind are necessary, if there is to be intellectual or spiritual progress. " Whoever could master the premises and combine the methods of both, would possess the entire English philosophy of his age." [3] The great danger in philosophy is that one will mistake a part of the truth for the whole. As the French Eclectics held, in controversies both sides are apt to be right in what they affirm, wrong in what they deny.

This frank recognition of the claims of a thoughtful conservatism is especially significant, when we remember what had been the early formative influences in Mill's case. Unlike his father and Bentham, he saw clearly that if we would improve upon the past, we must begin by understanding it, and by learning from it. In this connection, Mill pays a very high compliment to what he calls the ' Germano-Coleridgean ' school. He says : " They were the first (except a solitary thinker here and there) who inquired with any comprehensiveness or depth, into the inductive laws of the existence and growth of human society. . . . They thus produced, not a piece

---

[1] See *Autobiography*, p. 154.
[2] See *Dissertations*, vol. I., pp. 393 *et seq.*　　　[3] *Ibid.*, p. 397.

of party advocacy, but a philosophy of society, in the only form in which it is yet possible, that of a philosophy of history; not a defence of particular ethical or religious doctrines, but a contribution, the largest made by any class of thinkers, towards the philosophy of human culture." [1]

If Mill is to be criticised here, it must certainly be for conceding, not too little, but too much to those who had attempted to formulate a Philosophy of History. Indeed, as criticism of the school of thought which he is examining, this is not calculated to impress the reader; but, considered from another point of view, it is most important for those who would understand the difference between the new Utilitarianism (which practically dates from these earlier writings of Mill) and the old. The older form of the doctrine had been abstract in the extreme. Man had been considered as an isolated unit, moved in all respects by considerations of his own pleasure-pain, which, of course, made his social relations extraneous. This was, indeed, the natural view for those who started from, and throughout depended upon, the analytical method. But writers like Mill began to see that morality, like everything else, had had a development; that there were 'laws of permanence' and 'laws of progress' for society: and that our theorising in Ethics, in order to be sound, must be based upon at least a general comprehension of these laws.

This transition from the abstract to the (at least partially) concrete method of treatment was of the greatest importance for Utilitarianism. It is true that the doctrine rapidly lost much of its original simplicity, that many of its defenders, prominently Mill himself, fell into more or less palpable contradictions; but the compensations were great. More and more the doctrine came into touch with the historical and with the truly scientific spirit; more and more it was made to square with the moral consciousness; and if the result does not seem to most of us to have been a triumph for the

[1] See p. 425.

doctrine itself, it has certainly been to advance ethical theory, and to show that the original hard and fast distinction between hedonistic and non-hedonistic theory was based upon a misconception. In short, we have learned as much from Mill and his successors as from their antagonists, that, if we would know the truth about Ethics, we must go back to Bishop Butler, and base our theory, not upon one side of human nature, but upon human nature as a whole.

That this interest in what he was content to call by the rather vague name ' Philosophy of History ' was by no means a passing phase in Mill's own intellectual development, is shown by several of his best known essays published shortly after that on Coleridge, *viz.*, *M. de Toqueville on Democracy in America* (published later in 1840), *Michelet's History of France* (1844), and *Guizot's Essays and Lectures on History* (1845). It would be quite aside from our purpose to examine these essays at all in detail, but a few things may properly be noted. While Mill regards England as decidedly behind the continent in the scientific writing of history (though he has the most cordial, and, indeed, somewhat uncritical, praise for Carlyle's *French Revolution*), it is evidently the current historical literature of France, rather than of Germany, with which he is thoroughly acquainted at first hand. This takes away something from the force of his frank preference for the current French histories. Mill recognises three stages [1] in the evolution of historical method: (1) the naïve stage, which is characterised by constantly reading present conceptions into the past; (2) the merely accurate stage, which describes the facts as nearly as possible as they were, but without entering at all elaborately into the causes of progress or decadence; and (3) the ' scientific ' stage, where these causes are themselves subjected to the most thorough investigation. It is this third stage that the author has generally in mind when he speaks of the ' Philosophy of History,' though he hardly uses the term with perfect consistency. If these essays con-

[1] See *Dissertations*, vol. II., pp. 124 *et seq.*

tain little or nothing that is strictly original, and nothing directly applying to Ethics, it is certainly interesting to find the late disciple of Bentham making clear to his countrymen, as Michelet and others (not holding a brief for the Church) had made clear in their historical writings, how enormous had been the debt of Europe during the Middle Ages to the Catholic Church. Hardly less interesting is it when, in the essay on Guizot, he says that, when the history of the Middle Ages comes to be adequately treated, it will be universally recognised " that at no period of history was human intellect more active, or society more unmistakably in a state of rapid advance, than during a great part of the so much vilified feudal period ".[1] Plainly Mill is no longer under the spell of the eighteenth century.

In speaking of the later essays mentioned above, we have left unmentioned the fact that, as the reader will remember, Mill's *System of Logic* had been published in 1843. The sixth book of the *Logic*, which appears to have been written in 1840, dealt with the " Logic of the Moral Sciences ". This will call for careful consideration later, but first it will be desirable to notice Mill's well-known essay, *Dr. Whewell on Moral Philosophy* (1852).[2] This is quite different in tone from the essays which had immediately preceded it. For the most part, those had been decidedly appreciative of tendencies of thought very different from those to which the author had been subjected in childhood and early youth ; and, if the essay on Coleridge is hardly a success as a sympathetic study, it is at least a good deal more conciliatory in tone than the one on Bentham, which had been published in the same periodical (*London and Westminster Review*) two years before. In this essay on Whewell, it must be confessed that Mill's tolerance breaks down. This may have been partly due to the fact that his marriage with Mrs. Taylor had taken place the year before, and that her influence here, as certainly later, had been in the direction of confirming

---

[1] See *Dissertations*, vol. II., p. 273.
[2] *Westminster Review*, October, 1852.

him in the earlier and more uncompromising form of his doctrine. But it should also be remembered that Whewell's writings were specially calculated to arouse a polemical attitude in a critic belonging to the Utilitarian school, for, doubtless without in the least intending it, he had managed to give his contemporaries a lamentably warped and distorted notion of what Utilitarianism really was.

With most of Mill's particular criticisms of Whewell, we are, of course, not here concerned; but two of them have an important bearing upon the general question as to the end of moral action, and so demand notice. Whewell had allowed himself, in a rather rhetorical passage, to use some very characteristic question-begging epithets. As Mill says: " He appropriates to his own side of the question all the expressions, such as conscience, duty, rectitude, with which the reverential feelings of mankind towards moral ideas are associated. . . . Dr. Whewell is assuming to himself what belongs quite as rightfully to his antagonists. We are as much for conscience, duty, rectitude, as Dr. Whewell. The terms, and all the feelings connected with them, are as much a part of the ethics of utility as of that of intuition. The point in dispute is, what acts are the proper objects of those feelings; whether we ought to take the feelings as we find them, as accident or design has made them, or whether the tendency of actions to promote happiness affords a test to which the feelings of morality should conform. In the same spirit, Dr. Whewell announces it as *his* opinion, as the side *he* takes in this great controversy, ' that we must do what is right, at whatever cost of pain and loss'. As if this were not everybody's opinion: as if it was not the very meaning of the word right. The matter in debate is, what *is* right, not whether what is right ought to be done. Dr. Whewell represents his opponents as denying an identical proposition, in order that he may claim a monopoly of high principle for his own opinions. The same unfairness pervades the whole phraseology." [1]

It cannot be too strongly insisted that, while Mill expresses

[1] See *Dissertations*, vol. II., pp. 459, 460.

himself with perhaps needless emphasis, he is perfectly right here, not only as against Whewell, but as against the question-begging procedure of many later anti-hedonistic writers. The facts of our moral experience are what they are; their explanation is quite a different matter.    Since our principal interest here is historical, however, it may be well to pause a moment in order to see how it was possible that contemporary writers of such undoubted intellectual eminence as Mill and Whewell should be at issue on so seemingly simple a matter. The fact is, that the Utilitarianism which Mill is here upholding is something quite different from the narrower Utilitarianism of the preceding generation, to which (hardly with justice) Whewell had continued to direct his criticisms.    It is broader and deeper, more in touch with the ordinary moral and religious consciousness.    But there was some excuse for the Utilitarians of the earlier generation, if they were inclined to look a little askance at the vocabulary of conventional ethical discussion, inasmuch as these very terms were being constantly thrust in their faces, as if they were in themselves conclusive arguments against any attempt at a scientific explanation of the moral life.

Not less suggestive than the preceding, is Mill's answer to Whewell's contention that Utilitarianism must fall to the ground, because we cannot calculate *all* the consequences of any action.    This, unfortunately, is too long to be quoted at large; but the general line of argument may be gathered from the following.    "If Dr. Whewell can point out any department of human affairs in which we can do *all* that would be desirable, he will have found something new.    But because we cannot foresee everything, is there no such thing as foresight? . . . Dr. Whewell, in his zeal against the morality of consequences, commits the error of proving too much. Whether morality is or is not a question of consequences, he cannot deny that prudence is; and, if there is such a thing as prudence, it is because the consequences of actions *can* be calculated.    Prudence, indeed, depends on a calculation of consequences of individual actions, while for the establishment of moral rules it is only necessary to calculate the consequences of classes of actions—a much easier matter." [1] But if it be urged that, even so, Utilitarian morality seems to admit of possible exceptions to its own general rules, Mill shows that it is in no worse case than other forms of ethical theory.   He says: "That the moralities arising from the special circumstances of the action may be so important as to overrule those arising from the class of acts to which it belongs, perhaps to take it out of the category of virtues into that of crimes, or *vice versâ*, is a liability common to all ethical systems".[2]

What Mill says here is quite true, but he might easily have made his case even stronger.   An ethical writer who shuts his eyes to the evident fact, that a conscientious moral agent is sometimes confronted with duties, both of the highest order, which apparently conflict, hardly deserves the attention of any serious reader.   And yet there is a manifest tendency, even at the present time, for non-hedonistic writers to point triumphantly to these concrete difficulties of the moral life (which, of course, may be distressing in the extreme to a really conscientious person), as if, in themselves, such difficulties were a refutation of Utilitarianism.   Nothing could be more ridiculously unfair.   The difficulties just referred to, be it observed, are practical before they are theoretical — *i.e.*, the question *what* is right in this particular case arises before the question *why* is the one action or the other right.   The theoretical difficulty, therefore, arises for any system of Ethics which attempts to explain our moral life.   To say that these difficulties of actual moral experience are not difficulties for one's own particular type of ethical theory, is in itself enough to condemn the theory utterly.   In cases like those just mentioned, is the Self-realisation theory, *e.g.*, one whit better off than Utilitarianism?   Certainly not.   The question of 'more' or 'less,' 'whole' or 'part,' is much more extensive than that of the hedonistic calculus.   If it is difficult, in these

---

[1] See *Dissertations*, vol. II., pp. 473, 474.        [2] See p. 477.

hopelessly perplexing cases, to say which of two possible courses of action will bring more happiness to the greater number, is it easier to say which conduces more to self-realisation? Merely to put the question, is to answer it.

But while there is no logical justification for using against Utilitarianism the practical difficulties of our moral life—which are bound to remain difficulties for any form of ethical theory worthy of the name—there is an historical explanation for this still prevailing tendency, which is rather interesting. In spite of the undoubted variety of ethical theory which appears in the course of the development of English Ethics, the perennial conflict, almost down to the time that we are considering, had been between the various forms of Intuitionism and those of Hedonism. Now the earlier Intuitionism tended to refer back to a few convenient 'first principles,' and discoun· explanations; while Utilitarianism, with all its faults and weaknesses, which certainly were many, did try to provide explanations. The result was that the 'burden of proof' was constantly shifted to the side of the Utilitarian. If he could not explain away the difficulties outstanding, then Intuitionism was supposed to hold the field. In the past two generations, we have pretty generally outgrown this naïve method of argument (which the present writer would by no means attribute to thoughtful Intuitionists of the present day), seeing that it is generally admitted, that it is incumbent on one form of ethical theory not less than another to offer explanations that shall be satisfactory to the scientific intelligence.

# CHAPTER XI.

HAVING traced the development of Mill's views on Ethics, by means of the *Autobiography* and his contributions to various periodicals, from his first stage of enthusiastic Benthamism to what proved his relatively permanent, if not strictly final, position, we are now prepared to give careful attention to his later writings, which, though in no case amounting to a systematic treatment of Ethics, have at least the substantial advantage of being constructive and not merely critical. And first we have to notice Book VI. of his *System of Logic*, "On the Logic of the Moral Sciences". Here, indeed, as regards the chronological order, we have to retrace our steps. In the last chapter, it seemed best to include our mention of the essays on Michelet (1844), Guizot (1845), and Whewell's *Moral Philosophy* (1852), in order that the critical essays, later as well as earlier, might be considered together. The sixth book of the *Logic* was probably written in 1840, *i.e.*, in the same year as the essays on Coleridge and De Toqueville. The *Logic* was not published, however, till 1843, and we shall use the text of the standard eighth edition (1872).

Mill begins his treatment of the "Logic of the Moral Sciences" by remarking that, while we are practically agreed as to the method of investigation to be employed where the physical nature of man is concerned, this is by no means the case where the laws of mind, and especially those of society, are in question. In truth, it is even a matter of controversy whether these are capable of strictly scientific treatment.

But if we are really in earnest with these sciences, true scientific method must be applied here also; and general scientific method is always one and the same thing. Now, Mill says, "at the threshold of this inquiry we are met by an objection, which, if not removed, would be fatal to the attempt to treat human conduct as a subject of science. Are the actions of human beings, like all other natural events, subject to invariable laws?" [1]

This, of course, raises the whole controversy concerning the freedom of the will, which, from at least the time of Pelagius, has divided both the philosophical and the religious world. We find one side holding the doctrine of necessity, which regards human volitions and actions as necessary and inevitable; while the other side "maintains that the will is not determined, like other phenomena, by antecedents, but determines itself; that our volitions are not, properly speaking, the effects of causes, or at least have no causes which they uniformly and implicitly obey".[2] Mill complains of the misleading terms in which these doctrines are commonly set forth; and, in particular, he objects to the use of the word 'necessity,' as standing for determinism. Correctly understood, the doctrine called 'Philosophical Necessity' is merely this: that if we could know perfectly the motives present in the agent's mind, and also his character and disposition, we would be able to predict his action in a given case, just as we would be able to predict any physical event, if we could know all the conditions. Now our assurance of this does not conflict in the slightest degree with our 'feeling of freedom,' so constantly appealed to in this controversy. We may be free, and yet it may be practically certain to those who know us best, how we will use our freedom in a given case. And if this be true in the simpler cases, why would it not also be found true in the more complex ones, if only the observer could have an adequate knowledge of the character and circumstances?

Thus far, as will be seen, Mill's argument is merely the con-

---

[1] See *Logic*, vol. II., p. 419.     [2] *Ibid.*, p. 421.

ventional one for determinism. At this point, however, he
attempts to silence the scruples of the libertarian in a rather
peculiar way. What really troubles the libertarian, he thinks,
is the idea of compulsion commonly associated with the idea
of causality. We feel that we are not compelled, as by some
magical force, to obey a particular motive; and we are quite
right. "But neither is any such mysterious compulsion now
supposed, by the best philosophical authorities, to be exercised by any other cause over its effect." [1] In short, reduce
the conception of causality to that of invariable sequence, and
Mill seems to think that little or nothing remains, to which
the libertarian can object. It is rather difficult to take this
quite seriously. Most certainly it is proper, when discussing
freedom of the will, to clarify our ideas as much as possible
on the general subject of causality; but the plain fact is, that
what libertarians have always mainly objected to in determinism (whether rightly or wrongly), has been the putting of
physical and mental causality on the same plane. It will
readily be seen that, however we might see fit to modify our
general conception of causality, this difficulty would remain
exactly what it was before.

Mill goes on to show, by the usual line of argument, that
determinism and fatalism are two very different doctrines;
but he rather surprises one, almost at the beginning of his
discussion, by remarking that the determinist (or 'necessi-
tarian,' as he calls him), " is apt to be, with more or less of consciousness on his part, a fatalist as to his own actions, and to
believe that his nature is such, or that his education and
circumstances have so moulded his character, that nothing can
now prevent him from feeling and acting in a particular way,
or at least that no effort of his own can hinder it ".[2] This is
not an isolated instance of the facility with which Mill can at
times confuse metaphysical issues. And in this particular
case, the effect is, quite needlessly to detract from the force
of his own argument. In short, he confuses fatalism (the

---

[1] See p. 423.        [2] See p. 425.

doctrine that what is to happen will happen, all ordinary causes to the contrary notwithstanding) with a view which he attributes to many determinists regarding the unchangeability of individual character. It has often been shown—in recent years, *e.g.*, by Fouillée [1]—that the doctrine of fatalism does not arise from too much, but from too little, attention being paid to the ascertainable causes of human actions. Now the class of determinists to which Mill refers, and which can hardly have been as large as his language would seem to indicate, were doubtless wrong in over-emphasising the 'unchangeability of character'; but this does not at all make them fatalists. They, as much as Mill himself, were in search of the ascertainable causes; they, as much as he, were prepared to admit that actual effort in opposition to the unfortunate tendencies of one's own character would have its effect: they simply made the serious mistake of exaggerating what we may call the 'inertia' of individual character.

But, while Mill's discussion is hardly satisfactory as a treatment of the metaphysical question of freedom, it throws an interesting light upon his own ethical theory, for he goes, if anything, to the extreme in his view of the extent to which we may change our own characters. He begins by very properly remarking that, while the individual's character is formed by his circumstances, " his own desire to mould it in a particular way, is one of those circumstances, and by no means one of the least influential ". And he proceeds to show that we are exactly as capable of making our own character, if we will, as others are of making it for us. Later he makes the more original remark that, " if we examine closely, we shall find that this feeling, of our being able to modify our own character *if we wish*, is itself the feeling of moral freedom which we are conscious of ". [2] And he concludes this phase of the discussion by making the following suggestive observation. " The free-will doctrine, by keep-

---

[1] See *La liberté et le déterminisme*, ch. ii.
[2] See p. 427.

ing in view precisely that portion of the truth which the word
Necessity puts out of sight, namely the power of the mind to
co-operate in the formation of its own character, has given to
its adherents a practical feeling much nearer to the truth
than has generally (I believe) existed in the minds of necessi-
tarians. The latter may have had a stronger sense of the
importance of what human beings can do to shape the characters of one another; but the free-will doctrine has, I believe,
fostered in its supporters a much stronger spirit of self-
culture."

Now what shall be said of the possibility of a science of
human nature? In the preceding discussion, according to
Mill, we have seen no reason for denying that human actions
take place according to laws. But any class of phenomena,
subject to laws, is legitimate subject-matter for a science.
The mere difficulty of ascertaining all the laws, is not as serious as might at first appear. Take the case of meteorology.
Nobody doubts that the phenomena with which this science
attempts to deal are subject to law; and the extreme complexity of the phenomena, and the resulting difficulty of ascertaining the precise nature of the particular laws involved,
does not by any means keep the scientist from making them
the object of most careful research. This, to be sure, is the
case of a very imperfect science; but we need not look
far to find a science midway between this condition of extreme imperfection and the relative perfection of the more
developed physical sciences. The theory of the tides, 'Tidology,' as Dr. Whewell proposes to call it, is a convenient
example. What depends on the attraction of the sun and
moon is perfectly understood, and the results can be accurately
predicted even tor an unknown, but definite, part of the earth's
surface. But circumstances of a local nature, like the character of the sea-bottom, the degree of confinement from
shores, the prevailing direction of the winds, etc., come in to
complicate. These can be partly calculated and allowed for,
but not completely, with the result that the actual tides in
given places do not precisely agree with our predictions.

Still the approximation is sufficient to make 'Tidology' not only a science, like meteorology, but a science largely available in practice, as meteorology has not (or in Mill's day had not yet) become.

Now this is all that is, or should be, meant by sciences that are not 'exact sciences'. Once having admitted that human actions are conformable to law, there is no reason why the science of human nature should not, in time, become as much of a science as 'Tidology'. And one thing should never be forgotten. Even if the science of human nature could conceivably become perfect, which is absurd, certain prediction could be made only on the basis of complete data in the given case, which, of course, we never can have. We must not, therefore, underrate the probable usefulness of this proposed science, which, for obvious reasons, must to the end remain imperfect. Mill says: "An approximate generalisation is, in social inquiries, for most practical purposes equivalent to an exact one: that which is only probable when asserted of individual human beings indiscriminately selected, being certain when affirmed of the character and collective conduct of masses".[1]

After giving a brief outline of his own psychological views, which need not detain us, since it consists merely in the reaffirmation of the general principles of the traditional Associationist school (particularly as represented by James Mill's *Analysis of the Phenomena of the Human Mind*), Mill passes on to a consideration of 'Ethology,' the proposed new 'science of the formation of character'. And first he calls attention to what he has already, when treating of induction, had occasion to call 'empirical laws'. Such a law is "an uniformity, whether of succession or of coexistence, which holds true in all instances within our limits of observation, but is not of a nature to afford any assurance that it would hold beyond those limits".[2] General observations on human affairs, collected from common experience, are precisely of this nature. The really scientific truths which we are seek-

[1] See p. 434.     [2] See p. 448.

ing, however, are not these 'empirical laws,' but the causal laws which explain them. The 'empirical laws,' in fact, are at best almost always a more or less vague statement of the complex result of the operation of two or more laws of the scientific kind.

What, then, is the proper method of investigation for Ethology? Nobody who realises the extreme complexity of the phenomena to be explained can be seriously in doubt. Taken by itself, the inductive method would be almost useless, by reason of the amount of material to be treated and the resulting confusion. The deductive method, surely, which sets out from general laws (in this case, those of mind), and verifies their consequences by specific experience, is alone applicable. In fact, there are but two methods of discovering the laws of nature, the deductive method just mentioned and that of experimentation. But experimentation is obviously impossible here, and, if possible, experiments could not be performed with any approach to scientific accuracy. The deductive method, then, is our only resource. Mill says: " The laws of the formation of character are, in short, derivative laws, resulting from the general laws of mind ; and are to be obtained by deducing them from those general laws ; by supposing any given set of circumstances, and then considering what, according to the laws of mind, will be the influence of those circumstances on the formation of character ".[1] This new science, then, is to be called Ethology, or the Science of Character. It is the science which corresponds to the art of education in the widest sense, including the formation of national or collective character, as well as individual. If the possible results in this direction are not all that could be desired, we must remember that a degree of knowledge far short of the power of actual prediction, is often of much practical value. " It is enough that we know that certain means have a *tendency* to produce a given effect, and that others have a tendency to frustrate it." [2]

---

[1] See p. 457.        [2] See p. 458.

The relation between Ethology and Psychology must always be kept clearly in mind. Mill says : " While on the one hand Psychology is altogether, or principally, a science of observation and experiment, Ethology, as I have conceived it, is, as I have already remarked, altogether deductive. The one ascertains the simple laws of Mind in general, the other traces their operation in complex combinations of circumstances. Ethology stands to Psychology in a relation very similar to that in which the various branches of natural philosophy stand to mechanics. The principles of Ethology are properly the middle principles, the *axiomata media* (as Bacon would have said) of the science of mind : as distinguished, on the one hand from the empirical laws resulting from simple observation, and on the other from the highest generalisations." [1] And, in this connection, Mill naturally quotes Bacon's famous observation, that the *axiomata media* of every science principally constitute its value.

Such, then, is the greatly needed science of Ethology, without which, in Mill's view, there can be no truly scientific Sociology. The remainder of the sixth book of the *Logic* is devoted to a criticism of what the author regards as false methods, and an elaboration of what he regards as the true method, of the latter science. But we cannot follow Mill further in this direction. As would be surmised, since Ethology is regarded as the necessary connecting-link between Psychology and Sociology, the proper method of Sociology is held to be deductive also—" not," as the author explains, " after the model of geometry, but after that of the more complex physical sciences ". [2]

It is hardly necessary to state that Mill had to give up his project of founding the new science of Ethology, and that this made impossible the further, and more considerable, task of writing a work on Sociology along the lines laid down in the last part of the sixth book of the *Logic*. Such being the ease, it may seem needless to have examined Mill's treatment

---

[1] See p. 458.  [2] See p. 488.

of the Logic of the Moral Sciences at such length. This has been done, however, for a very definite reason. It will be remembered that the first draft of the sixth book of the *Logic* was probably written in 1840, only two years after the publication of the important essay on Bentham. In that remarkable but perplexing critique, Bentham's great merit in Ethics was held to have been his attempt to apply ordinary scientific method to the subject matter of that science. It was not claimed that the net result of his attempt was specially important, but the attempt itself was regarded as little less than epoch-making. It might seem to one reading the essay on Bentham without reference to Mill's other works, that the writer was here giving rather perfunctory praise to the elder moralist, whom he felt obliged in most respects to criticise so severely. But Mill's own perfectly serious attempt in the same general direction, which we have just been considering a good deal in detail, proves conclusively the contrary. To be sure, the science of Ethology was not to be a substitute for Ethics; but it was once for all to furnish that discipline with a strictly scientific basis. And in that sense (indirectly, if not directly), Ethics was at last to come within the scope of true scientific method.

Mill's inevitable failure here was, perhaps, as instructive as success in some other direction would have been. For success in this direction was found to be impossible, not from any individual fault or weakness on the part of Mill, but from the nature of the case. Whatever, in the last analysis, Ethics may be thought to be, one may hold with perfect confidence that it is not a natural science merely, nor an art founded upon a natural science—which is as far as possible from implying that it does not need to take cognizance of all the facts of moral experience and development that can possibly be obtained. In short, Mill had not, any more than the Evolutionists later, discovered a new 'method,' which was to revolutionise Ethics. And it can hardly be thought fanciful to suggest, that the essential barrenness of the method outlined in this part of the *Logic*, and Mill's lack of success in carrying out even the initial step in constructing, at least in outline, the new science of Ethology, was one important reason why he never undertook to write a systematic treatise on Ethics.[1]

In following the development of Mill's ethical views, it seems necessary here to depart from the order of publication. The reason will appear from the following passage, taken from the 'Introductory Notice' prefixed by Miss Helen Taylor to three of Mill's essays, *Nature*, *The Utility of Religion*, and *Theism*, first published (together) in 1874, the year following Mill's death. "The two first of these three Essays were written between the years 1850 and 1858, during the period which intervened between the publication of the *Principles of Political Economy* [1848], and that of the work on *Liberty* [1859]; during which interval three other Essays—on Justice, on Utility, and on Liberty—were also composed. Of the five Essays written at that time, three have already been given to the public by the Author. That on Liberty was expanded into the now well-known work bearing the same title. Those on Justice and Utility were afterwards incorporated, with some alterations and additions, into one, and published under the name of *Utilitarianism* [1863]. The remaining two — on Nature and on the Utility of Religion—are now given to the public, with the addition of a third—on Theism—which was produced at a much later period. . . . [This last] was written between the years 1868 and 1870, but it was not designed as a sequel to the two Essays which now appear along with it, nor were they intended to appear all together." This definite statement, from one who had such exceptional opportunities to know the exact facts of the case, must be accepted as authoritative. And the information which it conveys is interesting. The essay on "Nature" and that on the "Utility of Religion" may confidently be attributed to the period dur-

---

[1] It is rather strange that this chapter was not thoroughly revised, after Mill had given up the projected science of Ethology as an impossibility.

ing which the first draft of *Liberty* and that of *Utilitarianism*
were written. Moreover, since these two essays were apparently not recast, like the others, they may properly be considered first.

When Mill wrote the essay on "Nature," he must already
have given up the project of writing a book on Ethology, for,
according to Professor Bain,[1] his disappointment in this respect was what led him to go on with the *Political Economy*,
which, as will be remembered, was published in 1848. Thus
much, at any rate, his position must have changed since the
time when he wrote the sixth book of the *Logic*. What he
seems to have proposed to himself, in writing the essay which
we are to examine, was neither to attack the defunct doctrine
of Laws of Nature, nor precisely to attack Natural Theology,
but to clear up, as far as might be, what he regarded as the
fatally ambiguous, and often question-begging, use of the
concept 'nature' in ethical speculation. How, then, is the
word 'nature' actually used in philosophical discussions?
In one definite and justifiable sense, it may be taken to mean
"the sum of all phenomena, together with the causes which
produce them; including not only all that happens, but all
that is capable of happening; the unused capabilities of causes
being as much a part of the idea of Nature, as those which
take effect".[2] But 'nature' is constantly used in a popular
sense, as opposed to that which is 'artificial'. This obviously
conflicts with the preceding (strictly scientific) definition, according to which art is as much a part of nature as anything
else, since it is a part of the universal world-process.

Such being the two principal senses of the word 'nature,'
in which sense, if either, is it used to convey ideas of commendation, approval, and even moral obligation? For that
the word is thus used, even at the present time, seems to Mill
beyond question. He says: "Though perhaps no one could
now be found who, like the institutional writers of former

---

[1] See *J. S. Mill: a Criticism*, p. 79.
[2] See *Three Essays on Religion*, p. 5.

times, adopts the so-called Law of Nature as the foundation of ethics, and endeavours consistently to reason from it, the word and its cognates must still be counted among those which carry great weight in moral argumentation ".[1]  It looks at first, indeed, as if we were confronted with another actual use of the word ' nature' at the very threshold of our investigation.  "All inquiries are either into what is, or into what ought to be: science and history belonging to the first division, art, morals, and politics to the second.  But the two senses of the word Nature first pointed out, agree in referring only to what is."  Mill does not, however, admit a third use of the word here.  He says: " Those who say that we ought to act according to Nature do not mean the mere identical proposition that we ought to do what we ought to do.  They think that the word Nature affords some external criterion of what we should do . . . they have a notion, either clearly or confusedly, that what is, constitutes the rule and standard of what ought to be." [2]  Such, then, is the view which is to be examined in the present essay.

Now, when we are told to ' follow nature' in moral conduct, is ' nature' understood in what we have called the first, or philosophical sense?  Manifestly not, for then the admonition would have no meaning.  We *must* follow nature, in this sense, whether we will or no.  The only moral precept that could be given from this point of view would be, ' study nature '; and, however, important this precept may be, it can only lead to intelligent moral action.  Right moral action, to be sure, implies this, but also a great deal more.  Clearly we have no criterion of right conduct afforded here.  But how would it be, if we should take ' nature' in the second sense, as standing for that which takes place without human intervention?  Here the precept ' follow nature ' would be worse than superfluous and unmeaning; it would be palpably absurd and self-contradictory.  Mill says: " If the artificial is not better than the natural, to what end are all the arts of life?  To dig, to

---

[1] See *Three Essays on Religion*, p. 11.        [2] See p. 13.

plough, to build, to wear clothes, are direct infringements of the injunction to follow nature. . . . All praise of Civilisation, or Art, or Contrivance, is so much dispraise of Nature; an admission of imperfection, which it is man's business, and merit, to be always endeavouring to correct or mitigate." [1]

We must evidently look further, if we would understand the real hold which this vague principle still has in the minds of thinking men. Mill argues that this principle in the last resort depends upon the view that, since nature is the work of God, we may and do find in nature distinct traces of a divine moral order, which, of course, it is our duty to imitate. Here, obviously, we come to close quarters with Natural Theology. But before proceeding further, we must divest ourselves of certain preconceptions. We are often reminded of the awe which thoughtful men feel in the presence of some of the mightier aspects of nature. This awe, however, has no strictly moral significance; in fact, we feel it most, when viewing (at a sufficient distance) the phenomena of nature which are most capable of inflicting harm upon man. After this brief warning, the author comes to close quarters with the essential question at once; and his arraignment of 'nature,' taken as a moral order, is rather striking, if somewhat rhetorical and not wholly relevant.

He says: "In sober truth, nearly all the things which men are hanged or imprisoned for doing to one another, are nature's everyday performances. Killing, the most criminal act recognised by human laws, Nature does once to every being that lives; and in a large proportion of cases, after protracted tortures such as only the greatest monsters whom we read of ever purposely inflicted on their living fellow-creatures. . . . All this, Nature does with the most supercilious disregard both of mercy and of justice, emptying her shafts upon the best and noblest indifferently with the meanest and worst; upon those who are engaged in the highest and worthiest enterprises, and often as the direct consequence of the noblest

---

[1] See pp. 20, 21.

acts; and it might almost be imagined as a punishment for them. . . . Next to taking life (equal to it according to a high authority) is taking the means by which we live; and Nature does this too on the largest scale and with the most callous indifference. A single hurricane destroys the hopes of a season; a flight of locusts, or an inundation, desolates a district; a trifling chemical change in an edible root, starves a million of people. . . . All which people are accustomed to deprecate as 'disorder' and its consequences, is precisely a counterpart of Nature's ways. Anarchy and the Reign of Terror are overmatched in injustice, ruin, and death, by a hurricane and a pestilence." [1] The argument that all things are nevertheless 'for the best,' is not applicable here; for, if we are to imitate nature, it must be the nature that we know, and not the hidden ways of a mysterious Providence. Moreover, if good sometimes comes out of evil in the natural course of things, it must not be forgotten that this is quite as often the case with human crimes; and, still further, it must be recognised that it happens as frequently that evil comes out of good. On the whole, however, good produces good, and evil, evil. 'To him that hath shall be given.'

The inevitable conclusion for Mill is, that the order of nature, as we know it, is not a moral order—or, at any rate, only partially such. If an omnipotent God can will happiness, and does will misery, there is but one legitimate conclusion. But suppose that God has willed virtue instead of happiness. Then we can only say that His purpose has been equally frustrated. The natural theologians have failed lamentably in that they have proved practically nothing by trying to prove too much. "The only admissible moral theory of Creation is that the Principle of Good *cannot* at once and altogether subdue the powers of evil, either physical or moral; . . . but could and did make [man] capable of carrying on the fight with vigour and with progressively increasing success." This is evidently said by Mill, not in irony, but in perfect good

[1] See pp. 28-31.

faith, for he goes on to show that this view, whether specula-
tively tenable or not, would really satisfy our moral nature.
He even goes so far as to add : " And I venture to assert that
such has really been, though often unconsciously, the faith
of all who have drawn strength and support of any worthy
kind from trust in a superintending Providence ".[1]

But if only a part of the order of nature, at any rate, can
be as the Divine Being intended, it becomes highly important to discover what part. It would be most natural to
point out those primitive impulsive tendencies in man which,
not altogether fortunately, have received the name ' instincts '.
Apart from the very serious difficulty of saying just what are
' instincts,' however, it remains true that nearly every respect-
able attribute of humanity is the result, not of instinct, but
of a victory over instinct. Only in a highly artificialised
condition of human nature, could the notion grow up, that
goodness was natural. Indeed, the victory over fear, one of
the most powerful emotions of human nature, shows how
artificial is the condition even of the savage. Sympathy,
though in a sense natural, requires a great deal of cultivation.
Veracity, one of the highest virtues, is plainly artificial, for all
savages are liars. And the same might be proved of all the
other virtues.

And here we come to what, for Mill, is the gist of the
whole matter. He says : " If it be said, that there must be
the germs of all these virtues in human nature, otherwise
mankind would be incapable of acquiring them, I am ready,
with a certain amount of explanation, to admit the fact. But
the weeds that dispute the ground with these beneficent germs,
are themselves not germs but rankly luxuriant growths, and
would, in all but some one case in a thousand, entirely stifle
and destroy the former, were it not so strongly the interest
of mankind to cherish the good germs in one another, that
they always do so, in as far as their degree of intelligence
(in this as in other respects still very imperfect) allows. . . .

[1] See p. 39.

Even those gifted organisations which have attained the like excellence by self-culture, owe it essentially to the same cause; for what self-culture would be possible without aid from the general sentiment of mankind delivered through books, and from the contemplation of exalted characters real or ideal? This artificially created or at least artificially perfected nature of the best and noblest human beings, is the only nature which it is ever commendable to follow." [1]  Mill concludes from the above and similar arguments, that "conformity to nature, has no connection whatever with right and wrong".[2]

If it were worth while, one could easily show that this essay is by no means a complete success as a piece of destructive criticism. Of the two senses which Mill allows to the word 'nature,' the first or 'scientific' sense is by no means a common one in actual philosophical discussions—least of all in ethical discussions—while the second meaning of the word, in which it is merely opposed to 'artificial,' is left ambiguous. If by natural, in this sense, we are to mean only what is historically aboriginal, it is easy to prove that nothing of any value in human life as we know it, particularly in the moral life, is natural. But Shaftesbury had long ago shown the absurdity of this use of the word 'natural'. In short, Mill is unconsciously unjust to the real or supposed theory which he is attempting to controvert, in his very statement of the problem; and if the theory had possessed more vitality, it would hardly have been damaged by such criticism: but there are two respects in which the essay is important, as defining the author's own point of view.

First, this is the clearest statement we have of Mill's attitude toward Natural Theology, with the exception of the essay on Theism, also published in this volume, but belonging, as already explained, to a much later period, and therefore less valuable as a commentary upon his strictly ethical writings. He maintains, as we have seen, that the order of

---

[1] See pp. 53, 54.      [2] See p. 62.

nature is not a moral order, but that, on the contrary, it abounds in what we should condemn most strongly, if we could know that it was the result of intention accompanied by absolute power. If, then, there be a God of Nature (divinely good, as we must on other grounds suppose), He must be finite, and not infinite, as the theologians feel bound to assume. In short, we must suppose that there are two conflicting powers in the world, one making for good and one making for evil. In this case, it will be our duty and privilege to ally ourselves with the beneficent power; and we can have the assurance that, however, slight our influence may be, it will really count, and count on the right side. All this is hypothetical, however; the implication seems to be that there is not a sufficient basis for even such a Natural Theology. On the other hand, it must be admitted that, if such a theory does not wholly satisfy the mind, it does satisfy the heart. There is nothing in it which, like the conventional Natural Theology, is repugnant to our highest moral ideals. In the essay on Theism, Mill's last work, he remains constant to this view as to the moral aspect of the Manichæan doctrine—which, it will be remembered, he distinctly attributes to his father in the *Autobiography*—the difference being, that in the latter essay he seems to take a good deal more seriously the general arguments for Theism.

Secondly, we must notice the bearing of this essay upon Mill's view of human nature and the possibility of moral development. This is not quite easy to state in exact terms. The author is so concerned to disprove the theory that the order of nature is essentially a moral order, that he very nearly goes to the extreme of regarding it as not merely a non-moral, but what we might call an anti-moral, order. In other words, it looks as if he regarded the great forces of nature as making for evil decidedly more than for good. But if the general conditions and efficient forces, as much in man himself as in the external world, are so strongly set against the moral order, how can any artificial process of cultivating the good and eliminating the evil in human nature, such as that which Mill describes, be regarded as sufficient? The author seems to forget that, though cultivation may accomplish much, soil and climate, and, more particularly, the original nature of the plant, are most important considerations. Moreover, if we must employ this analogy, whence did the desire to cultivate arise? In the passage above quoted, Mill has seemed to refer this to a tendency on the part of each to encourage in others conduct calculated to conduce to his own good. This was perfectly consistent with the older Utilitarianism, which admitted of an extreme separation between the objective end of moral action and the motive of the moral agent; but such a view is hardly consistent with Mill's theory, which admits a certain primitive altruistic tendency in human nature. In short, it seems as if Mill, in arguing against a somewhat naïve form of Natural Theology, has overstated his case, with results distinctly detrimental to his own ethical system.

Let us now turn to the essay on the "Utility of Religion," which, as already explained, belongs to the same period as that which we have just been considering. The purpose of this essay may be stated in a few words. If the dogmas of religion must be regarded as certainly true, the 'utility' of religion follows as a matter of course. Our eternal weal or woe depends upon our making it the guide of our lives. But in a sceptical age like our own, when the theoretical grounds of religious belief are freely investigated and by many found wanting, such an inquiry can by no means be regarded as gratuitous. Of course, it would be gratuitous, if we had passed from perfect faith to complete doubt or negation; but nobody claims that this is the case. Now in this condition of uncertainty as regards the theoretical grounds of religion, it is natural that theologians should, perhaps unconsciously, insist more and more upon the supposed fact of our absolute need of religion as a moralising power, and that they should hold that this indirectly affords a strong presumption of its truth. Mill's purpose, then, is to investigate the questions:

(1) Is religion really, at the present time, as great a moralising power as is constantly assumed ? (2) Even if so, is it the only power capable of producing the desired results.

The keynote of the whole discussion is struck in the following remark by the author. " It is usual to credit religion *as such* with the whole of the power inherent in *any* system of moral duties inculcated by education and enforced by opinion." [1] The point, of course, is, that morality has almost always been taught in connection with religion during the past, so that we cannot assume, without further argument, that an equally systematic non-religious moral education would not produce equally good results. Mill first insists upon the enormous influence of authority upon the human mind. " Authority is the evidence on which the mass of mankind believe everything which they are said to know, except facts of which their own senses have taken cognizance." But next we have to consider the power of education. This, the author confidently holds, is almost boundless. He even goes so far as to say : " There is not one natural inclination which it is not strong enough to coerce, and, if needful, to destroy by disuse ". And he immediately adds, what, of course, is most important to his argument : " In the greatest recorded victory which education has ever achieved over a whole host of natural inclinations in an entire people—the maintenance through centuries of the institutions of Lycurgus —it was very little, if even at all, indebted to religion. . . . The root of the system was devotion to Sparta, to the ideal of the country or State." If we would understand the possibility of such a phenomenon, we must try to realise the full meaning of public opinion. " The love of glory ; the love of praise ; the love of admiration ; the love of respect and deference ; even the love of sympathy, are portions of its attractive power. . . . The fear of shame, the dread of ill-repute or of being disliked or hated, are the direct and simple forms of its deterring power." Moreover, " when once the

[1] See p. 77.

means of living have been obtained, the far greater part of the remaining labour and effort which takes place on the earth has for its object to acquire the respect or the favourable regard of mankind ; to be looked up to, or at all events, not to be looked down upon by them ".[1]

Turning from this great and almost compelling force of public opinion, let us examine what is peculiar to religious teaching.  It is not without significance, Mill thinks, that preachers and religious writers are always complaining of the inconsiderable effect that religious motives have, in ordinary life, and this in spite of the tremendous penalties denounced. The plain fact of the matter is, that the vagueness of men's ideas of future retribution and their belief that, if they repent before death, they will escape punishment altogether, take away a great part of the terrors that might be expected to attach to such a doctrine.  When a strong present tempta-tion arises, therefore, it is natural that it should often prevail. But Mill does not dwell upon this aspect of the question, which he rightly terms "the vulgarest part of it".  He is more than ready to admit that the higher advocates of religion are far from regarding it as "an auxiliary to the thief-catcher and the hangman".  "In their view of the matter, the best of mankind absolutely require religion for the perfection of their own character, even though the coercion of the worst might possibly be accomplished without its aid." [2]

But just here Mill is guilty of serious, though doubtless unintentional, unfairness to his opponents.  He wrongly identifies the position which he has just stated, in terms that no one could object to, with the theory that moral truth can be revealed only by religion.  It hardly needs to be pointed out that there is no necessary connection between these views.  One may perfectly well believe—many do believe— that the essential principles of moral conduct, so far at least as our human relations are concerned, may be demonstrated quite apart from religion, and yet hold that, while religion is

---

[1] See p. 87.                    [2] See p. 95.

by no means needed as " an auxiliary to the thief-catcher and the hangman," it is of inestimable value as affording a hope, which no mere examination of the facts of human experience could wholly justify, that good will finally prevail over evil, and that the struggle itself, even when it seems to be a losing one, is not wholly in vain. Mill himself says somewhat later : ' So long as human life is insufficient to satisfy human aspirations, so long there will be a craving for higher things, which finds its most obvious satisfaction in religion ".[1]

The author admits that some Christian precepts seem to be on a higher plane than any which have preceded them. But he argues that this benefit has been gained once for all. Precepts like the ' new commandment to love one another ' have become the common property of humanity, and could only be lost by a return to primeval barbarism. Moral truths of any sort are strong enough in their own evidence to retain the belief of mankind, when once they have acquired it. The supposed supernatural character of moral truths, moreover, is a positively dangerous view in one important respect, for it keeps us from analysing and criticising our moral principles, and separating the good from the bad. At the same time, Mill admits that " the value . . . of religion to the individual, . . . as a source of personal satisfaction and of elevated feelings, is not to be disputed "; and we saw, at the end of the last paragraph, that he was capable of defining that value in most appreciative terms.

But is religion the only source of such satisfaction ? Do we, in particular, have to assume personal immortality, in order to obtain such satisfaction ? If individual life is short, that of the species is long. " Its indefinite duration is practically equivalent to endlessness; and being combined with indefinite capability of improvement, it offers to the imagination and sympathies a large enough object to satisfy any reasonable demand for grandeur of aspiration." By referring to the sentiment of disinterested devotion to the Republic,

[1] See p. 104.

which existed for many generations among the Romans, who were otherwise a selfish people, Mill argues that the love of that larger country, the world, may be nursed into similar strength, both as a source of elevated emotion and as a principle of duty. As this moral education progresses, men will think less and less of definite personal rewards or punishments, and more and more of the approbation of the highest moral natures, whether among the living or the dead. " For," as the author very truly remarks, " the thought that our dead parents or friends would have approved our conduct is a scarcely less powerful motive than the knowledge that our living ones do approve it "; and the thought that Socrates, or Antoninus, or Christ would have sympathised with us and have approved our actions, " has operated on the very best minds, as a strong incentive to act up to their highest feelings and convictions ".[1]

And here follows one of the most impressive passages to be found in Mill's philosophical writings. " To call these sentiments by the name morality, exclusively of any other title is claiming too little for them. They are a real religion; of which, as of other religions, outward good works (the utmost meaning usually suggested by the word morality) are only a part, and are indeed rather the fruits of the religion than the religion itself. The essence of religion is the strong and earnest direction of the emotions and desires towards an ideal object, recognised as of the highest excellence, and as rightfully paramount over all selfish objects of desire."' This is the climax of the argument, and here the essay might will have ended. Mill's following apology for the Religion of Humanity, and his attempt to show its superiority to any form of supernatural religion, is by no means calculated to bring conviction. But we must never forget the seeming paradox with which we are here confronted, *viz.*, the fact that it was an agnostic who first brought the Utilitarian doctrine into closest touch, not only with our moral, but with our

[1] See p. 109.

religious consciousness. There is one characteristic remark, after the author has said all that he can for the Religion of Humanity. Speaking of the one "real and valuable consolation" which the sceptic loses, the hope of a reunion in the life to come with the friends whom he has lost here, Mill says: "That loss, indeed, in neither to be denied nor extenuated. In many cases it is beyond the reach of comparison or estimate; and will always suffice to keep alive, in the more sensitive natures, the imaginative hope of a futurity which, if there is nothing to prove, there is as little in our knowledge and experience to contradict." [1] After this concession to our human feelings, however, he remarks that one of the great Eastern religions offers, not immortality, but annihilation, as the end supremely to be desired; and he concludes the essay by saying: "It seems to me not only possible but probable, that in a higher, and, above all, a happier condition of human life, not annihilation but immortality may be the burdensome idea; and that human nature, though pleased with the present, and by no means impatient to quit it, would find comfort and not sadness in the thought that it is not chained through eternity to a conscious existence which it cannot be assured that it will always wish to preserve".

[1] See p. 120.

# CHAPTER XII.

## JOHN STUART MILL (*continued*).

IT will be remembered that we have reliable testimony to
the effect that the essays on " Nature " and on " The Utility
of Religion," which we have been examining, were written at
about the same time as Mill's well-known book *On Liberty*,
published in 1859. If this were not the case, it would be
natural to assign them to a somewhat different period; not
because the *Liberty*, which we are now to consider, exactly
contradicts what we have seen to be the doctrine of the two
other essays, but because it seems to represent the development of an earlier tendency of the author's thought. It hardly
need be pointed out how different Mill's whole treatment of
religion was from what would have been possible for an
eighteenth century writer of either party. Agnosticism *with*
a keen appreciation of at least much that is essential to religion, would have sorely puzzled a reader of even the preceding generation. Still less would Mill's idea of the perfectibility
of an originally unpromising human nature, and the possibility
of merging one's individual interests in the general interests of
society, not merely present but future, have met with a sympathetic response at an earlier time. Hartley, indeed, had
thrown out such a suggestion, though in a crude form, but
his immediate successors had let this idea severely alone. The
essay on *Liberty*, on the other hand, though decidedly of the
nineteenth century in certain essential respects, which will
be considered in due time, to all intents and purposes takes
eighteenth century individualism as its starting-point. In
short, the difference in tone between the essays on " Nature "

and " The Utility of Religion," on the one hand, and the book *On Liberty*, on the other hand, was the difference between emphasising the social character of man as against individualism and emphasising the claims of the individual as against society.

This difference in tone, which it is much easier to recognise than to describe in exact terms, makes it somewhat important to fix the date of the composition of the book. Fortunately Mill himself has given us very exact information, in the *Autobiography*, as to both the time and the circumstances of its composition. He says : " During the two years which immediately preceded the cessation of my official life, my wife and I were working together at the *Liberty*. I had first planned and written it as a short essay in 1854. It was in mounting the steps of the Capitol, in January, 1855, that the thought first arose of converting it into a volume. None of my writings have been either so carefully composed, or so sedulously corrected as this. After it had been written as usual twice over, we kept it by us, bringing it out from time to time, and going through it *de novo*, reading, weighing, and criticising every sentence. Its final revision was to have been a work of the winter of 1858-9, the first after my retirement, which we had arranged to pass in the South of Europe." After speaking of the death of his wife, he says : " After my irreparable loss, one of my earliest cares was to print and publish the treatise. . . . The *Liberty* was more directly and literally our joint production than anything else which bears my name. . . . The whole mode of thinking of which the book was the expression, was emphatically hers. . . . My great readiness and eagerness to learn from everybody, and to make room in my opinions for every new acquisition by adjusting the old and the new to one another, might, but for her steadying influence, have seduced me into modifying my early opinions too much." [1]

The dates given above may, of course, be accepted with

---

[1] See *Autobiography*, pp. 250-252.

perfect confidence, for not only is the author himself the witness, but the circumstances under which the book was written were obviously such as to impress themselves indelibly upon his memory. But what has just been quoted raises a general question of considerable interest: Was Mill's intellectual debt to his wife such as he would give us to understand, here and in other well-known passages in his writings? Conclusive evidence one way or the other would, of course, be practically impossible to obtain, since we have no reason to believe that there are existing manuscripts which would decide the matter; but it may safely be assumed that, when Mill expressed himself as he does in the present instance, the emotional element came in to such an extent as makes it necessary to take his statements with very great caution.

But while Mill's strictly intellectual debt to his wife was almost certainly far less than he himself would lead us to suppose, there is no question whatever that her influence upon his development was considerable. In the passage quoted from the *Autobiography*, her influence is described as a 'steadying' one, which kept Mill from departing too far from his earlier position. One may doubt whether the adjective is well chosen. So far as one can trace her influence in his writings, it would seem rather to have been merely reactionary. The difference in tone between the essay on Whewell (1852) and the immediately preceding essays has been noted. This was certainly not an improvement, but may plausibly be traced to his wife's influence, since their marriage had taken place the preceding year. In the *Liberty*, on the other hand, there is much less asperity of tone to criticise, but the apparent difference in the general drift of this book from that of his other writings of the same period may not unreasonably be attributed to the fact that his wife's influence comes out much more strongly here. At any rate, here, if anywhere, we must look for her influence, since Mill tells us definitely that the central idea of the essay was primarily hers rather than his own.

The problem of this little book is clearly developed by Mill in the introductory chapter. The old struggle between liberty and authority was at first between subjects, or some class of subjects, and the government. It might have seemed as if this conflict would necessarily cease, when what we call 'self-government' became, for a given nation, an accomplished fact; but the event has shown that this is by no means the case. The reason is that the 'people' who exercise power are not always the same people over whom it is exercised. In truth, the tyranny of majorities is perhaps the most dangerous of all tyrannies. Society tends "to fetter the development, and, if possible, prevent the formation, of any individuality not in harmony with its ways, and compel all characters to fashion themselves upon the model of its own ".[1] Restraints of some kind are, of course, absolutely necessary; without them neither life nor property would be safe. But how far should society interfere with the action of the individual? Governments, as a matter of fact, act upon no settled principles. The likes or dislikes of a particular society at a particular time decide the matter. Now, Mill tells us, the object of this essay is to assert one very simple principle, *viz.*, " that the sole end for which mankind are warranted, individually or collectively, in interfering with the liberty of action of any of their number, is self-protection. . . . His own good, either physical or moral, is not a sufficient warrant." [2]

The following chapters, as will be remembered, are devoted to " The Liberty of Thought and Discussion," " Individuality, as One of the Elements of Well-being," " The Limits to the Authority of Society over the Individual," and " Applications ". It should be noticed at the outset that one of these chapters, at least, the first mentioned, is not as closely connected with the general thesis as might appear. Mill's defence of freedom of discussion, on grounds of general utility, is not essentially different from what any enlightened Englishman might write at the present day on the same subject. It differed from con-

[1] See *Liberty*, p. 13 (third ed.).
[2] See pp. 21, 22. Mill explains that this principle applies only to civilised adults.

temporary discussions, only in that the principle was rather
more strongly emphasised.   In short, Mill's argument does not
necessarily depend upon the individualistic principle, which it
is the main purpose of this essay to maintain.   In the chapter
on the "Limits to the Authority of Society," on the other
hand, this principle is naturally brought out with perfect clearness.   Even when we agree with Mill's conclusions, however,
which is not difficult in most cases, the arguments employed
are hardly convincing to one who sympathises with the general
trend of ethical theory at the present day.

This chapter is, in fact, an interesting example of 'putting
the new wine into old bottles'.   We have already several times
had occasion to notice how far Mill had departed from the
older Utilitarian school, in holding to the original character
of sympathy, and therefore to the possibility of strictly disinterested action.   And yet, the present discussion depends
almost entirely upon the distinction between the self-regarding
and the other-regarding virtues—the question being: In how
far, if at all, have we a right to enforce upon others conduct in
accordance with the self-regarding virtues?   When a man's
conduct is, even in an inferior degree, anti-social, Mill admits
that we have a right to coerce him; but when he gives himself
up to bestial excess, like habitual drunkenness, he claims that
we have no such right—unless, of course, this makes him
transgress the recognised rights of others.   But the recognition of primitive sympathy would seem logically to break down
this hard and fast barrier between self-regarding and other-
regarding virtues, even if the general Utilitarian principle,
properly understood, had not done so already.   If man must
be regarded as really a social being from the first, it may,
indeed, be convenient to use some such classification of the
virtues as that just mentioned; but the classification should
always be regarded as a convenience only, and never as the
basis for an argument.   As a member of society—and Mill
would have been the first to recognise social obligations—a
man of bestial tastes and habits is worse than useless; in fact,
he may become a positive menace to society, in proportion to

his position in life and to his still unextinguished talents. Mill, indeed, partly recognises all this, but not to the extent of seeing how largely it vitiates his argument. It is hardly necessary to explain that what has just been said is not intended as an argument for the too paternal interest of the State in the habits of its citizens. The desirability of such control is a practical question, to be decided in each case on its own merits; in truth, no government could possibly afford to decide such questions on purely abstract principles. There is a good deal of legislation to-day that would have been branded as ' socialistic' thirty years ago. This is not, we may surmise, because we are becoming converted to socialism, but because the mere word ' socialism' has less terrors for us than it once had, and because we tend more and more to decide each question, as it comes up, on its own merits, only taking care not to establish dangerous precedents.

If the essay on *Liberty* had contained nothing different from what we have thus far noticed, it could hardly have been regarded as permanently important, except as pointing out the real danger to democracy which lies in the almost inevitable tyranny of public opinion. But by far the most original and important part of the essay is the third chapter, " Of Individuality, as One of the Elements of Well-being ". It is here that Mill's discussion of the general question of Liberty brings him into closest relation to Ethics proper. What is particularly interesting, however, is the fact that the arguments advanced in this chapter, whether good or bad, have a much looser relation to the general individualistic position of the book than would at first appear. It will be remembered that, in the preceding chapter, Mill had been vindicating perfect freedom of speech. Here he comes to the question, how far freedom of action should be permitted. Nobody pretends that actions should be as free as opinions. The individual should not make himself obnoxious to others; but in matters that do not primarily concern others, individuality should by all means assert itself. " As it is useful that while mankind are imperfect there should be different opinions, so is it that there should be different experiments of living; that free scope should be given to varieties of character, short of injury to others; and that the worth of different modes of life should be proved practically, when any one thinks fit to try them."[1] So far Mill is saying no more than might be urged from quite various points of view in favour of such freedom of action as will keep society from a condition of stagnation; but from this point onward, throughout the chapter, he takes for his text the saying of Wilhelm von Humboldt that "the end of man, or that which is prescribed by the eternal or immutable dictates of reason, and not suggested by vague and transient desires, is the highest and most harmonious development of his powers to a complete and consistent whole"; and that therefore the object "towards which every human being must ceaselessly direct his efforts, and on which especially those who design to influence their fellow-men must ever keep their eyes, is the individuality of power and development".[2]

It hardly need be pointed out that a good deal more is implied by this passage from von Humboldt than the assertion of the importance of individuality as such. And Mill himself, almost unconsciously, as it would seem, does a good deal to work out the principle to its logical conclusion. For instance, he says: "Among the works of man, which human life is rightly employed in perfecting and beautifying, the first in importance surely is man himself. . . . Human nature is not a machine to be built after a model, and set to do exactly the work prescribed for it, but a tree, which requires to grow ánd develop itself on all sides, according to the tendency of the inward forces which make it a living thing."[3] And again, he says: "'Pagan self-assertion' is one of the elements of human worth, as well as 'Christian self-denial'. There is a Greek ideal of self-development, which the Platonic and Christian ideal of self-government blends with, but does not supersede. It may be better to be a John Knox than an Alcibiades, but it is better to be a Pericles than either; nor would a Pericles, if we had

---

[1] See p. 101.     [2] See p. 103.     [3] See pp. 106, 107.

one in these days, be without anything good which belonged to John Knox." [1] Passages like this almost seem to imply that self-development is an end in itself, without direct reference to hedonic results, either to oneself or to others. While it would be unjust to insist too strongly upon the inconsistency of such passages with Mill's general hedonistic position, it is necessary always to keep them in mind as tending to show how complex his ethical theory really was. What Mill did not see was, that if one take this principle of self-development seriously, it by no means lends itself to the purposes of individualism, or even to those of hedonism.

In passing to the well-known *Utilitarianism*, first printed in *Fraser's Magazine* in 1861, and reprinted (without changes) in book form in 1863, we come, of course, to Mill's most complete statement of his mature views regarding Ethics. After our rather careful examination of his previous ethical writings, however, we shall find little that is strictly new here, and, since this small volume is more universally familiar than any other book in the whole literature of English Utilitarianism, it would be gratuitous to reproduce its arguments in any detail. It seems best, therefore, to take up the principal points of the essay as briefly as may be, and to see in each case, on the one hand, how this last statement of Mill's ethical views corresponds with his own earlier treatment and that of his immediate predecessors, and, on the other hand, how it corresponds with the recognised Utilitarian theory of the present day.

It is probably significant that in the " General Remarks," with which Mill prefaces his treatment, there is no parade of scientific method. He says : " The intuitive, no less than what may be termed the inductive, school of ethics, insists on the necessity of general laws. They both agree that the morality

---

[1] See p. 112. It will doubtless occur to the reader that the examples which Mill gives here are the reverse of instructive. John Knox presumably was not lacking in ' Christian self-denial,' but he had in addition a rather unusual amount of what might, not unfairly, be termed ' Pagan self-assertion '.

of an individual action is not a question of direct perception, but of the application of a law to an individual case. They recognise also, to a great extent, the same moral laws ; but differ as to their evidence, and the source from which they derive their authority." [1]   Mill seems no longer to be labouring under the delusion, that the thorough-going application of Bentham's 'method of detail' is sufficient to solve the difficulties of Ethics ; on the contrary, by this time the real issues are pretty well cleared up in his mind.   He does, however, insist upon one very important point, when he says, regarding non-hedonistic systems : " I might go much further, and say that to all those *a priori* moralists who deem it necessary to argue at all, Utilitarian arguments are indispensable ".[2]

This is a claim which, in various forms, had been advanced by nearly all Mill's Utilitarian predecessors, and, such being the case, one may well give it a final scrutiny.   It would be easy to brush this aside as an unproved assumption, but, in the opinion of the present writer, it is rather more than that. The fact is, that the very moralists who have spoken most scornfully of the 'doctrine of consequences' have without exception found it extremely difficult, if not impossible, to leave consequences altogether out of account.   By some strange fatality, however, the opponents of Utilitarianism have succeeded in putting themselves in the wrong by almost universally conceding to the Utilitarians that, *if* consequences are to be regarded, they must be construed in *hedonistic* terms.   There was nothing to do, then, from this point of view, but to deny that the rightness or wrongness of actions depends to any large extent upon their consequences—with the unfortunate result above indicated.   For, no matter how 'internal' one's conception of morality, one cannot safely deny that the 'consequences' of actions may be important to any degree whatever. To overlook or deny this fact, is to blind oneself to one of the most serious aspects of the moral life.   But these good or bad consequences are by no means necessarily such, merely be-

---

[1] See p. 3.          [2] See p. 5.

cause of the happiness or unhappiness which they imply.
They may consistently be shown to be good or bad, because
they tend for or against whatever one may regard as of
supreme importance in the moral life.

Mill next goes on to explain "What Utilitarianism Is".
He begins by defining utility as happiness, and happiness as
'pleasure, and the absence of pain'. In the same way, unhappiness is defined as 'pain, and the privation of pleasure'.
That concrete desirable things are as numerous for Utilitarians
as for others, he very properly insists; but holds, of course,
that they are "desirable either for the pleasure inherent in
themselves, or as means to the promotion of pleasure and
the prevention of pain". Moreover, he remarks that "there
is no known Epicurean theory of life which does not assign
to the pleasures of the intellect, of the feelings and imagination, and of the moral sentiments, a much higher value as
pleasures than to those of mere sensation".[1] But just here
Mill makes his famous distinction. He does not agree with
traditional Utilitarianism in holding that this superiority of
mental over physical pleasures is due to their greater permanence, safety, uncostliness, etc., but insists that pleasures
are essentially different in kind (or value) as well as in degree.
Quite in the spirit of Hutcheson, he appeals to that "sense of
dignity, which all human beings possess in one form or other,
and in some, though by no means in exact, proportion to their
higher faculties, and which is so essential a part of the happiness of those in whom it is strong, that nothing which conflicts with it could be, otherwise than momentarily, an object
of desire to them".[2] Moreover, he says: "If it may possibly
be doubted whether a noble character is always the happier
for its nobleness, there can be no doubt that it makes other
people happier, and that the world in general is immensely
a gainer by it".[3]

Since nothing in Mill's ethical writings has been so thoroughly discussed as this admission on his part of qualitative

---

[1] See p. 11.          [2] See p. 13.          [3] See p. 16.

distinctions between pleasures, and since there is perfect agreement at the present day among competent critics, of whatever
ethical convictions, as to the inconsistency of this view with
his general hedonistic position, it would be an impertinence
to argue the matter again here. The inconsistency, in truth,
may be expressed in a word: If all good things are good in
proportion as they bring pleasure to oneself or others, one
cannot add to this statement that pleasure itself, the assumed
criterion, is more or less desirable in terms of something else
(*e.g.*, human dignity) which is not pleasure. At the same time,
it would be a grave mistake to suppose that this was merely
one of Mill's many careless slips. The inconsistency is not
superficial, it is vital. In this very chapter, when criticising
the way in which Utilitarianism has commonly been presented,
Mill has said: "To do this in any sufficient manner, many
Stoic, as well as Christian elements require to be included ".[1]
And we have seen how, in the most important chapter of the
*Liberty*, he appropriates von Humboldt's impressive statement
of the all-importance of self-development as an essential constituent of well-being.

Mill next considers the objection that happiness cannot be
the end, because it is unattainable in this life. Incautiously
admitting, as it would seem, that the burden of proof is on
his side, he enters upon a brief and rather superficial argument for (hedonistic) optimism. Into this, we need not follow
him. As might be expected, he exaggerates, as usual, the
power of education to alter the manifestations of human nature,
particularly in the direction of sympathy and intelligence.
Even poverty and disease, as implying acute suffering on the
part of large numbers, are to disappear. It is hard to see
why hedonists have so commonly admitted that the concrete
difficulties of the moral life are difficulties for them, more than
for others. In the present case of optimism *versus* pessimism,
it would be a simple matter to show that hedonism is no better
and no worse off than any other recognised form of ethical

See p. 11.

theory. For surely there are as many possible forms of optimism and pessimism as there are possible definitions of the Good. And it may be observed that, if happiness is by no means universal, it is probably quite as frequent a phenomenon as moral perfection.

On the other hand, Mill is undoubtedly right, when he shows the absurdity of objecting to Utilitarianism as a ' godless doctrine,' and says: " Whatever aid religion, either natural or revealed, can afford to ethical investigation, is as open to the Utilitarian moralist as to any other ". He might very properly have added, what he has elsewhere pointed out, that, as a matter of fact, Theological Utilitarianism was for a long time the common orthodox view, as against those who held various forms of the ' Moral Sense ' theory. He is also right, as against those who brand Utilitarianism as the doctrine of ' expediency,' since this is plainly a question-begging epithet as here applied; but he is plainly careless when, speaking of the virtue of truthfulness, he says: " Yet that even this rule, sacred as it is, admits of possible exceptions, is acknowledged by all moralists ".[1] How about Kant, whom he has undertaken to criticise in the first chapter?

Somewhat earlier in this chapter, Mill considers a question that would more properly come up for discussion in the next chapter, where he treats of " The Ultimate Sanction of the Principle of Utility ". And he is again careless in the way just noted. He is answering the supposed objection that the Utilitarian doctrine is too high in its demands. " They say it is exacting too much to require that people shall always act from the inducement of promoting the general interests of society. But this is to mistake the very meaning of a standard of morals, and to confound the rule of action with the motive of it. It is the business of ethics to tell us what are our duties, or by what test we may know them; but no system of ethics requires that the sole motive of all we do shall be a feeling of duty. . . . It is the more unjust to Utilitarianism that

[1] See p. 33.

this particular misapprehension should be made a ground of objection to it, inasmuch as Utilitarian moralists have gone beyond almost all others in affirming that the motive has nothing to do with the morality of the action, though much with the worth of the agent." [1]

In the first place, it hardly need be remarked that a very important system of Ethics, just mentioned, which Mill has criticised in the course of his "General Remarks," does hold precisely that "the sole motive of all we do [if it is to be strictly moral] shall be a feeling of duty". It may, indeed with considerable justice be retorted, 'so much the worse for Kant'; but Mill betrays his lack of an intimate knowledge of modern ethical literature, when he allows himself to make sweeping statements with so little caution.   But in the second place, and more particularly, has Mill a right to appropriate the argument of the earlier Utilitarians, that the motive has nothing to do with the morality of the action?   That was part and parcel of what we may call the extreme 'dualism' of their ethical theory : their contention that the end of moral action and the motive which leads to it must be different since one can will only one's own happiness.   But, as we have seen, it was Mill's great merit to revive Hume's view (as given in the second form of his ethical system), and show that man is originally sympathetic, and that therefore he can, to a certain extent, directly will the common good, although other motives do, as a matter of fact, generally come in to complicate.

In the next chapter, to which, as already said, this discussion properly belongs, Mill shifts his position and says—speaking of the psychological basis of the feeling of obligation—" But there *is* this basis of powerful natural sentiment ; and this it is, which, when once the general happiness is recognised as the ethical standard, will constitute the strength of the Utilitarian morality.   This firm foundation is that of the social feelings of mankind. . . . The social state is at once

[1] See p. 26.

so natural, so necessary, and so habitual to man, that, except in some unusual circumstances, or by an effort of voluntary abstraction, he never conceives himself otherwise than as a member of a body; and this association is riveted more and more, as mankind are further removed from the state of savage independence." [1] Of course, this is Mill's true, and only consistent, position; but it at once separates him from the eighteenth century Utilitarians, whose characteristic arguments, for that reason, he has no right to use. And how does the last part of the passage just quoted square with Mill's conception of the 'natural' as developed in the essay on "Nature," apparently written at about the same time? This unconscious shifting of the point of view, in the course of an argument of any length, or in different writings, even of the same period, makes Mill a somewhat obscure writer on Ethics to those who take the trouble to read him carefully.

But, in the present case, there can be no doubt as to what Mill really means. Earlier in this same (third) chapter, when distinguishing between the 'external' and the 'internal' sanctions of morality, he says: "The principle of utility either has, or there is no reason why it might not have, all the sanctions which belong to any other system of morals. Those sanctions are either external or internal. Of the external sanctions it is not necessary to speak at any length. . . . The internal sanction of duty, whatever our standard of duty may be, is one and the same—a feeling in our own mind; a pain, more or less intense, attendant on violation of duty, which in properly cultivated moral natures rises, in the more serious cases, into shrinking from it as an impossibility. This feeling, when disinterested, and connecting itself with the pure idea of duty, and not with some particular form of it, or with any of the merely accessory circumstances, is the essence of Conscience. . . . The ultimate sanction, therefore, of all morality (external motives apart) being a subjective feeling in our own minds, I see nothing embarrassing to those whose standard

[1] See p. 46.

is utility, in the question, What is the sanction of that particular standard? We may answer, The same as of all other moral standards—the conscientious feelings of mankind." [1]　These 'conscientious feelings of mankind,' however, are of course not regarded by Mill as intuitive. In the last resort, the feeling of duty depends upon that powerful natural sentiment, social feeling or sympathy, which we have been examining. This, then, and nothing else, is " the ultimate sanction of the greatest-happiness morality ".[2]

The fourth chapter of the *Utilitarianism* treats " Of What Sort of Proof the Principle of Utility is Susceptible "—a question which might very properly have been considered first. After making the obvious remark, that questions of ultimate ends do not admit of proof, in the ordinary acceptation of the term, the author indicates the general drift of his argument, very concisely, as follows : " No reason can be given why the general happiness is desirable, except that each person, so far as he believes it to be attainable, desires his own happiness. This, however, being a fact, we have not only all the proof which the case admits of, but all which it is possible to require, that happiness is a good : that each person's happiness is a good to that person ; and the general happiness, therefore, a good to the aggregate of all persons. Happiness has made out its title as *one* of the ends of conduct, and consequently one of the criteria of morality." [2]　But to prove it to be the sole criterion, it is necessary to show that people never desire anything else. It will be seen that the method by which Mill would prove the general principle of utility is closely analogous to that by which Hume tried to prove the Utilitarian character of the particular virtues.

In the main, Mill's arguments are the conventional ones of Associationist-Utilitarianism, and so do not call for special examination. His position, of course, is defined by his often-quoted remark in this chapter, that " desiring a thing and finding it pleasant, aversion to it and thinking of it as painful, are

---

[1] See pp. 40-42.　　　　　[2] See p. 50.

phenomena entirely inseparable, or rather two parts of the same phenomenon ". One of his explanations, however— the crucial one, since he depends upon it to show that the Utilitarian theory provides for the fact, that the virtuous man may will that which is contrary to his own happiness—requires careful consideration. He says: " The distinction between will and desire . . . is an authentic and highly important psychological fact; but the fact consists solely in this—that will, like all other parts of our constitution, is amenable to habit, and that we may will from habit what we no longer desire for itself, or desire only because we will it. It is not the less true that will, in the beginning, is entirely produced by desire; including in that term the repelling influence of pain, as well as the attractive one of pleasure." [1]

This is perhaps all the more instructive, because it only brings out what is latent in the traditional Associationist-Utilitarian theory of the will. What, then, does this often reiterated theory mean? Suppose we leave out of account, for the moment, the question how this ' habit ' of the will has arisen, and accept the facts as we seem to find them. Lest it be thought that the above quotation is ambiguous in its admissions, the reader is reminded that just before Mill has said: " In case of an habitual purpose, instead of willing the thing because we desire it, we often desire it only because we will it ".[2] Now this cannot be a case where habit makes a mental process unconscious or only semi-conscious, because we still hear of desire and will. And that being the case, pleasure-pain must still, just as at the beginning of our conscious experience, come in as determining factors. Only here pleasure and pain attach respectively to actions in accordance with, or against, certain tendencies of the will (call them ' habits,' if you please) that we have to recognise as facts, however they may be explained.

This, then, would appear to be the meaning of the common, though seemingly paradoxical, statement that we desire a

[1] See p. 60.  [2] See p. 59.

thing at present because we will it. In other words, there are certain things toward which our nature, as at present constituted, tends. To let our nature, in these respects, have its way, produces pleasure; to balk our nature, in these respects, produces pain. But this is a very different thing from saying that at present we necessarily act for pleasure, or the avoidance of pain, as such. When Mill says that will goes back to desire (in the sense of desire for pleasure), this can, according to his own statement, be only historically true. We had no such tendencies as the ones just noticed at first; these are 'habits' that have developed as a result of our acting, in the first place, solely for pleasure and the avoidance of pain.

Now suppose we do not agree that the character was a *tabula rasa* at first; but hold rather that some of the tendencies which are so apparent in adult life were potentially present at the beginning—what becomes of this traditional form of the hedonistic theory of desire? In short, in how far does this theory depend upon the extremely dubious *tabula rasa* assumption? It is hardly necessary to say that the above is not intended as a summary refutation of the general doctrine of hedonism, but as an attempt to state a really serious difficulty which constantly presents itself, when one is dealing with the apparently simple and unambiguous theory of the will held practically in common by the Associationist-Utilitarians. At the same time, when the full force of this difficulty is appreciated, one has taken the first and most important step toward recognising the substantial truth of Butler's analysis of desire, which does so much to transform the problems of Ethics.

It will be remembered that we have the reliable testimony of Miss Helen Taylor, Mill's step-daughter, in her preface to the posthumously published *Three Essays on Religion* (1874), that the long chapter on Justice, which concludes the little volume we are examining, was first composed as a separate essay. We are told that this essay on Justice and another on Utility, written at about the same time, "were afterwards incorporated, with some alterations and additions, into one, and published under the name of *Utilitarianism*". While this chapter is a most admirable exposition of Justice, from the Utilitarian point of view, it will hardly require extended notice here, first, because it is little more than a consistent application of the traditional Utilitarian method, and secondly, because it is perhaps as familiar as any chapter in Mill's philosophical writings.

The general drift of the argument may be indicated very briefly. In all ages of speculation, one of the strongest objections to the Utilitarian doctrine has been found in the absolute character which common sense has attributed to Justice. Since this has been so long the stronghold of Intuitionism, Mill accepts it as a test case. In the first place, he analyses the notion of Justice with some care, and in a way that partly reminds one of Professor Sidgwick's later and much more elaborate analysis in the *Methods of Ethics*. The question then arises, whether the feeling or sentiment which attaches to the idea of Justice is such as would have originated in considerations of general expediency. And Mill bluntly states his thesis as follows: "I conceive that the sentiment itself does not arise from anything which would commonly, or correctly, be termed an idea of expediency; but that, though the sentiment does not, whatever is moral in it does".[1]

The author's preceding analysis has shown that the two essential elements in the sentiment of Justice are: (1) the desire to punish a person who has done harm, and (2) the knowledge or belief that there is some definite individual, or individuals, to whom harm has been done. Now the desire to punish is held by Mill to be "a spontaneous outgrowth from two sentiments, both in the highest degree natural, and which either are or resemble instincts; the impulse of self-defence,[2] and the feeling of sympathy". The former has nothing moral in it, when considered apart from the social sympathies, to which it should be subordinated. If, on the

---

[1] See p. 76.
[2] This should be distinguished from Mr. Spencer's 'instinct of personal rights' (*Social Statics*, 1851), which is also supposed to be helped out by sympathy.

other hand, it be moralised by sympathy for others, it will be
brought into play only when conformable to the common good
—in which case, the Utilitarian test is inevitable.

But we are constantly told that Utility is an uncertain
standard, that we must obey the immutable dictates of Justice,
which are self-evident, and therefore independent of the fluctu-
ations of private or public opinion.   Here Mill suggests what
would seem to be the obvious line of argument, though it had
been practically overlooked both by the orthodox Intuitionists
and by Mr. Spencer in *Social Statics* (1851).   We have no
right whatever to assume that the notion of Justice *is* free from
ambiguity.   Indeed, Mill says :   " So far is this from being the
fact, that there is as much difference of opinion, and as fierce
discussion, about what is just, as about what is useful to
society ".[1]   After citing a number of cases which go to prove
this contention, he argues that an external standard of some
kind is absolutely necessary, and that the only practicable
standard is Social Utility.   This is by no means to assign to
Justice a minor place in the moral code.   Mill says in conclusion :   " Justice remains the appropriate name for certain
social utilities which are vastly more important, and therefore
more absolute and imperative, than any others are as a class
(though not more so than others may be in particular cases) ;
and which, therefore, ought to be, as well as naturally are,
guarded by a sentiment not only different in degree, but also
in kind ; distinguished from the milder feeling which attaches
to the mere idea of promoting human pleasure or convenience,
at once by the more definite nature of its commands, and by
the sterner character of its sanctions ".[2]

[1] See p. 82.   It will be remembered that Professor Sidgwick, though by no
means wholly opposed to Intuitionism, comes to much the same conclusion in
his *Methods of Ethics*.

[2] See p. 96.   All of Mill's writings bearing at all directly upon Ethics have now
been noticed, with the exception of the last of the posthumously published *Three
Essays on Religion*, the rather long essay on " Theism ".   Even a brief examination of this may safely be omitted here, in spite of the pathetic interest which
attaches to this last, if also least satisfactory, of the author's many philosophical
writings.   Though rather more systematic than the other two essays, on " Nature "

In estimating the significance of Mill's position in the development of English Utilitarianism, it is particularly important that we should keep in mind both the nature of his early environment and training, and the various changes that his ethical views underwent even after the important essay on Bentham (1838), which marks the beginning of his really independent work in Ethics, and therefore the beginning of a new phase of Utilitarian theory. Quite apart from what may be thought of the unique pedagogical experiment which was performed upon Mill by his father, in place of the conventional school and university training of his generation, it must be counted a distinct misfortune, on the whole, that he inherited ready-made his earliest views on Ethics and Politics, as well as on Psychology. Not that these views were necessarily, or probably, further from the truth than those which he would have adopted, if left to himself; but it is nothing less than pathetic, when we view the situation at this distance, that the young apostle of freedom and reform should have lived in an atmosphere such that anything like real intellectual freedom was for himself an impossibility.

Mill began writing for various periodicals as early as 1824,

and on " The Utility of Religion "—which cover much the same ground, but which appear to have been written more than ten years earlier—it does not, like them, belong to a period when Mill was doing important work, and so is of much less value as a commentary upon his other writings bearing more directly upon Ethics. Moreover, as Miss Taylor states in the preface to the volume in which it appears, this last essay was not revised by the author, as it certainly would have been before he himself would have given it to the world. But even apart from this, just in proportion as the treatment is more elaborate than that in the two earlier essays, it shows Mill at a disadvantage, for he was never less at home than in these theological discussions. The difference in tone between this last essay and the two others, which has often been commented upon, is undeniable. Mill is at the end much more sympathetic toward Theism than he had been at any previous time—a fact which did not fail to suggest edifying reflections when the *Three Essays on Religion* were first published. But this apparent change of personal attitude affects his treatment of the arguments themselves less than might be expected. The principal difference is that, in the essay on Theism, he concedes more than he had in the others to ' The Utility of Religion '. Properly speaking, Mill remained an agnostic to the last, but with an increasing appreciation of the ethical value of religious ideals.

while still a mere boy, but for the next twelve years the opinions which he expressed could from the nature of the case be only partly his own—or his own, in the sense that they were largely accepted from others—although at first they appear to have been surrounded with all the halo of youthful enthusiasm. His father, the stern task-master of his childhood, was the tacitly recognised censor of all that he wrote. The nature and degree of this control is evident, when one compares the essay on Sedgwick's *Discourse* (1835) with the very different essay on Bentham (1838). Indeed, Mill himself says of the former essay in the *Autobiography*, in a passage previously quoted: "My relation to my father would have made it painful to me in any case, and impossible in a Review for which he wrote, to speak out my whole mind on the subject at this time".[1] The very important essay on Bentham, then, published two years after his father's death, was at once his 'Declaration of Independence' and his first noteworthy contribution to Ethics.

In the exercise of his newly asserted freedom, Mill expressed himself regarding the fatal shortcomings of Benthamism with an emphasis which he might possibly have avoided later. And as he is generally right in this destructive part of the essay, the result is one of the most damaging critiques in the whole range of English ethical literature. But while his whole moral personality revolted against the hidebound doctrine which had done so much to fetter his own earlier development, he still made a very high claim for Bentham. Though not a 'great philosopher,' he was to be regarded as a 'great reformer in philosophy,' since he was the first to apply 'scientific method' to the treatment of moral problems, from the hedonistic point of view. This does not, of course, mean what it might mean to us now, for Bentham was as innocent of any intimate knowledge of the Biology or the Psychology of his day, as he was of the previous development of ethical theory. The 'scientific method,' or

[1] See p. 201.

'method of detail,' as Mill sometimes calls it—which in one passage he admits to be "as old as philosophy itself"—consisted in the employment of elaborate analysis and classification in place of what Bentham and his followers doubtless regarded as the barren, semi-rhetorical method of the past.

Mill's description of the 'scientific method' which he attributes to Bentham in this essay is extremely vague, if not partly self-contradictory; but one cannot doubt the sincerity of his praise of the elder moralist for what he attempted in this direction, since in Book VI. of the *Logic*, on "The Logic of the Moral Sciences," which appears to have been begun about two years later, he himself made a much more elaborate attempt to provide a 'scientific' foundation for Ethics, by developing in outline the idea of a new science, 'Ethology,' or the 'Science of the Formation of Character'. The inductive science, Psychology, was to be the ultimate foundation; and the new science, Ethology, necessarily deductive, because of the complexity of the data with which it would have to deal, was to form the necessary connecting-link between Psychology, on the one hand, and Sociology, on the other, the latter also, of course, being conceived as necessarily deductive in its method.

It was highly characteristic of Mill's more than catholic acceptance of partly conflicting principles, that in 1840, when he was beginning to work out, more or less on the lines of Benthamism, this hopelessly abstract, and therefore practically valueless 'scientific method' for the treatment of the moral sciences, he should also have published the essay on Coleridge, in which he seems to be meeting what he calls the 'Germano-Coleridgean' school fully half-way. And still more significant is the fact that Mill retained this chapter in his *Logic* to the end, and therefore long after he had given up the proposed science of Ethology as impracticable—which meant the implicit surrender of the whole position.

After the very appreciative essay on Coleridge, just mentioned, and the equally sympathetic essays on De Toqueville (1840), Michelet (1844), and Guizot (1845), which show that

Mill was coming more and more to appreciate the significance of the historical method, not only for itself, but for its bearing upon the moral sciences, and which therefore indicate a still further divergence from the spirit of Benthamism—which had been above all things unhistorical—one is hardly prepared for the very severe essay on Whewell (1852), parts of which sound almost like the very early essay on Sedgwick's *Discourse* (1835). Making due allowance for the fact that Whewell had justified rather severe criticism by his use of ' question-begging epithets,' etc., this essay seems really to indicate a partial and temporary reaction toward the earlier phase of Mill's thought, while he was still under the spell of Bentham. As explained in the proper context, this change of attitude may plausibly be attributed to the influence of Mill's wife, whom he had married the year before, and whose influence, where it can be located, seems always to have been in the direction of confirming him in the earlier and more uncompromising form of his doctrine.

The two posthumously published essays on " Nature " and on " The Utility of Religion " (probably written between 1848 and 1859) by no means show Mill at his best in philosophical argumentation : but they serve to bring out in an interesting way, first, his partial acceptance of the Manichaean doctrine, which in the *Autobiography* he attributes to his father, at least in the sense that the elder Mill entertained it as a speculative possibility ; and secondly, his almost naïve belief in the perfectibility of human nature—and this, in spite of the fact that, according to his own account of the matter as here given, the great forces not only in external nature, but in man himself, are strongly set against the moral order. In the latter essay, in particular, he urges that religion, as ordinarily understood, is by no means the indispensable moralising factor that it is commonly assumed to be, though his attitude toward religion in this essay, as in nearly all of his later writings, is partly one of appreciation for the ideals it represents. In fact, he would apply the name ' religion ' to the higher morality for which he himself pleads, for he says: " The essence of religion is the strong and earnest direction of the emotions and desires towards an ideal object, recognised as of the highest excellence, and as rightfully paramount over all selfish objects of desire ".[1]

In the case of the *Liberty* (1859)—which belongs to about the same period, though it was probably written somewhat later—we again find evidence of conflicting tendencies in Mill's intellectual development. The main idea of the essay, which he distinctly attributes to his wife, is the assertion of the rights of the individual as such, almost in the sense of eighteenth century Individualism. But the argument in the chapter on " Individuality, as One of the Elements of Well-being " (by far the most important one for Ethics) really depends upon the implicit assumption that harmonious self-development is practically an end in itself, an assumption which carries him far beyond what at least seemed to be his original thesis, and by no means in the direction of consistent Utilitarianism.

When we finally turn to the *Utilitarianism* (1863), we find little that is strictly new, but much to confirm us in the opinion that the partial divergence from the Utilitarian method, which had been so noticeable in some of Mill's previous ethical writings, was not a matter of chance, depending upon the nature of the particular discussion, but indicative of tendencies which, if they had been completely developed, would have meant the practical surrender of the Utilitarian position itself. The classic instance, of course, is Mill's emphatic assertion of the existence of ' qualitative distinctions ' between pleasures. As already pointed out, this must be very carefully distinguished from the author's many careless slips in the course of particular arguments. It was a distinct and most important concession, if not to Intuitionism, at least to the ideal of the harmonious development of the human personality, as an end in itself.

But over against this most important concession to non-hedonistic ethical methods, must be placed Mill's not infre-

[1] See p. 109.

quent employment of arguments which properly belong to the older type of Utilitarianism, and not to the more modern form of the doctrine which he had himself done so much to inaugurate. A typical example, which we have noticed in the *Utilitarianism*, is the way in which he appropriates the characteristic argument of the earlier Utilitarians, that the motive has nothing to do with the morality of the action, considered in itself. This is a manifest inadvertence, since in the next chapter, as we have seen, sympathy is regarded—quite consistently with Mill's general position, and that of all the later Utilitarians—as " the ultimate sanction of the greatest happiness morality ". So, too, in the essay on " Nature," he had allowed himself to argue for the 'artificial' character of all the virtues, which, according to his view as there expressed, would never have come into being, " were it not so strongly the interest of mankind to cherish the good germs in one another ". This, of course, is the familiar argument of the older type of Utilitarianism, which logically results from the assumption that all motives are ultimately selfish. In the *Utilitarianism*, on the other hand, Mill avoids this confusion of the two points of view in the corresponding discussion. Though the moral feelings are " not innate, but acquired," in his own opinion, " they are not for that reason the less natural ". And he adds : " It is natural to man to speak, to reason, to build cities, to cultivate the ground, though these are acquired faculties ".[1] This, of course, means that man is a social (and therefore partly sympathetic) being from the first, and that therefore civilisation and morality are 'natural' and not merely ' artificial '—which is the exact contrary of the position which Mill had carelessly taken not long before in the other essay, on " Nature ".

But this almost mechanical combination of the old and the new, which one so often discovers in Mill's ethical writings, must not blind us to the fact, that to him we owe the modern form of Utilitarianism more than to any other single influence.

[1] *Cf. Three Essays on Religion*, p. 53, and *Utilitarianism*, p. 45.

Indeed, these inconsistencies were doubtless in the first instance largely due to the fact that he was a pioneer in the new ethical movement. His incautious admission of 'qualitative distinctions' between pleasures has, of course, been avoided by later writers of the same school; but it would hardly be possible to estimate the extent of his influence in the direction of humanising the Utilitarian doctrine, and making it square with the highest concrete moral ideals. The social nature of man, and the complexity of that nature, were recognised by him almost from the first, and though he never himself accepted the theory of organic Evolution, he did much to prepare his contemporaries to recognise the importance of the idea of development as applied to Ethics. In his hands, the older analytic Utilitarian method was gradually transformed into the synthetic method of to-day. And not least remarkable is the fact, that this professed agnostic did more than any of his theological predecessors to bring Utilitarianism into touch with the higher, more ideal side of religion. Seldom, indeed, has a personality counted for more in the whole history of Ethics.

From first to last critics have dwelt altogether too much upon the manifest inconsistencies in Mill's ethical writings, and have failed to do anything like justice to the perfect candour and broad-mindedness that made him take serious account of the very facts of our moral experience which presented the most serious difficulties to his own ethical theory. Just because of this fair-mindedness, this constant endeavour to do justice to our moral nature as a whole—not because of his inconsistencies, as some would hold—Mill belongs, not merely to the Utilitarians, but to those who have found the Utilitarian theory insufficient, and have attempted to transcend it, while doing full justice to the measure of truth which it contains.

# CHAPTER XIII.

## HERBERT SPENCER.

AFTER the publication of the *Origin of Species* (1859), it was inevitable that the idea of evolutional development should sooner or later be applied to morality. In truth, it appeared to certain writers of the following two or three decades that the theory of Evolution afforded a perfectly new method of Ethics, from which the most important results might confidently be expected. Nothing could be more natural; but it happened in this case, as generally, when epoch-making theories are exploited, that the collateral issues were at first somewhat confused. We have seen that Mill was grievously disappointed, when he earlier made the attempt to apply ' scientific method' to the subject-matter of Ethics. This was not because Ethics is a discipline which cannot permit of the same rigorous analysis that we employ in the case of the physical sciences, but because the writer on Ethics primarily attempts, what the physical scientist, *qua* scientist, can never for a moment permit himself—an evaluation, as opposed to a mere explanation, of the facts with which he has to deal. In a similar way, we have quite generally, if only somewhat gradually, come to see that the idea of development according to law, while of great importance for Ethics, as tending to bring into prominence a multitude of facts that had previously been far too generally neglected, does not of itself inform us as to the worth or meaning of life, or as to the essential nature of morality. Not that the work of the so-called Evolutional moralists has by any means been in vain. Quite as much as any other recent school, they have helped to broaden the whole field of ethical discussion. But their contribution has mainly been to the data of the science; they have by no means supplied it with a new and definitive method.

It would, of course, be wholly apart from the purpose of this book to examine Evolutional Ethics as such. In spite of the varying tendencies represented by the writers usually assigned to this school, they all agree in differentiating their method more or less sharply from that of traditional Utilitarianism. Their most prominent representative, however, can by no means be neglected, partly because he enjoys a popular reputation second to none among the English hedonists of the latter part of the nineteenth century, but more particularly because his ethical theory is much less dependent upon the Evolutional method which he adopts than is commonly recognised. It will be remembered that Mr. Spencer's first book having a bearing upon Ethics was published eight years before the *Origin of Species*, his last only nine years ago. During these forty-two years, most of which have been devoted to other subjects, his views on Ethics have naturally undergone some modifications, yet there is an underlying consistency which one misses in the ethical writings of J. S. Mill —and this, although Mr. Spencer shows a frankness equal to that of Mill in pointing out the modifications of his doctrine of which he is himself conscious.

In truth, a special reason for considering his ethical writings at length in this connection is, that his doctrine is presented in what may be called a pre-Evolutional form in *Social Statics* (1851), as well as in a form ostensibly depending upon the theory of Evolution in the *Principles of Ethics* (1879-1893). A comparison of the later with the earlier form of the system is as interesting as it is instructive. Moreover, the extreme claims for Evolutional Ethics, made in the *Data of Ethics* (1879), are considerably diminished before the completion of the *Principles*. We must not anticipate on this point, but no passage in Mr. Spencer's works does more credit to his single-minded love of truth, all his own former prepossessions to the contrary notwithstanding, than that in the Preface to his concluding contribution to Ethics, *Negative Beneficence and Positive Beneficence* (1893), where he says : " The Doctrine of Evolution has not furnished guidance to the extent I had hoped. Most of the conclusions, drawn empirically, are such as right feelings, enlightened by cultivated intelligence, have already sufficed to establish."

The earliest draft of Mr. Spencer's ethical theory is to be found in the first, or theoretical, portion of his well-known *Social Statics* (1851), and also in the concluding chapters of the same book. The long, but rather unsystematic, Introduction is mainly devoted to a severe criticism of the Doctrine of Expediency, the gist of which is as follows. All men seek a guide for conduct, but a practical guide in the form of a general principle seems to remain a desideratum. The Doctrine of Expediency (Bentham's principle of ' the greatest happiness of the greatest number ') has indeed been confidently recommended as such a guide ; but a rule, principle, or axiom, in order to have any theoretical or practical value, must have a definite meaning. We must therefore take it for granted that, when Bentham announced ' the greatest happiness of the greatest number ' as the canon of social morality, he supposed mankind to be unanimous in their definition of ' greatest happiness '.

" This was a most unfortunate assumption," says Mr. Spencer, " for no fact is more palpable than that the standard of happiness is infinitely variable. In all ages—amongst every people —by each class—do we find different notions of it entertained." After giving a number of rather striking examples, he says : " Generalising such facts, we see that the standard of ' greatest happiness ' possesses as little fixity as the other exponents of human nature ". And he goes on to show that the reason for this is simple enough. Happiness signifies a gratified state of all the faculties. The gratification of a faculty is produced by its exercise, provided that the exercise be proportionate to the power of the faculty. But the faculties of men differ as regards their ratio to each other in each case ; moreover, there is in each a different balance of desires. "Consequently the notion of happiness must vary with the disposition and character; that is, must vary indefinitely." According to the author's view, this leads to the inevitable conclusion that "a true conception of what human life should be, is possible only to the ideal man. . . . And as the world yet contains none such, it follows that a specific idea of 'greatest happiness' is for the present unattainable."[1] But even if we were agreed as to what constitutes the 'greatest happiness,' there would yet remain the unwarranted assumption that it is possible for the self-guided human judgment to determine, with something like precision, by what methods it may be obtained. In support of this latter position, Mr. Spencer mentions a number of cases of mistaken legislation. And he characteristically adds: "But why cite individual cases? Does not the experience of all nations testify to the futility of these empirical attempts at the acquisition of happiness? What is the statute-book but a record of such unhappy guesses? or history but a narrative of their unsuccessful issues?"[2]

Here, in fact, the drift of the argument changes somewhat. The author proceeds to criticise the Expediency Philosophy less as a method of Ethics than as a mistaken political theory. A fatal objection to this theory is, that it assumes the eternity of government, while in reality government is not essential, but incidental. "Daily is statecraft held in less repute. . . . As civilisation advances, does government decay. To the bad it is essential; to the good, not. . . . Its continuance is proof of still-existing barbarism."[3] Note, then, the predicament of the Expediency Philosophy: "A system of moral philosophy professes to be a code of correct rules for the control of human beings. . . . Government, however, is an institution originating in man's imperfection; an institution confessedly begotten by necessity out of evil. . . . How, then, can that be a true system of morality which adopts government as one of its premises?"

[1] See Introduction: 'The Doctrine of Expediency,' § 2.
[2] See *ibid.*, § 3.            [3] See *ibid.*, § 4.

Mr. Spencer sums up his objections as follows: " Of the Expediency Philosophy it must therefore be said, in the first place, that it can make no claim to a scientific character seeing that its fundamental proposition is not an axiom, but simply an enunciation of the problem to be solved.

" Further, that even supposing its fundamental proposition were an axiom, it would still be inadmissible, because expressed in terms possessing no fixed acceptation.

" Moreover, were the Expediency theory otherwise satisfactory, it would be still useless; since it requires nothing less than omniscience to carry it into practice.

" And, waiving all other objections, we are yet compelled to reject a system, which, at the same time that it tacitly lays claim to perfection, takes imperfection for its basis." [1]

The rest of the Introduction is taken up with a vindication of the Moral Sense doctrine in a qualified form. This we may pass over somewhat rapidly, both because the author's views on the subject were at this time very imperfectly worked out, and because they later were fundamentally changed. The drift of the argument is as follows. It seems probable that the *moral* law of society, like its other laws, originates in some attribute of human nature. Answering to each of the actions which we need to perform for the sake of physical health, we find in ourselves some prompter called a desire. May we not therefore assume that there is also some inner tendency or principle impelling us to morality, *i.e.*, a Moral Sense? It is not enough to disprove the existence of such an instinct, to insist upon what are properly to be regarded as perversions of the instinct. All instincts may be perverted. Moreover, even the disciples of Bentham are, in the last resort, obliged to depend upon an intuition of this much derided Moral Sense for the foundation of their own system. In truth, only the hopelessly prejudiced can fail to recognise, on every hand, the workings of such a faculty.

" But how, it may be asked, can a sentiment have a percep-

---

[1] See Introduction: ' The Doctrine of Expediency,' § 5.

tion? How can a desire give rise to a moral *sense*? Is there not here a confounding of the intellectual with the emotional?" Mr. Spencer admits that the objection—which, as will be seen, he states very clearly—seems a serious one, and would be fatal, were the term 'sense' to be understood in its strictest acceptation. Indeed, his answer to the objection is by no means convincing. The problem, as he himself points out, is to explain "how from an *impulse* to behave in the way we call equitable, there will arise a *perception* that such behaviour is proper—a *conviction* that it is good". He says: "This instinct or sentiment, being gratified by a just action, and distressed by an unjust action, produces in us an approbation of the one, and a disgust towards the other; and these readily beget beliefs that the one is virtuous, and the other vicious".[1] Speaking of the Moral Sense and Intuitional schools of Ethics, he says: "Unsuccessful as these writers have been in the endeavour to develop a philosophical morality, all of them, if the foregoing reasoning be correct, have consulted a true oracle. Though they have failed to systematise its utterances, they have acted wisely in trying to do this. An analysis of right and wrong so made, is not indeed the profoundest and ultimate one; but, as we shall by-and-by see, it is perfectly in harmony with that in its initial principle, and coincident with it in its results." One other passage is well worth reproducing: "If Bentham is right in condemning Moral Sense, as an 'anarchical and capricious principle, founded solely upon internal and peculiar feelings,' then is his own maxim doubly fallacious. Is not the idea, 'greatest happiness,' a capricious one? Is not that also 'founded solely upon internal and peculiar feelings'? . . . At the worst therefore, in so far as want of scientific precision is concerned, a philosophy founded on Moral Sense, simply stands in the same category with all other known systems." [2]

Such are the principal ideas of the Introduction, expressed largely in the author's own words. Before proceeding with

[1] See Introduction: 'The Doctrine of the Moral Sense,' § 5.
[2] See *ibid.*, § 6.

our examination of the rest of the book, in so far as that is necessary for our purpose, it will be well to pause for a little, in order to grasp the fundamental conception upon which both the critical and the (at least implicitly) constructive part of the Introduction depend. It would be quite possible for a careless reader to mistake the drift of Mr. Spencer's earlier criticism of what he terms the Expediency Philosophy. His is not one of the familiar attempts to show in detail the difficulties attending the hedonistic calculus. If such were the case, it would have been wholly unnecessary to reproduce his criticism at such length. As a matter of fact, his point of view is not easy to define in brief terms, but it plainly depends upon his conception of the perfect man in a perfect society, as the necessary postulate in a scientific system of Ethics. This paradoxical conception, which has remained to the end an important feature of Mr. Spencer's ethical theory, will later require careful consideration. Here we are concerned with it only as affording his point of departure in criticising Utilitarianism. His meaning seems to be, that a direct computation of the consequences of actions, in terms of happiness and unhappiness, can never afford the foundation for a scientific Ethics, not merely, or principally, because experience shows that individuals derive pleasure or pain, as the case may be, from very different things ; but because it is absolutely certain, on general principles, that every advance in morality involves a shifting of the scale of hedonistic values. Otherwise expressed, individuals and nations are constantly, if generally very slowly, discarding one scale of hedonistic values for another, previously assumed to be ultimate, and this in proportion to the development of moral character. Reduced to its lowest terms, this means that hedonistic values vary as moral character varies.

By many ethical writers of the present day, this is regarded as perhaps the strongest argument for holding that, in some sense or other, character or personality is the ultimate for Ethics, and not happiness. Mr. Spencer, however, does not seem to entertain this view even as an abstract possibility ;

but, assuming that moral values must ultimately be interpreted
in hedonistic terms, without anything like a careful examination of other types of ethical theory, he concludes that only
the scale of hedonistic values that would appeal to the perfect
man in a perfect society (in which alone, apparently, he could
exist) is the true scale of such values. Apparently, then,
this postulate of the perfect man in a perfect society, however
great the difficulties which it involves, is far from being a
merely arbitrary and eccentric assumption on the part of the
author, in this earlier exposition of his ethical theory; he
seems here to regard it, rather, as the only possible salvation
of hedonism. Nothing could well be more instructive than
such an implicit criticism of hedonism itself, coming from
one of its most prominent and able advocates. It is rather
important to remember that this view, when first set forth by
Mr. Spencer, was held in connection with the Moral Sense
doctrine. Such an intuitional adjunct to his system would
tend to prevent that further analysis which might have suggested to him, that he was really making hedonism depend
upon some other undefined principle. It is probably significant that Mr. Spencer's later criticisms of Utilitarianism vary
considerably in method from this earlier and, in the present
writer's opinion, much more effective one.

We have now to see how the principles of the Introduction
are worked out in the earlier and later parts of the
body of the book, the intermediate portions not being to the
present purpose, as they have not to do with theoretical
Ethics. The title of the first chapter, "Definition of Morality," is somewhat misleading. Instead of attempting
clearly to differentiate the subject-matter of Ethics from
that of other sciences or disciplines, the author insists still
further upon the necessity of regarding the moral law as the
law of the perfect man. He argues that a system of pure
Ethics cannot recognise evil, or any of those conditions which
evil generates. Indeed, he says : " It entirely ignores wrong,
injustice, or crime, and gives no information as to what must
be done when they have been committed. It knows no such

thing as an infraction of the laws, for it is merely a statement of what the laws are. It simply says, such and such are the principles on which men should act; and when these are broken it can do nothing but say that they *are* broken." [1] And he argues in justification of this position, that he is merely putting Ethics on the same plane with the several sciences. The geometrician, *e.g.*, has to assume that the various figures with which he deals are perfect each after its kind. In a similar way, physiology treats of the functions of our different organs in their normal state; it has nothing to say of disease or any of the problems arising in connection with disease.

It does not seem to have occurred to Mr. Spencer that such comparisons amount to little more than figures of speech, unless re-enforced by arguments which, in his own treatment, are not forthcoming. Even apart from the important distinction between the normal and the abnormal, the method of the sciences is necessarily abstract in a sense that is not always appreciated by those who triumphantly point to science as that which describes things or events as they are or take place in the concrete, the principal reason being that the scientist has to take one thing at a time. A given physical law, *e.g.*, states what would take place under certain definite conditions, abstracting from all other complicating conditions. In this sense, science is quite as abstract as Mr. Spencer would make it; but one must carefully observe that the abstractions of the scientist, if legitimate, are always perfectly clear. We are never left in doubt as to what is meant by a perfectly straight line or a perfect curve of a particular order; nor do we fail to understand the physicist, when he tells us that things would happen exactly thus and so in the external world, if the conditions specified were the only conditions present. But the perfect man is an abstraction of an entirely different kind—an abstract and ultimate ideal, the true meaning of which, at any given stage of ethical reflection, can be only very vaguely indicated. To say, then,

[1] See Pt. I., ch. i., § 3.

that the very possibility of a scientific Ethics depends upon our beginning with, and perpetually referring to, an ideal which by no possibility can be made perfectly definite, is surely to put Ethics itself in a most dangerous position. Moreover, an Ethics which should refuse to take account of moral evil as well as moral good, and to define the relations of those standing for the good to those responsible, so far as human beings are responsible, for the evil in the world, would surely have little to do with what we all understand by moral conduct.     One must hasten to remark that Mr. Spencer's own ethical system is by no means such as to come under this necessarily sweeping condemnation, but we must clearly recognise the danger of the methodological principle with which he starts out.

The next topic treated is " The Evanescence of Evil ". Here biological science affords the point of departure, although it must be remembered that the author was not yet writing in the light of modern evolutional theory.[1]   All evil results from the non-adaptation of constitution to conditions.   But evil perpetually tends to disappear ; adaptation is going on all the time.   This universal law of physical modification is the law of mental modification also.   Now the best condition of society plainly requires that each individual shall have such desires only as may be satisfied without trenching upon the ability of other individuals to obtain like satisfaction. Of course, we are not thus perfectly adapted at present ; and the principal reason is, that we retain certain traits that were necessary in the original predatory life of the race. All sins of men against each other, in the last resort, reduce to sacrificing the welfare of others to one's own.   This was once necessary, but is no longer so.   We are still in the pro-

[1] Of course ' adaptation of constitution to conditions ' conveniently indicates the general direction of evolutional development ; but what is most characteristic in modern evolutional theory is the attempt to show how such adaptation is brought about—what are the ' factors of evolution,' and how they operate.   It is hardly necessary to say that no account of the ' factors of evolution ' is given in *Social Statics*, which, as we have seen, was published eight years before the *Origin of Species*.

cess of adaptation to the changed conditions. Progress, which can only consist in such adaptation, is not an accident, but a necessity.[1]   The belief in human perfectibility merely amounts to the belief that man will finally become completely suited to his mode of life. " Thus," to quote Mr. Spencer's own words, " the ultimate development of the ideal man is logically certain—as certain as any conclusion in which we place the most implicit faith ; for instance, that all men will die." [2]

Various things might be said regarding this decidedly summary treatment of the problem of evil. Even admitting the unproved assumption that there is nothing in any sense essential in morality, but that it consists merely in the complete adaptation of the individual to his environment, it is plain that the biological analogy is misleading, particularly when made to do service as an argument. In the first place, complete adaptation to environment, in the case of any given species, is always rather an ideal than a fact. The most we can say is, that there is always a tendency toward such complete adaptation. But secondly, adaptation of an animal species to its environment means adaptation to relatively permanent and comparatively simple physical conditions. On the other hand, adaptation of man to his environment—if, as is here certainly the case, man is to be regarded as more than a mere physical organism—means indefinitely more than this. Even physically considered, his environment is subject to constant, and sometimes radical, change as the result of his own exertions, in his capacity as an intellectual being capable of devising means to the attainment of his desired ends. But what we may call his ' psychical environment ' is much more important, and this plainly is subject to almost endless modi-

---

[1] It is rather curious that Mr. Spencer has never questioned the legitimacy of this optimistic assumption. In the later form of his system, where he professes to depend upon the theory of Evolution, Evolution itself is always regarded as that which makes for 'progress'. But how about the phenomena of 'degeneration'?   (*Cf.* the book on that phase of Evolution by Professor E. R. Lankester.)

[2] See Pt. I., ch. ii., § 4.

fication. Every stage of intellectual or moral progress or
decadence on the part of the social group to which he belongs
means a change in what we here call the 'psychical environment'. To say that, in the last resort, this constantly changing psychical environment is wholly dependent upon physical
environment, would really be practically to beg the whole
question; and what the complete adaptation of man to his
total environment, psychical as well as physical, would
mean—that, surely, would be a problem for omniscience
itself.

Having thus cleared the ground, and acquainted us with
his own fundamental postulates, in large part, at least, Mr.
Spencer proceeds to a still further criticism of the Expediency
Philosophy, as introductory to the constructive portion of the
book, which is immediately to follow. He says: "If, instead
of proposing it as the rule of human conduct, Bentham had
simply assumed 'greatest happiness' to be the creative purpose, his position would have been tenable enough. Almost
all men do in one way or other assert the same. . . . The doctrine is taught by all our religious teachers; it is assumed
by every writer on morality: we may therefore safely consider it as an admitted truth." [1]  But he goes on to show that
it is something quite different to assume that 'greatest happiness' should be the *immediate* aim of man. That has been
the fatal error of the Expediency Philosophers. "They have
not observed that the truth has two sides, a Divine side and
a human side." We, as human beings, must confine ourselves
to the attempt to ascertain the general conditions, by con-
forming to which this greatest happiness may be obtained.

First and foremost among these conditions is the social
state itself. There is really no option as to whether we shall
live in or out of society; that is decided for us. Now it is
evident that, in order to realise the greatest sum of happiness in society, men must be such that "each can obtain
complete happiness within his own sphere of activity, without

[1] See Pt. I., ch. iii., § 1.

diminishing the spheres of activity required for the acquisition of happiness by others ".[1]    This, then, is the first and most fundamental of those fixed conditions to the attainment of greatest happiness, necessitated by the social state; and it is the fulfilment of this condition which we express by the word Justice.    But this non-interference is not all that is required, though in itself more important, as we shall see later, than any other single principle whatever.    We must add: " The human constitution must be such as that each man may perfectly fulfil his own nature, not only without diminishing other men's spheres of activity, but without giving unhappiness to other men in any direct or indirect way ".    This may be called Negative Beneficence.    Later we shall see that this principle needs to be kept quite separate from the preceding. But further, the sum-total of happiness will be greatly increased, if men are so constituted that each, in addition to the pleasures that come to him immediately, can sympathetically participate in the pleasurable emotions of all others.    The observance of this condition of happiness may be called Positive Beneficence.    But even still the enumeration is incomplete.    Another principle must be recognised, which, indeed, has been tacitly presupposed throughout.    " Lastly," says Mr. Spencer, " there must go to the production of the greatest happiness the further condition, that, whilst duly regardful of the preceding limitations, each individual shall perform all those acts required to fill up the measure of his own private happiness." [2]

Such, then, are the conditions absolutely requisite, in order to the attainment of greatest happiness.    The author says : " We have no need to perplex ourselves with investigations into the expediency of every measure, by trying to trace out its ultimate results in all their infinite ramifications—a task which it is folly to attempt.    Our course is to inquire con-

---

[1] Later in *Social Statics* appears the more exact formula for the same principle : " Every man has freedom to do all that he wills, provided he infringes not the equal freedom of any other man " (see Pt. I., ch. vi., § 1).

[2] Pt. I., ch. iii., § 2.

cerning such measure, whether or not it fully recognises these fundamental necessities, and to be sure that it must be proper or improper accordingly. Our whole code of duty is comprehended in the endeavour to live up to these necessities." [1] If it be objected that the foregoing classification of the conditions needful to greatest happiness is in some degree artificial, the author admits that, under a final analysis, all such distinctions as those above made must disappear; [2] but he insists that similar criticisms may be passed upon all classifications whatever.

At length we have, in briefest possible outline, the essentials of Mr. Spencer's own ethical system, in its earlier form. And it will be seen at a glance that, however much he may have changed his mind on special points, he has employed the same classification and, roughly speaking, the same method to the end. This, then, is the 'scientific' method, which we are to accept and rigorously to carry out, in place of the discredited Expediency Philosophy. We must now inquire, and that very carefully, whether we have here a really new theory, or the unconscious revival of an old one. We have been told that we must not pursue the greatest happiness directly, for that would mean committing ourselves to the perfectly hopeless task of computing exactly the consequences of actions in the particular case; we must rather act with a view to the fundamental conditions of the greatest happiness, or, in other words, according to certain general rules. So far, it must be denied emphatically that the doctrine above set forth is new. In truth, it would be possible to show a rather startling similarity between this earlier, pre-Evolutional form of Mr. Spencer's ethical theory, in which he recognises the greatest happiness of man as the Divine Idea in creation, and the later form of so-called Theological Utilitarianism. Both theories recognise the Divine Idea, or creative purpose, as being the greatest happiness of man; both show that for

---

[1] Pt. I., ch. iii., § 2.

[2] He admits this verbally, but is inconsistent in his peculiar treatment of Justice, as will be seen later.

very practical reasons, reasons of utility itself, one must act according to general rules, which plainly make for the common welfare, and not either follow the will-o'-the-wisp of selfish gratification or entangle oneself with special problems of what Bentham only too aptly termed 'moral arithmetic'.

But we must be warned by some of the author's own mistakes, and not carry a tempting comparison too far. The reader has doubtless already noted Mr. Spencer's insistence upon the all-importance of Justice. This, to be sure, does not in itself differentiate his treatment of Ethics from that of preceding hedonistic writers. In fact, any sane moralist is pretty sure to recognise the extreme importance of the principle of Justice, however defined, and to grant it a certain primacy over other principles. But it is to be noted that Mr. Spencer—unlike earlier, or indeed later, hedonistic writers —first, practically identifies the principle of Justice with that of non-interference with the free activities of others, and secondly, gives to the principle a special intuitive character, as will be explained immediately, which comes very near to putting it on a plane by itself, *i.e.*, making it differ from other ethical principles, not only in degree, but in kind. This last feature of the author's treatment was perhaps not unnatural, considering the rather vague and confusing Intuitionism of his earlier ethical position; but it is hardly necessary to remind the reader that this same discrimination in favour of Justice, which makes it in a sense more ultimate than even hedonism itself, is fully as characteristic of Mr. Spencer's later as of his earlier treatment. At the proper time, this very serious difficulty in the system which we are examining will have to be squarely met; here it is mentioned merely by way of anticipation.

At the beginning of Part II. of the *Social Statics*, which immediately follows the discussion which we have been considering, the author attempts to deduce his fundamental principles somewhat less abstractly for the benefit of those who may find the previous argument difficult to follow. This attempted simplification of the same general argument we may, of course, safely omit. But in this connection we shall find stated, more clearly than elsewhere in this book, the exact relation between the primary principle, Justice, and the secondary principles, Prudence, Negative Beneficence, and Positive Beneficence. Mr. Spencer says : " Justice imposes upon the exercise of faculties a primary series of limitations, which is strictly true as far as it goes. Negative beneficence imposes a secondary series. It is no defect in the first of these that it does not include the last. The two are, in the main, distinct ; and, as we have just seen, the attempt to unite them under one expression leads us into fatal errors." [1] Then, after repeating that the secondary laws are greatly inferior, as regards exactness, to Justice, he says : " Not being able to define *specifically* the constitution of the ideal man, but being able to define it *generically* only ... we are quite incompetent to say of every particular deed whether it is or is not accordant with that constitution. Or, putting the difficulty in its simplest form, we may say, that as both of these supplementary limitations [2] involve the term *happiness*, and as happiness is for the present capable only of a generic and not of a specific definition, they do not admit of scientific development. Though abstractedly correct limitations, and limitations which the ideal man will strictly observe, they cannot be reduced to concrete forms until the ideal man exists." [3] The last passage, in particular, is important. The supplementary principles, of whatever sort—and these are three, according to Mr. Spencer, Prudence, Negative Beneficence, and Positive Beneficence—are subordinate to Justice, not only because they lack the definite, intuitive character of Justice, but because they all equally involve the conception

---

[1] See Pt. II., ch. iv., § 4. (It should be noted that the chapters are numbered continuously, without regard to the part to which they belong.)

[2] The supplementary principles directly referred to, as the context would show, are due regard for one's own welfare (Prudence) and Negative Beneficence. What Mr. Spencer says in this passage would, of course, apply with equal force to Positive Beneficence.

[3] See *ibid.*, § 5.

of happiness, which latter is capable only of a generic, and not a specific, definition—until the advent of the perfect man.

Before passing on to the latter part of the *Social Statics*—for of course we are not here concerned with the numerous chapters in which the author applies his fundamental principles to the solution of special political and social problems—it will be well to notice a few passages in what he calls his "Secondary Derivation of a First Principle". He is here concerned to show that there is in man a special faculty by virtue of which he tends both to assert his own rights and to recognise the rights of others. As might be expected, this faculty turns out to be the Moral Sense itself, exercising its most characteristic function. Mr. Spencer definitely lays down and defends the thesis, that "this first and all-essential law [Justice], declaratory of the liberty of each limited only by the like liberty of all, is that fundamental truth of which the moral sense is to give an intuition, and which the intellect is to develop into a scientific morality". He then says: "From the above accumulation of evidence it is inferred that there exists in man what may be termed an *instinct of personal rights*—a feeling that leads him to claim as great a share of natural privilege as is claimed by others—a feeling that leads him to repel anything like an encroachment upon what he thinks his sphere of original freedom".[1] Somewhat later he adds: "Seeing, however, that this instinct of personal rights is a purely selfish instinct, leading each man to assert and defend his own liberty of action, there remains the question—Whence comes our perception of the rights of others?"

In general, Mr. Spencer agrees with the method adopted by Adam Smith in his *Theory of Moral Sentiments*, where, of course, this and other important phenomena of our moral life are explained by the principle of Sympathy. But he makes the following criticism of Smith's actual treatment: "Not recognising any such impulse as that which urges men to maintain their claims, he did not see that their respect for the

---

[1] See Pt. II., ch. v., § 2.

claims of others, may be explained in the same way. He
did not perceive that the sentiment of justice is nothing but
a sympathetic affection of the instinct of personal rights—
a sort of reflex function of it. . . . It was elsewhere hinted,
that though we must keep up the distinction between them,
it is nevertheless true that *justice* and *beneficence* have a
common root, and the reader will now at once perceive that
the common root is—Sympathy." [1] It is further argued that,
if our perceptions of justice are generated in the way alleged,
" it will follow that, other things equal, those who have the
strongest sense of their own rights, will have the strongest
sense of the rights of their neighbours ". Of course it is not
claimed that this is absolutely true, but only that, " in the
*average* of cases, we may safely conclude that a man's sense
of justice to himself, and his sense of justice to his neighbours,
bear a constant ratio to each other ".[2]

The passages above quoted contain, perhaps, the most
satisfactory statement to be found in the *Social Statics* regarding that constitution of human nature, by virtue of which the
moral law is at once to be apprehended and gradually realised.
They also throw an interesting light upon Mr. Spencer's
earlier conception of the Moral Sense. We have already seen
that this has to do mainly with the one ethical principle which
is perfectly free from ambiguity, and therefore capable of
strictly scientific development—Justice. And we are now led
to see, what has probably been suspected by the reader
hitherto, that, in its operation, the moral sense manifests itself
more as an instinct (implying an impulsive tendency) than as
a faculty of abstract moral intuitions. In fact, the author is
always comparing it with the instincts which lead us to satisfy
our various bodily wants.

It is difficult to see, from the hints afforded, how this fundamental tendency of human nature, primarily impulsive in
character, is capable of such development as to make possible
a scientific Ethics. Is it too much to suggest that, here

---

[1] See Pt. II., ch. v., § 5.     [2] See *ibid.*, § 6.

again, Mr. Spencer is partly misled by his dependence upon biological analogies? Most assuredly the moralist, of whatever school, should take the most careful account of those forces of human nature which make for conduct. But those same forces, or tendencies, of human nature, no matter how fundamental, must be morally justified, if justified at all, by showing that they make for the ultimate end of conduct, the *Summum Bonum.* Logically, the only escape from an Ethics of the Good is to stop with naïve Intuitionism, the essential characteristic of which is an implicit denial that the several parts of the moral law can be rationalised by being brought under a single higher principle. And this, without question is the very antithesis of scientific ethical method. In the earlier form of his system, at any rate, Mr. Spencer seems to run great risk of becoming entangled with two ultimates: Justice, considered as an absolute principle, which therefore needs no further justification, and Happiness, considered as an ultimate, though an ultimate not capable of exact comprehension; and two methods, the one Intuitive, the other Hedonistic—and this quite apart from his questionable interpretation and explanation of the Moral Sense itself.

As already suggested, it would be quite apart from our present purpose to consider Mr. Spencer's own applications of his first principle, or axiom, of freedom from interference, *i.e.* Justice, to prove the several rights upon which he so strongly insists—the rights of life, personal liberty, use of the earth, property, exchange, free-speech, etc. Nor are we concerned with his discussions (in Part III.), also from the point of view of Justice, interpreted as the principle of non-interference, regarding the proper constitution of the State. It may be doubted whether any prominent writer belonging strictly to the present generation would attempt the solution of so many practical problems, mainly of state-craft, by the application of a single abstract principle. So far from being a matter of strict logic, such application is necessarily a matter of individual judgment, even allowing, for the sake of the argument, the validity of the first principle assumed. An interesting illustration of this rather obvious truth may be found in the author's earlier treatment of the land question, where, quite contrary to his later judgment in the matter, he advocates the nationalisation of land, on the ground that a monopoly of land-ownership by individuals interferes with the equal freedom of others.

Part IV. of the *Social Statics*, which concludes the work, is essentially different in character from what precedes. Not that the views set forth are incompatible with those which we have already examined; but what the writer here attempts is something radically different. He says: "Social philosophy may be aptly divided (as political economy has been) into statics and dynamics; the first treating of the equilibrium of a perfect society, the second of the forces by which society is advanced towards perfection. . . . Hitherto we have concerned ourselves chiefly with the statics, touching upon the dynamics only occasionally for purposes of elucidation. Now, however, the dynamics claim special attention."[1] The treatment here given, however, is both very brief and quite unsystematic, a last word being devoted to various subjects. Hence, probably, the title of the long chapter which practically constitutes this final part of the book—"General Considerations".

The course of civilisation, we are told, could not have been different from what it has been. What might have been in the abstract (*i.e.*, according to a different scheme of creation), we cannot say. "But given an unsubdued earth; given the being—man, appointed to overspread and occupy it; given the laws of life what they are; and no other series of changes than that which has taken place, could have taken place."[2] The primitive man had to be a savage, for it was his function to clear the earth of races endangering his life and occupying the space required for mankind. It was necessary that he should have the desire to kill, and that he should be devoid of sympathy, or possess but the germ of it. A thoroughly civilised community could not be formed out of men qualified

---

[1] See Pt. IV., ch. xxx., § 1.    [2] See *ibid.*, § 2.

to wage war with the pre-existing occupants of the earth The barbarising of colonists, who live in close contact with the lower races, is universally admitted. The gist of the matter is : the primitive man had to be one whose happiness was obtained largely at the sacrifice of the happiness of others. But we have already seen that the ultimate man must be one who can obtain happiness without deducting from the happiness of others. Moreover, we have seen that progress, what we call 'moral progress,' is a necessary law. Why, then, does the needed adaptation to new conditions, in which progress consists, take place so slowly?

The reason is, that the new conditions themselves have arisen but slowly. Warfare between man and the creatures at enmity with him has continued up to the present time, and over a large portion of the globe is going on still. The destructive propensities which inevitably thus arise, are perpetuated by the custom of game-preserving. But, what is more important, the old predatory instinct is in a sense self-maintained for it generates between men and men a hostile relationship, similar to that which it generates between men and inferior animals. In short—and here we come to the earlier statement of one of the author's most characteristic views—human character has changed slowly, because it has been subject to two conflicting sets of conditions. " On the one hand," to use his own words, " the discipline of the social state has been developing it into the sympathetic form ; whilst on the other hand, the necessity for self-defence partly of man against brute, partly of man against man, and partly of societies against each other, has been maintaining the old unsympathetic form." [1] The two codes thus resulting are, of course, what the author in his later writings terms the 'ethics of amity' and the 'ethics of enmity'. Only when warfare has largely ceased, can the former code, which is to develop into the code of the perfect man, have a normal, and reasonably rapid, development.

[1] See Pt. IV., ch. xxx., § 3.

At this point Mr. Spencer somewhat complicates his argument by showing that warfare itself has had its uses, even on the social side. For what are the pre-requisites to a conquering race? Numerical strength or improved methods of warfare, both of which are indications of advancement. " Evidently, therefore, from the very beginning, the conquest of one people over another has been, in the main, the conquest of the social man over the anti-social man ; or, strictly speaking, of the more adapted over the less adapted." But we must very carefully observe what may at first seem to the reader a rather fine distinction. Mr. Spencer says : " Whilst the injustice of conquests and enslavings is not perceived, they are on the whole beneficial ; but as soon as they are felt to be at variance with the moral law, the continuance of them retards adaptation in one direction, more than it advances it in another : a fact which our new preacher of the old doctrine, that might is right, may profitably consider a little ".[1]

Before sympathy arises, indeed, hero-worship plays a humanising part. It is found among all savage and barbarous peoples, as well as among those of higher development. Indeed, without such a check upon anti-social propensities, it is difficult to see how many primitive societies could exist. But we must recognise it for what it is : " a sentiment which leads men to prostrate themselves before any manifestation of power, be it in chief, feudal lord, king, or constitutional government, and makes them act in subordination to that power ". In proportion to the lack of moral sense, will be the degree of such submission to mere authority. This, in fact, is absolutely necessary. Where reverence for the moral law is lacking, reverence for mere authority must take its place ; otherwise there would be complete lawlessness or barbarism. In short, as the author says : " We must admit that this power-worship has fulfilled, and does still fulfil, a very important function, and that it may advantageously last as long as it can ".[2] All this is quite as characteristic of the later, as of the

---

[1] See Pt. IV., ch. xxx., § 4.    [2] See *ibid.*, §§ 6, 7.

earlier, form of Mr. Spencer's ethical theory. He consistently holds throughout, that what he calls the 'pro-moral' paves the way for the strictly moral, the latter, of course, being an ideal to which humanity tends always to approximate, rather than an accomplished fact. The civilised races are at present in an intermediate position, and the radical confusion to be found in their ethical ideals is largely to be explained by the essential inconsistency between the 'ethics of amity' and the 'ethics of enmity'.

Perhaps it may seem that a disproportionate amount of space has been devoted to this rather minute reproduction and criticism of the earlier, and confessedly inadequate, statement of Mr. Spencer's ethical theory. Such a mode of treatment, however, has seemed necessary for two principal reasons. First, the *Social Statics*, in its original and complete form, is now withdrawn from circulation, being superseded by a revised and greatly abridged edition (1892), which is almost useless for our present purpose. Secondly, there is a special reason for presenting the earlier form of the system in detail, before considering the later form. Far more adequately than any other single writer, Mr. Spencer is commonly supposed to represent Evolutional Ethics. It is generally assumed, alike by friendly and adverse critics, that his success or failure in solving the problems of Ethics is due principally to his rigorous application of Evolutional principles. But it is highly important, in an historical and critical examination like the present one, not to take things for granted. We shall have to look as carefully for similarity as for dissimilarity between the later and the earlier form of this important system, remembering always that the earlier form, which has just been reviewed, appeared eight years before the publication of the *Origin of Species*, and that, whatever its merits, we have found it to be nothing if not highly abstract in character. And one must not, by any means, permit oneself here that hopelessly vague use of the word 'Evolution' which makes it stand merely for continuous development according to some undefined law or laws. That is what the scientist very properly criticises in some writers who constantly urge that we must go back to the early Greek philosophers to find the first Evolutionists. The theory of Evolution, from which Evolutional Ethics takes its name, is, of course, the modern scientific theory of the development of organic forms by means of certain more or less definitely determined 'factors of Evolution,' as Mr. Spencer has called them. And it is hardly necessary to point out that, of ethical systems really depending upon the theory of Evolution, one which should employ the principle of 'the inheritance of acquired characteristics,' and base important arguments upon this principle (as Mr. Spencer actually does in his later ethical writings), would differ in many important respects from one which should either deny the validity of this principle altogether, or allow to it only a secondary rôle. For the influence of the theory of Evolution proper upon Mr. Spencer's ethical system, then, we must of course look to the later form of his doctrine; and the extent of such influence can hardly be greater, at any rate, than that represented by the divergence of the later from the earlier form.

# CHAPTER XIV.

## HERBERT SPENCER (*continued*).

BETWEEN the publication of the *Social Statics* (1851) and that of the *Data of Ethics* (1879), nearly thirty years had elapsed, and during this time the sciences, particularly the biological sciences, had made unexampled progress. Moreover, it is probable that no single scholar, in the English-speaking world, at least, had followed this progress with keener interest or with a more comprehensive grasp of its general significance than Mr. Spencer. His equipment, therefore, on the strictly scientific side, was most complete, when he attempted to realise his early ideal of a scientific Ethics. Unfortunately, however, he had retained almost undiminished two of his early prejudices: first, a frank contempt for History as such; and secondly, a decided lack of appreciation, at least, for the classic works of Philosophy, even those in the field of Ethics itself. The natural result was that, while a polymath in quite the literal sense, so far as the literature of science was concerned, Mr. Spencer had never taken the trouble to master the literature of the discipline which he proposed to reform; nor had he, by any means, fitted himself to take the historical point of view, even when his own treatment logically required this. In the case of any but a highly original thinker such a mixed preparation for the task in hand could hardly have failed to lead to disastrous results. As it is, we are bound to recognise a considerable debt to the author of the *Synthetic Philosophy* for his later contributions to a discipline in which he was, perhaps, never completely at home.

The *Data of Ethics*, ostensibly only the first of the six Parts of the proposed (and now happily executed) *Principles of Ethics*, is a great deal more than either its title or its place in the scheme of the whole work would suggest. From it, in truth, one could obtain a satisfactory general knowledge of the later form of Mr. Spencer's ethical system, though the great importance of Part IV.—*Justice* (1891)—is by no means to be questioned. The decidedly inferior importance of the remaining parts, interesting as these are, will call for explanation and discussion later. Here it may be premised that the reason is not to be found in the failure of Mr. Spencer's powers as a thinker and writer, but rather in the peculiar structure of the system itself. But what one would particularly insist upon at present, is the extreme importance of the *Data of Ethics*, as giving an intelligible, and fairly adequate, statement of the author's system as a whole.

Nothing could well seem to differ more, as regards method, from the highly abstract *Social Statics* than the first two chapters of the *Data of Ethics*, on " Conduct in General " and " The Evolution of Conduct ". In the former work, we were somewhat abruptly introduced to the conception of the ideal man in an ideal society, as the necessary starting-point for Ethics ; in the latter, we are told that we must begin by regarding conduct as a whole, in a sense an organic whole, of which moral conduct, ordinarily so-called, is only a part, inextricably bound up with the rest. By conduct is here meant the adjustment of acts to ends, whether on the part of man or of the lower animals. This adjustment, of course, may be unconscious or conscious,[1] relatively simple or almost indefinitely complex. And, exactly as in the case of biological investigations, we must interpret the more developed by the less developed. This naturally leads to a consideration of the evolution of conduct. Plainly such evolution, when we take

[1] This is rather implied than stated in the passages we are discussing, and Mr. Spencer's emphasis on the complexity rather than the consciousness of human adjustments, as that which differentiates man from the lower animals, is itself an error and the source of others in his system.

the whole animal kingdom into consideration, must mean at least a more and more perfect adjustment of acts to ends subserving individual life and the rearing of offspring. But something else is presupposed, or neither of the above kinds of adjustment could attain its highest form. The multitudinous creatures which fill the earth are interfered with by each other. A grim 'struggle for existence' is being carried on all the time, so that the gain of one animal or species means the loss of another.

" This imperfectly-evolved conduct," says Mr. Spencer, " introduces us by antithesis to conduct that is perfectly evolved. Contemplating these adjustments of acts to ends which miss completeness because they cannot be made by one creature without other creatures being prevented from making them, raises the thought of adjustments such that each creature may make them without preventing them from being made by other creatures." But even this is not all. The author adds : " A gap in this outline must now be filled up. There remains a further advance not yet even hinted. For beyond so behaving that each achieves his ends without preventing others from achieving their ends, the members of a society may give mutual help in the achievement of ends." And he urges in conclusion that " Ethics has for its subject-matter, that form which universal conduct assumes during the last stages of its evolution ".[1]

When examining the *Social Statics*, we were obliged to conclude that Mr. Spencer was not infrequently led astray by scientific analogies that did not hold. How is it with his use of the idea of ' Evolution ' in the present case ? Conduct, we have been told, is a whole, and " we must interpret the more developed by the less developed ". Organic evolution is to afford us the clue. But, without warning, we take leave of the struggle for existence, without which organic evolution means exactly nothing, and consider how rational beings, not so much do as should, behave toward each other—Justice and

[1] See ch. ii., §§ 6, 7.

Beneficence being thus represented as pertaining to the 'last stages' of the 'evolution of conduct'. Are we any longer interpreting the 'more developed' by the 'less developed'? Are we still holding to the original meaning of the word 'Evolution'? Or are we not rather using 'Evolution' for development in general, and assuming a development that implies reason and moral personality? Assuming, however, the legitimacy of the author's conception of a perfectly continuous evolution of conduct, from the lowest animals up to ideal man, we are prepared for his definition of good and bad conduct. The conduct which we call good is the relatively 'more evolved' conduct; and bad is the name we apply to conduct which is relatively 'less evolved'. But why, on scientific grounds merely, should Evolution be thus constantly identified with what we, from our human point of view, call progress? Degeneration (*e.g.*, of cave animals) is as good a case of evolutional development (*i.e.*, adaptation to a given environment) as any other.

But now a further question arises, according to the author: "Is there any assumption made in calling good the acts conducive to life, in self or others, and bad those which directly or indirectly tend towards death, special or general?" And he himself makes the following reply: "Yes, there is one postulate in which pessimists and optimists agree. Both their arguments assume it to be self-evident that life is good or bad, according as it does, or does not, bring a surplus of agreeable feeling. . . . The implication common to their antagonistic views is, that conduct should conduce to preservation of the individual, of the family, and of the society, only supposing that life brings more happiness than misery." Mr. Spencer concludes: "If we call good every kind of conduct which aids the lives of others, and do this under the belief that life brings more happiness than misery; then it becomes undeniable that, taking into account immediate and remote effects on all persons, the good is universally the pleasurable".[1]

[1] See ch. iii., §§ 9, 10.

Such is Mr. Spencer's very summary vindication of hedonism. The criticism of other types of ethical theory, which immediately follows, adds little or nothing to the force of the argument, as it almost wholly lacks the originality which characterised the early attack upon the Expediency Philosophy in *Social Statics*. Generally speaking, the argument contained in the passages just quoted is an excellent example of what may be called the 'either—or' method of solving philosophical problems. It is, of course, possible to state almost any problem in Metaphysics or Ethics, so as to make one of two conclusions seem inevitable. In fact, it takes a great philosopher even to state fairly, in the first instance, the essential problems of philosophy. But taking the argument as it stands, and looking at it a little more closely, it will readily appear that there may logically be just as many forms of Optimism or Pessimism as there are different theories regarding the nature of the Good. If the Good, whatever the Good may be, is attainable; then life is worth living—otherwise not. Moreover, the fact—which can hardly be denied—that the Good has some relation to happiness, even a very close relation, by no means proves that it is itself identical with happiness. In truth, this argument of Mr. Spencer's is perhaps the shortest cut to hedonism, with which the present writer is acquainted. He seems to have no suspicion of the many pitfalls that lie in the way of one, who would solve the oldest puzzles of Moral Philosophy in such summary fashion.

Lest this criticism—which, of course, implies that Mr. Spencer has not taken the trouble to understand certain types of ethical theory differing from his own—may seem too severe, let us carefully examine the well-known chapter on "Ways of Judging Conduct," which immediately follows. After quite properly insisting that intellectual progress is by no one trait so adequately characterised, as by development of the idea of causation, and indicating briefly how long it has taken for the full implications of this idea to be recognised, the author says: "Why do I here make these reflections on what seems an irrelevant subject? I do it because on studying the various ethical theories, I am struck with the fact that they are all characterised either by entire absence of the idea of causation, or by inadequate presence of it. Whether theological, political, intuitional, or utilitarian, they all display, if not in the same degree, still, each in a large degree, the defects which result from this lack." [1]

At first, this general indictment of all previous ethical theories may seem rather staggering; but if the reader pursues the argument further, he will see reason as he proceeds to distrust its validity, and will end by retaining a large portion of his respect for the ethical speculation of the past. Note first the division of all ethical theories into theological, political, intuitional, and utilitarian. Of 'theological' theories, we are told: "Religious creeds, established and dissenting, all embody the belief that right and wrong are right and wrong simply in virtue of divine enactment. And this tacit assumption has passed from systems of theology into systems of morality. . . . We see this in the works of the Stoics [*sic*], as well as in the works of certain Christian moralists." [2] It is interesting to learn that the Stoics, with their pantheistic tendencies, were guilty of making morality depend upon the arbitrary will of God; and the 'Christian moralists' referred to are unnamed, except Jonathan Dymond, a recent Quaker writer, who of course cannot properly be taken as typical. To attribute this error to theological moralists indiscriminately, is most unjust. To say nothing of more recent writers, the so-called 'Theological Utilitarians' (who apparently would have to be classed in this category, since Utilitarianism is here, as elsewhere, treated by Mr. Spencer as a non-theological system) were as far as possible from holding this view, though they have sometimes been misunderstood, as by J. S. Mill in his early essay on Sedgwick's *Discourse*. It will be remembered that this error was tacitly corrected by Mill three years later, in the essay on Bentham.

As regards 'political' systems of morality, which imply " the

---

[1] See ch. iv., § 17.     [2] See *ibid.*, § 18.

belief that moral obligation originates with Acts of Parliament, and can be changed this way or that way by majorities," we must confess that this type of ethical theory has escaped our observation.    The fling, apparently, is at all those who " ridicule the idea that men have any natural rights, and allege that rights are wholly results of convention "—another example of the 'either—or' method, previously mentioned. That the ' pure intuitionists ' have not paid a due regard to natural causation, may be cheerfully conceded to the author. But the ' pure intuitionists ' seem here to be identified with those who " affirm that we know some things to be right and other things to be wrong, by virtue of a supernaturally given conscience ".[1]   What is to distinguish them from the class of theological moralists ?

Mr. Spencer's startling indictment of all previous Moral Philosophy, then, reduces itself to his old dissatisfaction with the Expediency Philosophy, so forcibly expressed in *Social Statics*.   In fact, a comparison would show that the criticism here given is much less effective than the earlier one.   Is this because Mr. Spencer no longer cares, in this particular connection, to avail himself of his conception of the perfect man in the perfect society as the initial postulate of a scientific Ethics?   The gist of the earlier criticism, as will be remembered, was : that every advance in morality involves a shifting of the scale of hedonistic values, so that only the scale of such values that would appeal to the perfect man could be regarded as the true or permanent scale.   Hence the hedonistic calculus will at any rate remain impossible until the advent of the perfect man.   In its way, this earlier mode of attack was most effective, for it went to show that hedonistic values vary with the development (or decadence) of moral character ; but it plainly was dangerous to hedonism in any form.   Perhaps it is significant that Mr. Spencer does not return to it in his later criticisms of Utilitarianism.

He proposes, indeed, a method of treatment for Ethics

---

[1] See ch. iv., §§ 19, 20.

which might seem the very antithesis of his earlier method. He says: " A preparation in the simpler sciences is presupposed. Ethics has a physical aspect; since it treats of human activities which, in common with all expenditures of energy, conform to the law of the persistence of energy: moral principles must conform to physical necessities. It has a biological aspect; since it concerns certain effects, inner and outer, individual and social, of the vital changes going on in the highest type of animal. It has a psychological aspect; for its subject-matter is an aggregate of actions that are prompted by feelings and guided by intelligence. And it has a sociological aspect; for these actions, some of them directly and all of them indirectly, affect associated beings. What is the implication? Belonging under one aspect to each of these sciences — physical, biological, psychological, sociological—it can find its ultimate interpretations only in those fundamental truths which are common to all of them." [1] Hence, of course, the four chapters—better known by title, perhaps, than any others in the book—" The Physical View," " The Biological View," " The Psychological View," and " The Sociological View ".

There is something at first sight tempting in this proposal to reduce the relatively indefinite science, or discipline, of Ethics, to terms of sciences as definite in their scope and method as Physics, Biology, and Psychology—though, perhaps, even the prudent scientist would prefer, for the present, to steer clear of Sociology. And the case of Physiology might plausibly be cited in justification of such a mode of procedure, since the progress of that science has plainly been in the direction of reducing its facts and principles, as far as possible, to terms of physics and chemistry. But one very important difference must be noted between what Mr. Spencer proposes here and what the physiologist has found an extremely useful, if not indispensable, methodological principle. Physics, chemistry, and physiology are alike explanatory

---

[1] See ch. iv., § 22*a*.

sciences pure and simple. They do not for a moment admit of evaluations or appreciations : ' good ' and ' bad ' are for them—as for all explanatory sciences, whether dealing with the external or with the internal world—meaningless terms. Ethics, on the contrary, while by no means neglecting the mere facts of human character and conduct, always discriminates between that which has worth and that which has not— the standard, of course, being that which is assumed to be the Good, except in the case of Intuitionism, where the evaluation is made with direct reference to certain immediate feelings or intuitions of the moral agent, assumed to be ultimate.

But while, to the present writer, the method here involved seems highly questionable, for reasons partly indicated, it is frankly to be admitted that Mr. Spencer is not alone in failing to recognise, or refusing to admit, this line of demarcation between the descriptive and explanatory sciences, on the one hand, and the normative sciences, on the other. Let us, then, consider his ' physical view ' of Ethics. This, as the author explains, means considering conduct " as a set of combined motions ". And he says: " Taking the evolution point of view, and remembering that while an aggregate evolves, not only the matter composing it, but also the motion of that matter, passes from an indefinite incoherent homogeneity to a definite coherent heterogeneity, we have now to ask whether conduct as it rises to its higher forms, displays in increasing degrees these characters; and whether it does not display them in the greatest degree when it reaches that highest form which we call moral ".[1] The author argues that this is the case. From the lower animals up to man, there may be observed an increasing degree of the coherence of motions. And the same thing is equally manifest, as we trace the condition of man from a savage state to the highest modern civilisation. All this, observe, is the coherence of physical motions, considered strictly as such—an abstraction, to realise the exact import of which is a considerable intellectual feat.

[1] See ch. v., § 24.

(The present writer must acknowledge that he has never accomplished it, to his complete satisfaction.) Mr. Spencer adds: "Now mark that a greater coherence among its component motions, broadly distinguishes the conduct we call moral from the conduct we call immoral. The application of the word dissolute to the last, and of the word self-restrained to the first, implies this. . . . In proportion as the conduct is what we call moral, it exhibits comparatively settled connections between antecedents and consequents. . . . Contrariwise, in the conduct of one whose principles are not high, the sequences of motions are doubtful." [1]

Frankly speaking, this seems to me one of the most unhelpful abstractions ever made in the name of Ethics. From the proposition that the 'coherence' of physical motions increases, as we ascend from the lower to the higher manifestations of life, we are led on to the very different proposition that, the more moral conduct is, the greater will be this coherence of the motions involved. This last proposition seems more than doubtful. Some forms of dissipation, particularly drunkenness, might appear to bear out the statement; but how about a life more or less deliberately devoted to crime? Certainly there is greater coherence in the manipulations of the counterfeiter and the expert safe-opener than most moral men, not manually expert, could ever lay claim to. And as for the possibility of predicting conduct (whether considered as a mere series of physical motions or otherwise), what conduct could be easier to predict than that of a man hopelessly given over to a particular vice? Almost precisely the same criticisms apply to the author's contention, that increasingly moral conduct implies an increasingly 'definite' set of physical motions. It is not to the point to urge that "the conscientious man is exact in all his transactions". The defaulting bank clerk, who falsifies his accounts, in order to conceal his own crime, has to be as exact as if he were keeping the books properly; and generally he needs to be more,

[1] See ch. v., § 25.

rather than less, expert than the honest man. But this exactness, or expertness—do they, as applied to a series of physical
motions, considered merely as such, really mean anything at
all? More plausible is the final argument, which goes to
show that the highest morality implies an increasing 'heterogeneity' of motions. But what a ridiculously unsafe criterion
this would be, by which to distinguish moral from immoral
conduct!

The 'physical view' of morality, then, turns out to be not
only highly abstract, but extremely fanciful. We now pass
on to the 'biological view'. From the standpoint of biology,
the perfectly moral man is one in whom the physiological
functions of all kinds are duly fulfilled. Either defect or excess in the performance of function results in a lowering of
life for the time being. Hence the performance of every
function is, in a sense, a moral obligation. The author hastens
to remark that this principle, *viz.*, that the performance of
every function is a duty, strictly applies to ideal humanity
only, not to humanity as now existing. At present, the performance of every function by each would involve interference
of one individual with another;[1] but when man is completely
evolved, this will not be the case. Another important result
of such complete evolution will be, that immediate pleasures
and pains, accompanying the exercise of our various functions,
will be safe guides of conduct, as of course they are not now—
though it is universally true that every pleasure increases
vitality for the time being, while every pain decreases vitality.
While freely admitting that, as we are at present constituted,
pleasures are not always connected with actions which should
be performed, nor pains with actions which should be avoided,
Mr. Spencer says: "Along with complete adjustment of
humanity to the social state, will go recognition of the truths
that actions are completely right only when, besides being
conducive to future happiness, special and general, they are
immediately pleasurable, and that painfulness, not only ulti-

---

[1] *I.e.*, 'injustice,' which, as will be remembered, is the cardinal sin, according
to Mr. Spencer.

mate but proximate, is the concomitant of actions which are wrong ".[1]

It cannot be denied that the ' biological view ' of morality possesses at least one very important advantage over the ' physical view,' *viz.*, the propositions involved are sufficiently definite to admit of clear comprehension. Let us begin by examining the first, that complete or ideal morality means, among other things, the due performance of all physiological functions. There is, undoubtedly, an important element of truth in this statement. Complete mental health, so desirable for the moral life, is hardly possible without a fair degree of physical health ; and this, of course, implies the due perform- ance of at least many physiological functions. That the moral agent should have a conscientious regard for his health, even under existing conditions, goes without question. But it is only too evident that, as things are now, the teachings of biology (or rather, of hygiene) and those of Ethics by no means necessarily coincide. And one must carefully observe that this is not all. Strictly moral considerations apart, every man who fills a real place in society, no matter how humble, often finds himself obliged to work when it is undoubtedly more or less detrimental to his health ; and those whose ser- vices are at all indispensable to their fellow-men, particularly at critical times, not infrequently have to take considerable personal risks. It should be noted that one does not here refer to cases of unnecessary hardship. The difficulty is, that each has, or should have, his own work, which no other can perform equally well—at least, without some slight prepara- tion. Moreover, that all-round physical development here im- plied, which is so desirable in itself, is practically impossible for those who have to devote themselves constantly to any specialised form of labour, whether physical, or mental, or both.

Such considerations may seem irrelevant, as they plainly refer to existing conditions, while Mr. Spencer claims only

[1] See ch. vi., § 39.

that the due performance of all physiological functions will be a moral duty in the ideal, or completely evolved, society. But why is it that a perfectly normal physical life—implying, as Mr. Spencer would say, 'the due performance of all physiological functions'—is impossible for the great majority at the present time? The principal reason would seem to be that very tendency toward specialisation of physical and mental activities, which is the most characteristic feature of modern civilisation. How far specialisation should go, is, of course, a perfectly fair, and indeed a very serious, question; but is it conceivable that future generations will succeed in doing away with specialisation, either altogether or in any large measure? If not, Mr. Spencer's physiological ideal will hardly be attainable even in a society 'completely evolved'—whatever that may mean.

So far, as will be remembered, we have left out of account strictly moral considerations. When we take the point of view of Ethics proper, it becomes evident that a necessary result of increasing specialisation has been a great increase in the complexity of human relations — including, of course, moral relations. More and more it has become morally reprehensible, even if not socially impossible, for a man to 'live unto himself alone, or die unto himself alone'. Will this complexity of human relations decrease as social evolution approaches its goal—granting that there is any definite, and therefore stationary, goal? If not, we shall apparently have to remain to the end 'members of one body,' whether one take this as the language of Christian theology or that of the most recent Evolutional Ethics, with its fundamental conception of society as an organism. Hence, from the strictly ethical point of view, it would seem still more improbable, that the individual member of the society of the future will necessarily have either the duty or the privilege of duly performing *all* physiological functions.

We must now examine the second principal thesis which Mr. Spencer defends in this chapter on the 'biological view' of morality. This, as will be remembered, is: that pleasures and pains will finally become so adjusted to the performance of special functions, that each will exactly correspond to acts to be performed or avoided. This may seem like trenching on the field of psychology; but the author urges that this immediate connection between feeling and function must be considered here, since it has played such an important part in organic evolution. Among the lower animals, indeed, a fair degree of adaptation such as that described must be assumed, since without it a given animal species would tend to become extinct. Through the different stages of human civilisation, however, it must be confessed that this adjustment has been far from perfect. This has been mainly due to the necessity of a continuous partial readjustment to continually changing conditions of life. But when the final stage of evolution is reached, the adjustment will be perfect; and hence the immediate pleasures and pains accompanying functions will be a safe indication as to whether they are to be performed or avoided. In fact, as Mr. Spencer explicitly says, in the passage previously quoted, actions will then be completely moral, only if they are immediately pleasurable to the agent, as well as calculated to bring future pleasures to himself and others.

This very argument for what Mr. Spencer would call complete 'æstho-physiological' adaptation in the future, tends to bring out in strong relief the difficulties of his conception of the perfectly evolved society. These we shall have to touch upon almost immediately; but it seems necessary to pause a moment, in order to note another example of the habit which the author has of running one principle into another. The only excuse, as he himself admits, for introducing psychical phenomena at this point, is that the immediate connections between pleasures and pains and the performance of particular physiological functions play a very important part in organic evolution itself. Now, after arguing that this kind of adjustment will become perfect in the completely evolved condition of man, he draws, as a sort of corollary, the ethical conclusion that when such perfect adjustment obtains, moral actions will be immediately pleasurable to the agent, as well as ultimately pleasant in their effects on the agent and others. This is a radically different principle, involving the whole moral nature of the completely evolved man, for it is too plain to admit of argument, that the rightness or wrongness of a moral action of any consequence involves very different, and generally much more complicated, considerations than does the due performance of any particular physiological function, considered as such. Otherwise expressed : granting that immediate pleasures and pains, connected with the performance of physiological functions, should become even infallible hygienic guides for the individual, they would not necessarily, or even conceivably, be therefore trustworthy guides to the complete satisfaction of the agent himself, according to any recognised form of Egoism ; and they would wholly leave out of account the moral relations of the agent to others. It is disconcerting to find such inadvertencies in a ' scientific' treatment of Ethics.

Let us now pass on to our delayed examination of the general difficulties involved in Mr. Spencer's conception of an ideal, or completely evolved, society. Such an examination seems necessary here, for this is the first time in the *Data of Ethics* that he has allowed himself to base an important argument on the assumed certainty of an ideal society in the remote future ; and the question immediately arises, whether his conception of the ideal society has become more definite since the publication of *Social Statics*. There is nothing, in the present volume, at any rate, to indicate this. The ideal society is still regarded merely as a society composed of individuals completely adjusted to their environment. In our examination of *Social Statics*, we saw that this conception of the complete adjustment of man to his environment involved serious difficulties, of which the author took no account. Roughly speaking, these were : that man is constantly, and in many cases materially, changing even his physical environment ; and, secondly, that what we may call the ' psychical' environment of any group, whether larger or smaller, is subject to still greater modification. In short, we saw that while, for organic evolution, the environment is relatively stationary, and not too complex for fairly adequate comprehension, the total (physical and 'psychical') environment to which the completely evolved man is to become perfectly adapted, is so largely a matter of his own creation— so constantly changing, and by no means necessarily always in the direction of improvement [1]—that the perfect adaptation or adjustment predicted is difficult even to conceive.

Now in the *Data of Ethics*, where, of course, the author attempts to do justice to both the 'dynamic' and the 'static' view of morality, these difficulties, so far from diminishing, become considerably accentuated. We have seen that Mr. Spencer admits, with his usual candour, that the adjustment of immediate pleasures and pains to the performance of particular physiological functions is less reliable in man than in the lower animals, and less reliable in a high civilisation, up to the present, than in the original savage condition of man; and he suggests what is doubtless the true explanation, that the continually changing conditions of life have necessitated continuous partial readjustment. This, observe, is considering the matter from what Mr. Spencer, at any rate, would call the merely biological point of view. The 'changing conditions of life' referred to are not modifications in his environment produced by man himself, but the changing conditions involved in the development of humanity from a savage, and therefore wholly militant, condition to a completely civilised, and therefore wholly industrial, condition, through the rather complicated transitional condition of militant-industrialism in which we find ourselves at present. The fact that all this involves a good deal that is peculiar to Mr. Spencer's sociological views, may be neglected for the present. But what we must insist upon observing is, that perfect adjustment (whether of the particular kind which we have been considering, or any other) has hitherto been impossible, on the author's

---

[1] *Cf.* periods of decadence in history. But Mr. Spencer despises the 'gossip' of history.

own showing, because society as a whole has never—crystallised. One must be pardoned for the physical comparison, since no other would exactly express the sinister meaning. The actual attainment of a stationary goal, no matter how many æons ahead, would mean, not highest life, but death—this from the point of view of sociology, but much more from the point of view of Ethics.

This is the really fatal objection; but, leaving out of view all such difficulties, however unsurmountable, and assuming for the moment that the complete adaptation of man to his environment is no more difficult to conceive than a correspondingly perfect adaptation of a given animal species to its merely physical environment, the very serious question remains: By what 'factors of evolution' is such complete adjustment to be effected? Natural selection, which plays such an important—even if not, as some have claimed, a nearly all-important—part in organic evolution proper, is largely done away with in civilised human society. The 'unfit' are not allowed to be eliminated by the simple, if ruthless, methods of nature, owing to our deeply-rooted conviction of the sanctity of human life. We shall, indeed, find that Mr. Spencer's later interpretation of the principle of Justice makes it largely consist in letting the individual take the natural consequences of his actions; but, as just pointed out, the all-important consequence, elimination or death as the result of 'unfitness,' is not permitted. The possibility of the perfect adaptation of man to his environment, therefore, would seem to depend almost entirely upon the 'inheritance of acquired characteristics'. If the increment of adaptation to environment, which has taken place in the individual (in this case, the human) organism, as a result of its life-experience, can be transmitted in part to offspring, then a constant progress in the direction of complete adaptation may conceivably go on without the operation of natural selection; otherwise, apparently not.

So far as the present writer is aware, this 'factor' of evolution ('inheritance of acquired characteristics') had hardly been called in serious question at the time when the *Data of Ethics* was published (1879), though there had, of course, been the greatest diversity of opinion as to its relative importance. One would be far from assuming that Weismann has entirely proved the non-inheritance of acquired characteristics; but, so far as an outsider can judge of the results of this highly technical controversy, they have at least gone to show that this principle must be employed with very much greater caution than has been customary hitherto. To have an ethical postulate of the last importance for his system practically depend upon a biological principle by no means universally recognised, is certainly an unfortunate predicament for one who would found a ' scientific' Ethics.

The interesting chapter in which Mr. Spencer sets forth his ' psychological view' of morality need not detain us long. In terms of his own psychological system, which it is wholly unnecessary to criticise here, he traces briefly the development of motives from the lowest, such as would appeal to organisms barely endowed with sentiency, to the most complex, re-representative, or ideal, that can appeal to the highly civilised man. This development from simple to complex, from what we call ' lower' to what we call ' higher' motives, manifestly implies an increasing degree of subordination of present to future ends. " Hence," as the author says, " there arises a certain presumption in favour of a motive which refers to a remote good, in comparison with one which refers to a proximate good." [1] But he very properly argues that this presumption must not be transformed into an ascetic dogma. The feelings, *e.g.*, which prompt one to comply with the fundamental requirements of health, may, and often do, have as high an authority as any. Moreover, one must admit that it is quite possible to go too far in subordinating present to future good.

The earliest regulation of human conduct, we are told, is by means of three external controls, political, religious, and

[1] See ch. vii., § 42.

social. These, for the most part, operate simultaneously, leading men to subordinate proximate satisfactions to remote satisfactions; yet it must be observed that they do not constitute the moral control proper, but are only preparatory to it—"are controls within which the moral control evolves". Mr. Spencer says: "The restraints properly distinguished as moral, are unlike these restraints out of which they evolve, and with which they are long confounded, in this—they refer not to the extrinsic effects of actions but to their intrinsic effects".[1] His meaning is made plain by the context: motives truly moral cannot spring from a foresight of rewards or punishments that may be expected at the hands of the State, of one's fellow men, or even of a Divine Being; they are constituted by representations of consequences which the acts *naturally* produce. He says: "These representations are not all distinct, though some of such are usually present; but they form an assemblage of indistinct representations accumulated by experience of the results of like acts in the life of the individual, super-posed on a still more indistinct but voluminous consciousness due to the inherited effects of such experiences in progenitors: forming a feeling that is at once massive and vague".

In further justification of this view, he quotes a passage from his well-known letter to J. S. Mill, a part of which may be given here, as it indicates his later [2] attitude toward Intuitionism. "Just in the same way that I believe the intuition of space, possessed by any living individual, to have arisen from organised and consolidated experiences of all antecedent individuals who bequeathed to him their slowly-developed nervous organisations—just as I believe that this intuition, requiring only to be made definite and complete by personal experiences, has practically become a form of thought, ap-

---

[1] See ch. vii., § 45.

[2] Not necessarily his latest. His "Inductions of Ethics" (Part II. of the *Principles*, published in 1892) seem to imply throughout an unconditional rejection of Intuitionism, which is rather more than is expressed by the passage here quoted.

parently quite independent of experience; so do I believe that the experiences of utility organised and consolidated through all past generations of the human race, have been producing corresponding nervous modifications, which, by continued transmission and accumulation, have become in us certain faculties of moral intuition—certain emotions responding to right and wrong conduct, which have no apparent basis in the individual experiences of utility."[1]

So much for the origin of what are taken to be particular moral intuitions. How does there arise the feeling of moral obligation in general? We are told: "The answer is that it is an abstract sentiment generated in a manner analogous to that in which abstract ideas are generated".[2] All particular moral feelings have in common complexity and re-representative character, being occupied with the future rather than the present. Hence[3] the idea of 'authoritativeness' has come to be connected with them, and this idea is naturally carried over, so as to form an essential moment of the abstract sentiment of duty. But, besides authoritativeness, there is the further, and apparently more characteristic, element of 'coerciveness. This has arisen mainly as the result of the agent's fear of political and social (and probably one should add, religious) penalties. Now since this second element of 'coerciveness,' or moral obligation proper, has arisen in connection with the 'extrinsic,' as opposed to the 'intrinsic,' or natural, consequences of actions, it may be expected to diminish in proportion as moral conduct ceases to depend upon merely external restraints. This leads to the author's characteristic, but rather startling conclusion, that the sense of duty or moral obligation is transitory; that it will diminish until it finally disappears with the complete adaptation of man to the social state.

We have seen that the 'physical' and the 'biological' views of morality are open to serious criticism, not only as to results, but as to method. It might appear that, from the

---

[1] See ch. vii., § 45.    [2] See *ibid.*, § 46.

[3] It will be noted that this is one of the author's many facile inferences.

point of view of method, at any rate, the present chapter, on the 'psychological view,' would call for substantially the same criticism, since the general introduction to these four 'views' of morality puts them ostensibly on the same plane. But what Mr. Spencer actually attempts in this chapter, is not, properly speaking, to reduce Ethics to terms of something else; he attempts, rather, to give a psychological account of the origin of our particular moral intuitions and of our general feeling of duty. As an attempt, this is perfectly legitimate; and to use such results, if obtainable, for the purposes of Ethics, is, of course, equally legitimate. In truth, so far from this attempt being peculiar to the author of the *Data of Ethics*, it is one that had been made by all previous hedonist-empiricists, and that is certain to be made as long as such a school exists.

The question as to whether Mr. Spencer has succeeded in this attempt, is, of course, quite another matter. In his own opinion, he has successfully mediated between Empiricism and Intuitionism, as they have existed in the past, by his character-istic theory, that the results of the moral experience of the individual have been transmitted from generation to genera-tion, until the fundamental 'moral intuitions,' so-called, like those concerning the spatial relations of things, have become for the individual, as at present constituted, practically innate 'forms' of thought or feeling—though, of course, ultimately explainable as the result of the experience of the race. This theory raises epistemological and metaphysical questions, which cannot properly be discussed here, even superficially; but it will readily be seen that, from the point of view of epistemology, the theory does not really transcend empiricism and methods opposed to it, but rather decides in favour of empiricism itself. Moreover, the essential difficulties of empiricism—whatever those may be thought to be—are not in any true sense done away with, but merely thrust further back. In truth, it may be seriously doubted if Mr. Spencer has really improved at all upon the traditional arguments for empiricism, as applied to Ethics, since he has again staked everything upon the validity of the biological principle of the ' inheritance of acquired characteristics '.

What calls for more special consideration, in the present connection, is the author's well-known, but paradoxical view, that the feeling of duty will finally become extinct, with the perfect adaptation of man to the social condition. It hardly need be pointed out that this view, however startling in itself, is a practically necessary corollary from the general theory of a ' completely evolved ' society, with which we have by this time become so familiar. And it serves, in a very interesting way, to illustrate still further the difficulties of that highly abstract theory. But first, let us realise, as clearly as may be, what this view is in itself. The argument briefly is, that the feeling of duty, or moral obligation proper, implying the idea of ' coerciveness,' has arisen mainly in connection with the three external controls of conduct ; and that therefore, when the thought of ' extrinsic ' consequences makes way for the thought of ' intrinsic,' or natural, consequences on the part of the agent—as will necessarily take place with the moral progress of the individual and of the race—inclination will take the place of duty, and man will become spontaneously, if not mechanically, moral. As the author expresses it : " The higher actions required for the harmonious carrying on of life, will be as much matters of course as are those lower actions which the simple desires prompt ".[1]

It is difficult to see how morality necessarily becomes internal and spontaneous, as opposed to external and constrained, by the mere fact that the agent passes from a consideration of ' extrinsic ' to a consideration of ' intrinsic,' or natural, consequences—granting that such a thing is ever wholly possible. The development of altruism, to a proper degree and under control of reason, would seem to be the desideratum—not disregard for the approval of one's fellowmen or even for that of the Divine Being. In truth, this hard and fast distinction between ' extrinsic ' and ' intrinsic ' con-

[1] See ch. vii., § 46.

sequences is another of the misleading abstractions which one
so often meets with in Mr. Spencer's ethical writings. What
could be a more 'natural' consequence of any form of recognised wrong-doing than the disapproval, perhaps abhorrence,
of one's fellow-men? But let us not tamper with the author's
terminology; it is most convenient in the present connection.
Granting that any human being could perform the psychological and moral feat here indicated—granting that he could
wholly neglect all 'extrinsic' consequences, including the
approval or disapproval of his fellow-men, and fix his mind
upon the 'intrinsic,' or natural, consequences alone—how
would it fare with his moral life? The 'intrinsic' consequences would obviously supply as many egoistic motives as
the 'extrinsic,' and he would wholly lose the moralising influence of enlightened public opinion. One may be an individualist in theoretical Ethics, like Mr. Spencer; most
fortunately one cannot be a practical individualist in the sense
just indicated. To be that would mean, to be a moral monster.
But, it may be objected, the rise and growth of altruism has
really been presupposed by the author. To this it may be
replied, that we must not make of altruism still another abstraction : in the social nature of man, without which morality
would be impossible, regard for the feelings of others and regard for their opinions are so inextricably involved, that
neither can develop, or even continue to exist, in isolation from
the other.

But, neglecting these and similar considerations, the force
of Mr. Spencer's argument seems also to depend upon the
assumption that, if we ever outgrow the feeling of duty, as
something external and coercive, nothing but inclination can
take its place. Are these, then, the only alternatives? The
whole History of Ethics goes to prove the contrary: from
Socrates to the present time—Mediævalism apart—Ethics has
nearly always been regarded by some influential school or
schools as the doctrine of the Good. From that point of view,
this antithesis between duty, in the grimly forbidding sense,
and inclination tends to disappear. On the one hand, indeed,

the Good is regarded as something which appeals to one's higher, or whole nature ; but, on the other hand, to identify it with the necessary object of inclination would be fatally misleading. 'Desirable'—even 'above all things desirable'—and 'desired' are, unfortunately, not convertible terms. True, as moral progress is made, 'desirable' and 'desired' tend to approximate ; but there is one fatal difficulty with all truly human ideals, whether ethical or other, and that is, that the more we attain, the more do new and unimagined vistas open up before us. Now it is perfectly conceivable that, in the course of the moral development of the race, duty may take on a very different aspect from that which it now presents ; but that the 'springs of action' will ever by themselves be sufficient to make us automatically live up to our highest ideals of the moral Good is wholly inconceivable. And this is because man is not a mere organism to be adjusted to a comparatively stationary external environment, but a personality, capable of practically endless development.

There ostensibly remains to be considered the 'sociological view' of morality ; but, as a matter of fact, the chapter devoted to this subject contains little or nothing of importance for Ethics that had not been at least implied, either in Book IV. of the *Social Statics*, or in the preceding chapters of the *Data of Ethics*. It will therefore be sufficient to notice very briefly, partly by way of review, Mr. Spencer's highly characteristic theory of the evolution of society. All along we have seen that, generally speaking, this evolution has been from a wholly militant condition toward a wholly industrial condition, though the latter condition is still far ahead. Now in the militant condition two codes will necessarily spring up, one of 'enmity' toward alien societies, and one of 'amity'[1] toward other individuals of the same society. The one, in fact, is as necessary as the other : co-operation within and antagonism

---

[1] Of course 'amity,' as here used, is a relative term. The 'code of amity' does not necessarily signify more than a code, as between members of the same society, which makes co-operation of the necessary kind and to the necessary degree possible.

to all that which is without. While this militant condition continues, either wholly or in any large degree, the very existence of society demands a constant subordination of the interests of the individual to those of the State; but, in so far as mutual aggression between societies ceases, this need for the sacrifice of private claims to public claims ceases also. Moreover, as mutual external aggressions cease, mutual internal aggressions will also tend to cease. Not only so, but co-operation will become more complex and effective. But we must go further still—and the reader will readily see that from this point Mr. Spencer's sociology, so far as here set forth, practically coincides with his ethics. After pointing out that non-interference (Justice, in its more obvious phase) is not enough, he says: "Daily experiences prove that every one would suffer many evils and lose many goods, did none give him unpaid assistance. The life of each would be more or less damaged had he to meet all contingencies single-handed. Further, if no one did for his fellows anything more than was required by strict performance of contract, private interests would suffer from the absence of attention to public interests. The limit of evolution of conduct is consequently not reached, until, beyond avoidance of direct and indirect injuries to others, there are spontaneous efforts to further the welfare of others." [1] And it is hardly necessary to remark that for the later, as well as for the earlier, form of Mr. Spencer's ethical theory, Justice and Beneficence (Negative and Positive), together with a due regard for his own welfare on the part of the agent, constitute the whole of Ethics.

Having followed Mr. Spencer through the arguments contained in the first eight chapters of the *Data of Ethics*, which explain his views on scientific ethical method, and which happen to form exactly the first half of the book, we are in a position to make some interesting comparisons. In the *Social Statics* both the very interesting destructive criticism of the Expediency Philosophy and the outline of the author's

[1] See ch. viii., § 54.

own system are frankly shown to depend upon his characteristic, but paradoxical, conception of the perfect society of the
future. We are told that the moralist must deal with the
perfect man, just as the mathematician deals with the hypothetically perfect geometrical figure ; hence evil cannot even
be recognised by a scientific system of Ethics. When stated
in such terms, it is evident that the system, whatever its other
defects or merits may be, is one of the most abstract ever
formulated ; and, moreover, that the abstract criterion constantly referred to, the perfect man in the perfect society,
can never be completely understood until the millennial condition of society actually arrives. Now in the *Data of Ethics*
the method adopted seems at first to be almost the opposite of
that employed in the earlier book. Organic evolution is to
afford the clue ; so we begin by considering the evolution
of conduct in its most general sense, *i.e.*, the mere adaptation
of acts to ends, whether conscious or unconscious. After noting that such adaptation becomes more and more complex
and efficient, as we ascend from the lowest animals up to man,
we are, apparently, invited to regard the evolution of human
conduct as on the same plane, except that men 'look before
and after,' and are thus able to contrive means for the attainment of the ends desired. But, before we are fully aware
of what has happened, the grim struggle for existence has
been banished from our mental vision, and social evolution — a 'power which makes for righteousness,' whether
we will or no — is represented as necessarily leading up
to a state of things where man is 'completely adapted' to
the social condition. This, upon inspection, turns out to be
precisely Mr. Spencer's old, pre-Evolutional ideal of 'the
perfect man in the perfect society'. It is true that the
expression 'completely adapted,' already used in *Social Statics*,
may seem to define the perfect man in evolutional terms ;
but we have elsewhere considered in some detail the difficulty of even conceiving what such 'complete adaptation'
would mean.

More particularly, Mr. Spencer objects to all previous

systems of Ethics, on the ground that they either wholly, or in
very large measure, neglect the principle of causation.   As we
have seen, however, this alarming indictment practically reduces itself to his old objection to the Expediency Philosophy.
He then attempts to put Ethics on a strictly scientific basis,
by (at least ostensibly) reducing certain of its most general
principles to terms of Physics, Biology, Psychology, and
Sociology.   The results, as we so recently found, are hardly
reassuring.   The 'physical view' turned out to be not only
so abstract as almost to baffle definite comprehension, but
extremely fanciful, and, where one can test it, by no means
uniformly in accord with the facts.   The 'biological view'
—that the 'completely adapted' man will find it not only his
privilege, but his duty, to perform duly all physiological functions, and, moreover, that for him the immediate pleasures or
pains, attending the performance or avoidance of functions,
will be safe guides, not only to hygienic, but to moral conduct—we found to involve the most serious difficulties, unless
the highest civilisation of the future prove to be almost the
antithesis of what we understand by civilisation now.   The
'psychological view' turned out to be Mr. Spencer's own
version of the empirical explanation of the origin of our
recognition of particular moral principles and of duty in
general; and we saw that he had by no means necessarily
improved matters by staking everything upon the 'inheritance of acquired characteristics'.   The evanescence of the
feeling of duty predicted also appeared to present the gravest
difficulties, though doubtless a legitimate, and perhaps necessary, corollary from his fundamental conception of a perfect,
or completely evolved, society.   Finally, the 'sociological
view' presented little or nothing really novel, since it represented merely the author's characteristic theory (already indicated in *Social Statics*) as to the route to be followed by
humanity in its progress toward perfection.

We must now ask: Is this later treatment really new?   Is
the author really *depending* upon the most advanced modern
science as the foundation for his ethical system?   Or is he

not rather, quite unconsciously, of course, providing us with an ostensibly scientific (in particular, evolutional) development of the very same conception which, nearly thirty years earlier, and eight years before the publication of the *Origin of Species*, had dominated the *Social Statics*? Now, apart from the author's abandonment of the Moral Sense theory, not only does this seem to the present writer to be the case, but the newly-provided scientific approaches to this long-cherished ideal seem dubious in the extreme. Evolution is appealed to as the universal solvent of difficulties; but, as here employed, it is no longer analogous to the principle of organic evolution, with its ruthless destruction of the unfit. It is rather the principle of universal and continuous progress on the part of human society, conceived as a hope rather than proved as a fact—with a convenient disregard for what history has to say of periods of political and social decadence, or even for what biology has to say of the highly interesting, if not morally inspiring, phenomena of organic degeneration. So far, then, all the aids of modern science to the contrary notwithstanding, the author seems to stand practically where he did in the *Social Statics*—always excepting his later rejection of the Moral Sense theory—and to base everything upon his apparently arbitrary belief in the necessity of a perfect society in the remote future.

The remainder of the *Data of Ethics* may be considered very briefly, for the ground covered will become increasingly familiar to one who has read the *Social Statics* at all carefully. Mr. Spencer never seems perfectly satisfied with his later criticisms of Utilitarianism, for he returns to the subject again and again. He is never tired of insisting that the hedonistic calculus, as ordinarily understood, is an impossibility; but, on the other hand, he never gives sufficiently definite information as to what we are to employ in place of it. The suggestions, however, always take the form of insisting that certain very general principles of conduct are necessary in any properly organised society, no matter what the external environment and therefore the prevailing mode of life of the individual members, and no matter what the stage of development of the given society; and, moreover, these general principles finally turn out to be adumbrations of his own ethical principles—Justice, Negative Beneficence, and Positive Beneficence, enlightened Self-Interest being always presupposed.

This, of course, is merely the doctrine of the *Social Statics* over again; and one must remark here, as in the last chapter, that this insistence upon the necessity of general rules, as the direct guides of action, is by no means a novelty in English Utilitarianism. Nobody but Bentham, in fact, seems to have failed to recognise the need of depending upon such general rules. The principal difference between Mr. Spencer and other hedonists, writing before and after the publication of the *Data of Ethics*, is, that he prefers to represent the general principles of Ethics as general conditions of the efficiency of society, while the others are content to represent them merely as general conditions of the greatest happiness. For ordinary purposes, the two methods practically coincide in their results; and, where there is divergence, the advantage is by no means necessarily on the side of Mr. Spencer—*if* happiness be really the ultimate end. A society, *e.g.*, might conceivably be ideally efficient in a practical way, and yet neglect all things æsthetic. Presumably this would result in a great diminution of happiness; but we are not quite sure that such considerations would move the author of the *Synthetic Philosophy*. One always has a suspicion that, like Plato, he would banish the poets from his ideal state.

As we have just seen, Mr. Spencer is not always fortunate in his attempts to differentiate his own treatment of Ethics from that of traditional Utilitarianism, since he generally tends to over-emphasise differences in method; but it should be noted that the later chapters of the *Data of Ethics* are a decided improvement upon some of the earlier chapters in one respect, at any rate, *viz.*, they keep to the real problems of Ethics. Highly interesting, even if by no means satisfactory, are the four chapters in which he defines the relations between

egoism and altruism in his own system. In the chapters
"Egoism *versus* Altruism" and "Altruism *versus* Egoism," as
the titles themselves would indicate, he gives an *ex parte*
statement of what may be said for egoism and for altruism,
separately considered. In spite of the confessedly abstract
method here adopted, he discusses the problems involved with
admirable candour and great ability. After exhibiting this
opposition between egoism and altruism in a perhaps too
striking light, even for his purpose—which manifestly is to
state the difficulty rather than to indicate his own solution—
he goes on to show how impossible it is to construct an ethical
system in terms of either the one or the other. The chapter
devoted to this discussion, "Trial and Compromise," while
evidently correct as regards its main thesis, is open to criticism, as the author is plainly unfair to Utilitarianism, *e.g.*, in
representing it as logically a system of mere altruism. Moreover, while egoism and altruism are thus held apart almost as
if they were separate entities, in a way that Mr. Spencer himself could not admit when treating the problem of their
relation constructively, he does a good deal to prejudice the
case in favour of egoism, by insisting upon such evident truths
as that, "other things equal, ideal feelings cannot be as vivid
as real feelings"; that "much of the happiness each enjoys
is self-generated and can neither be given nor received";
and that "the pleasures gained by efficient action—by successful pursuit of ends, cannot by any process be parted with,
and cannot in any way be appropriated by another".[1] Still,
one should observe, he does not really attempt (in this discussion, at least) to reduce altruism to egoism in the way that
the earlier Associationists had done; but, on the contrary,
regards them as co-essential. Hence the title of the next
chapter, "Conciliation".

Here, without giving quite sufficient notice, the author
drops his confessedly abstract method of treatment, and proceeds to give his own solution of the apparent antinomy upon

[1] See ch. xiii., §§ 86-88.

which he has dwelt so long. He argues that during evolution there has been going on a conciliation between the interests of the species, the interests of the parents, and the interests of the offspring. More exactly, he says: " As we ascend from the lowest forms of life to the highest, race-maintenance is achieved with a decreasing sacrifice of life, alike of young individuals and of adult individuals, and also with a decreasing sacrifice of parental lives to the lives of offspring ".[1] Similarly, he argues that, with the progress of civilisation, like changes have taken place among human beings. Parental altruism is, of course, already highly developed; and, with further evolution, causing, along with higher nature, diminished fertility, and therefore smaller burdens on parents, it may be expected to develop still further. Now altruism of a social kind cannot, of course, be expected to equal parental altruism in degree; but it may confidently be expected to become equally spontaneous, and such that lower egoistic satisfactions will continually be subordinated to this higher egoistic satisfaction—and this, not from a feeling of obligation, but rather from natural inclination. Before such general sympathy can develop on a large scale, however, society must outgrow the condition of habitual militancy; and it goes without saying that, even then, a long time will be required by society, in which to outlive the effects of that pernicious *régime*. But finally, with complete adaptation of man to the social condition, this most desirable result will be attained.

Does this mean that man, beginning as an individual with merely selfish interests, will finally become, in the true sense of the word, a social being? Mr. Spencer says: " In natures thus constituted, though the altruistic gratifications must remain in a transfigured sense egoistic, yet they will not be egoistically pursued—will not be pursued from egoistic motives ".[2] This passage is made still more ambiguous by its context, for the time-honoured example of the miser and his money—so popular, as we have seen in previous chapters,

---

[1] See ch. xiv., § 92.          [2] See *ibid.*, § 95.

with the earlier Associationist-Utilitarians, who held to the necessary egoism of the moral agent—is employed by the author. But it would hardly do to class Mr. Spencer with the older school of Utilitarians, the lineal descendants of Gay, as regards this important matter of the moral motive, for he has just argued for the necessity of a certain degree of altruism from evolutionary considerations.

In truth, it is most difficult satisfactorily to define Mr. Spencer's position; and the reason, apparently, is that he has ended, as he began, an individualist—not as a result of his devotion to the general theory of Evolution, but in spite of this. Here, as so often, we have to note the striking correspondence between the Evolutional and the pre-Evolutional form of his ethical theory. In this case, indeed, it is a correspondence practically amounting to identity. Evolution is generally supposed to develop a tendency only when it is needed, and only in proportion as it is needed; but in the later, so-called 'Evolutional,' form of Mr. Spencer's ethical theory, as in the earlier one set forth in *Social Statics*, it is made to appear that, in the triumphal progress of humanity toward perfection, altruism will be developed in proportion as it is *not* needed. This is not an imaginary difficulty. In this very chapter we are told: "Sympathy can reach its full height only when there have ceased to be frequent occasions for anything like serious self-sacrifice ".[1]

The last chapter of any length in the *Data of Ethics* is most appropriately devoted to "Absolute and Relative Ethics". This, in fact, is the one fundamental distinction, based on Mr. Spencer's early faith in a perfect society in the remote future, which has both given unity to the book as a whole and served principally to distinguish the author's treatment of Ethics from that of traditional Utilitarianism. The chapter is of importance, not because it represents any appreciable change of opinion on the part of the author, but because the first part is somewhat more definite than the

[1] See ch. xiv., § 96.

corresponding discussion in *Social Statics*, and therefore more subject to exact criticism.    In the earlier book we began with the point of view of 'Absolute Ethics,' and saw that from that standpoint all considerations of evil—or pain, which for Mr. Spencer is the same thing—had to be ruled out.    In the *Data of Ethics*, on the contrary, we have been largely concerned with the conception of a gradually developing, or 'evolving,' morality, and accordingly have had our attention frequently directed to the fact that, as things are now constituted, there are multitudinous cases where there is no absolute right or wrong, but only a right which, on inspection, turns out to be a least wrong.    One must observe that the author is not insisting upon the apparent conflict of real duties, as a result of the complex relations which are inevitable in modern civilisation.    Duty, in fact, as we have seen, is regarded by him as only a passing phase of the moral experience of the race.

As Mr. Spencer defines it, " the absolutely good, the absolutely right, in conduct, can be that only which produces pure pleasure—pleasure unalloyed with pain anywhere.    By implication, conduct which has any concomitant of pain, or any painful consequence, is partially wrong ; and the highest claim to be made for such conduct is, that it is the least wrong which, under the conditions, is possible—the relatively right." [1] The author freely admits that humanity must still, for a very long time, content itself principally with the 'relatively right' ; but he pauses to give two concrete illustrations of what he means by the 'absolutely right,' taken from the existing order of things.    He first asks us to consider the relation of a healthy mother to a healthy infant, and says : " Between the two there exists a mutual dependence which is a source of pleasure to both.    In yielding its natural food to the child, the mother receives gratification ; and to the child there comes the satisfaction of appetite—a satisfaction which accompanies furtherance of life, growth, and increasing enjoyment.    Let the relation be suspended, and on both sides there

[1] See ch. xv., § 101.

is suffering. . . . Thus the act is one that is to both exclusively pleasurable, while abstention entails pain on both; and it is consequently of the kind we here call absolutely right." [1]

It will be noted that the author confines himself to a single, and that a merely physiological, relation between mother and child—and one which, by the way, is far less likely to be perfectly normal in civilisation than in a savage state of society. Does Mr. Spencer mean to imply that, in general, the relations of mother to child can conceivably become wholly pleasurable on both sides, no matter how healthy both may be? It will no longer suffice to say, as an ordinary Utilitarian might do, that the mother's pleasures may, and should, be greatly in excess of her pains. That would not at all answer the requirements of the author's characteristically abstract ideal. As long as any suffering whatever is involved, the relation is ' imperfectly moral '. In fact, this relation between mother and child is one of the least happy that could have been chosen, as an example of the ' absolutely right,' for here, at any rate, we may assert with perfect confidence that some degree of suffering and self-sacrifice will always be necessary, no matter how ' completely evolved ' society may be. Would it, in fact, be going too far to say that, according to Mr. Spencer's paradoxical standard, maternity is bound to remain to the end one of the most ' imperfectly moral ' of human relations? If any *reductio ad absurdum* of the conception of ' absolute morality ' were needed, this ought to serve.

The author's other example of ' absolutely right ' conduct, is that of a father of healthy mind and body, who takes a keen interest in the sports and tasks of his young children. But here again, it must be remembered that the predominantly pleasurable will not serve the purpose. As long as the male parent permits himself to indulge in any acts of real self-devotion for the benefit of his offspring, so long will this relation also remain ' imperfectly moral '—and this, no matter how necessary the sacrifice or how worthy those for whom it has been made may prove themselves in later years.

[1] See ch. xv., § 102.

The above examples, be it observed, are supposed to represent the nearest approach to 'absolute morality' at present attainable. The author admits that the intercourse of adults yields relatively few cases that fall completely within the same category. The rank and file of humanity do not find their necessary work in life an unmixed pleasure; but it is argued that 'social discipline' will finally bring this about. And, with his fatal infelicity in the choice of examples, Mr. Spencer says: "Already, indeed, something like such a state has been reached among certain of those who minister to our æsthetic gratifications. The artist of genius—poet, painter, or musician—is one who obtains the means of living by acts that are directly pleasurable to him, while they yield, immediately or remotely, pleasures to others." Plainly the man of genius is here mentioned merely as one who is so fortunate as to be able to live by congenial work. Up to the present, the man of genius has far too often found it difficult to support himself at all by his own exertions; but this is perhaps the least important aspect of the matter. With his abnormally sensitive temperament, his striving, often hopeless, after ideals the highest, if not actually unattainable, and the grudging recognition accorded him by the world at large during his years of probation, he is about as far as possible from being the satisfied, and therefore happy man—the man 'perfectly adjusted to his environment' — of Mr. Spencer's imagination. In fact, of all men, the man of genius is, and must remain, one of the least adjusted to the society in which he finds himself. In this very paragraph, by an odd juxtaposition, is a most significant reference to the so-called 'absolute morality' of a benevolence that costs nothing. "Some one who has slipped is saved from falling by a bystander: a hurt is prevented and satisfaction is felt by both. A pedestrian is choosing a dangerous route, or a fellow-passenger is about to alight at the wrong station, and, warned against doing so, is saved from evil: each being, as a consequence, gratified." [1]

[1] See ch. xv., § 102.

After these examples, which are instructive only as exhibiting, in a concrete way, the difficulties of Mr. Spencer's hopelessly vague, and otherwise more than paradoxical, conception of ideal morality, he proceeds to treat of the relation between ' Absolute Ethics ' and ' Relative Ethics ' in what he terms a ' systematic ' way. All that follows on this score is an almost literal reproduction of the treatment in *Social Statics*, and so calls for no special notice here. As before, the gist of the argument is, that Ethics must deal with the perfect man in the perfect society for just the same reason that the geometrician deals with hypothetically perfect figures, the physiologist with normal, as opposed to pathological, organic processes, etc. And, as before, we must remark that such scientific analogies are seriously misleading, even apart from the distinction already referred to between explanatory and normative sciences ; since the legitimate abstractions of science are always indispensable aids to clearness, while the abstract ideal of the perfect man becomes always more vague upon repeated examination. But all this has been discussed at length in the proper context. Here the important thing to notice is, that while Mr. Spencer's later criticisms of Utilitarianism differ from his earlier ones, in that they do not so obviously depend upon his fundamental conception of the perfect man in the perfect society, he never for a moment gives up his distinction between ' Absolute Ethics ' and ' Relative Ethics,' but rather expounds it in precisely the same way, and makes it equally essential to the structure of his ethical system as a whole.

The final chapter of the *Data of Ethics*, on " The Scope of Ethics," is also, for the most part, a mere reproduction of what had been given in the *Social Statics*. Here, as there, the interests of self are regarded as largely separate from the interests of others, so that we have a personal ethics (that of Prudence) and a social ethics. The latter, again, is divided into Justice, Negative Beneficence, and Positive Beneficence, which are defined precisely as before. Moreover, as the author points out, each of these divisions and subdivisions has to be conceived first as a part of ' Absolute Ethics ' and then as a part of ' Relative Ethics '—though under ideal conditions Negative Beneficence (which consists in avoiding acts that would give unnecessary pain to others) " has but a nominal existence ".  The relations between these general principles of conduct are much less clearly indicated here than in the corresponding discussion in *Social Statics ;* but a comparison of the two will show that the author's later view, so far as here developed, corresponds exactly with his earlier one.  Here, as there, Justice is regarded as the one exact principle, while Negative Beneficence and Positive Beneficence are regarded as necessarily inexact, since they involve (at least indirectly) calculations of pleasures and pains.  This absolute priority of the principle of Justice, retained in the later form of the system, will almost immediately call for careful consideration.  In the *Social Statics*, as will be remembered, a Moral Sense was assumed, and its one clear intuition was held to be precisely that of Justice.  In the *Data of Ethics*, the Moral Sense has been tacitly given up.  That, in fact, is the one essential difference, as regards method, between the later book and the earlier one. We shall have to ask ourselves, in the following chapter, whether the peculiar treatment of Justice, retained in the later form of Mr. Spencer's system, is a logical deduction from his revised premises or a mere survival from the earlier form of his system.

# CHAPTER XV.

### HERBERT SPENCER (*continued*).

IT now remains to examine, somewhat briefly, Mr. Spencer's later ethical writings, in which he develops the principles set forth in the *Data of Ethics*. As he explains in the Preface to *Justice* (1891), declining health and decreasing power of work during the years following the publication of the *Data* made it necessary for him to depart from the order of treatment originally intended. Passing over Part II. of the *Principles of Ethics*, "The Inductions of Ethics," and Part III., "The Ethics of Individual Life," he proceeded at once, after four years of compulsory inaction (1886-1890), to the composition of Part IV., "The Ethics of Social Life: Justice". Such a choice was, indeed, a foregone conclusion. It was already evident from numerous statements in the *Data of Ethics*, that for the later, as for the earlier form of the system, Justice was the one ethical principle susceptible of rigorously scientific treatment. Following the order of publication, we shall now proceed to examine the earlier, and more strictly theoretical, portion of this book.

Since we found in the *Data of Ethics* that it is necessary to begin with a consideration of 'conduct in general,' regarded from the Evolutional point of view, it is evident that here we must first consider animal ethics. The cardinal and opposed principles of animal ethics, as conceived by the author, are stated as follows: "During immaturity benefits received must be inversely proportionate to capacities possessed. Within the family group most must be given where least is deserved, if desert is measured by worth. Contrariwise, after maturity

(329)

is reached benefit must vary directly as worth : worth being measured by fitness to the conditions of existence." [1]    These principles are alike essential to the continuance of the species, and hence equally fundamental to animal ethics ; but, as we are here concerned only with the principle of Justice, we may properly neglect the necessary care of offspring, which would belong to another branch of animal ethics, and confine ourselves to a consideration of sub-human justice.    Under its biological aspect, this is the well-known principle of 'the survival of the fittest'; in ethical terms (which the author assumes are applicable here), it means that "each individual ought to be subject to the effects of its own nature and resulting conduct".    Now it is to be observed that, throughout sub-human life, 'ought,' as here used, and 'is' would coincide, but for one very important complication.    This is, that the wholesale destruction of many of the lower forms of life often interferes seriously with the survival of the variations that would otherwise prove themselves 'the fittest'.    Among such lower organisms, a high rate of multiplication is necessary, in order to counteract this indiscriminate destruction.    The manifest implication is, that sub-human justice is extremely imperfect among the lowest organisms, but tends to become more and more perfect as organisation becomes higher.

If all animals led solitary lives, the above description of sub-human justice would be sufficiently exact ; but among gregarious creatures another element emerges, and one of the greatest importance.    Mr. Spencer says : "Each individual, receiving the benefits and the injuries due to its own nature and consequent conduct, has to carry on that conduct subject to the restriction that it shall not in any large measure impede the conduct by which each other individual achieves benefits or brings on itself injuries.    The average conduct must not be so aggressive as to cause evils which out-balance the good obtained by co-operation.    Thus, to the positive element in sub-human justice has to be added, among gregarious creatures,

---

[1] See ch. i., §§ 2 *et seq.*

a negative element." [1]  But even this is not all.  Among certain of the higher gregarious animals, more or less concerted action on the part of the stronger males for the defence of the females and the young, in case of danger, is an established, and, as one can readily see, a necessary custom.  This, of course, means a temporary subordination of the interest of the individual to that of the herd ; but evolution itself necessarily provides that such self-subordination shall go no further than the actual needs of the species demand.  In the absence of external enemies, this last qualification of the original principle of Justice would, of course, have no meaning.

Thus far the author's treatment has been simple and consistent, because up to this point the ordinary distinction between what is and what ought to be has not arisen.  'The survival of the fittest' has been limited only by the indiscriminate destruction of certain of the lower forms of life.  When he begins the treatment of human justice, this is at first represented as a mere extension of animal justice, more perfect in degree, but not differing in kind.  The only clear intimation we receive that we are passing beyond the *inevitable* working of the biological principle of 'the survival of the fittest,' is afforded by a passage in which the natural effects of bad, or imperfectly adapted, actions are mentioned.  " To what extent such ill, naturally following from his actions, may be voluntarily borne by other persons, it does not concern us now to inquire. The qualifying effects of pity, mercy, and generosity, will be considered hereafter in the parts dealing with ' Negative Beneficence ' and ' Positive Beneficence '.  Here we are concerned only with pure Justice." [2]  On the assumption, then, that we are still on the plane of the previous discussion, we are asked to note that human justice is more perfect than that holding among the higher animals, as was to be expected from man's higher organisation.  The lower rate of mortality, which results from man's foresight and greater ability to provide for the future, makes it possible for the individual members of

[1] See ch. ii., § 8.          [2] See ch. iii., § 12.

human society to experience the good or bad effects of their conduct for a correspondingly longer time. Hence well adapted and ill adapted conduct are far more likely to lead to their legitimate results in human society than even among the higher animals.

If the matter were as simple as this, it is safe to say that Mr. Spencer's book would never have been written. The most striking form of 'sub-human justice' is the constant elimination of the unfit. Now the mere fact that, in civilised human society, the unfit are not weeded out in this convenient fashion, introduces a serious complication, if, with the author, we conceive of justice in quasi-biological terms. With his unfailing habit of arguing from analogy, when an analogy is in sight, Mr. Spencer has assumed, rather than proved, that human justice, as here defined, is more perfect than animal justice, in proportion to man's higher organisation—and this, in spite of the obvious fact, that the principle of 'the survival of the fittest,' which is the very essence of 'sub-human justice,' is only allowed a comparatively restricted range in civilised human society. In truth, it is one important thesis of the present book, that human justice ought, in this respect, to correspond a good deal more closely to animal justice than is actually the case.

We have seen that, among the higher animals, the partial or complete sacrifice of individuals to the good of the species is already occasionally necessary. Mr. Spencer admits that, in the highest gregarious creature, man, this qualification of primitive justice assumes large proportions. "No longer, as among inferior beings, demanded only by the need for defence against enemies of other kinds, this further self-subordination is, among human beings, also demanded by the need for defence against enemies of the same kind." But he hastens to add: "The self-subordination thus justified, and in a sense rendered obligatory, is limited to that which is required for defensive war".[1] And, in accordance with his characteristic view, now

---

[1] See ch. iii., § 15.

so familiar, he urges that even such self-subordination is only a passing phase of human morality, which will disappear on the advent of universal peace. Such being the case, it belongs to ' Relative ' and not to ' Absolute ' Ethics. That self-sacrifice in all its forms will be unnecessary in a 'perfectly adapted' society, is one of the author's many puzzling assumptions.

So far we have considered human justice, as it were, from the outside, and as a sort of inevitable extension of animal justice. It now remains to see how our conception of justice has arisen. We found that Mr. Spencer's earlier account of this matter in *Social Statics* was extremely vague and unsatisfactory. There, of course, he ostensibly takes the Intuitional point of view; but, after stating his thesis—that "this first and all-essential law [Justice], declaratory of the liberty of each limited only by the like liberty of all, is that fundamental truth of which the moral sense is to give an intuition, and which the intellect is to develop into a scientific morality"— he makes it appear that, in the last resort, the Moral Sense is reducible to a merely egoistic 'instinct of personal rights'. Even with the help of his Intuitional assumptions, therefore, the author regards the conception of justice, as actually entertained, as being inexplicable without assuming the co-operation of sympathy. Indeed, he complains that even Adam Smith "did not perceive that the sentiment of justice is nothing but a sympathetic affection of the instinct of personal rights".

The confusion here between Intuitionism and Empiricism is evident. In the *Data of Ethics*, on the other hand, Intuitionism has already been tacitly given up, and Mr. Spencer attempts to mediate between the two methods by his characteristic theory, that what we take to be moral intuitions are to be explained as results of the accumulated experience of the race, as transmitted by the 'inheritance of acquired characteristics'. This theory, however, as we saw, is only Empiricism in disguise, with the additional disadvantage of making the explanation depend entirely upon a biological principle by no means universally admitted, and one which, even when admitted, is now employed with very much greater caution than hitherto.  Moreover, the explanation given in the *Data of Ethics* is unsatisfactory for the further reason, which more particularly concerns us here, that it does not tell with sufficient definiteness how we come to apprehend the one ethical principle which is perfectly free from ambiguity, *viz.,* Justice. This, of course, is precisely what the author here attempts to explain.  And it is instructive to note the similarity between this later explanation, which is supposed to depend upon the theory of Evolution, and the one given in *Social Statics* forty years before.

Mr. Spencer begins by distinguishing between the 'sentiment' and the 'idea' of Justice, the principal difference being that the former is somewhat vague, while the latter is capable of becoming perfectly distinct.  He finds no difficulty with the 'egoistic sentiment of justice,' since this, as in the earlier work, is practically assumed as a sort of instinct (*i.e.,* 'instinct of personal rights'), which is sure to develop with the general development of the individual and of the race.  The real question is: How are we to explain the development of the 'altruistic sentiment of justice'?  This is not easy from the author's individualistic point of view, for, as he himself points out: "On the one hand, the implication is that the altruistic sentiment of justice can come into existence only in the course of adaptation to social life.  On the other hand the implication is that social life is made possible only by maintenance of those equitable relations which imply the altruistic sentiment of justice.  How can these reciprocal requirements be fulfilled?" [1]

The answer given is on lines already suggested in the *Data of Ethics,* where it was explained how we pass from the 'extrinsic' to the 'intrinsic' view of morality, though the previous discussion is not referred to here.  Since the 'altruistic' sentiment of justice is, by hypothesis, lacking, a 'pro-altruistic' sentiment of justice must take its place.  This develops as a result of the four 'extrinsic' controls of con-

---

[1] See ch. iv., § 19.

duct, with which we are already familiar: the dread of retaliation, the dread of social dislike, the dread of legal punishment, and the dread of Divine vengeance. By these four controls, united, as the author says, 'in various proportions,' social co-operation is made possible even before sympathy develops in any considerable degree. But given a common life, whether of the herd or of any group in primitive society, and sympathy tends to develop.

The explanation of the development of sympathy which follows is by no means new. It is really very similar to the one so long ago given by Tucker in his *Light of Nature* (1768), and substantially identical with the one which Mr. Spencer himself had given in his *Principles of Psychology*. The nature of the explanation is sufficiently indicated by the following passage: "In a permanent group there occur, generation after generation, incidents simultaneously drawing from its members manifestations of like emotions—rejoicings over victories and escapes, over prey jointly captured, over supplies of wild food discovered; as well as laments over defeats, scarcities, inclemencies, &c. . . . Thus there is fostered that sympathy which makes the altruistic sentiment of justice possible." [1] The similarity between this and Tucker's explanation may not at first be evident; but comparison will show that both begin by assuming primitive egoism, and proceed to argue that, since men are bound to feel more or less *like* each other, in similar circumstances, they must end by feeling *for* each other. How this transition is effected, *viz.*, that from feeling like to feeling for others (which, of course, is what we mean by altruism), is left almost, if not quite, as mysterious by Mr. Spencer as by Tucker. If man really begins as a practical individualist, sympathy must necessarily remain factitious to the end. It is interesting to see that, in this, as in many other respects, Mr. Spencer stands in much closer relations to the eighteenth century British moralists than to the more recent Evolutional school, which takes

[1] See ch. iv., § 20.

seriously the helpful, if by no means ultimate, conception of society as an organism.

But, to proceed, Mr. Spencer argues that, when sympathy is once developed, the 'altruistic' sentiment of justice is sure to develop alongside of the 'egoistic' sentiment of justice. Men will come to feel strongly, even if still somewhat vaguely, for the rights of others as well as for their own. It goes without saying that this development is conditioned in important respects by the growth of 'the faculty of mental representation'; and here, as so often elsewhere, it is argued that the sentiment of justice, like moral development in general, must remain imperfect until society has completely outgrown the militant condition. In short, the only real difference between this later, and last, explanation of the derivation of the sentiment of justice and that given in the *Social Statics*, is that here, as in the *Psychology*, an explanation of the origin of sympathy has also been given. The author remains true to his original position, that "the sentiment of justice is nothing but a sympathetic affection of the instinct of personal rights—a sort of reflex function of it". And this explanation, surely, is by no means dependent upon the theory of Evolution.

Thus much as to the origin of the relatively vague 'sentiment' of justice. By itself, this would be insufficient; the 'idea' of justice must become definite and objective. How is this possible? The explanation given is rather surprising: "The idea emerges and becomes definite in the course of the experiences that action may be carried up to a certain limit without causing resentment from others, but if carried beyond that limit produces resentment. Such experiences accumulate; and gradually, along with repugnance to the acts which bring reactive pains, there arises a conception of a limit to each kind of activity up to which there is freedom to act." [1] And it is important to note that, according to Mr. Spencer, not equality, but inequality, is the primordial ideal suggested.

[1] See ch. v., § 21.

If each is to receive the benefits and evils due to his own nature and consequent conduct, then, since men differ in their powers, there must be differences in the results of their conduct. Such, at any rate, is the author's rather abstract explanation. More convincing is his contention that, where habitual war has developed political organisation, the idea of inequality necessarily becomes predominant. In fact, he points out that, in such a condition of society, " the inequality refers, not to the natural achievement of greater rewards by greater merits, but to the artificial apportionment of greater rewards to greater merits ". Regimentation pervades the civil, as well as the military organisation; and the idea of justice conforms to the social structure. Such an ideal of justice could not, of course, be permanent; but the modern revolt from it has been to the other extreme. Instead of an artificial inequality, an at least equally artificial equality is held by many, especially by Bentham and his followers, to represent the essential character of justice. By a decidedly strained interpretation of the Utilitarian formula, the author argues that its logical result would be nothing less than communism.

Here, again, Mr. Spencer proposes to mediate. He says : " If each of these opposite conceptions of justice is accepted as true in part, and then supplemented by the other, there results that conception of justice which arises on contemplating the laws of life as carried on in the social state. The equality concerns the mutually-limited spheres of action which must be maintained if associated men are to co-operate harmoniously. The inequality concerns the results which each may achieve by carrying on his actions within the implied limits. No incongruity exists when the ideas of equality and inequality are applied the one to the bounds and the other to the benefits. Contrariwise, the two may be, and must be, simultaneously asserted." [1] It remains only to find a formula for the compromise here suggested. This must unite a positive

[1] See ch. v., § 25.

with a negative element. As the author says: "It must be positive in so far as it asserts for each that, since he is to receive and suffer the good and evil results of his actions, he must be allowed to act. And it must be negative in so far as, by asserting this of every one, it implies that each can be allowed to act only under the restraint imposed by the presence of others having like claims to act. . . . Hence, that which we have to express in a precise way, is the liberty of each limited only by the like liberties of all. This we do by saying:—Every man is free to do that which he wills, provided he infringes not the equal freedom of any other man." [1]

At length we have obtained a formula for the principle which Mr. Spencer regards as absolutely fundamental to Ethics, being thus on an entirely different plane from Prudence, Negative Beneficence, and Positive Beneficence, all of which share in the general ambiguity of the conception of happiness, upon which they equally depend. That this principle is identical with the principle of Justice, as formulated in *Social Statics*, is evident. [2] There, however, the principle was represented as being our one perfectly clear intuition coming from the Moral Sense, the existence of which the author then assumed. At the same time, as pointed out a few pages back, it was apparently only the 'instinct of personal rights' that was regarded as strictly intuitive—a rather curious intuition of justice, which, however formulated, is generally supposed to imply impartiality, if it implies anything. In order to the development of the sentiment of justice, as universally understood, the co-operation of sympathy (assumed rather than derived, though not necessarily assumed as an ultimate) was held to be necessary, so that justice was represented as a sort of 'reflex function' of the 'instinct of personal rights'. We have already remarked

---

[1] See ch. vi., § 27.

[2] In fact, the final form given to the principle in *Social Statics* is as follows: "Every man has freedom to do all that he wills, provided he infringes not the equal freedom of any other man". See ch. vi., § 1.

upon the confusion of Intuitionism and Empiricism which one
finds here. Now, according to Mr. Spencer's explanations in
the present volume, as we have so recently seen, the 'sentiment' of justice is developed in much the same way. The
'egoistic sentiment of justice' is practically assumed here, as
the 'instinct of personal rights' had been in the earlier
volume. In order to the development of the 'altruistic sentiment of justice,' sympathy must co-operate, as was also held
in *Social Statics.* The difference is, that here sympathy is
not assumed, but shown to have been developed while society
was being held together by a provisional sentiment—the 'pro-
altruistic sentiment of justice,' which results from the four
external controls of conduct. But when once sympathy is
sufficiently developed, the 'altruistic sentiment of justice' will
necessarily develop as the counterpart of the 'egoistic sentiment of justice'. Whether these two forms of the 'sentiment'
of justice, at first so sharply differentiated, tend later to
blend into a general 'sentiment' of justice, we are not informed; but such would seem to be the implication.

The author's peculiar method of explaining the transition
from the 'sentiment' to the 'idea' of justice, has already been
indicated. Evidently it reduces itself to the rather surprising
statement that men obtain the 'idea,' as opposed to the mere
'sentiment,' of justice, by experience of the fact that there
are certain limits beyond which their fellows will not tolerate
interference! Well may he add: "It is a long time before the
general nature of the limit common to all cases can be conceived".[1] If this were the true origin of our idea of justice,
it would be long indeed. Not only so; but there would inevitably be a different 'idea' of justice for every race, if not
for every minor social group, for the degree of human long-
suffering is plainly a variable. And, in truth, it has been
argued by the author that, up to the present time, two radically
different ideals or 'ideas' of justice have actually been developed, one implying a more or less artificial inequality, the

[1] See ch. v., § 21.

other a decidedly artificial equality. The true formula—which, so far from being evidently true, has been left for Mr. Spencer to enunciate—is supposed to unite the elements of truth in the two prevailing, but antagonistic views.

It is not strange that Mr. Spencer feels it necessary to subjoin a defence of 'the authority of this formula'.[1] He laments the general contempt for 'abstract principles,' and argues that " it is only where the ethics of amity are entangled with the ethics of enmity, that thoughts about conduct are confused by the necessities of compromise". This last is itself quite confusing, since the author has just urged strongly in favour of his own formula for justice, that it stands for a highly satisfactory compromise between the two one-sided views. Again, he answers the supposed objection that this principle belongs to the class of *a priori* beliefs, though his own derivation of the principle, as indicated above, has suggested anything but that difficulty ; and, in this connection, he repeats his old argument, which goes to show that what often pass for *a priori* principles are the inherited results of race experience. From such general considerations, he concludes : " No higher warrant can be imagined ; and now, accepting the law of equal freedom as an ultimate ethical principle, having an authority transcending every other, we may proceed with our inquiry ".[2]

It will thus be seen that the author's later explanation of the genesis of the 'sentiment' and the 'idea' of justice consists merely in working out in some detail the suggestions already made in *Social Statics*—unless we except the peculiar account given of the transition from the 'sentiment' to the 'idea' of justice, which, as we have seen, is by far the weakest part of the whole explanation. Moreover, it is plain that this similarity between the explanation given in *Social Statics* and that given in the present volume, is made possible only by the fact, that the earlier view involves something rather less than a Moral Sense, while the later view involves something

---

[1] See ch. vii.　　　　[2] See *ibid.*, § 35.

rather more than ordinary Empiricism would admit in that characteristic ultimate, which, though not so called, is in reality the old 'instinct of personal rights'.

All this, of course, does not by any means involve the theory of Evolution. In how far does Mr. Spencer's general treatment of Justice, in the present volume, depend upon that all-important biological theory? The answer is not difficult: Merely in professedly regarding [1] human justice — as conceived by himself and defined in his favourite formula—as being an inevitable evolutional development from sub-human justice, which he has shown to be practically identical with the 'survival of the fittest'. It has often been demonstrated that what we commonly mean by justice cannot be explained in terms of anything analogous to this brute survival of the merely strongest in the struggle for existence. It has not, perhaps, so often been pointed out that, while Mr. Spencer's conception of the essential nature of justice is undoubtedly different from the ordinary one, it equally implies a departure from the inevitable course of Evolution considered strictly as such. In short, the opposition between what merely is and what ought to be, really exists quite as much for Mr. Spencer as for any other moralist—except in so far as he takes refuge in his unproved assumption that human society will eventually become perfect.

Let us consider this a little more closely. 'Animal justice' is reducible to the 'survival of the fittest'. Now the 'survival of the fittest'—and the originator of this useful phrase doubtless knew, best of all men, that by 'the fittest' is here meant only 'the fittest to survive'—is a fact. It would have to be recognised as such even by one who should deny the validity of the theory of Evolution itself; much more is it recognised by the enormous majority who do accept the general theory of Evolution, however they may differ as to the particular factors involved, and the relative importance of these factors. Is human justice—defined as the principle that 'every man is

---

[1] Often, when it suits the needs of a particular argument; not consistently, as the sequel will show.

free to do what he wills, provided he infringes not the equal freedom of any other man '—also a statement of what inevitably happens in the natural course of events? By no means; for '*is* free,' we must read '*ought* to be free,' in order to give the formula an intelligible meaning. And that is what Mr. Spencer himself really does, though one is obliged to suspect that his use of the indicative mood here is not wholly a matter of chance. In fact, this facile transition from what evidently is to what he thinks ought to be, or *vice versa*, in the course of an argument of any length, is a source of almost endless ambiguity, which conceals a radical confusion of thought, in the author's later ethical writings, where he professes to depend upon the theory of Evolution for guidance. One of the early passages in the *Data of Ethics*, already quoted, conveniently illustrates this. It may be the more pardonable to quote it again, since it plainly refers to the very principle which we are considering. " This imperfectly-evolved conduct *introduces us by antithesis* to conduct that is perfectly evolved. *Contemplating* these adjustments of acts to ends which miss completeness because they cannot be made by one creature without other creatures being prevented from making them, *raises the thought* of adjustments such that each creature may make them without preventing them from being made by other creatures." [1]

In short, human justice, even as conceived by Mr. Spencer, is no inevitable extension of ' animal justice,' of which latter it is only too obviously the ' antithesis '. It is rather what one man, at any rate, thinks *ought* to be, and this not so much because he is an evolutionist—for he held the doctrine firmly, and stated it in precisely the same way, before he or any one else had adequately formulated the theory of Evolution—but rather because he is, and has been, first, last, and always an individualist. To be sure, this conception of justice happens to be less obviously inconsistent with Evolutional theory than some of the other results of the author's individualism. It

---

[1] See ch. ii., § 6.   Of course the italics are not in the original.

involves no manifest absurdity from the evolutionary point of view, as when it was seriously argued in the last part of the *Data of Ethics*, that sympathy will be developed with the future moral progress of the race, very much in proportion as it is not needed. At the same time, it makes individual welfare an end in itself in a way that the theory of Evolution would never suggest, and that the perfectly consistent Evolutionist could by no means admit without reservations that never occur to Mr. Spencer.

Indeed, one may go further than this. The highly abstract principle of Justice, as here defined, so far from being shown to have been necessarily involved in the actual evolution of society, is practically treated as a 'categorical imperative,' an 'absolute ought'. 'Though the heavens fall,' Mr. Spencer would seem to say, 'every man must be granted the right to do as he pleases, so long as he does not interfere with any one else in the exercise of this divine right.' In other words, though the principle of Justice is no longer held by Mr. Spencer to be the one intuition of our Moral Sense, as was at least ostensibly done in the earlier form of his theory, it is actually treated as such by him, after he has explained its derivation in empirical terms. Of course he admits that Justice is not the only principle of Ethics ; that Prudence, Negative Beneficence, and Positive Beneficence must also be taken into account. But these latter principles all depend upon the indefinite conception of general happiness, while Justice does not. Is such a combination of practical Intuitionism, as regards Justice, and Universalistic Hedonism, as regards the remaining principles of morality, really workable? This very serious question can only be answered, if answered at all, in the sequel.

We are as little concerned here, as in our treatment of the earlier form of Mr. Spencer's ethical system, to take account of the numerous applications of this highly abstract principle of Justice. Such applications must necessarily be a matter of individual judgment ; and, moreover, any such attempt to solve many of the most important practical problems of government by the application of a single abstract principle is a proceeding which logically belongs to the methods of eighteenth century, as opposed to nineteenth century thought. It will be remembered that the author contends for the following Natural Rights : ' the right to physical integrity,' ' the rights to free motion and locomotion,' ' the rights to the uses of natural media,' ' the right of property,' ' the right of incorporeal property,' ' the rights of gift and bequest,' ' the rights of free exchange and free contract,' ' the right of free industry,' ' the rights of free belief and worship,' ' the rights of free speech and publication,' not to mention the less definite ' rights ' of women and children.

Do these rights, however understood, owe their origin to the principle of Justice, as here defined ? On this point an early reviewer of *Justice* admirably said : " Of the various Natural Rights specified by Mr. Spencer, I think it must be said that not one of them is, or can be, deduced from the law of equal freedom. They are the conditions which have been found, in some cases, necessary, in others, expedient, for the maintenance of human society. . . . We learn them from history, not from deduction ; and we see at the same time that they are not universally applicable. The ' right of free speech and publication ' may at times be properly withheld, and I have not observed any censure of the Indian government for its recent withdrawal of the right from certain native writers. ' The right of free exchange ' exists nowhere in the world outside of Great Britain ; and certainly American citizens are peculiarly sensitive to their rights. If we believed that ' freedom of worship ' imperilled the public welfare, no assertion of individual rights would prevent its abolition (*cf.* the great Mormon case, Reynolds *versus* United States). ' The right to property ' is one of the most sacred of rights ; yet it may be modified or set aside for the good of the community, as is illustrated by recent land-legislation in England. Even ' the right to life ' is qualified by the state's need of soldiers." [1]

[1] See review of *Justice* by President J. G. Schurman, *Philosophical Review*, vol. I., No. 1, p. 84.

We have now examined all that is really distinctive in the later form of Mr. Spencer's ethical theory. The remaining Parts of the *Principles of Ethics*, published during the two years following the publication of *Justice* (Part IV.), need not detain us long. In 1892 appeared Part II., " The Inductions of Ethics," and Part III., " The Ethics of Individual Life," completing the first volume of the *Principles ;* and in 1893 appeared Part V., "Negative Beneficence," and Part VI., "Positive Beneficence," completing the second volume, and the work as a whole. The topics treated in these concluding Parts are, of course, intrinsically of great importance ; but the author's handling of them is almost exactly such as could have been predicted on the basis of what is contained in the *Social Statics* and the *Data of Ethics*. Moreover, as we shall see, there is comparatively little in Parts III., V., and VI. to distinguish the author's treatment from that of traditional Utilitarianism.

" The Inductions of Ethics " (Part II.) consists almost wholly of a mass of sociological details, so arranged as to illustrate the moral development of the race, according to the author's point of view. As might be expected, Mr. Spencer constantly takes occasion to justify his characteristic distinction between the 'ethics of enmity' and the 'ethics of amity' by reference to the sociological facts here collected. At first, these supposed facts, taken from the most various sources, seem to be accepted most uncritically ; but the author himself warns us, in his closing "Summary of Inductions," against taking particular statements with too much confidence. After speaking of the difficulty of dealing with phenomena so complex as those which form the data of sociology, he very justly says : " To the difficulties in the way of generalisation hence arising, must be added the difficulties arising from uncertainty of the evidence—the doubtfulness, incompleteness, and conflicting natures, of the statements with which we have to deal. Not all travellers are to be trusted. Some are bad observers, some are biassed by creed or custom, some by personal likings or dislikings ; and all have but imperfect opportunities of getting at the truth. Similarly with historians. Very little of what they narrate is from immediate observation. The greater part of it comes through channels which colour, and obscure, and distort; while everywhere party feeling, religious bigotry, and the sentiment of patriotism, cause exaggerations and suppressions. Testimonies concerning moral traits are hence liable to perversion." [1]

After all deductions have been made, however, the author holds that one conclusion must be drawn from the sociological material here collected: the Moral Sense theory, as ordinarily understood, is wholly untenable. Mr. Spencer's definite statement regarding his own change of view on this important matter is well worth quoting. He says: "Though, as shown in my first work, *Social Statics*, I once espoused the doctrine of the intuitive moralists (at the outset in full, and in later chapters with some implied qualifications), yet it has gradually become clear to me that the qualifications required practically obliterate the doctrine as enunciated by them". [2]

But while he has changed his mind regarding the existence of a Moral Sense, he gives emphatic testimony to his continued belief in the perfectibility of human society. He says: "There needs but a continuance of absolute peace externally, and a rigorous insistence on non-aggression internally, to ensure the moulding of men into a form naturally characterised by all the virtues". [3]

When we turn to "The Ethics of Individual Life" (Part III.), it is to be remembered that we are dealing with the Part of the *Principles* immediately preceding "Justice". The chapters belonging to this third, and concluding, Part of Vol. I. contain almost nothing that is new, at least concerning the essential principles of Ethics, as understood by the author. The general title itself is, of course, significant as indicating that Mr. Spencer remains true to his original individualism. There is, it seems, an "Ethics of Individual Life," as opposed to the "Ethics of Social Life"—Justice and Beneficence. This is developed on the lines already suggested in the *Data*

---

[1] See Pt. II., ch. xiv., § 188.    [2] See *ibid.*, § 191.    [3] See *ibid.*

*of Ethics ;* the only difference between the treatment here given and that of ordinary recent Utilitarianism being, that the good of the individual is regarded as something not necessarily connected with the good of the whole—which, of course, again suggests the author's affinity to the eighteenth century moralists. The bulk of these chapters, however, is devoted to good advice rather than to the systematic treatment of Ethics. It may be interesting to know what are Mr. Spencer's personal views on 'activity,' 'rest,' 'nutrition,' 'stimulation,' etc.; but these cannot be said to belong to the History of Ethics.

More important are " Negative Beneficence " (Part V.) and " Positive Beneficence " (Part VI.), since we must look here for the necessary mitigation of the stern principle of Justice ; but it cannot be denied that these concluding Parts of the *Principles* are seriously disappointing. That the principle of Justice, all-important though it may be in its own sphere, is not the whole of Ethics, is fully recognised by Mr. Spencer. Indeed, as we have just seen, he has already (in Part III.) attempted to treat systematically of the duties which we owe merely to ourselves, and which thus, according to his own point of view, fall entirely outside the sphere of Justice. We have seen, however, that the actual treatment is hardly important, since—apart from the practical counsels above referred to—it amounts to little more than a reiteration of the author's view of the claims of the individual, considered merely as such. The method of treatment adopted, so far as it has to do with theoretical Ethics at all, is practically reducible to the Utilitarian method in its earlier, and by this time somewhat antiquated, form. The difficulty of adjusting this method of treatment to the peculiar treatment of Justice—in which, of course, Mr. Spencer stands alone among English hedonists—is, indeed, apparent; but it does not come up in an acute form, for the " Ethics of Individual Life " and that *part* of the " Ethics of Social Life " which belongs to the sphere of Justice are, at any rate, alike consistent deductions from the individualistic assumptions of the system.

When, however, the author begins to treat systematically of Beneficence, this difficulty arising from the employment of two apparently distinct methods becomes a serious matter. As already said, the principle of Justice, though no longer held to be our one clear intuition derived from a Moral Sense,[1] is actually regarded by Mr. Spencer, in the later as in the earlier form of his system, as a practical ultimate, and therefore as not depending upon considerations of ' greatest happiness '.     On the other hand, Beneficence—a principle with which the author can dispense as little as any other moralist— is, to all intents and purposes, treated in terms of traditional Utilitarianism.[2]     What will happen in the case of the (at least apparent) conflict between the principle of Justice and that of Beneficence?     One would by no means hold Mr. Spencer responsible for the practical difficulties of the moral life, *viz.*, the occasional conflict of duties, as some anti-hedonist critics are in the habit of doing in similar cases.     As we have repeatedly seen, such difficulties are practical before they are theoretical; hence they are bound to be difficulties for any system of Ethics.     But the peculiar difficulty which we have to recognise here is : the lack of any single, clearly-defined, organising principle, upon which the particular principles of morality—Justice as much as any other—can be shown to depend.     Probably this is why the author's treatment of all moral principles besides Justice is as empirical as his treatment of Justice had been abstract and theoretical.     From his point of view, indeed, very little of a strictly theoretical character can be said of any moral principle other than Justice—the only one, as he has so often insisted, that is capable of a perfectly definite, and therefore strictly scientific, treatment.

The difficulties which attend an individualistic treatment of Beneficence are avoided at the outset in the introductory chapter on " Kinds of Altruism ".     Mr. Spencer says, *e.g.:*

---

[1] As in the earlier, not necessarily the later, part of *Social Statics*.

[2] *Cf.* the author's admission on this point in the passage already quoted from the Preface to *Negative Beneficence* and *Positive Beneficence*.

" As distinguished from egoistic actions, altruistic actions include all those which either negatively by self-restraint, or
positively by efforts for their benefit, conduce to the welfare
of fellow-men : they include both justice and beneficence ".[1]
As will readily be seen, this use of ' egoistic ' and ' altruistic,'
as applied to actions, leaves out of account the moral motive
altogether. That justice and beneficence, however defined,
should be kept distinct, so far as possible, Mr. Spencer very
properly insists. He further maintains " that the primary law
of a harmonious social co-operation may not be broken for the
fulfilment of the secondary law ; and that therefore, while en-
forcement of justice must be a public function, the exercise of
beneficence must be a private function ".[2] When stated in such
general terms, this principle also may at first commend itself ;
but one must remember that by justice is here meant the principle of non-interference, which has important corollaries as
regards theory of government. While many practical states-
men have a healthy dread of a too paternal government, it
is safe to say that no practical statesman ever did, or ever will,
try to keep justice and beneficence, in whatever sense understood, separate in the way that Mr. Spencer would seem to
require. It would, *e.g.*, take but a famine or a pestilence to
show how unworkable such an abstract theory would be. Moreover, every government is, and must be, ' paternal ' in the
sense that it provides for the common good in many ways
that can by no means be included under the single head of
Justice, according to any legitimate interpretation of that
principle.

The distinction between Negative Beneficence and Positive
Beneficence, here again insisted upon and made the basis of
treatment, is that which the author had already clearly drawn
in *Social Statics*. Negative Beneficence, of course, consists
in avoiding the infliction of unnecessary pain upon others,
when strict Justice, as here understood, would permit this ;
while Positive Beneficence consists in voluntarily adding to

---

[1] See Pt. V., ch. i., § 389.    [2] See *ibid.*, § 390.

the pleasures of others. It is implied here, as elsewhere, that under the latter head are included "those kinds of actions alone recognised in the ordinary conception of beneficence". If this be so—and the statement could probably be controverted—it is only because justice is ordinarily understood not only in a different sense from that of Mr. Spencer, but in a larger sense. To the ordinary moral consciousness, it doubtless seems only just that one should avoid causing others unnecessary pain; and when the writer on systematic Ethics prefers not to include this under the head of Justice in the strict sense, he nearly always provides for the principle in his own way. This distinction, then, between Negative Beneficence and Positive Beneficence, so far from being an important invention of Mr. Spencer's, can hardly be regarded as more than a subdivision convenient for himself, and partly necessitated by his narrow and peculiar conception of Justice. Often, indeed, this distinction must have proved inconvenient even to its originator. He more exactly defines Negative Beneficence as "the species of beneficent conduct which is characterised by passivity in deed or word, at times when egoistic advantage or pleasure might be gained by action".[1] It has frequently been pointed out by moralists of the most diverse tendencies, that 'activity' and 'passivity,' as applied to moral conduct, are very misleading terms for Ethics; since, in a great number of possible cases, 'passivity' is the full equivalent of 'activity'. It is only fair to say that the author avoids such difficulties in his own treatment; but this is only by the careful choice of examples.

It is wholly unnecessary to consider in detail these concluding Parts of the *Principles of Ethics*, for here, as in Part III., "Ethics of Individual Life," Mr. Spencer contents himself, for the most part, with giving and defending his individual opinion with respect to each of the practical problems discussed. These are by no means without interest, particularly as being the opinions of one who has impressed his personality

---

[1] See Pt. V., ch. i., § 394.

so strongly upon his contemporaries ; but here, as before, we must remark that such discussions do not belong to the technical treatment of Ethics. It would hardly be going too far to say that it is only in the final chapter of Part V., on " The Ultimate Sanctions " (*i.e.*, of Negative Beneficence), that the author reverts, for the time being, to theoretical Ethics. Here it is held merely, that " the admitted desideratum being maintenance and prosperity of the species, or that variety of the species constituting the society, the implication is that the modes of conduct here enjoined under the head of Negative Beneficence, have their remote justification in their conduciveness to such maintenance and prosperity "—the assumption, of course, being that 'maintenance and prosperity of the species,' if adequately provided for, will ultimately conduce to 'greatest happiness'. The author pertinently adds : " Of course these considerations touching the nature of Beneficence at large, here appended as a commentary on the actions classed under the head of Negative Beneficence, equally apply, and indeed apply still more manifestly, to the actions classed under the head of Positive Beneficence ".[1]

It should perhaps be noted that little is said in these concluding Parts of the *Principles* regarding the distinction between ' Absolute ' and ' Relative ' Ethics. Presumably, however, this is not because the author has by any means given up his belief in a perfect society in the remote future, so strongly reaffirmed in Part II., " Inductions of Ethics," published the year before. It is doubtless because the treatment here given is almost wholly practical, as already indicated, and so naturally keeps to the present conditions of social life. There are, indeed, passages almost pathetic, in which the author points out how completely, in his own opinion, ' the time is out of joint '; but it would be wholly unwarranted to infer from these that he has given up his original optimism with regard to the future of society, so firmly held through a long life of almost unremitting labour, under adverse physical conditions that

---

[1] See Pt. V., ch. viii., §§ 426, 427.

would long ago have discouraged a literary worker of less heroic mould.

Little need be said by way of *résumé*, after our somewhat extended examination of both the earlier and the later form of Mr. Spencer's ethical system, since this examination has already involved the necessary general, as well as special, comparisons and criticisms. Nothing more than the merest outline of results will be attempted in what follows. In the earlier (what we have ventured to term) 'pre-Evolutional' form of the system, we have found an interesting but highly abstract theory of morality, confessedly based upon the author's characteristic, though paradoxical, conception of the perfect man in the perfect society—with which alone, indeed, he holds that scientific Ethics properly speaking has to do. From this point of view, as he himself insists, not even the existence of evil can be recognised. The perfect man is the only object of interest for the scientific moralist, just as the hypothetically perfect geometrical figure of whatever kind for the scientific mathematician. Moreover, a Moral Sense must be recognised—though this, upon further examination, resolves itself into an 'instinct of personal rights,' which is supposed to be helped out by 'sympathy'.

The 'Expediency Philosophy,' as represented by Bentham, is discredited, not merely, or perhaps principally, because experience shows that the hedonistic calculus involves insuperable difficulties, but because it may be proved *a priori* to be impossible, if only we consider that, with every stage of intellectual or moral progress (or decadence) on the part of the individual, the community, the nation, or the race, there would necessarily be a partial shifting of the scale of hedonistic values. In place of this wholly inadequate method, which involves the impossibility of particular computations, we must employ one which shall determine the general conditions to efficient social life and therefore, indirectly, to the 'greatest happiness,' which must still be regarded as the ultimate ideal. These are reducible to the principles of Justice,

Negative Beneficence, and Positive Beneficence, enlightened self-interest being always pre-supposed. Even from the author's abstract statement of these principles, however, a serious difficulty was apparent. Though all were designed to supplant the 'hedonistic calculus,' all except Justice were admitted to depend in the last resort upon the conception of happiness, which, as the severe criticism of the 'Expediency Philosophy' went to show, is bound to remain indefinite until the perfect society shall become an accomplished fact.

Justice, on the other hand, already defined as the principle that "every man has freedom to do all that he wills, provided he infringes not the equal freedom of any other man,"[1] was held to be our one perfectly clear moral intuition, derived from an ultimate Moral Sense — though, as we have seen, the author's direct treatment of the Moral Sense in *Social Statics* is decidedly wavering. As a result, we have found that, in this earlier work, at any rate, the author is practically an Intuitionist as regards Justice, while his proposed treatment of the remaining principles of morality, hardly more than indicated here, practically coincides with that of traditional Utilitarianism, the inadequacy of which he has been at such pains to point out. In so far as he has merely insisted upon the necessity of general rules instead of particular computations, he has reverted unconsciously to the traditional Utilitarian position as against Bentham, or at any rate as against the interpretation that has generally been put upon Bentham's doctrine.

It will be remembered that, in the earlier form of Mr. Spencer's ethical theory, our attention was directed almost wholly to the 'static' aspect of morality, as the title of the book itself would indicate. In the *Data of Ethics*, on the other hand, in which the later form of the system as a whole was at least clearly indicated, the author attempts to do justice to both the 'static' and the 'dynamic' views, but with

---

[1] See *Social Statics*, ch. vi., § 1.

special emphasis upon the latter. As a result, it looks at first as if the method employed were as concrete as the earlier method had been confessedly abstract. Organic evolution is to afford the clue, and we are invited to consider carefully what makes for the 'evolution of conduct'. It appears, however, that the 'last stages of evolution,' to which we must hopefully look forward, mean practically the doing away with that 'struggle for existence' which has been recognised hitherto as the very essence of organic evolution. In fact, the author's cardinal principle, Justice—still defined as the principle of non-interference, but now supposed to have an evolutional origin—seems to imply the precise opposite of the actual trend of Evolution; for so long as there is any real 'struggle for existence,' it is only too obvious that interference of the ultimate kind is always present.

In truth, as we proceed further with the *Data of Ethics* and the remaining parts of the *Principles*, it becomes more and more evident that we are being conducted as directly as possible to what practically amount to Mr. Spencer's earlier ethical conclusions, not because these are the result of the Evolutional method as applied to ethical problems, but rather in spite of what Evolution itself would appear to dictate. The four chapters devoted respectively to the 'Physical View,' the 'Biological View,' the 'Psychological View,' and the 'Sociological View' of morality, seem to have been intended as a preliminary statement of the method adopted; but we have seen, in perhaps wearisome detail, how vulnerable this 'scientific' method is, and how elaborately it seems to have been contrived to lead up to the desired results.

The one really important change in the *Principles of Ethics*, so far as method is concerned, is the rejection of Intuitionism; but the difference even in this respect is less than would at first appear, for in the later chapters of *Social Statics* the Moral Sense, originally taken as ultimate, had already been reduced to a sort of 'instinct of personal rights,' which had to be helped out by 'sympathy,' and to this latter assumption Mr. Spencer really adheres to the end. According to the later and more elaborate, but hardly more convincing argument, the general 'sentiment' of Justice is developed much as before, the factors being the so-called 'egoistic sentiment of justice' (*i.e.*, the original 'instinct of personal rights') and 'sympathy' (this latter now being treated as derived, instead of assumed as given). When sympathy has developed sufficiently, the 'altruistic sentiment of justice' will necessarily develop as the counterpart of the 'egoistic sentiment of justice'; and the implication would seem to be that the two will eventually blend into a general 'sentiment of justice'.

So far, of course, the apprehension of Justice is confessedly indefinite. Must we then give up the perfectly definite 'idea' of Justice, as opposed to the vague 'sentiment' of the same —that 'idea' which was assumed in the earlier part of *Social Statics* to be the one clear intuition of the Moral Sense? By no means. After a satisfactory conclusion has once been reached, Mr. Spencer is never greatly troubled with his revised premises. And in this case, the short cut to the desired conclusion is rather staggering, for apparently he argues that men obtain the perfectly definite 'idea' of Justice, still expressed by the original formula, by experiencing the fact that there are certain limits beyond which their fellows will not, as a matter of fact, tolerate interference! From all such difficulties the author may be depended upon to emerge triumphant. After his strangely confused argument, he says, in a passage previously quoted: "No higher warrant can be imagined; and now, accepting the law of equal freedom as an ultimate ethical principle, having an authority transcending every other, we may proceed with our inquiry".[1]

All this is highly instructive. A reader unfamiliar with the earlier form of Mr. Spencer's ethical system might well wonder how it came about that a principle thus empirically derived, and in such roundabout fashion, should straightway be treated, to all intents and purposes, as a 'categorical imperative'. The explanation is simple. Though this highly abstract

---

[1] See *Justice*, ch. vii., § 35.

principle of Justice is far from resulting from any legitimate application of the theory of organic Evolution, it pointedly illustrates the evolution of Mr. Spencer's own theory. Manifestly it is a survival from the 'pre-Evolutional,' Intuitional form of the theory. But this is not all; for its logical origin we must go back further still. This emphatic assertion of the rights of the individual as such was by no means a new doctrine, when set forth in *Social Statics* half a century ago; rather was it a definite and picturesque application of eighteenth century Individualism, though carried to an extreme that the average eighteenth century philosopher would probably have avoided. In fact, it seems to the present writer that, in order to do Mr. Spencer justice, one must regard him as the last great Individualist, in the eighteenth century sense of the word, rather than as the true exponent of Evolutional Ethics.

In the earlier form of the system, again, we found that, while the principle of Justice was treated as an ultimate intuition, the remaining principles of Ethics, Prudence, Negative Beneficence, and Positive Beneficence, were apparently left to be treated in the traditional Utilitarian fashion, depending as they all do upon what the author regarded as the hopelessly indefinite conception of happiness. In the later form of the system, as given in the *Principles of Ethics*, this strange combination of practical Intuitionism, as regards one ethical principle, and Utilitarianism, as regards all the rest, is unmistakable. We have repeatedly seen that the author's absolute principle of Justice by no means results from evolutionary considerations. Now Mr. Spencer himself seems finally to have conceded that Negative Beneficence and Positive Beneficence, as defined by himself, are principles that must stand on their own merits. In the passage already quoted from the Preface to *Negative Beneficence and Positive Beneficence*, he admits: "The Doctrine of Evolution has not furnished guidance to the extent I had hoped. Most of the conclusions, drawn empirically, are such as right feelings, enlightened by cultivated intelligence, have already sufficed to establish."

Since, then, these principles depend upon the variable quantity, happiness, they are not at present susceptible of exact scientific treatment; and Mr. Spencer contents himself almost wholly with practical counsels, instead of approaching the problems involved from the point of view of systematic Ethics. For the truly scientific treatment of these principles, we must wait until the perfect society actually exists—a somewhat novel form of moral agnosticism, which must have been anything but satisfactory to one with the most genuine moral convictions, whose long-cherished, and indeed highest, ambition had been to place Ethics once for all upon a strictly scientific foundation.

# CHAPTER XVI.

## HENRY SIDGWICK.

NEARLY a quarter of a century after *Social Statics*, but five years before the *Data of Ethics*, appeared the first edition of Professor Sidgwick's *Methods of Ethics* (1874). This was early seen to be a work of very considerable importance, not merely as an elaborate criticism of the various forms of ethical theory recognised by the author, but as an independent contribution to the literature of Utilitarianism; and it is hardly necessary to say that it has continued to be so regarded by competent critics up to the present time. We shall therefore be justified in treating it as the last authoritative utterance of traditional Utilitarianism.

The purpose of the book may best be expressed in the author's own words. In the Preface to the first edition he says: "Its distinctive characteristics may be first given negatively. It is not, in the main, metaphysical or psychological: at the same time it is not dogmatic or directly practical; it does not deal, except by way of illustration, with the history of ethical thought: in a sense it might be said to be not even critical, since it is only quite incidentally that it offers any criticism of the systems of individual moralists. It claims to be an examination, at once expository and critical, of the different methods of obtaining reasoned convictions as to what ought to be done which are to be found—either explicit or implicit—in the moral consciousness of mankind generally: and which, from time to time, have been developed, either singly or in combination, by individual thinkers, and worked up into the systems now historical."

Though the *Methods of Ethics* has been carefully revised five times (the revised editions bearing the dates 1877, 1884, 1890, 1893, and 1901 [1]), the author has never permitted himself to deviate from the programme which he first announced. The titles of some chapters have been changed, and many passages have been carefully rewritten, sometimes with the implicit confession of a slight change of view regarding the particular point at issue; but the framework of the book remains almost precisely what it was, even down to its minor details, while by far the greater part of the treatment is unchanged in essential respects. It is rather important to keep this fact in mind, for the numerous references to current ethical literature in the later editions of the *Methods* might give the impression that the book in its present form had been more recently planned and written than is actually the case. In the following exposition and criticism, the text of the last edition will be followed, except where notice is given to the contrary; but the treatment in the first edition will always be kept in mind, and will be referred to when comparison seems desirable.

It will readily be seen that Professor Sidgwick has undertaken a most difficult task. Ostensibly critical, for the most part, his treatment is almost bound to be implicitly constructive from the very beginning, and this not from any mere bias on his own part, but from the nature of the case. Abstracting, as he purposely does, from the historical development of ethical theory, he could not have attempted an answer to such questions as that of the number of possible ' Methods of Ethics,' and

---

[1] The edition just published (1901) represents Professor Sidgwick's final revision of the work up to p. 276. The passages quoted from this edition in the following chapters, however, are practically identical with the corresponding ones in the fifth edition (1893). In the Preface to the last edition is printed, from one of the author's manuscripts, a very condensed account of the development of his ethical views down to the time of the publication of the first edition of the *Methods*, showing what he owed successively to Mill, Kant, Butler, and Aristotle, in working out his own system. It is interesting to know that the valuable analysis of the morality of common sense (Bk. III., chaps. i.-xi.) was the part of the book first written.

the relation of these to " the moral consciousness of mankind generally," with any hope of success, except from a somewhat definite point of view of his own. For this reason we need to see, in the first place, how the author, consciously or unconsciously, defines his own position, particularly with regard to the feeling of moral obligation and the related problem as to the motive of the moral agent.

Traditional Intuitionism had consistently held that the feeling of obligation was *sui generis*, not by any means to be reduced to terms of anything else. Moreover, it had held that the mere consciousness that an action was right or wrong could in some way become a motive for performing it or abstaining from it. Traditional Utilitarianism, on the other hand, had always tended to regard the feeling of obligation as reducible to terms of interest, though not in the sense of conscious personal interest, operating at the moment of action. English Utilitarians had generally attempted to explain this, like so many other phenomena of our moral life, by means of the principles of 'association of ideas' and 'translation'. This, however, was not the strongest part of their argument. Their truly characteristic position—which they regarded as unassailable, and from which their treatment of obligation was a sort of corollary—was, of course, that no merely rational considerations can move the agent to action, but only his own pleasurable or painful feelings.

So long as these contrary, if not, as they long seemed, absolutely contradictory, doctrines were set forth in such abstract terms, there could be little hope of an understanding. Down to the time of J. S. Mill they may be said to have had a practically independent, though parallel, development; but in Mill's ethical writings certain intuitional elements, or what had previously passed for such, began to appear. The most prominent, of course, was the author's insistence upon 'qualitative distinctions' between pleasures. So flagrant an inconsistency as this could hardly prove a permanent influence in the further development of Utilitarian theory; but Mill did much to make both his contemporaries and his successors take account of the worth and meaning of human personality and regard self-development as practically an end in itself. It thus became a question how far Utilitarianism could rationalise these and other concrete aspects of the moral life, which had at least been pointed out with considerable effect by Intuitional writers.

But this was not all. We have seen that, in his earliest important contribution to Ethics, his well-known essay on Bentham (1838), Mill had complained that the elder moralist, when he dismissed all ethical theories differing from his own as ' vague generalities,' " did not heed, or rather the nature of his mind prevented it from occurring to him, that these generalities contained the whole unanalysed experience of the human race ". The reference apparently was to certain supposed moral intuitions, and the language of appreciation used was certainly a novelty in the literature of Utilitarianism. Only thirteen years later, Mr. Spencer published his *Social Statics*, in which, while confessedly a Hedonist, in spite of his rejection of the ' Expediency Philosophy ' of Bentham, he went so far as to proclaim himself also an Intuitionist, though in a somewhat qualified sense. His position in this respect, though it was one from which he retreated later, must be counted among his early inconsistencies ; but the mere fact that moralists representing such different tendencies as Mill and Mr. Spencer should both have come so near to Intuitionism, was not wholly a matter of chance. It was undoubtedly a sign of the times, showing that the older Utilitarianism, admirably consistent for the most part, but so abstract that it simply failed to take account of much that was highly significant in the moral life, was entering upon a new stage of development.

Professor Sidgwick had far too logical a mind to combine Intuitionism with Utilitarianism in this merely mechanical way ; but his attitude toward the data of the moral life was, from the first, similar in that he insisted upon certain aspects of morality which the earlier Utilitarians had practically neglected. Unlike Mill and Mr. Spencer, however, he seems to have appreciated the difficulties of the task which he had undertaken. Probably it is not without significance that chapter iii. of Book I. of the *Methods of Ethics* has successively borne the titles "Moral Reason," "Reason and Feeling," and "Ethical Judgments". The more important changes, however, seem to have been made in the second edition (1877), in the Preface to which the author says: "Even before the appearance of Mr. Leslie Stephen's interesting review in *Fraser* (March, 1875), I had seen the desirability of explaining further my general view of the 'Practical Reason,' and of the fundamental notions signified by the terms 'right,' 'ought,' &c. With this object I have entirely rewritten chap. iii. of Book I., and made considerable changes in chap. i." The fact of these alterations is not mentioned with the purpose of suggesting, that Professor Sidgwick has changed his mind in any essential respect on the very important subject to which this chapter is devoted; but the difficulty which he has found in satisfactorily expounding his views is worthy of notice, for it is in this chapter that he first makes that serious attempt to do justice to Intuitionism, which has so largely determined the peculiar form of his own ethical theory.

The treatment in the first edition is very brief, and may be indicated sufficiently for our present purpose in a few words. The author points out that two difficulties are often raised with regard to the conception of Practical Reason. "It is maintained, first, that it is not by the Reason that we apprehend moral distinctions, but rather by virtue of some emotional susceptibility commonly called a Moral Sense; and, secondly, that the Reason cannot be a spring of action, as it must always be Feeling that stimulates the Will." [1] As regards the first objection, that it is not by Reason that we apprehend moral distinctions, the author indicates his own position quite clearly as follows: "It seems, therefore, to belong to reason not merely to judge of the relation of means to ends, or of the consistency of maxims: but also to determine the ultimate ends and true first principles of action". [2] This might seem like Intuitionism (or Intellectualism) pure and simple, but the

[1] See p. 22.     [2] See p. 26.

author holds that " such an intuitive operation of the practical reason seems . . . to be somewhere assumed in all moral systems ". Earlier in the chapter he has argued that Hobbes identifies Reason with Rational Self-love, Bentham with conduct calculated to conduce to 'the greatest happiness of the greatest number,' etc.[1] It will readily be seen that ' Reason ' is here used in a sense by no means free from ambiguity.

As regards the second objection to the conception of ' Practical Reason,' *viz.*, that Reason cannot itself be a spring of action, the author suggests a characteristic compromise. After stating that, in his opinion, it is needless to ask whether a mere cognition can act upon will and prompt to action—since " no one is competent or really concerned to maintain that the apprehension of duty is a state of consciousness which occurs without any emotional element "—he says: " It is enough if it be granted that there exists in all moral agents as such a permanent desire (varying, no doubt, very much in strength from time to time, and in different persons) to do what is right or reasonable because it is such ".[2] As a note appears the following altogether too liberal concession to Intuitionism. " It can hardly be said that Intuitional Moralists generally have been disposed to over-estimate the actual force of the practical reason. Certainly neither Clarke nor Kant have fallen into this error." The author concludes: " We may assume then as generally admitted that the recognition of any action as reasonable is attended with a certain desire or impulse to do it: and that in this sense the Reason may be affirmed to be a spring of action ".[3] All this, it must be remembered, is supposed to represent not merely the author's own point of view, but the concensus of opinion among moralists. It is not strange that he found it necessary to state his position more clearly. Moreover, in spite of the ambiguous use of ' Reason,' referred to above, it is evident that the treatment here given is already implicitly constructive, and concedes a good deal more to Intuitionism than had been customary among previous Utilitarian writers.

[1] See p. 23.      [2] See p. 27.      [3] See p. 28.

As already indicated, the important changes in this chapter were made in the second edition of the *Methods* (1877); but for the sake of brevity, we shall turn at once to the latest version (1901). Here 'reasonable' conduct is identified with that which 'ought' to be done; 'non-rational' conduct, therefore, being regarded as that which takes place in accordance with mere desires and inclinations. Of course, the question at once arises, whether this antithesis between 'reason' and 'desire' is not a misapprehension, *i.e.*, whether the conflict is not after all a conflict between different desires and aversions, "the sole function of reason being to bring before the mind ideas of actual or possible facts, which modify . . . the resultant force of our various impulses".[1] Now Professor Sidgwick argues that this is *not* the case. The gist of the whole chapter, in its revised form, is, that strictly moral judgments are essentially different from any prudential judgments whatsoever, and that therefore the notion of 'ought' is in the last resort irreducible to terms of anything else.

His own language on this very important matter should be noted : "It seems then that the notion of 'ought' or 'moral obligation' as used in our common moral judgments, does not merely import (1) that there exists in the mind of the person judging a specific emotion (whether complicated or not by sympathetic representation of similar emotions in other minds); nor (2) that certain rules of conduct are supported by penalties which will follow on their violation (whether such penalties result from the general liking or aversion felt for the conduct prescribed or forbidden, or from some other source). What, then, it may be asked, does it import? What definition can we give of 'ought,' 'right,' and other terms expressing the same fundamental notion? To this I should answer that the notion which these terms have in common is too elementary to admit of any formal definition."[2]

[1] See p. 25.

[2] See pp. 31, 32. In what follows the author explains that, when he speaks of this notion as ultimate and unanalysable, he does not mean to rule out mental development; but only to insist that "as it now exists in our thought, [it] cannot be resolved into any more simple notions".

In this later version, as in that which appeared in the first edition of the *Methods*, Professor Sidgwick refuses to admit that he has made any concessions to Intuitionism as a differentiated form of ethical theory. He says explicitly : " Nothing that has been said . . . is intended as an argument in favour of Intuitionism, as against Utilitarianism or any other method that treats moral rules as relative to General Good or Wellbeing ". In fact, he holds that " the notion ' ought '—as expressing the relation of rational judgment to non-rational impulses—will find a place in the practical rules of any egoistic system, no less than in the rules of ordinary morality, understood as prescribing duty without reference to the agent's interest ". And he adds : " According to my observation of consciousness, the adoption of an end as paramount—either absolutely or within certain limits—is quite a distinct psychical phenomenon from desire : it is a kind of volition, though it is, of course, specifically different from a volition initiating a particular immediate action ".[1]

Such, in substance, is one of the four most significant chapters in the *Methods of Ethics*, in its earliest and in its latest form. Perhaps it may now be surmised why the original title of the chapter, " Moral Reason," was changed, first to " Reason and Feeling," and then to " Ethical Judgments ". In the earlier treatment it was held that Reason (in a sense not sufficiently defined) does determine ends, and particularly the ultimate end, in moral conduct ; and, moreover, that it is *as if* reason were itself capable of affording a motive to right conduct, though not necessarily the only one, since " we may assume . . . as generally admitted that the recognition of any action as reasonable is attended with a certain desire or impulse to do it ". Indeed, as we saw, the author made the much too generous admission that " it can hardly be said that Intuitional Moralists generally have been disposed to over-estimate the actual force of the practical reason ". In this earlier version of the chapter, then, the concession to

[1] See pp. 35-37.

Intuitionism seems unmistakable, and the only reason why it cannot be still more clearly proved is to be found in the ambiguous use of the word 'reason,' to which we have already referred.

Is this ambiguity cleared up in the later version? It is difficult to see that this is the case. As already indicated, the greater part of the chapter is devoted to showing that the conception of 'ought' is irreducible to terms of anything else. Not that this notion may not have been developed, like all our others, but that it now has all the simplicity which introspection would seem to show. And still the claim is made that all this is not to be counted against Utilitarianism, or even against Egoism. Evidently 'ought' is here used in a more general sense than that of ordinary Intuitionism, but the author's absolute refusal to resolve the conception of obligation, as had been done by all the earlier English hedonists, at least down to the time of J. S. Mill, is most significant; while he plainly remains true to his original position that, while it may not, perhaps, properly be held that reason, apart from all feeling, can afford the moral motive, it is nevertheless much *as if* this were the case, since we nearly all desire, more or less strongly, to do that which is reasonable merely because it is such—a position which at least brings him into a good deal closer relation to traditional Intuitionism than to traditional Utilitarianism.

So much, then, concerning Professor Sidgwick's treatment of "Moral Reason," as given in the first of what we have ventured to call the four most significant [1] chapters of the book. The others will be found to be: chapter iv. of Book I., which, in its latest as in its earliest form, bears the title, "Pleasure and Desire"; chapter vi., also of Book I., first called "The Methods of Ethics," and later, "Ethical Principles and Methods"; and chapter xiii. of Book III., on "Philosophical Intuitionism," which contains the most important part of the author's proof of Utilitarianism. The chapter on

---

[1] *I.e.*, significant, as tending to define the author's own position.

"Pleasure and Desire" has been a good deal less modified in successive editions than the one which we have just examined, and so can be considered rather more briefly, though it is hardly less important as preparing us for the author's characteristic treatment of Ethics. Evidently we here come to close quarters with the problem as to what can constitute a motive. We say 'can' advisedly, for the psychological question: What *can* constitute a motive? is very properly treated as logically preceding the question: What *ought* the motive to be, if the action is to be truly moral?

It will hardly be necessary to compare the earliest and the latest versions of this chapter, since the gist of the argument is the same in both. Perhaps it is worth noticing, however, that the author was careless in the first edition, to the extent of seriously misinterpreting Mill's theory of desire. After quoting the well-known passage in the *Utilitarianism,* in which Mill maintains that "desiring a thing and finding it pleasant, aversion to it and thinking of it as painful, are phenomena entirely inseparable, or rather two parts of the same phenomenon," and further that "we desire a thing *in proportion* as the idea of it is pleasant," the author says: "On this view the notions 'right' and 'wrong' would seem to have no meaning except as applied to the intellectual state accompanying volition: since if future pleasures and pains be truly represented, the desire must be directed towards its proper object. And thus the only possible method of Ethics would seem to be some form of Egoistic Hedonism."[1]

This is the familiar mistake, now generally recognised as such, of treating this problem too much in the abstract. It may plausibly be urged that, if that motive is always followed which appeals most strongly to oneself, then all motives are on the same plane, *i.e.*, equally selfish; but the fallacy is not far to seek. What attracts or repels depends very largely upon the character of the particular moral agent, and characters vary almost indefinitely. Psychologically the motives

[1] See p. 31.

of Judas and his Master may have been alike, in that they were equally strong; ethically, of course, they were as different as the extremes of character which they represented. In other words, so far from Mill's theory of desire necessarily leading to Egoistic Hedonism, it is compatible with any degree of altruism which, on other grounds, may be attributed to human nature.[1]

But the author is not really attacking a phantom. He seems to confuse with Mill's theory of desire the very different position of traditional Utilitarianism, which was, not merely that " desiring a thing and finding it pleasant, aversion to it and thinking of it as painful " are the same thing considered from different points of view, but that ultimately only *pleasure as such* can be desired, and consequently only the agent's own pleasure. This is really the theory to a consideration of which this chapter is principally devoted; and it will be found that the author's conclusions are not only in conflict with those of the older Utilitarians, but come perilously near to carrying him beyond Utilitarianism altogether. Neglecting other differences of treatment in the earlier and the later editions, which are immaterial, so far as the main argument is concerned, we shall now confine ourselves to the latest version.

The point of departure is afforded by Butler's familiar analysis of desire, which had been so strangely disregarded by nearly all previous hedonistic writers. Butler, of course, had held that particular passions or appetites are " necessarily presupposed by the very idea of an interested pursuit; since the very idea of interest or happiness consists in this, that an appetite or affection enjoys its object ". After arguing that Butler has over-stated his case—since pleasures of sight, hearing, and smell, as well as many emotional pleasures, do not seem to imply previous desires—Professor Sidgwick concedes the essential point. He says : " But as a matter of fact, it appears to me that throughout the whole scale of my impulses, sensual, emotional, and intellectual alike, I can distinguish

---

[1] Of course we are not here concerned with the question as to whether Mill's theory was correct.

desires of which the object is something other than my own pleasure ".[1] Of hunger, *e.g.*, he gives practically the same account as Butler had done. It is a direct impulse to the eating of food. Of course, pleasure may be anticipated as a result of the satisfaction of this craving, and such is very often the case ; but there could be no pleasure of satisfaction, and therefore no anticipation of such pleasure, were not the craving itself an original, objective tendency.

The same line of argument would obviously apply to our other so-called 'natural' appetites and desires ; but, as a matter of fact, Professor Sidgwick does not take the trouble to develop the argument further in this direction. What he does particularly insist upon is the fact that, in the case of the so-called 'pleasures of pursuit,' which, as he remarks, " constitute a considerable item in the total enjoyment of life," a certain disinterestedness is always implied. One could not, *e.g.*, experience the pleasures of the chase, if one did not for the time become objectively absorbed in it. In all such cases—and they really include nearly all the so-called 'active' pleasures, mental as well as physical—self-conscious Epicureanism would defeat its own end. Here, indeed, the particular end which is for the time disinterestedly, in the sense of objectively, sought, is not organic to our nature like our various original appetites. It may even be a thing as insignificant as success in some game which we play for a first and only time. This might seem to constitute a very important difference ; but the author would doubtless have explained, if it had seemed to him necessary to explain anything so obvious, that the impulse to activity of some sort, whether physical or mental, is as original as any of our bodily appetites.

Professor Sidgwick is rather more cautious than Butler in employing this theory of the objective character of our primary desires to prove the possibility of disinterested action ; but he pertinently urges, *e.g.*, that " the much-commended pleasures of benevolence seem to require, in order to be felt

[1] See p. 45.

in any considerable degree, the pre-existence of a desire to do good to others for their sake and not for our own ". Of course, arguments like this are not intended to emphasise the extra-regarding impulses at the expense of the self-regarding ones. The two alternate with such rapidity that they often seem to blend. But, so far as concerns what is actually in the mind, Professor Sidgwick says : " A man's conscious desire is, I think, more often than not chiefly extra-regarding ; but "— as he is careful to add—" where there is strong desire in any direction, there is commonly keen susceptibility to the corresponding pleasures ; and the most devoted enthusiast is sustained in his work by the recurrent consciousness of such pleasures ".[1] This seems to be a perfectly just analysis, as far as it goes, and, as will be seen, it wholly avoids the confusion which we had occasion to notice in the earlier version of the first part of this chapter, where the author was arguing, as against J. S. Mill's contention that " we desire a thing in proportion as the idea of it is pleasant," that this would commit one to Egoistic Hedonism. At the same time, this present account of the matter shows that Mill's analysis of desire, like that of his predecessors, was insufficient.

It will be seen, then, that Professor Sidgwick is as far as possible from admitting, what appeared to most of the earlier English Utilitarians so obviously true, that each can only desire pleasure as such, and consequently only his own pleasure. In fact, he says : " Our conscious active impulses are so far from being always directed towards the attainment of pleasure or avoidance of pain for ourselves, that we can find everywhere in consciousness extra-regarding impulses, directed towards something that is not pleasure, nor relief from pain " [2] The logic of all this is clear : there is, according to his view, no theoretical difficulty in admitting a certain degree of original altruism, if this seems necessary on other grounds. As regards the traditional view of Associationism, that our original impulses were all directed toward pleasure or from

---

[1] See pp. 50, 51.     [2] See p. 52.

pain, and that any impulse otherwise directed must be explained by the principles of 'association' and 'translation,' he says explicitly: "I can find no evidence that even tends to prove this: so far as we can observe the consciousness of children, the two elements, extra-regarding impulse and desire for pleasure, seem to coexist in the same manner as they do in mature life. In so far as there is any difference, it seems to be in the opposite direction; as the actions of children, being more instinctive and less reflective, are more prompted by extra-regarding impulse, and less by conscious aim at pleasure. No doubt the two kinds of impulse, as we trace back the development of consciousness, gradually become indistinguishable: but this obviously does not justify us in identifying with either of the two the more indefinite impulse out of which both have been developed." [1]    All this is most admirably expressed. The abstractions of the older Associationist-Utilitarianism have been left far behind; we are beginning with what practically amounts to Butler's analysis of desire. It remains to be seen how far the author will commit himself to what would appear to be the logical implications of this analysis.

After these discussions, the importance of which for the constructive part of the book could not easily be exaggerated, Professor Sidgwick takes up the 'freedom of the will,' in the sense of indeterminism. Both sides of the argument are very clearly and impartially presented. On the determinist side, there is held to be "a cumulative argument of great force," against which is to be set "the immediate affirmation of consciousness in the moment of deliberate action"; [2] and the two seem to be regarded by the author as about equally convincing. It may seem a little strange that the immediate verdict of consciousness should be taken quite so seriously in a book, the most prominent characteristic of which is a tendency toward almost painfully rigorous analysis; for, whatever may be the merits of this wearisome controversy, it is plain that the verdict of consciousness in this case is, after all, only a fact of

[1] See p. 53.          [2] See pp. 62-65.

consciousness, and one which may itself quite possibly be susceptible of explanation.

Perhaps it would be fair to regard this as one of Professor Sidgwick's partly unconscious concessions to Intuitionism; but, on the whole, his attitude is most fortunate, for he is able to show very clearly that one's decision in this matter does not commit one for or against any recognised form of ethical theory. Whether happiness or perfection be regarded as the end of action, this end cannot properly be held to be either more or less desirable because our actions are supposed to be either free or determined. Certain theological problems, *e.g.*, that regarding 'retributive justice,' are indeed involved; but it is far wiser not to entangle ourselves with such problems in the present connection. And it is fair to add, what the author does not happen to mention, that a developed theological system is almost sure to have quite as much trouble with the conception of an absolute freedom of the will as with determinism.

The ground having thus been cleared, Professor Sidgwick proceeds at once, in Chapter vi., to an investigation of the possible Methods of Ethics. Considering its very important consequences, this preliminary discussion is much too brief, occupying in fact only about twelve pages of the elaborate treatise in its final form. In truth, it is rather necessary to compare the latest version of this chapter with the one to be found in the first edition of the *Methods*, in order fully to understand how the author arrives at his conclusions, identical in both and of the very greatest importance as determining the whole method of treatment followed in the body of the book.

Let us examine briefly the substance of the chapter in its original form. As we have before had occasion to notice, the prevailing motive in conscious action is not always an impulse toward the attainment of pleasure or the avoidance of pain. Among our disinterested motives "we may place the desire to do what is right and reasonable as such, of which the characteristic is that, as Butler says, it claims supremacy: *i.e.*, that in so far as we are moral beings we think that it *ought* to prevail, whether it does or not ".[1]   Now the methods of systematising conduct that claim to be reasonable are limited in number.   In the first place, Happiness seems to be a reasonable end; but, if it be regarded as the ultimate end, the question immediately arises: *Whose* happiness is to be assumed as the ultimate end of action?   The author holds that there are " two views and methods in which Happiness is regarded as the ultimate and rational end of actions : in the one it is the agent's happiness which is so regarded, in the other the happiness of all men, or all sentient beings ".   Of course it would be possible to adopt an intermediate position, and regard the happiness of some limited portion of mankind as the end, but such a limitation would plainly be arbitrary.   So much for Happiness; but Perfection or Excellence is also thought a rational end, and may be regarded as an end in itself.   And, as in the case of happiness, the perfection aimed at may be either individual or universal, though in actual systems of Ethics one's own perfection seems to be the ideal presented. Moreover, it is a common opinion that a great part of truly moral action is done merely because it is right or good, because duty so dictates.   This is what is commonly called the Intuitional theory of morals.

It may at first appear that this list is not exhaustive.   Many religious persons, *e.g.*, regard the Will of God as the highest reason for acting in a given way, while philosophical schools which are at least historically important have advanced the principle of ' living according to Nature ' as the true ultimate. At first these principles may seem distinct from those above mentioned ; but further examination will show that they either lie beyond the scope of this inquiry, or that they resolve themselves into the others—or perhaps into a confused blending of two or more of these.   While fully admitting the difficulties inevitably encountered, when such classifications are attempted, the author says : " In the meantime the list of first principles

[1] See pp. 58 *et seq.*   Note the concession to Intuitionism.   This passage does not occur in later versions.

already given seems to include all that have a *primâ facie* claim to be included: and to afford the most convenient classification for the current modes of determining right conduct. At the same time I do not wish to lay stress on the completeness or adequacy of the classification. I do not profess to prove *à priori* that there are these practical first principles and no more. They have been taken merely empirically from observation of the moral reasoning of myself and other men, whether professed moralists or not: and though it seems to me improbable that I have overlooked any important phase or point of view, it is always possible that I may have done so." [1]

Let us inspect a little more carefully our proposed classification. When Perfection is taken as the end of action, the agent's own perfection seems nearly always to be what is meant, and, moreover, this is commonly understood as moral perfection. But what is to be the test of such perfection? One seems almost inevitably to be thrown back upon intuitive moral judgments, so that this method may properly be taken as a form of Intuitionism. On the other hand, if we conceive Happiness to be the end, it is necessary to distinguish very sharply between Egoism and Utilitarianism (*i.e.*, Universalistic Hedonism). This, it should be remembered, is one of the author's fundamental positions. Speaking of the tendency to confuse the two forms of hedonistic theory, he says: "Such a *rapprochement* encourages a serious misapprehension of both the historical and the philosophical relations of these methods to the Intuitional or Common-Sense Morality".[2]

Indeed, as he goes on to urge, the distinction between one's own happiness and that of people in general is so natural and obvious, and so continually forced upon us by the circumstances of life, that we must look for some good reason for the persistent confusion between the two which we so commonly find. "And," he adds, "such a reason is found in the theory of human action held by Bentham (and generally speaking by

[1] See pp. 64, 65.
[2] As we shall see later, this statement requires considerable modification.

his disciples), which has been discussed in a previous chapter. Though ethically Epicureanism and Benthamism may be viewed as standing in polar opposition, psychologically Bentham is in fundamental agreement with Epicureans. He holds that a man ought to aim at the maximum felicity of men in general; but he holds, also, that he always does aim at what appears to him his own maximum felicity—that he cannot help doing this—that this is the way his volition inevitably acts." [1]

The above almost literal reproduction of the substance of this chapter in its original form has seemed desirable, first, because the first edition of the *Methods* is not, of course, readily accessible to most readers, and secondly, because this earliest version shows exactly how the author came to classify the Methods of Ethics as he has once for all done. Before criticising this classification, it is important to note certain differences in the latest version, published twenty-seven years afterward (1901).[2] One modification had long before become necessary. Some reference, at least, had to be made to the principle of Self-realisation as affording a possible Method of Ethics, for this had actually become one of the most important 'methods' in the hands of contemporary ethical writers. Curiously enough, however, this principle is hardly more than mentioned in the later form of the present chapter, in which the author explains and defends his own classification. Practically the only reference to it is to be found in the revised form of the passage in which 'God's Will' and 'living according to Nature' are considered only to be rejected, as principles not deserving the position of separate Methods of Ethics.

Professor Sidgwick says: "Many religious persons think that the highest reason for doing anything is that it is God's Will: while to others 'Self-realisation' or 'Self-development,' and to others, again, 'Life according to Nature' appear the

---

[1] See p. 67.

[2] The latest version is not essentially different from some which preceded it, but is referred to here as indicating the author's final position.

really ultimate ends ". But he almost immediately adds: " God, Nature, Self, are the fundamental facts of existence ; the knowledge of what will accomplish God's Will, what is ' according to Nature,' what will realise the true Self in each of us, would seem to solve the deepest problems of Metaphysics as well as of Ethics. But just because these notions combine the ideal with the actual, their proper sphere belongs not to Ethics as I define it, but to Philosophy — the central and supreme study which is concerned with the relations of all objects of knowledge." [1]

There follows a further examination of the conceptions of ' conformity to God's Will ' and ' life according to Nature,' as affording guides for conduct ; but we are informed in a note, that the notion of ' Self-realisation ' will more conveniently be considered in the following chapter, which is devoted to an examination of Egoism. It will thus be seen that, at the crucial point of the discussion, where the author is once for all deciding what shall be regarded as the typical Methods of Ethics, the issue with Self-realisation is avoided rather than met. This would be very difficult to understand, if we were not able to refer back to the earliest version of this chapter (1874), where the author quite naturally overlooked the significance of this possible method,[2] which, if taken seriously, tends so materially to discredit the classification here adopted. But, even so, it is rather puzzling to find that, while the earliest form of this chapter represented the classification of ethical methods adopted as tentative rather than as logically complete and final, the later versions are much more dogmatic in tone, and do not appear to suggest any doubt as to the complete adequacy of the classification. Perhaps it became evident to Professor Sidgwick himself, that, if the classification should prove seriously defective, this would have to be regarded as very seriously detracting from the validity of the results obtained ; for, as we shall soon see, given the classification, the results are almost a foregone conclusion.

[1] See p. 79.

[2] It will be remembered that Bradley's *Ethical Studies, e.g.*, was published two years later.

But, before we venture to criticise this classification further, it will be well to avoid possible misconceptions by noticing certain additional explanations of the terms Egoism and Intuitionism, as here used, which will be found in the concluding chapters of Book I. And, as before indicated, under the discussion of Egoism we shall find the author's further, and final, explanation of his refusal to recognise Self-realisation as an independent Method of Ethics. Neglecting the order of exposition, we may first notice that what is here said of Intuitionism, though admirably clear and to the point, as far as it goes, does not really add much to our understanding of the author's position. He very properly suggests that we must distinguish three forms of Intuitionism: (1) the ' ultra-intuitional' view, which " recognises simple immediate intuitions alone [referring to the particular act in question] and discards as superfluous all modes of reasoning to moral conclusions"; (2) the ordinary intuitional view, " of which the fundamental assumption is that we can discern certain general rules with really clear and finally valid intuition "; and (3) what may be called Philosophical, as opposed to Perceptional or Dogmatic, Intuitionism—*i.e.*, the form of Intuitionism which, " while accepting the morality of common sense as in the main sound, still attempts to find for it a philosophic basis which it does not itself offer: to get one or more principles more absolutely and undeniably true and evident, from which the current rules might be deduced, either just as they are commonly received or with slight modifications and rectifications ".[1]

It is to be observed, that no further attempt is here made to show that systems which regard Perfection as the end necessarily come under the head of Intuitionism. If, as the author has previously assumed, the ' perfection' meant is merely ' moral perfection,' no objection can well be made; but if, as certain later passages in the book would seem to indicate, the principle of Self-realisation is regarded as one form of the perfection doctrine, it will readily be seen that the classification is, in this respect, rather seriously misleading.

[1] See pp. 100-102.

As already indicated, however, the only further reference made to Self-realisation, in the chapters which we are considering occurs in the discussion as to the precise meaning of Egoism. The chapter devoted to this discussion we shall now briefly examine. One possible ambiguity in the use of the term Egoism would be almost sure to suggest itself. Egoism might stand for 'self-preservation' as well as for the consistent pursuit of one's own happiness. In fact, it is often self-preservation rather than pleasure that Hobbes appears to have in mind in the development of his system. Professor Sidgwick does not, however, point out that there is also a possible ambiguity in the use of 'self-preservation'; but rather immediately remarks that " in Spinoza's view the principle of rational action is necessarily egoistic, and is (as with Hobbes) the impulse of self-preservation ". By itself this would be seriously misleading, but the author himself adds: " Still it is not at Pleasure that the impulse primarily aims, but at the mind's Perfection or Reality: as we should now say, at Self-realisation or Self-development ".[1]

Even if this were all that needed to be said on this point, it would be evident that 'self-preservation' in this sense is by no means the equivalent of 'egoism,' as ordinarily understood, for the realisation of an ideal self is plainly something very different from the satisfaction of what may be called one's 'empirical self,' with all its peculiarities and even perverted tendencies. Moreover, if allied with any metaphysical theory, Egoism, in the strict sense, could only go with one which should regard the individual being as, at least practically, a metaphysical ultimate; whereas it is only too evident that, in Spinoza's system, the individual as such is only a passing phase or manifestation of the Universal Substance.

But, neglecting this historical reference, which can hardly be regarded as fortunate, let us consider the author's final reason for neglecting Self-realisation as a separate Method of Ethics. He says: " It may be said, however, that we do not,

[1] See p. 90.

properly speaking, 'develop' or 'realise' self by yielding to
the impulse which happens to be predominant in us; but by
exercising, each in its due place and proper degree, all the
different faculties, capacities, and propensities, of which our
nature is made up. But here there is an important ambiguity.
What do we mean by 'due proportion and proper degree'?
These terms may imply an ideal, into conformity with which
the individual mind has to be trained, by restraining some of
its natural impulses and strengthening others, and developing
its higher faculties rather than its lower: or they may merely
refer to the original combination and proportion of tendencies
in the character with which each is born. . . . According to the
former interpretation rational Self-development is merely another term for the pursuit of Perfection for oneself: while
in the latter sense it hardly appears that Self-development
(when clearly distinguished) is really put forward as an absolute end, but rather as a means to happiness." [1]  Hence the
author concludes that, on the whole, "the notion of Self-
realisation is to be avoided in a treatise on ethical method,
on account of its indefiniteness".

It is doubtless true, that writers standing for the Self-
realisation theory have often laid themselves open to the
charge of indefiniteness in their treatment of ethical problems;
but it is only fair to say, that neither of the two interpretations
of the principle of Self-realisation which Professor Sidgwick
here allows could be admitted as adequately characterising
the method, even when somewhat carelessly employed. The
second of the supposed alternatives may, of course, be dismissed at once. No ethical writer worthy of consideration
has held that the 'due proportion and proper degree' of
development of the various sides of our nature "merely refer
to the original combination and proportion of tendencies in
the character with which each is born".

On the other hand, it is rather misleading merely to speak
in general terms of "an ideal, into conformity with which

[1] See p. 91.

the individual mind has to be trained, by restraining some of its natural impulses and strengthening others, and developing its higher faculties rather than its lower," for this is adopting precisely the language of ordinary Intuitionism rather than that of Self-realisation. 'Higher' and 'lower' are, indeed, conceptions which exist for Self-realisation, as for all other recognised Methods of Ethics;[1] but they are by no means necessarily regarded by the moralist of that school as intuitive ultimates. On the contrary, they are supposed to be explainable in terms of the more or less complete; moreover, the Self which is to be developed is, of course, a social or ideal self, with all the implications which this involves, and not merely what we have just ventured to call the 'empirical self,' which latter is obviously the result of heredity and environment in each particular case. It is hardly necessary to say that no attempt is here made to explain, much less to vindicate, the Self-realisation theory. I would merely suggest that, even in the last edition of the *Methods*, it is not stated in terms that could be accepted by its supporters.

Professor Sidgwick concludes this discussion as follows: "To sum up, Egoism, if we merely understand by it a method that aims at Self-realisation, seems to be a form into which almost any ethical system may be thrown, without modifying its essential characteristics. And even when further defined as Egoistic Hedonism, it is still imperfectly distinguishable from Intuitionism if quality of pleasures is admitted as a consideration distinct from and overruling quantity. There remains then Pure or Quantitative Egoistic Hedonism, which, as a method essentially distinct from all others and widely maintained to be rational, seems to deserve a detailed examination."

---

[1] Of course the hedonist recognises the *primâ facie* distinction between 'higher' and 'lower,' but explains it in his own way.

# CHAPTER XVII.

### HENRY SIDGWICK (*continued*).

AFTER these careful, if also somewhat tedious preliminaries, we are at length in a position to appreciate the exact significance of the author's classification, upon which so much depends. It is hardly necessary to say more at present regarding his failure to recognise Self-realisation as one of the Methods of Ethics. Such an omission would hardly be possible in a recent ethical treatise; but we are always to remember that Professor Sidgwick has strictly adhered to the lines laid down in the first edition of the *Methods* (1874), which, to mention only two significant dates, was published two years before Bradley's *Ethical Studies* (1876) and nine years before Green's *Prolegomena to Ethics* (1883). Neglecting, then, what would otherwise seem so strange an omission, and confining ourselves to the classification as actually given in all editions of the *Methods*, we shall do well to scrutinise this classification somewhat carefully before we proceed.

We find what purport to be three distinct Methods of Ethics, Egoism (or Egoistic Hedonism), Intuitionism, and Utilitarianism (or Universalistic Hedonism); and the implication, at least in the later editions of the *Methods*, would seem to be that this division must be regarded as exhaustive. No objection, of course, could possibly be made to regarding Intuitionism as a separate Method of Ethics; but it is the author's peculiar view, that what he terms Egoism is even more distinct from Intuitionism and Utilitarianism than these are from each other. In fact, it is largely by emphasising the antithesis between Egoistic Hedonism and Universalistic Hedonism,

(381)

that he is able to show what he conceives to be the comparatively close relation between Universalistic Hedonism and Intuitionism.

But a very serious objection at once presents itself. Is Egoism a Method of Ethics at all, even according to the author's carefully formulated definitions? There is, indeed, no question that many English moralists, from the time of Hobbes down at least to the time of J. S. Mill, held that the motive of the moral agent was necessarily egoistic; and nobody held this view more strongly than Bentham himself, as Professor Sidgwick candidly admits. If, then, all were to be classed as Egoists who held this theory of the moral motive, we should plainly have to include all the English Utilitarians before Mill, with the exception of Cumberland, Hartley, and Hume (*i.e.*, as represented by the second form of his theory). In truth, we should have to go much further than this, and include other moralists wholly outside the Utilitarian school, for the selfish theory of the moral motive was a natural result of eighteenth century individualism. Even the greatest of English moralists, Butler himself, would not wholly escape, according to Professor Sidgwick's interpretation of his doctrine, for he elsewhere says: "It is by no means Butler's view (as is very commonly supposed) that self-love is naturally subordinate to conscience. . . . He treats them as independent principles, and so far co-ordinate in authority that it is not 'according to nature' that either should be over-ruled. . . . He even goes so far as to 'let it be allowed' that 'if there ever should be, as it is impossible there ever should be, any inconsistence between them,' conscience would have to give way."[1]

Plainly, then, the egoistic theory of the moral motive cannot be what Professor Sidgwick means, when he speaks of Egoism as constituting a separate Method of Ethics. A 'Method of Ethics,' as clearly indicated in the Preface to the first edition, is one of "the different methods of obtaining reasoned convictions as to what ought to be done which are to be found—either explicit or implicit—in the moral consciousness of man-

---

[1] See *History of Ethics*, pp. 194, 195.

kind generally: and which, from time to time, have been developed, either singly or in combination, by individual thinkers, and worked up into the systems now historical". Now it may confidently be maintained that not one of the many moralists referred to above, as holding or seeming to hold the egoistic theory of the moral motive, ever so much as suggested that one could obtain "reasoned convictions as to what ought to be done" by merely computing what would bring the most pleasure to one's self. It was characteristic of the essential dualism of their general view of Ethics to consider the *subjective* end of action, or the motive of the moral agent, quite apart from the *objective* end, or standard of whatever sort, which was supposed to determine the morality of human actions. Even Hobbes, the arch-egoist, according to the ordinary conception of Egoism, was no exception, for he explicitly held that those things are 'right' or 'wrong' which are declared to be such by the constituted civil authority; and perhaps no English moralist would have been more averse to having the individual decide for himself what was 'right' or 'wrong' on the basis of a deliberate computation of his private chances of happiness.

Who, then, is the Egoist intended? It would not do to urge that certain depraved characters do, as a matter of fact, appear to seek their own happiness regardless of all else; for, even when free rein is given to the self-seeking impulse, it is apparently never claimed by the agent himself that a given action is to be regarded as moral, on general principles, merely because it promises to conduce to his own selfish pleasure,[1] though, of course, his moral judgments in particular cases may be fatally warped by selfish considerations. Moreover, it is wholly needless to point out that Egoism is used by the author, not by any means as a term of reproach, but as a convenient designation for what he conceives to be one of the three possible Methods of Ethics. All this is puzzling in a writer so logical, for the most part, as Professor Sidgwick. One can

---

[1] This would be too flagrant a contradiction even for the *im*moral consciousness.

only conclude that, in his very serious, and largely successful, attempt to differentiate the modern form of Utilitarianism, for which he himself stands, from the older form which based upon the assumed necessary egoism of the moral agent, he has unconsciously developed, in what he terms Egoism, the conception of a form of hedonistic theory which in reality has never existed in Modern Ethics, and which never could exist as a 'Method of Ethics,' if by this we are to understand a method of " obtaining reasoned convictions as to what ought to be done ".

It would almost seem that Professor Sidgwick wished to forestall this criticism in a passage which appeared for the first time in the fifth edition of the *Methods* (1893). This is at the beginning of Book II., which is devoted to an examination of the 'method' of Egoism. In the first four editions of the treatise, he seems to have suspected no difficulty, for he had said: " It is, perhaps, a sufficient reason for considering this [*i.e.*, Egoism] first of the three systems [1] with which this treatise is principally concerned, that there seems to be more general agreement among reflective persons as to the reasonableness of its fundamental principle, than exists in the case either of Intuitionism or of that Universalistic Hedonism to which I propose to restrict the name of Utilitarianism ".[2] On the other hand, the passage referred to above, as having first appeared in the fifth edition, reads as follows : " It may be doubted whether this [*i.e.*, Egoism] ought to be included among received 'methods of *Ethics*' ; since there are strong grounds for holding that a system of morality, satisfactory to the moral consciousness of mankind in general, cannot be constructed on the basis of simple Egoism. In subsequent chapters I shall carefully discuss these reasons : at present it seems sufficient to say—what will hardly be denied—that no principle of conduct is more widely accepted than the proposition that it is reasonable for a man to act in the manner most conducive to his own happiness." [3] Then, as in all

---

[1] 'Methods' in fourth edition.
[2] See p. 107 (first edition).          [3] See p. 119 (fifth edition).

previous editions, he goes on to show that ethical writers as different as Bentham, Butler, Clarke, and Berkeley, alike, though in somewhat different terms, concede the ultimate reasonableness of acting for one's own happiness.

But if the object of this belated passage really was to forestall the very serious criticism, that the first of the author's three Methods of Ethics is not a 'method' of Ethics at all, it is not difficult to show that it wholly fails in its purpose. With all respect to Professor Sidgwick, one must submit that it is by no means sufficient to point out that " no principle of conduct is more widely accepted than the proposition that it is reasonable for a man to act in the manner most conducive to his own happiness ". In truth, there is a double ambiguity here. Does 'reasonable,' as here used, mean 'reasonable, other things being equal' or 'ultimately reasonable'? If the former, the principle is indeed generally admitted by those who admit the claims of happiness at all, but it is irrelevant in a discussion with regard to what mode of conduct is 'ultimately reasonable'. Again, if 'ultimately reasonable' is what is meant, it becomes extremely important to know in what sense acting for one's own happiness is to be so regarded.

It proves altogether too much to refer to the concessions of Bentham, Butler, Clarke, and Berkeley on this point. Each of the first three, at any rate, had a method different from that of either of the others for determining the rightness or wrongness of actions ; but all, being alike of the eighteenth century, were inclined to admit that it must be for the agent's selfish interest to be moral. So we are brought back to the selfish theory of the moral motive, which, as we have already seen, and as this mention of Bentham, Butler, Clarke, and Berkeley aptly illustrates, cannot by itself possibly be regarded as affording the basis for a separate Method of Ethics. In a word, while many of the older English moralists, otherwise representing the most diverse tendencies, held the egoistic theory of the moral motive, or at least used language that would permit of that interpretation, not one of them ever claimed, or so much as suggested, that one could determine the morality of actions by computing one's private chances of happiness.

In fact, a careful reading of Book II., on "Egoism," in any one of the slightly differing versions, will show that what is really considered is the *practicability* of ordering one's life on the principle of Egoistic Hedonism, not whether morality itself can be rationalised by the application of that principle. It is hardly necessary to say that the method of treatment, in this respect, differs very materially from that employed in Book III., on "Intuitionism," and in Book IV., on "Utilitarianism". Still, the substance of Book II. is by no means unimportant, for it is here that Professor Sidgwick first considers in detail both the implications and the real or supposed difficulties of Hedonism in general. Indeed, it will be found, in many cases, that important problems connected with Hedonism are discussed only in this book.

The fundamental assumption of Hedonism as such is shown to be 'the commensurability of pleasures and pains'.[1] Unless a more or less definite quantitative comparison be possible, it is plain that both Egoism and Utilitarianism must be rejected as impracticable methods. It is sometimes claimed that certain pleasures and pains are so intense that any comparison between them and others is out of the question, but this particular objection to the hedonistic calculus can hardly be sustained. We commonly assume that "all the pleasures and pains that man can experience bear a finite ratio to each other in respect of pleasantness and its opposite". This idea of an arrangement of pleasures and pains in a scale, as greater or less in some finite degree, might seem to involve the assumption of a 'hedonistic zero,' or perfectly neutral feeling. It is not necessary to decide whether this strictly neutral feeling ever occurs; but it is worth noticing that a state very nearly approximating to this is even common. At the same time this fact would not seem to present any special

---

[1] See pp. 123 *et seq.*

difficulty. The celebrated dictum of Epicurus, that the state of painlessness is equivalent to the highest possible pleasure, is too paradoxical to require definite refutation.

The first real difficulty occurs, when we try to define pleasure and pain for purposes of quantitative comparison. Mr. Spencer defines pleasure as " a feeling which we seek to bring into consciousness and retain there "; but, while adequate for purposes of distinction, this definition is hardly appropriate for purposes of quantitative comparison, since it can hardly be held that pleasures are greater or less, exactly in proportion as they exercise more or less influence in stimulating the will to actions tending to sustain or produce them.[1]  For the present purpose, it will be convenient to define pleasure as " feeling which, when experienced by intelligent beings, is at least implicitly apprehended as desirable or—in cases of comparison—preferable ".  As regards the old problem concerning the so-called ' qualitative distinctions ' between pleasures, we may fairly conclude that, " when one kind of pleasure is judged to be qualitatively superior to another, although less pleasant, it is not really the feeling itself that is preferred, but something in the objective conditions under which it arises "; for it seems impossible to find in feeling as such any other preferable quality than that which we call ' pleasantness '.[2]

After this admirably clear statement of the general aspects of the problem, Professor Sidgwick proceeds to examine carefully and most impartially certain of the more common objections to the hedonistic calculus.  It is impossible here to go into details ; but, on the whole, it must be conceded that he allows to the objections mentioned fully as much weight as they deserve.  Unfortunately, however, he does not consider the objection which Mr. Spencer had urged with such force in *Social Statics* (1851), *viz.*, that the hedonistic calculus is impossible, because there would necessarily be an important shifting of the scale of hedonic values with every stage of intellectual or moral progress (or decadence), whether on the part of the individual, the community, the nation, or the

[1] See p. 126.          [2] See p. 129.

race.[1]  In the opinion of the present writer, this is the one really fatal objection to the hedonistic calculus.  And it will be seen to have an important theoretical, as well as practical, bearing; for if the assumed ultimate, happiness, be found to vary in proportion as something else varies, external conditions remaining the same, there is at least a very strong presumption that it may prove not to be the true ultimate after all.

On the other hand, altogether too much weight seems generally to have been attached to the objection, that the quantitative comparison of particular pleasures and pains cannot be carried to the point of scientific precision; for the comparison actually attempted nearly always is, not between particular pleasures and pains, but between the pleasurable or painful results of certain classes of actions, where the known actual preferences of ourselves and others are at least of considerable assistance.  The difficulties involved in such a comparison are, indeed, very serious from any point of view; but they would not necessarily be unsurmountable, if it were not for the inevitable shifting of the scale of hedonic values referred to above.  In truth, as we had occasion to notice in a previous chapter, the question of more or less, whole or part, is one which arises not only in connection with the hedonistic calculus, but for any method of Ethics which seriously attempts to explain how we are to determine the rightness or wrongness of particular classes of actions.  Otherwise expressed, this difficulty is practical before it is theoretical; for the moment we transcend the crudest form of Intuitionism, which refuses to go beyond what is conceived to be the infallible verdict of 'conscience' in each individual case, we discover that the regulation of conduct must depend upon a comparison of values, extrinsic or intrinsic, which, from the very nature of the case, can never become mathematically exact.

---

[1] It will be noted that this is a somewhat free rendering of Mr. Spencer's objection, but the attempt has been made to state it in its most comprehensive form.

The final chapter of Book II., originally called "Other Forms of the Egoistic Method," then "Other Methods of Egoistic Hedonism," and finally, "Deductive Hedonism," has been considerably changed since it first appeared; but the modifications are not of a kind to detain us. What the author has throughout been concerned to prove is, that no hedonistic method is in the last resort able to dispense with the hedonistic calculus. In the first edition it was clearly shown that, though Mr. Spencer had objected so strongly to the hedonistic calculus, he had in reality by no means supplied a deductive method which would take its place, and, moreover, that the other less ambitious indirect methods of determining what will make for happiness or its contrary are too vague to be of much practical assistance. In the later form of the chapter, 'Scientific Hedonism' is examined a good deal more carefully, but with practically the same result. The author very justly concludes that, try as we may to avoid it, we are inevitably thrown back upon the empirical method, *i.e.*, some form of the hedonistic calculus, so long as we hold to Hedonism at all. It would hardly be possible to do justice to his very cogent argument by any brief paraphrase; and perhaps this is the less necessary since, in our detailed examination of Mr. Spencer's ethical writings, we have already found how little is really accomplished here by the parade of scientific method.

At this point Professor Sidgwick somewhat abruptly takes leave of Hedonism for a considerable time, and devotes Book III. to a sympathetic, but at the same time very searching, examination of Intuitionism. We have seen that the title of Book II., *i.e.*, "Egoism," is a little misleading, since the greater part of the book is really devoted to a consideration of the more general aspects of Hedonism. In fact, we have purposely abstracted from the particular applications to Egoism, since this is so far from deserving the dignity of a separate Method of Ethics. Now it should be carefully noted that by far the greater part of Book III., which itself is about twice the length of any other book in the treatise, is devoted, not to an examination of Intuitionism as a separate Method of Ethics, but to an extremely careful analysis of what the author terms ' the morality of Common Sense '.

Such a method of treatment was perfectly logical, and perhaps necessary; but it is important to keep in mind that the moral judgments of Common Sense, whatever these may turn out to be, are by no means the peculiar property of Intuitionism. They may be thought more or less significant, and obviously they are susceptible of quite different interpretations and evaluations from the points of view of the various types of ethical theory; but, as facts of the moral life, they must be taken account of in any adequate treatment of Ethics, provided, of course, that they are not too vague and conflicting to admit of fairly satisfactory formulation. To the present writer it seems, that Professor Sidgwick has contributed something of great importance to Ethics by carrying through this rigorous analysis of our common moral judgments, before making any serious attempt to evaluate them or to prove or disprove anything by them. The common defect of such discussions is, that the writer who attempts them carries a brief in his hand; but every candid reader must admit that nothing could well be more judicial than the temper which Professor Sidgwick manifests throughout. Of course, it is easy to criticise any work of this kind. ' Common Sense ' is a vague term, and what are given as the apparent moral judgments of the plain man may seem alternately naïve and sophisticated; but, on the whole, it may fairly be conceded that the author has performed this very important and difficult task more satisfactorily than any other English writer has done up to the present time.

It would be quite impossible to examine this part of the *Methods of Ethics* in detail, without devoting to such an examination more space than would here be warranted. Only a few points will be noticed. In this case, no stress is laid by the author upon the provisional classification adopted. The verdict of the common moral consciousness regarding the principal recognised virtues is subjected to the most minute and searching examination. The greatest importance is naturally attached to Benevolence and Justice, to each of which a long chapter is devoted. It is not strange that the result of such careful analysis should be much the same in all cases. The original dogmatic propositions of common sense are found to require important limitations, these limitations also being at least partly recognised by common sense itself. But the further the analysis is carried, the more difficult it becomes to state the exact nature of the limitations required. Common sense is found often to be at variance with itself, so that in many cases it looks as if the original principles threatened to elude us altogether—at any rate, unless we should take refuge in some definite form of ethical theory, which would at once carry us beyond the point of view of the ' plain man,' with which alone we are concerned at present.

We should naturally expect to find the greatest clearness and consistency in the case of our conception of Justice, but this turns out to be especially difficult to define satisfactorily. Nothing, in fact, could well afford a greater contrast to Mr. Spencer's recklessly dogmatic treatment of this virtue than Professor Sidgwick's very elaborate and extremely able analysis of our actual everyday judgments as to what things are just or the contrary. Incidentally, indeed, he shows how perfectly impossible it is to regard ' freedom from interference ' as a principle at once practically intuitive and sufficient to rationalise our ordinary conceptions of Justice.

After this very elaborate examination of the actual moral judgments of Common Sense, Professor Sidgwick raises the question : Do we find here a sufficient basis for dogmatic Intuitionism ? He himself, though by no means wholly opposed to Intuitionism as such, is far from drawing this conclusion. We require of an axiom, that it shall be (1) stated in clear and precise terms, (2) really self-evident, (3) not conflicting with any other truth, and (4) supported by an adequate ' concensus of experts '. Now he admits that, in the previous examination of the morality of Common Sense, he has discovered few, if any, maxims that fulfil these conditions. Of these maxims of Common Sense, he very truly says : " So long as they are left in the state of somewhat vague generalities, as we meet them in ordinary discourse, we are disposed to yield them unquestioning assent, and it may be fairly claimed that the assent is approximately universal—in the sense that any expression of dissent is eccentric and paradoxical. But as soon as we attempt to give them the definiteness which science requires, we find that we cannot do this without abandoning the universality of acceptance. We find, in some cases, that alternatives present themselves, between which it is necessary that we should decide ; but between which we cannot pretend that Common Sense does decide, and which often seem equally or nearly equally plausible." [1]

All this, of course, is not to be understood as implying that we are left in doubt as to what is right or wrong in ordinary conduct. On this point, Professor Sidgwick carefully defines his position at the end of the chapter. He says : " The notions of Benevolence, Justice, Good Faith, Veracity, Purity, etc., are not necessarily emptied of significance for us, because we have found it impossible to define them with precision. The main part of the conduct prescribed under each notion is sufficiently clear : and the general rule prescribing it does not necessarily lose its force because there is in each case a margin of conduct involved in obscurity and perplexity, or because the rule does not on examination appear to be absolute and independent. In short, the Morality of Common Sense may still be perfectly adequate to give practical guidance to common people in common circumstances : but the attempt to elevate it into a system of Intuitional Ethics brings its inevitable imperfections into prominence without helping us to remove them." [2]

It remains to see whether some other form of Intuitionism may not promise success, where ordinary dogmatic Intuitionism is so manifestly doomed to failure. The attempt has sometimes been made to show that moral judgments strictly

---

[1] See p. 342.     [2] See pp. 360, 361.

apply, not to acts, but to desires or affections. It is natural to fall back upon this view, when the difficulties of ordinary Intuitionism become too apparent; but Professor Sidgwick very truly observes, that nearly all the difficulties which we have previously encountered reappear in a different form, when we try to arrange motives in order of excellence, while " such a construction presents difficulties peculiar to itself, and the attempt to solve these exhibits greater and more fundamental differences among Intuitive moralists, as regards Rank of Motive, than we found to exist as regards Rightness of outward acts ".[1] In the pages which follow, these criticisms are abundantly sustained; but the particular arguments employed hardly need detain us. It is perhaps enough to notice that the tendency toward subjectivity, which is commonly recognised as the greatest danger of Intuitionism as such, is needlessly accentuated in this form of the doctrine. We may therefore properly pass on at once to Philosophical Intuitionism.

Here, again, it seems desirable to notice the author's earlier treatment, as contained in the first edition of the *Methods*, before taking up the later form of the same discussion. He begins with an important word of caution. We must very carefully guard against a certain class of ' sham axioms,' which have not infrequently deluded even moralists of considerable repute.[2] For example, it has been urged that the dictates of Wisdom and Temperance may be reduced to the following intuitive principles : (1) It is right to act rationally ; and (2) it is right that the lower parts of our nature should be governed by the higher. But the tautology becomes obvious, when we find that ' acting rationally' is merely another phrase for ' doing what we see to be right,' and that the ' higher part' of our nature, to which the ' lower parts ' are to defer, is nothing other than ' reason' itself. These definitions may be found in modern writers; but it must be observed that nearly the whole of the ethical speculation of

---

[1] See p. 365.          [2] See pp. 353 *et seq.*

Greece, though in many respects of the greatest interest and value, has this incurable defect. Is there any way of avoiding such circular reasonings, and attaining clear intuitive truths of substantial value? The author replies: "I believe that there is such a way: though we must be careful not to exaggerate the amount of the moral knowledge to which it conducts us. And I think we may find it by following the two thinkers who in modern times have most earnestly maintained the strictly scientific character of ethical principles: *viz.*, Clarke in England, and Kant in Germany."[1]

Abstracting from the particular form of Clarke's theory, which is largely determined by his anxiety to exhibit the supposed parallelism between ethical and mathematical truths, we may note that he recognises two fundamental 'rules of righteousness'; the first of which he terms 'Equity,' and the second 'Love,' or 'Benevolence'. The clearest of his three slightly differing statements of the Rule of Equity is as follows: "Whatever I judge reasonable or unreasonable that another should do for me: that by the same judgment I declare reasonable or unreasonable, that I should *in the like case* do for him". This principle is accepted by the author as really self-evident, "as much so as the axioms of mathematics, whether or not it be desirable to classify it with them". At the same time, he admits that this principle is *primâ facie* insufficient for the complete determination of just or equitable conduct.

As for Clarke's 'second branch of the Rule of Righteousness' with respect to our fellow creatures, his well-known principle of 'universal Love or Benevolence,' the elaborate formula which he actually gives is not altogether fortunate ; but it should be observed that "what Clarke urges is, that the Good of any one individual cannot be *more* intrinsically desirable, *because it is his*, than the equal Good of any other individual. So that our notion of Ultimate Good, at the realisation of which it is evidently reasonable to aim, must include the Good of *every* one on the same ground that it

[1] See p. 357.

includes that of *any* one."[1] This principle, again, seems to be as much a self-evident truth as the principle of Equity.

There follows an interpretation and criticism of Kant's ethical theory (the details of which are omitted in later editions), which is intended to show that two propositions, substantially identical with those just examined, are there propounded as the chief ultimate principles of conduct. These are: "First, that nothing can be right for me which is not right for all persons in similar circumstances: and secondly, that I cannot regard the fulfilment of my desires, or my own happiness, as intrinsically more desirable (or more to be regarded by me as a rational end) than the equal happiness of anyone else". The author concludes: "But now, of these two propositions, the first is a necessary postulate of *all* ethical systems, being an expression of what is involved in the mere conception of objective rightness and wrongness in conduct: while the second is the fundamental principle of that particular system which (in Book I.) we called Utilitarianism".[2]

The significance of this second principle in such a connection is particularly emphasised. In fact, the author maintains that "we have found it as the final outcome of philosophical Intuitionism, the final result of inquiry after really clear and self-evident ethical axioms, as conducted by philosophers who are commonly regarded as eminent examples of the Intuitional mode of thought". And he closes the chapter with a criticism of Mill's proof of the principle of Utility, as given in Chapter iv. of the *Utilitarianism*. Mill argued that, since each does actually desire his own happiness, it must be admitted that 'the greatest happiness is desirable'—in the sense that this is what each individual *ought* to desire, or at least to aim at realising in action. But it may fairly be claimed that this argument leads primarily to the principle of Egoistic, instead of Universalistic Hedonism, and that the only way of meeting this objection is to show, substantially as Clarke and Kant have done, the necessary universality of the

---

[1] See p. 360.  [2] See p. 364.

ultimate end, as recognised by Reason. " Thus Utilitarianism appears as the final form into which a really scientific Intuitionism tends to pass."

But there is one remaining difficulty here, which the author very pertinently points out, after having seemed to overlook it altogether. Omitting details, it is this: " The hedonistic interpretation which Mill and his school give to the principle of Universal Benevolence, seems inadmissible when the principle is enunciated as a self-evident axiom. In thus enunciating it, we must use, as Clarke does, the wider terms ' Welfare ' or ' Good,' and say that each individual man, as a rational being, is bound to aim at the Good of all other men. This brings us naturally to the question, What is ' Good '? which, it seems, still remains to be determined." [1]

When the later form of this very important chapter is compared with the above reproduction of the treatment in the first edition, it will be found that certain differences worth mentioning begin to appear at the point where the question is raised: What may really be accepted as valid intuitions? Instead of directly appealing to the well-known axioms of Clarke and to his own manifestly one-sided interpretation of Kant, Professor Sidgwick directly argues that " whatever action any of us judges to be right for himself, he implicitly judges to be right for all similar persons in similar circumstances ". [2] And he holds that a corresponding proposition may be stated with equal truth in respect of what ought to be done *to*—not *by*—different individuals. These principles appear in the Golden Rule, ' Do to others as you would have them do to you '; but that formula is obviously inexact, for one might wish for another's co-operation in sin, and be willing to reciprocate it. " In short the self-evident principle strictly stated must take some such negative form as this; ' it cannot be right for *A* to treat *B* in a manner in which it would be wrong for *B* to treat *A*, merely on the ground that they

---

[1] See p. 366. The author's answer to this question will be carefully considered later.

[2] See pp. 379 *et seq.*

are two different individuals, and without there being any difference between the natures or circumstances of the two which can be stated as a reasonable ground for difference of treatment." While such a rule manifestly does not give complete guidance in respect to just conduct, its practical importance cannot be questioned, and its truth, so far as it goes, appears to be self-evident. A somewhat different application of the same fundamental principle, that individuals in similar circumstances should be treated similarly, appears in that ' impartiality in the application of general rules ' which is so important an element in the common notion of Justice. In fact, the author's extremely careful analysis of the ordinary conception of Justice went to show, that no other element than this could be intuitively known with perfect clearness and certainty.

Besides the principle just explained, which is regarded as affording an intuitive foundation for the conception of Justice, there are two others, referring respectively to rational Prudence and Benevolence, which to Professor Sidgwick appear also to be intuitively apprehended. He says : " The proposition ' that one ought to aim at one's own good ' is sometimes given as the maxim of Rational Self-love or Prudence : but as so stated it does not clearly avoid tautology ; since we may define ' good ' as ' what one ought to aim at '. If, however, we say ' one's good on the whole,' the addition suggests a principle which, when explicitly stated, is, at any rate, not tautological. . . . All that the principle affirms is that the mere difference of priority and posteriority in time is not a reasonable ground for having more regard to the consciousness of one moment than to that of another." It is rather important to note that, while this principle is often stated in hedonistic terms, it does not seem to have any logical connection with the principle that ' pleasure is the sole Ultimate Good '. All that is necessarily implied is, that the Good be " conceived as a mathematical whole, of which the integrant parts are realised in different parts or moments of a lifetime ".[1]

[1] See pp. 381, 382. The validity of this assumption will be examined later.

And now we come to the crucial point of this argument, which, on account of its great importance for the author's treatment of Ethics, has been literally reproduced. Professor Sidgwick says: " So far we have only been considering the ' Good on the Whole ' of a single individual: but just as this notion is constructed by comparison and integration of the different ' goods ' that succeed one another in the series of our conscious states, so we have formed the notion of Universal Good by comparison and integration of the goods of all individual human — or sentient — existencies.   And here again, just as in the former case, by considering the relation of the integrant parts to the whole and to each other, I obtain the self-evident principle that the good of any one individual is of no more importance, from the point of view (if I may say so) of the Universe, than the good of any other; unless, that is, there are special grounds for believing that more good is likely to be realised in the one case than in the other.   And it is evident to me that as a rational being I am bound to aim at good generally,—so far as it is attainable by my efforts,— not merely at a particular part of it.   From these two rational intuitions we may deduce, as a necessary inference, the maxim of Benevolence in an abstract form:   *viz.* that each one is morally bound to regard the good of any other individual as much as his own, except in so far as he judges it to be less, when impartially viewed, or less certainly knowable or attainable by him." [1]

From the whole preceding argument, the author concludes that in the principles of Justice, rational Prudence, and Benevolence, as commonly recognised, there is at least a self-evident element, immediately cognisable by abstract intuition.   And he adds: " I regard the apprehension, with more or less distinctness, of these abstract truths, as the permanent basis of the common conviction that the fundamental precepts of morality are essentially reasonable ".   It will be remembered that, in the first version of this chapter, these principles, or what corresponded to them, were supposed to be taken from

[1] See p. 382.

Clarke and Kant, the Intuitional moralists *par excellence.* In the later form of the chapter, which we have just been examining, the reference to Clarke and Kant follows the much more elaborate, though hardly more satisfactory, vindication of the principles which are accepted by the author as ultimate intuitions. And it is to be noted that the present reference to Kant is much more guarded than the earlier one. In fact, the earlier careful, if by no means satisfactory, interpretation of Kant is reduced to a single colourless paragraph. The concluding criticism of Mill is presented in practically the same form, the author's claim, of course, being, that Utilitarianism absolutely requires the Intuitional basis which he has himself attempted to supply, particularly in his vindication of the intuitive character of the principle from which that of rational Benevolence is deduced.

In order to do justice to this interesting attempt to exhibit Utilitarianism as, on the one hand, the logical result of Philosophical Intuitionism itself, and, on the other hand, as absolutely requiring the Intuitional basis above indicated, it will be necessary somewhat later to examine carefully the final chapter of Book III., which is devoted to a consideration of " Ultimate Good "—for Professor Sidgwick's proof of Utilitarianism is confessedly not yet complete, the nature of the Good having been left indeterminate. Here we are only concerned to understand the general significance of this final, and, as he believes, decisive part of the argument. At first this might look like forsaking the Intuitional method altogether, for apparently it is the very essence of Intuitionism to hold that certain actions are intrinsically right or wrong, not right or wrong because they conduce to some ultimate end of action conceived to be the Good. But Professor Sidgwick defends himself, in all of the slightly differing versions of this chapter, by arguing that the ultimate intuitive principles at which he has arrived, as a result of his careful analysis of the Morality of Common Sense, *viz.,* Justice, rational Prudence, and Benevolence, all have to do with *the apportionment of the Good,* which itself has been left undefined.

# CHAPTER XVIII.

## HENRY SIDGWICK (continued).[1]

IN his examination of Intuitionism, and his attempt to discover in it a residuum of tenable doctrine, Professor Sidgwick has, in one respect at least, observed most commendable caution. He has pitilessly analysed the conventional tautological propositions, and candidly pointed out the inconsistencies that are inevitable, so long as Intuitionism is regarded as affirming an aggregate of independent, but at the same time absolutely valid, particular principles, corresponding in detail to the various recognised virtues. The result of this searching examination, as will be remembered, is a good deal the same in the latest as in the earliest edition. In the first edition of the *Methods* (1874), Samuel Clarke's maxims of Equity and Beneficence were accepted as really intuitive—"as much so as the axioms of mathematics". In the later editions (*e.g.*, sixth edition, 1901), the statements are somewhat more guarded; but it is still held that in the principles of Justice and Benevolence, as commonly recognised, "there is at least a self-evident element, immediately cognisable by abstract intuition,"[2] while a third intuitive principle, that of rational Prudence, is also admitted. The explicit formulation of this third principle in the later

---

[1] A paper entitled "An Examination of Professor Sidgwick's Proof of Utilitarianism," based upon the first part of this chapter, and closely following the present text, was read before the Philosophical Section of the American Psychological Association at the Baltimore Meeting, December, 1900, and was afterward printed in the *Philosophical Review*, May, 1901.

[2] See p. 382.

editions need not be regarded as in itself particularly significant, since it might very reasonably be held that the principle
was implicitly recognised as intuitive in the earlier treatment ;
but it is to be noted that, in the later and more elaborate
form of the author's proof of Utilitarianism, with which we are
here more particularly concerned, this principle of rational
Prudence is regarded as in a sense more ultimate than that of
Benevolence, since it is accepted as logically co-ordinate with,
if not logically prior to, the more general principle (not named,
as we shall see) from which that of Benevolence is deduced.

Assuming, then, as of course we must, that this later
enumeration of three intuitive principles, corresponding to the
virtues, rational Prudence, Benevolence, and Justice, accurately
represents the author's later, if not also his earlier, view as to
the Intuitional foundation of Ethics, it may be well first to
recall the precise form in which these principles are given.
The two which are certainly treated as intuitive are : (1) the
principle which is supposed to underlie the ordinary conception
of Justice, *viz.*, that "it cannot be right for $A$ to treat $B$ in a
manner in which it would be wrong for $B$ to treat $A$, merely
on the ground that they are two different individuals, and
without there being any difference between the natures or
circumstances of the two which can be stated as a reasonable
ground for difference of treatment ";[1] and (2) the principle
of rational Prudence just mentioned, *viz.*, that one part of a
given conscious experience is not to be regarded, other things
being equal, as of more importance than any other equal part
of the same experience. The precise formulation of the
third supposed intuition, from which the abstract principle of
rational Benevolence is directly deduced, will be considered
when we come to see how it is actually derived by the
author.

Now, in connection with these supposed intuitions, three
closely related questions at once present themselves : (1) Are
any or all of these principles to be accepted as really intuitive,

---

[1] See pp. 380 *et seq.*

without further examination? (2) What, exactly, does each of these principles imply? (3) Are they all to be regarded as strictly on the same plane? If the first question be answered in the affirmitive, the two others may perhaps be regarded as superfluous; otherwise they will most certainly be relevant. As regards the first question, it is difficult to see that Professor Sidgwick has taken the necessary steps to *prove* that any of these principles are intuitive, even granting for the time that they all may very well be such. Throughout the treatise he has studiously avoided all metaphysical and epistemological questions, and, on the whole, this has been most fortunate for his treatment of Ethics; but it is difficult to see how one is to prove that the principles in question are strictly intuitive, without for the time passing over into Epistemology. Professor Sidgwick says, indeed: " No psychogonical theory has ever been put forward professing to discredit the propositions that I regard as really axiomatic "; but this is evading the issue rather than meeting it. The question is one, not of the psychological origin, but rather of the epistemological significance, of these principles; and to call principles intuitive without committing oneself to any particular theory of knowledge looks almost like begging the question. The mere fact that, when separately considered, they commend themselves to common sense—which seems to be the test actually depended upon by the author—is plainly insufficient; for the result of philosophical reflection very commonly is, to show that what common sense unites, must be separated, and that what common sense separates, must be united.

Since, then, we cannot accept these principles as intuitive without further examination, and since we cannot directly raise epistemological questions without entering into those very discussions which the author explicitly avoids, it seems fairest to pass on at once to the two remaining very closely related questions: What, exactly, does each of these principles imply? And, in particular, are they all to be regarded as strictly on the same plane? Professor Sidgwick himself suggests one important difference, in making the transition from his treatment of the so-called intuition of Justice to that of the intuitions which are supposed to correspond to rational Prudence and Benevolence. He says: " The principle just discussed [Justice], which seems to be more or less clearly implied in the common notion of ' fairness ' or ' equity,' is obtained by considering the similarity of the individuals that make up a Logical Whole or Genus. There are others, no less important, which emerge in the consideration of the similar parts of a Mathematical or Quantitative Whole." [1]

Now it is partly because the principle of Justice, as here formulated, does not depend upon this conception of a merely quantitative whole, which to many seems inapplicable to Ethics, that it almost inevitably appears more ultimate than the other two principles, in the particular form here given, whether or not we think proper to ascribe to it a strictly intuitive character. Moreover, it is to be carefully noted that this principle, *viz.*, that " it cannot be right for *A* to treat *B* in a manner in which it would be wrong for *B* to treat *A*, merely on the ground that they are two different individuals," is much more extensive in its application than what is ordinarily understood by Justice. This fact seems hardly to be recognised by the author. Yet from the mere statement of the principle, it is evident that it applies at least to all our moral relations to others. It is thus a regulative principle, applicable to rational Benevolence quite as much as to Justice, though so abstract that the subordinate principles, Justice and Benevolence, as ordinarily understood, need to be formulated before this very general principle can be of much practical assistance in directing moral conduct. But if one consider the matter more closely, it will be evident that this same abstract principle, here called that of Justice, applies not merely to all our conduct which directly concerns others, but equally to that part of our conduct which more immediately concerns ourselves ; for any recognised form of ethical theory requires some reason for our treating ourselves differently

[1] See pp. 380, 381.

from others, though the reasons accepted as valid no doubt vary considerably.

It thus gradually becomes evident, that the principle which we are examining is not a particular ethical principle at all, but rather an abstract statement of that postulate of objectivity, or impartiality, which is implied in all ethical reasoning as such. Whether or not one call this postulate an intuition, depends, of course, upon one's theory of knowledge. At any rate, from the epistemological point of view, it would appear to be on a plane with the most fundamental methodological postulates of the various sciences and disciplines; it is not a particular principle referring to any one side of our moral experience more than to all others.

When we come to consider the supposed intuitions corresponding to rational Prudence and Benevolence, as here formulated, it soon becomes evident that we are dealing with relatively subordinate principles, and principles that involve certain assumptions that are likely to make them less universally acceptable. The principle of rational Prudence, *viz.*, that one should aim at one's good on the whole, looks at first very innocent, at any rate so long as the Good is left undefined, and so long as the point insisted upon merely is that " difference of priority and posteriority in time is not a reasonable ground for having more regard to the consciousness of one moment than to that of another ". But when it becomes evident that this principle is regarded as logically separate from, and apparently as logically prior to, that of Benevolence, it needs little argument to prove that this supposed intuition is by no means free from certain assumptions which themselves assuredly have no intuitive basis.

The most important, perhaps, is the extremely dangerous assumption that there is a good for me that is originally and to the end separate from the good of others. This inevitably commits one to that " dualism of the Practical Reason " which Professor Sidgwick himself frankly admits in the final chapter of the *Methods*. But that is not all. When Professor Sidgwick argues that all that is necessarily implied is, that the

Good be "conceived as a mathematical whole, of which the integrant parts are realised in different parts or moments of a lifetime," he partly suggests a really serious difficulty. As a matter of fact, the Good is here assumed to be not merely a mathematical whole—which might vaguely suggest certain internal relations—but a quasi-physical aggregate, as opposed to an organic whole. And this plainly begs the question, as against certain forms of ethical theory for which the author has no sympathy, as, for instance, Self-realisation.

How important this latter assumption really is, can readily be seen from the use which Professor Sidgwick makes of it; for he immediately proceeds to base his further argument upon this questionable analogy. Just as the notion of individual good is "constructed by comparison and integration of the different ' goods ' that succeed one another in the series of our conscious states," so the notion of Universal Good may be found " by comparison and integration of the goods of all individual human—or sentient—existencies ". In other words, consider the Good, whatever that may prove to be, in abstraction from the nature of the being for whom it is the Good, and the question of more or less is all that remains.[1] Mathematics, the most abstract of all the sciences, is at least ideally applicable here in the most thoroughgoing fashion, precisely because we are dealing with something that is already abstract.

It should be observed that we have not even yet obtained the desired intuition of rational Benevolence — which is emerging rather slowly for an intuition—*viz.*, the principle " that each one is morally bound to regard the good of any other individual as much as his own, except in so far as he judges it to be less, when impartially viewed, or less certainly knowable or attainable by him ".[2] This is confessedly a deduction, though a perfectly logical one, from the more

---

[1] It should be noted that the question of more or less may be an important question for Ethics, without by any means being the only one. This whole matter has been discussed in preceding chapters.

[2] See p. 382.

general principle—here employed, but unnamed—that 'the good of one individual is not as such to be preferred to that of any other individual'.

Now what is this unnamed principle, here treated as the real ultimate, from which the principle of rational Benevolence is regarded as merely a corollary? Professor Sidgwick does injustice to the strength of his own argument, such as it is, by representing this principle as suggested by a mathematical analogy, *i.e.*, by arguing that, just as one part of the individual's good is of no more importance than any other equal part, so one part of the total Good (or good of all) is of no more importance than any other equal part of the same. This is making the all-important transition from the subjective, in the sense of merely self-regarding, attitude to the objective ethical attitude altogether too easily.[1] As a matter of fact, this unnamed principle, here treated as an ultimate, is merely the original so-called principle of Justice, translated into terms of the Good. Any deduction from it, therefore, like the abstract principle of Benevolence, involves the same assumption, *viz.*, that moral distinctions are to be interpreted in terms of the Good, instead of in terms of Duty, Good Will, etc.—an assumption which, no matter how capable of being justified by argument, can by no means be regarded as intuitive. Regarding the author's abstract principle of Benevolence, then, we must conclude: (1) that it is a deduction from another principle, rather than a separate intuition; and (2) that the principle from which it is deduced cannot possibly be regarded as an intuition, even though we should accept the so-called principle of Justice as such.

So much, then, for the three fundamental so-called 'intuitions,' which are regarded by Professor Sidgwick as affording the needed Intuitional foundation for Ethics.[2] By themselves,

---

[1] Note again the author's difficulty with "the dualism of the Practical Reason" in the final chapter.

[2] Of "the axiom of Rational Benevolence" in particular, he has said a little before, that it is, in his view, "required as a rational basis for the Utilitarian system".

however, these abstract principles are insufficient, according to his own admission; for he holds that they all equally imply a Good, still undetermined, of which they are to be regarded as *distributive* principles. That this is true even of Justice, is asserted in the following definite statement: " Justice (when regarded as essentially and always a Virtue) lies in distributing Good (or evil) impartially according to right rules ".[1]

Before passing on to this second main division of the author's proof of Utilitarianism, which fortunately will not detain us long, *viz.*, the determination of the nature of the Good, which all of the so-called 'intuitions' are supposed to imply, and of which they are regarded as 'distributive' principles, two preliminary criticisms require to be made. (1) The very abstract principle of Justice, at any rate—which has turned out to be merely the postulate of objectivity, or impartiality, implied in all ethical reasoning—does not logically imply an apportionment of the Good, as the author holds that all of these principles do, precisely because it is so abstract that it applies to the Duty Ethics as well as to the various forms of the Ethics of the Good. (2) It must not hastily be assumed that even the subordinate principles, rational Prudence and Benevolence—which, as here formulated, do undoubtedly imply the conception of the Good—are necessarily to be regarded as *distributive*, rather than as *regulative*, principles. Whether they are to be the one or the other, depends entirely upon the nature of the Good, still undetermined.

It is impossible here to enlarge upon this distinction between 'distributive' and 'regulative' principles; but fortunately it is at once fairly obvious and quite commonly recognised. If the Good be conceived as something, *e.g.*, Happiness, which is to be portioned out, as nearly as may be, into equal parts, these principles will of course have to be regarded as externally distributive. If, on the other hand, the Good be conceived as organic in character, *e.g.*, Self-realisation or even Health of the Social Organism, we can no longer speak of

[1] See p. 393.

distribution merely, as if a lump sum of money were to be impartially divided. On the contrary, all the principles of Ethics—these as much as any others—must then be regarded as internally regulative, and as deriving their specific character from the concrete nature of the Good.

But let us return to Professor Sidgwick's own argument. What is the Good, which is supposed to be implied by all three of these principles, here treated as distributive? It should be carefully noted that this problem, by far the most important of all for any form of ethical theory except pure Intuitionism, is not here discussed with anything like philosophical thoroughness. The attempt rather seems to be to show what, on the whole, commends itself to common sense as the Good. This is particularly disappointing, since the investigation of this problem has been deferred so long.

Professor Sidgwick begins by arguing that it will not do to say that 'Virtue is the Good'. That would involve one in an obvious logical circle, since we have just seen that our three ultimate intuitions regarding what is virtuous all have to do with the apportionment of the Good. The purely logical difficulty may perhaps be avoided, if the 'good will' itself be affirmed to be the Good; but this is fundamentally opposed to common sense, "since the very notion of subjective rightness or goodness of will implies an objective standard, which it directs us to seek, but does not profess to supply".[1] From this point the argument moves only too rapidly. "Shall we then say that Ultimate Good is Good or Desirable conscious or sentient Life?" This seems to accord with common sense; but it must be observed that not all psychical existence can be regarded as ultimately desirable, "since psychical life as known to us includes pain as well as pleasure, and so far as it is painful, it is not desirable". This, of course, frankly *assumes* that 'desirable' consciousness is Happiness or Pleasure. Now the author urges that this is the only possible criterion of feeling as feeling; and further that both

[1] See p. 394.

cognition and volition, taken strictly by themselves, are quite neutral in respect of desirability. The further details of the argument may safely be neglected, for, as will readily be seen, the result is a foregone conclusion. By this highly abstract method—which practically begs the question, by arbitrarily isolating the different sides of consciousness—Happiness, or Pleasure, is vindicated as the only practicable test of what is desirable in conscious life. And the Good being thus defined, the author holds that we are finally at liberty to regard the three genuine moral intuitions, relating respectively to rational Prudence, Justice, and Beneficence, as affording the needed Intuitional basis of pure Universalistic Hedonism, or Utilitarianism.[1]

Little need be said by way of summary. As the chain is no stronger than its weakest link, it is evident that Professor Sidgwick's proof of Utilitarianism equally involves the validity of his treatment of what he regards as the fundamental moral intuitions and his hasty determination of the nature of the Good, which he holds that all of these intuitions imply. As regards the three supposed intuitions, we found that they were by no means on the same plane. The so-called intuition of Justice turned out to be merely the postulate of objectivity, or impartiality, implied in all ethical reasoning, and not a separate intuition, referring to one part of moral conduct more than to others. From the epistemological point of view, therefore, it appeared to be closely analogous to the most fundamental methodological postulates of the various sciences and disciplines.

Moreover, to the relatively subordinate principles of rational Prudence and Benevolence, also assumed as intuitive, and apparently as being on the same plane with that of Justice, two special criticisms were found to apply. (1) The assumption of an original separateness between the interest of each individual

---

[1] Sometimes the axiom of rational Benevolence is referred to as if it alone afforded the requisite Intuitional basis for Utilitarianism. See p. 387.

and that of all others could not be conceded. (2) We found that only the principle of rational Prudence was really treated as a separate intuition, that of Benevolence having been arrived at indirectly. The first step was the disguised translation of the original principle of Justice into terms of the Good—a conversion which itself should have been justified by argument. The second step was a deduction from this principle in its modified form. The principle of Benevolence, therefore, as here formulated, is at least twice removed from being an intuition in the proper sense, even if the author's abstract principle of Justice be regarded as such.

Again, we have seen that these principles do not, as the author claims, all imply a Good, still undetermined, of which they are to be regarded as 'distributive' principles. The so-called principle of Justice is so abstract that it does not necessarily imply the conception of the Good at all. Even rational Prudence and Benevolence, as here formulated, are not necessarily to be regarded as 'distributive' principles merely. That will depend upon the nature of the Good, still left undetermined; for if the Good, *e.g.*, turn out to be Self-realisation, or even Health of the Social Organism, no particular principle of Ethics can be regarded as externally distributive; but all must rather be regarded as internally regulative, and as deriving their specific character from the concrete nature of the Good. Finally, even assuming these principles to be 'distributive,' the author's hasty determination of the nature of the Good hardly pretends to be a philosophical treatment of this all-important problem; but is rather an attempt to justify Utilitarianism to common sense. When he practically rests his case upon the argument, that pleasure is the only possible criterion of the value of feeling as feeling, he unconsciously begs the question, which is, and must remain, whether or not the value of conscious life is to be determined solely in terms of feeling.

It is a natural, if also rather unexpected, result of Professor Sidgwick's order of treatment, which follows from his peculiar classification, that the concluding book of the *Methods of Ethics*, Book IV., "Utilitarianism," contains comparatively little that is of importance for systematic Ethics. The general implications of Hedonism as such, together with the special difficulties that are sure to arise in connection with any form of hedonistic theory, have already been considered at length in Book II., "Egoism"—with the result, indeed, that many of the difficulties of Utilitarianism have probably been either long forgotten by the reader, or confounded with those which more particularly belong to the so-called method of Egoism. Moreover, by far the most important constructive argument of the treatise, the author's elaborate proof of Utilitarianism, which we have just examined in considerable detail, comes at the end of Book III., "Intuitionism". This is perhaps natural enough, since it is the whole point of the argument to provide Utilitarianism with an Intuitional basis; but the fact remains that, before the reader begins the concluding book of the treatise, which, from its title, one would naturally expect to be devoted to a judicial examination of Utilitarianism, he is wholly committed to that method, provided that he has accepted the preceding arguments as valid.

In truth, what the author seems to have attempted, in this concluding book of the *Methods*, was not a further and more elaborate examination of the method of Utilitarianism as such, but rather a justification of that method to common sense. Apart from the two brief introductory chapters, which mainly consist in a *résumé* of what is given in more satisfactory form elsewhere, and the equally brief concluding chapter, on "The Mutual Relations of the Three Methods," nearly the whole book is devoted either to tracing out in detail the correspondence between Utilitarian morality and the morality of Common Sense, or to settling questions connected with the practical application of the Utilitarian method. While, therefore, these discussions are in themselves both interesting and valuable, they are hardly of a kind to detain us here; and we may best pass on almost immediately to the final chapter, referred to above, which will be found to afford an interesting commentary upon certain of the author's presuppositions.

It is perhaps worth noticing that, while Book IV. of the *Methods of Ethics* has been modified less (or in less important respects) in succeeding editions than any other book of the treatise, some of the chapters have received titles quite different from the original ones in the later editions. For example, the third chapter, which is the first of any length in the book, originally had the title, " The Proof of Utilitarianism (continued) ". This chapter, though very little modified, has received in later editions the much more appropriate title, " The Relation of Utilitarianism to the Morality of Common Sense "—which, in fact, exactly describes the nature of the discussion. The final chapter, on the other hand, which we are now to examine, has in later editions the title, " The Mutual Relations of the Three Methods," though this is less accurately descriptive of its real character, even in its somewhat modified form, than the original title, " The Sanctions of Utilitarianism ".

The real problem considered, in the later as in the earlier form of this chapter, is the reconciliation of duty and interest ; and the solution of the problem, so far as any solution is offered, is much less important than the very prominent place given to the discussion itself. In short, the last chapter of this elaborate treatise on the Methods of Ethics frankly emphasises the " Dualism of the Practical Reason," as the author himself elsewhere calls it. This is more significant than might at first appear, for the problem, as here stated, is a manifest survival from eighteenth century individualism. Referring to this chapter, Professor Sidgwick says, in the Preface to the second edition of the *Methods :* " I hold with Butler that ' Reasonable Self-love and Conscience are the two chief or superior principles in the nature of man,' each of which we are under a ' manifest obligation ' to obey ".

It might reasonably be held that the dualism in Butler's system is by no means so serious as this would imply, at any rate, if we take into account the logic of his system as a whole ;

but Professor Sidgwick does not permit us to mistake his own position. While never suggesting a real doubt as to our complete obligation to do what we believe to be right, he holds that morality must be regarded as only incompletely rationalised, unless it can be shown to be for the agent's individual interest to be moral. Yet even so, his unflinching honesty, which never shows in a more admirable light than here, will not permit him for a moment to juggle with this crux of eighteenth century Ethics. He refers, indeed, to his own argument, which goes to prove that it is 'reasonable' for one to aim at Good in general, and not merely at one's own individual, selfish good.[1] But he does not see fit to pursue this line of argument further, in the present connection. He admits also the reasonableness of the Egoist's demand that it shall be for his 'interest' to be moral, and, after carefully pointing out what can, and what cannot, be proved by the conventional appeal to sympathy, etc., he finally comes to the inevitable conclusion that there is no way of demonstrating that, in all cases, it is strictly for the agent's selfish interest to be moral, *unless* we take into account strictly theological considerations.

The clearest statement of his conclusion is to be found in the final paragraph of the first edition of the *Methods*, the gist of which is as follows : " The old immoral paradox, 'that my performance of Social Duty is good not for me but for others,' cannot be completely refuted by empirical arguments : nay, the more we study these arguments the more we are forced to admit, that if we have these alone to rely on, there must be some cases in which the paradox is true. And yet we cannot but admit with Butler, that it is ultimately reasonable to seek one's own happiness. Hence the whole system of our beliefs as to the intrinsic reasonableness of conduct must fall, without a hypothesis unverifiable by experience reconciling the Individual with the Universal Reason, without a belief, in some form or other, that the moral order which we see im-

[1] See pp. 495 *et seq.*

perfectly realised in this actual world is yet actually perfect." [1]
In the later editions Professor Sidgwick expresses himself
much more guardedly, but to practically the same purpose.
And we may add that, given the presuppositions, this appeal
to the theological sanction is the only way out of a more or
less complete ethical agnosticism.

The presuppositions, however, all centre about the fatal
assumption that the ultimate interest of the individual is
something which can be considered apart from that of the
society to which he belongs. If a ' sanction ' for morality
be demanded from this point of view, Gay's answer is the only
possible one, *viz.*, that, since God only can in all cases make
us happy or miserable, He only can reconcile duty with interest.
And that was what all the so-called ' Theological Utilitarians '
meant by saying that ' complete obligation ' to morality could
come only from the Divine Being himself. If we shrink from
such a conclusion, it is in no spirit of hostility to theology,
much less to the essential teaching of Christianity ; it is merely
because the philosophical methodology of the present day will
not permit us thus to invoke Divine assistance to extricate
us from speculative difficulties which we can avoid by the
exercise of our natural reason.

But it would be very unjust to Professor Sidgwick to allow
his own too emphatic statement of the " Dualism of the
Practical Reason " to serve as a final commentary upon his
system. As a matter of fact, he himself is one of the very
moralists who have enabled us to transcend this position,
which here he seems to define as his own. Both historically
and logically this demand for the reconciliation of duty and
interest, in the sense of separate individual interest, which
could be effected only by the theological sanction, is intimately connected with the theory of obligation which Gay
once for all perfectly expressed, when he said : " Obligation
is the necessity of doing or omitting any action in order to be
happy ".

[1] See p. 473.

The eighteenth century Intuitionists did not by any means wholly escape confusion regarding the problem as to the relation between duty and interest; but their characteristic theory of the absolute nature of moral obligation, intuitively apprehended, did not at all commit them to this Dualism of the Practical Reason, while they were influenced in the contrary direction by their view, that the mere consciousness that an action was right or wrong could in some way become a sufficient motive for performing it or abstaining from it. Professor Sidgwick himself, here, as elsewhere, has much in common with traditional Intuitionism, and could easily have avoided this characteristic crux of eighteenth century Utilitarianism. As we saw in the early part of Chapter xvi., he utterly refuses to reduce the notion of 'ought' to terms of anything else, as the earlier Utilitarians had done. For him, as much as for any Intuitionist, 'ought' is an irreducible datum of moral consciousness, although he uses the term in a sense rather more abstract than that of ordinary Intuitionism. Moreover, he distinctly holds, in his latest as in his earliest treatment, that, while it may not perhaps properly be maintained that reason, apart from all feeling, can afford the moral motive, it is nevertheless much *as if* this were the case, since we nearly all desire, more or less strongly, to do what is reasonable merely because it is such.

Much more important, however, in the present connection, than this abstract statement, which merely points in the direction of traditional Intuitionism, is Professor Sidgwick's highly significant analysis of desire. The characteristic position of the older Utilitarianism, that only pleasure as such can be desired, and consequently only the agent's own pleasure, he rejects as patently false. In discarding this theory, together with the theory of obligation inseparably connected with it, he really cut loose from the eighteenth century position. He was, indeed, the first Utilitarian to see the real significance of Butler's analysis of desire. And, in spite of minor differences, he agrees with Butler on the essential point. In a passage previously quoted, he says, after remarking that Butler has somewhat overstated his case: " But as a matter of fact, it appears to me that throughout the whole scale of my impulses, sensual, emotional, and intellectual alike, I can distinguish desires of which the object is something other than my own pleasure ".[1]  And a little later he adds: " Our conscious active impulses are so far from being always directed towards the attainment of pleasure or avoidance of pain for ourselves, that we can find everywhere in consciousness extraregarding impulses, directed towards something that is not pleasure, nor relief from pain ; and, indeed, a most important part of our pleasure depends upon the existence of such impulses ".[2]

The logic of all this is plain, at least to ourselves at the present day.  Not only is the possibility of an original altruism provided for, but the individual moral agent no longer has to be regarded as an isolated centre of desires, whether for the happiness of self or of others.  He is rather seen to be an organic part of society, in a sense that carries one far beyond eighteenth century individualism.  Butler, indeed, was too often obliged to employ the *argumentum ad hominem*, in order to meet the problems and difficulties of individualism in the working out of his system ; but the logic of his system as a whole was clearly in the direction of what we would have to regard as most modern in ethical speculation.  And it surely is not too much to say that, in so far as Professor Sidgwick follows Butler in this all-important analysis of desire, which does so much to transform the problems of Ethics, he also is logically one of the true moderns, in spite of all apparent evidence to the contrary.

It was a notable event in the development of recent ethical theory, when Utilitarianism thus for the first time really took account of Butler's starting-point and method ; and if the result would seem to be the inevitable dissolution of traditional Utilitarianism itself, there is perhaps little ground for regret. Neither J. S. Mill nor Professor Sidgwick were adepts in rigid logical consistency; but the very fact that they could for the time hold together the half-truths of seemingly anti-thetical systems, enabled them to perform a service for the development of systematic Ethics which only the future can duly appreciate. Both were essentially seekers after truth, and not system-makers. In fact, it would be difficult to mention two moralists who have shown more perfect candour in pointing out difficulties of their own systems, of which they were themselves conscious; and if they helped to lead a succeeding generation to the recognition of truths which they never definitely formulated for themselves, their contribution to Ethics was not the less, but the greater. Few English moralists of the nineteenth century, so recently ended, are deserving of more grateful appreciation than these two eminent Utilitarians, who did their work so well that they helped their successors even to transcend the Method of Ethics for which they themselves stood.

# INDEX OF NAMES, SUBJECTS, AND WORKS.

GEORGE ALLEN & UNWIN LTD
*London: 40 Museum Street, W.C.1*

*Auckland: 24 Wyndham Street*
*Bombay: 15 Graham Road, Ballard Estate, Bombay 1*
*Calcutta: 17 Chittaranjan Avenue, Calcutta 13*
*Cape Town: 109 Long Street*
*Karachi: 254 Ingle Road*
*New Delhi: 13-14 Ajmeri Gate Extension, New Delhi 1*
*Sao Paulo : Avenida 9 de Julho 1138-Ap. 51*
*Sydney, N.S.W.: Bradbury House, 55 York Street*
*Toronto: 91 Wellington Street West*